LEFTY KREH'S
PRESENTING THE FLY

Other Books by Lefty Kreh

LEFTY KREH'S
PRESENTING THE FLY

A Practical Guide to the Most Important Element of Fly Fishing

Lefty Kreh

Illustrations by Rod Walinchus

THE LYONS PRESS
Guilford, Connecticut
An imprint of The Globe Pequot Press

To buy books in quantity for corporate use
or incentives, call **(800) 962–0973, ext. 4551,**
or e-mail **premiums@GlobePequot.com.**

10 9 8 7 6 5 4 3 2 1

Printed in the United States of America

Designed by Compset, Inc.

ISBN-13: 978-1-59228-974-5
ISBN-10: 1-59228-974-6

The Library of Congress has previously cataloged an earlier (hardcover) edition as follows:

Kreh, Lefty.
  Presenting the fly/Lefty Kreh.
        p. cm.
  Includes index.
  ISBN 1-55821-788-6
  1. Fly fishing. I. Title.
SH456.K755 1999
799.1'24-dc21   98-25828
                                              CIP

I realize that both publishers and reviewers hate redundancy-repetition throughout the manuscript. But for much of my life I have been teaching fly fishing and I am convinced that people absorb concepts much better if important factors are repeated. In this book I will make an important point concerning presentation; later, I felt it essential to repeat that point at various places in the book when dealing with different kinds of situations. I felt it necessary to make the reader realize that a point made many pages before also applied to a specific situation. I hope that readers—and reviewers!—will forgive me for what I think was a necessary evil.

*This book is dedicated to EV,
my wife of sixty years—the best
friend that ever happened to me.*

CONTENTS

INTRODUCTION

Nothing is as important in successful fly fishing as properly presenting the fly. No matter what rod, reel, line, or fly is used, unless the presentation is correct, the game is over. Anglers often emphasize presenting an exact fly pattern. But I have known many trout fishermen who carry only three or four patterns in their fly box, yet catch more fish than their friends. The same could be said of fly fishing in salt water. These anglers, of course, have learned the lessons of good presentation.

Presentation is much more than dropping your fly in the best position in relation to a fish. It involves the clothes you wear, the way you rig your tackle, how and where you approach the fish, the types of fly lines and reels you use, the direction of the light, the type of cover, your retrieve method—and so on, and so on.

I know a number of fine fly casters who catch few fish, simply because they so often use the wrong cast, or else don't understand how to present the fly. I also know fishermen who'll make the proper cast but don't know how to correctly retrieve—which is one of the most important factors in a good presentation.

What I hope to do in this book, then, is first help you realize the many factors that govern successful presentation. I'll follow this with specific techniques to help you make better presentations.

PART ONE

1

SOME GUIDELINES FOR PRESENTATION

The following presentation guidelines apply to many fishing situations. I have indicated the types of fishing for which each guideline is most important—but these tips are often applicable to other areas of the sport as well.

1. General—Always approach the fish as quietly as possible before you cast.
2. General—Wear clothes that blend in with your background.
3. General—On small streams, stay in the shade whenever possible.
4. General—Always consider your position before you cast. Is your backcasting area clear? Can you make the right cast? Finally, will you be able to fight and land the fish from this position?
5. General—The calmer and shallower the water—in both fresh and salt—the longer the leader you'll need.
6. General—The spookier the fish, the longer your leader must be.
7. General—Most of the time the quietest cast is at eye level or slightly above. Only when you're casting into the wind or trying to throw under an object should you direct your fly downward on a forward cast.
8. General—When you're sight-fishing try to keep the sun either behind you or behind and to one side of you for best visibility.
9. General—Changing the color of your polarized glasses can be a big help under different light conditions.
10. Trout—With difficult-to-catch trout it's often best to get upstream from the fish and at a very slight angle, then allow your dry fly to drift downstream to it. This way, your leader remains unseen.

11. General—Know which direction your fish is facing before you make a cast—then cast to its eating end.
12. Trout—Never wade into a small stream if you can cast from the bank.
13. General—Never cast farther than is comfortable for you.
14. General—Never rush a cast, no matter how much a guide or companion may be talking or how excited you are. Rushing only destroys your accuracy and distance.
15. Flats—Always try to approach a single fish, or school of fish, from upwind.
16. Flats—When you're in a boat, never cast directly ahead. You may hook your guide.
17. General—When you're fishing from a boat in salt or fresh water, it's a good idea to have two different rods rigged.
18. General—If you can see your fly line in flight, you can make a more accurate cast. Because wearing a long-billed hat blocks much of your cast from you, wear a hat with a short bill.
19. General—Make as few false casts as possible. One sure sign of a good fly fisherman is how few false casts he makes.
20. Flats—Never rock the boat in shallow water while you're casting. It sends shock waves to the fish.
21. General—If you retrieve your fly 5 feet underwater with a fish closely following, and the fish doesn't strike—change your retrieve.
22. Flats—On windy days in salt water, you can shorten your leader.
23. Trout—Learn to use more than one line on your rod. On days when extra-short casts are called for, use a heavier line. On a windy day, a lighter line can add to your casting distance.
24. General—Never make a backcast until you've lifted *all* of your line from the water.
25. General—Never false-cast over a fish, especially not in calm water.
26. General—In fresh water it's usually best to fish out poor casts, but if you make a bad cast in salt water you should generally pick it up quietly and quickly, and make another cast.
27. General—Never attack a fish with an underwater fly.
28. General—Use the countdown method to retrieve at a specific depth. By casting a sinking line and counting ("One thousand one, one thousand two," et cetera) up to a certain number, you can determine the depth at which fish are taking your flies. This is an essential and accurate method of determining your fly's swimming depth.
29. General—To get your fly deeper in the water column use a sinking line, cast upcurrent, and allow the fly to sink fast and deep before retrieving.
30. General—Understand how the prey swims or moves around so that you can retrieve in a manner similar enough to interest predators. For example, sculpins are nocturnal and swim along the bottom,

because they have no swim bladder. Crabs don't dart forward in spurts; they swim in one continuous movement.

31. Flats—If large saltwater fish won't strike your streamer, switch to a popping bug, which makes a lot of noise. Keeping it in motion often gives big fish a false impression of its size. If you stop a bug in salt water, the fish will usually ignore it.

32. Trout—A dry fly should generally float drag-free.

33. Trout—To check your dry fly for a drag-free drift, cast it near drifting foam. If the fly and the foam don't float at the same speed, adjust your tippet.

34. Trout—To get a longer drag-free float, make your tippet longer.

35. Bass—When you're fishing a popping bug for bass in calm water, a very slow retrieve is usually best. On rivers with current, usually a faster retrieve is best.

36. General—If you need more line for a longer cast while you're retrieving an underwater fly, grasp both the line coming off the spool and the line you're retrieving at once. This way you can pull off additional line with each strip as you retrieve.

37. General—Sharpen your hooks. If you miss two strikes, check your points.

38. Trout—After you dress a dry fly, be sure to remove any oil before you make your next cast.

39. General—Shooting line on your backcast saves time and makes a longer cast possible; this often gives you a chance at a strike you wouldn't have otherwise gotten.

40. Flats—When you're in a boat, check your line constantly to see that it's clear of all obstructions.

41. Flats—When you're with a companion in a bonefish or tarpon boat, the one not fishing should monitor the angler's fly line to make sure it's free of tangles.

42. Flats—Learn the clock system. When your guide indicates a fish, point to it with your fly rod to locate it quickly.

43. General—When you're fishing for bottom feeders you should generally start by offering flies that blend in with the bottom's coloration.

44. General—After catching any sharp-toothed fish, examine your tippet. And after catching several fish of any species, make it a point to remove the tippet near the fly.

45. Trout—Try fishing the side of a trout stream that fewer people frequent. Trout soon learn to look for anglers who approach from the heavy-traffic side.

46. General—When you fish extremely clear waters, switch from bucktail and natural-hair streamer flies to those made from the more transparent synthetic wing materials.

47. General—When you and a companion are trying to figure out what the fish are hitting, fish two different patterns or water depths.

2

SOME GENERAL OBSERVATIONS

Before I delve more deeply into the subject, let me give you some random thoughts about making a better presentation. They're not in any order of importance—just thoughts that come to my mind that might be helpful.

Best Time to Fish

When I was a kid, I worshiped an old man who lived along the Monocacy River, a 75-yard-wide stream in central Maryland close by my home. He lived alone in a shack; that's the only word I can think of to adequately describe it. No one caught as many catfish and smallmouth bass as he did—nor as big. These were the only two species he sought. I wanted to know how he did it so I spent a lot of time with him, hoping to win his friendship and confidence—and to get the information I needed to catch the same kind of trophy fish he did, especially the smallmouths.

It took several enjoyable years before I screwed up enough courage to pose the question. Then I watched as he sat there, looking at the river. Finally he said, "Fish very early and late." I waited for him to say more—to tell me where to fish, what to use, how to approach the fish, and all his other pearls of wisdom. But he said nothing. He just slowly got up, walked to the river, and started fishing. I followed, wanting to ask more questions, but his manner indicated that the subject was closed.

Early or late in the day is often the best fishing time. Here Bill Anderson helps launch the author's boat as early-morning mist shrouds the bridge pilings. The target is small-mouth bass.

It took me quite a few years of fishing before I really understood what he had said. And he was dead right. Certainly the equipment you use, the quality of your knots, the proper selection of flies, where you fish, and the season or time of year you fish are all vital to success. But if you're after trophy fish, often the key factor is to fish very early in the morning and very late in the evening.

Some trophy fish only feed at these times. Others seem to be less wary, and it's easier to get them to take your fly. Many examples come to mind. For several years in the 1960s, Bart Foth caught the biggest bonefish entered in local tournaments in the Florida Keys. Bart once confided in me that a major factor in his success was that he lived only minutes from Shell Key, a shallow flat west of Islamorada. He fished for the first hour every morning, and again for the last hour in the evening. Some of the biggest bonefish in the Keys still roam these flats—and they're among the most difficult to convince to take your offering. Yet even today the best times to fish here are the times Bart used to fish.

Experienced anglers who chase big rainbow or brown trout in shallow waters soon learn that just at dawn and dusk, the chances that these wary trout will take their fly increase greatly. During summer months smaller trout streams heat up in the daytime to the point where trout become lethargic, so fishing early and late is best. Hard-fished bass waters produce far more fish just at dawn, and again just before dark, than they do during midday periods.

Tarpon seem to be greedy early in the morning. At night they lay up—suspend and rest just below the surface in a calm area, often with their dorsal fins and some of their backs sticking out of the water. Later, as the sun brightens the day, they sink deeper. But sneak up quietly on a laid-up tarpon just at daybreak, make a soft presentation, and you're almost assured of a savage strike. At dawn, too, tailing redfish are patsies for any succulent shrimp, lure, or fly teased right in front of their noses.

Farm ponds hold some big bass. Most of these trophies are very much aware of and evade the anglers who try to catch them. But early in the morning, as fog and mist are rising, these bass will move to the very edge of the pond banks. Drop a soft fly cast in front of these feeding bass and you can depend upon a solid strike.

Fish have no eyelids and bright sunlight must cause them some discomfort, for they seem to seek shade or other cover from it. This is especially true where waters are very clear. In fact the clearer the lake, stream, or body of water, the better your chances of scoring on its trophy fish early and late in the day. The worst times to fish such places are on bright, sunny days. Many anglers will tell you how poor the fishing is after a front moves through and high barometric pressure occurs. A high is associated with bright, sunny days. It has been my belief for some time that it's not the pressure that causes fish to go off their feed—or to feed well as the front moves in. Instead, I believe that fish feed well as the front approaches because the light level drops; they stop feeding as the high takes over mainly because the light intensity increases.

If you can fish very early or late in the day, then certainly the best times to go are when the conditions are overcast. Many old-timers used to say that rainy days produced their best fishing. But was it the rain that caused the fish to feed? I doubt it. *Light levels are low during rainy periods—and I believe that's why the fish are on the feed.*

But remember that when you're fishing early and late in the day, noise and surrounding disturbances are at a minimum. Thus it's vital that you make as silent an approach as possible. Clanking the oars, running a motor close to fish, wading too quickly, or making any other unnatural noises or commotion will reduce your chances.

This also applies to presenting your fly early or late. The fish are often in shallow water, easily spooked, or near the surface. If possible, locate a fish before making your cast. Then use a fly that, when cast correctly, will fall to the water without alarming the fish.

The old man who caught so many big bass in local waters when I was a youngster was indeed giving me very good advice. If you seek truly big fish, try fishing early and late in the day.

Switch to Lighter Fly Lines

It was during a two-day stay at Spruce Creek near State College, Pennsylvania, that I first found out how to drastically improve my dry-fly fishing. What I learned was a technique that's vital in calm, shallow-water fly fishing, and it has increased my hookups from beaver ponds to bonefish flats ever since.

Spruce Creek is maybe the best limestone spring creek in the eastern United States. George Harvey, whom I regard as the best trout fisherman in this country, fished it for decades, sometimes daily in summer. It's rather slow moving, with few riffles and many long, quiet pools that meander through pastures. The brown trout here are educated. They've been fished over since they were juveniles, and they'll turn down any fly that drags, or any cast that's poorly placed.

On my first day here the trico hatch was in full bloom. These tiny insects came out right on schedule that morning and fell to the surface, where scores of trout were greedily sucking them in. After a careful stalk and what I thought was a good cast, I dropped my spent-wing fly a foot in front of a brown that appeared to be at least 18 inches long. There was ample slack in my leader tippet, so I knew I'd get a good drift. The fish immediately dropped 6 inches deeper in the water and didn't feed again for more than 10 minutes, despite the many tricos floating over it.

I took six fish that morning, but none were the real trophies I wanted to land. Each large fish had instead refused my offering. I was puzzled: My leader had seemed right. My fly seemed to float drag-free. I could even catch the little fellows—just not the wiser, older, and larger fish.

The following morning I decided to leave my 6-weight rod-and-line combination on the porch and picked up a new 4-weight whose reel was loaded with 3-weight line. This all happened many years ago, back when a size 3 line was almost unheard of. Manufacturers were making a few samples for some of us who had requested them, but they weren't in production.

With the same leader and fly imitation I had the day before, I returned to Spruce Creek. I could see tricos dancing in a ball above the stream. Soon I spotted a big brown, rising steadily. I crawled into position, made a cast, and dropped the fly a foot in front of this 20-incher. The fish tipped up, sucked in my fly, and was hooked. Five minutes later I released the beauty. That day I went on to catch all but one of the larger fish I made good casts to. At lunch I sat on the porch and began to wonder what I was doing so differently from the day before, and realized that my only real change was the lighter line.

It was an important lesson: *For the first time, I began to realize how critical to shallow-water fishing success is the weight of the fly line.* Most dry-fly anglers use a line between 5- and 7-weight. They've found that a leader of at least 9 feet is needed to successfully catch fish. And if it's a slick beaver pond, quiet lake, or other calm water that's easily disturbed, they need a leader exceeding 12 feet.

Why?

The major reason is simply that the heavy splashdown of the fly line must occur far enough away from the fish to prevent alerting or frightening it. As I sat on the porch thinking that day, it became clear that the heavier my line was, the more likely I was to drop it to the surface with force. For this reason, I was using a longer leader. Yet anyone who throws a long leader knows that it's less accurate than a shorter one. Try casting a 10-foot leader and then switch the same fly to a 20-footer and you can see the difference.

The first 30 feet of a size 6 line weighs 160 grains. The same length of size 3 line weighs 100 grains—close to half as much. The six 6 line falls to the surface with a heavy *crunch* when compared to the 3-weight, which settles to the water like a thistle. Although a 9- to 12-foot leader may be called for under calm conditions with a 5- to 7-weight line, you can use a 7- to 8-foot leader with a 3-weight line. Obviously, the lighter impact and shorter leader will result in spooking fewer fish and making more accurate casts.

But what about fishing in the West, where winds are tough and longer casts are necessary? First, it's rarely advisable to fish a dry fly farther than you can see it well. This usually means less than 45 feet. Second, a 3-weight line is so much thinner than a 6-weight that it offers considerably less air resistance during the cast. Third, dry flies are nearly weightless, so a 3-weight line handles them well. If you're a good caster, you can throw a size 3 line and fly easily to 70 feet.

For about 15 years I've been using a 3-weight for most of my trout fishing. The exception is spots where trout may run more than 5 pounds—for this I like a 5-weight outfit, only because I can fight the fish a little better. But for fish of less than 5 pounds, from New Zealand to England and all over Canada and the United States, I've found that a 3-weight will outfish all my other rod-and-line combinations.

Thin, light fly lines will help you catch more fish in salt water, too. John Emery and I were fishing for sharks on the murky flats off Frank Key in Florida Bay at Flamingo years ago. These were big blacktips, maybe 5 feet or more in length. In shallow waters such large fish are extremely wary and easily frightened. I was casting an 11-weight rod-and-line combination, with a large red-and-orange fly. After making what I felt were four good casts to cruising blacktips—and scaring three of them and getting a refusal from the other—I realized the lesson I'd learned at Spruce Creek was being repeated. The heavy splashdown of my bulky 11-weight line was seriously disturbing the sharks.

I switched to a 9-weight rod and lengthened my leader from 5 to 8 feet. Another shark came down the flat in that zigzag swimming motion so typical of the species. When it was 30 feet away I made a cast and watched the fly line settle quietly to the surface. The retrieve brought the fly right alongside the eye of the big shark, which hit it instantly. I lost that fish when it rolled in the line. But during the rest of that tide phase we hooked three others—and never spooked another shark.

Stretching a floating line prior to fishing, as Charley Wells is doing here, gets rid of those unruly coils.

Certainly bonefishermen can profit by using a lighter line. Of course, if it's windy and you're forced to use an 8- or 9-weight line, that's different. On windswept flats you'll sometimes need a line of this size to punch your fly into the breeze. But when bonefish are tailing in inches of water on a slick flat, you might consider switching to a much lighter line. I often use a 7-weight, especially when I'm wading in very slick, calm situations. This line is light enough for you to get it close to the fish, yet heavy enough to throw the size 8, 6, or 4 hooks dressed for such occasions.

Anytime you're fishing in shallow water for fish that may be easily frightened, consider using the lightest fly line you can for the fishing conditions. I really believe that this will improve your fly-fishing success.

Using Shade as a Tool

Fishing gets tougher all the time as more people enter the sport, waterways become more crowded, and pressure on the fish increases. Modern equipment can help you catch more fish—depth finders, Global Positioning System, videotapes, books, and so on. But common sense (which isn't too common) is still the angler's best tool. Applying it means you'll come up with practical methods that make your fishing either more fun or more successful. One practical application that will help you catch more fish, from brook trout to species swimming in the sea, is the awareness that shade will help you in your pursuit.

Consider that fish have no eyelids. This means they can't handle the sun as humans do. There are many situations in which you can exploit shade as you fly fish; maybe the way to understand this is to analyze specific ways that you can use shade in some special fishing situations.

If you fish the open sea for species that enjoy lying beneath boards, logs, or other debris—almost anything that floats—you're using shade as a tool. Dolphinfish, tripletails, and a host of other saltwater species are attracted to these structures. There are several reasons for this. The debris is a good place for small prey to both hide and feed, especially if it's floating grass, which holds smaller prey. Debris on the open ocean surface also furnishes an ambush spot for predators.

One of the major reasons why bridge piers and similar water structures hold lots of fish is that these formations furnish shade. If you're a bass fisherman and fish lakes, you soon learn that docks and other floating structures are hot spots. The major reason is shade, which draws both the minnows and the bass that feed on them. Lakes that suffer excessive drawdowns leave bare stone or mud banks that often produce few fish—in part because the shade supplied by overhanging trees, floating docks, anchored boats, and so on, is lost.

Walleye experts have known for some time that one of the best places to explore for this tasty fish is along the edges of weed lines. The weed lines furnish shade, easy access to the vegetation to escape predators, and an ambush spot for smaller prey. Furthermore, if you locate a weed line, most of the time the better-lit edge will be less successful than the side in shade.

Again, fish have no eyelids for protection from bright glare, and you can use this knowledge to your advantage in both fresh and salt water. A log that's suspended in the water will have fish holding either under it or on its shaded side. Any standing timber in the water will almost always have fish on its shaded side. The same holds true for fish suspending near markers and buoys—you'll usually find them on the shady side.

Shade can work for trout fishermen, too. Consider a meadow stream that has an even depth of flowing water. One side has an undercut bank, while the other drops vertically to the streambed. Without question the undercut side will hold more fish: It offers shade, protective cover, and an ambush spot. Another example is a large boulder in the stream with equal current flowing on both sides. The fish will surely be on the shaded side of the boulder. There are two reasons for this: The fish's eyes will be better shaded here, and ospreys and other overhead predators can't see the fish as well if it lies in the shade.

Which side of a stream you should fish is (or should be) governed by which side is shaded at a given time of day. Through long years of experience I've determined to my satisfaction that certain portions of a stream are better fished in the morning; others in the late afternoon or evening. Why? It's simple: Small-stream fish have to know what's going on around them, and especially what's moving along the bank that may threaten them. *The angler who fishes carefully along the stream bank in deep shade is much less likely to be seen by the fish than the angler working in sunlight.* Approaching from the shaded side gives you an advantage. This is often obvious when you're fishing streams in the East, but it might seem not to apply to bigger western rivers. Most western riverbanks are fairly light in color, however, as is the brush in many areas. By approaching from the shaded side you'll reduce the contrast between yourself and the bank, lessening your chances of being seen by the fish.

When you're fishing the smallmouth rivers of the Mid-Atlantic early on a hot summer morning, it's always best to fish the shaded side, where the water is a few degrees cooler and the bass more active. Bass fishermen working farm ponds can also use shade to their advantage. A boat dock, a large tree that overhangs the water, or even an anchored boat—all produce shade that will attract bass.

On many trout streams almost everyone tends to fish from one particular bank. For many years I've fished the famed Letort in Carlisle, Pennsylvania. This was the home of Charley Fox and Vince Marinaro, the two men most responsible for developing terrestrial flies. The Letort is a limestone spring, fished often by top fly rodders. After several years I learned that everyone fished from one side of the stream. One day I took the trouble to get to the other side. Admittedly, it was difficult fishing—there was so much brush that backcasting was often difficult. But I often scored better than I ever did from the popular bank. On heavily fished streams, particularly smaller ones, fishing from the bank most anglers avoid is thus profitable.

Fly Entry

Too often we fishermen concern ourselves with which pattern to use, or how to retrieve it, without ever realizing the importance of how the fly enters the fish's domain. But the way an underwater fly enters the water can determine success or failure.

A good example of this is a trip I made a number of years ago to the Gallatin River north of West Yellowstone, Montana. Bob Lewis, my friend and guide, dropped me off along the river and explained that I should fish upstream until I met him and his companion. The first hour I caught a few fish, but nothing really large. Rounding the bend, I could see Bob and his friend in the distance.

At the head of the pool where I was standing, there was an old log. The forward portion of it lay up in the riffle, the rest of it close to and along the left bank. "What a good place for a nice brown to hide," I thought as I approached. Getting into position just to the right of and downstream from the log, I made a cast that would let my dry fly drift along its length. The hopper bobbed along in a nice drift. Suddenly a huge head broke the surface and sucked down the fly. I struck and within seconds the fish was back under the log—and then the leader tippet broke.

Bob and his companion, unbeknownst to me, had been watching. As I crawled out of the water I saw them and commented, "That was tough luck. It was a big fish." Bob said quietly and a bit reluctantly, "Lefty, if you'd gotten into the right position before casting, you might have landed that fish."

And then he explained—a lesson on fly entry that I'll not forget. What he said made a lot of sense. Instead of getting into position below and slightly to the side of the log, he suggested that I should have waded to a spot where I could get a drift at right angles to it. If I had then made my cast and the fish took, I could have used side rod pressure to work the trout away from the log and out into the current, where I stood a much better chance of landing it.

The following year I returned to this pool. Doing just as Bob had suggested, I got into the correct position and made my cast. The fish took, and I landed it. It wasn't as big as the monster from the year before, but it was one I could be proud of. Most of all, the lesson had been well learned.

How the fly enters the water is important. When most fly fishermen shoot line, they turn it loose and let it go. When the fly touches down, they're looking at the line so they'll be ready for the retrieve to begin. But consider what the fly is doing. It lands near a fish and, because the angler has slack in his line and no control over his retrieve yet, the fly tumbles and sinks in a manner that must be unattractive to the fish. But if the angler shooting line had instead allowed it to flow through a circle made with his thumb and first finger (simulating a rod guide), he could have trapped and stopped the line over his target. In this situation, he could begin a retrieve as soon as his fly hit the water. There are also times when being able to drop your fly on the water so that it's swimming away from a fish will enhance the possibility of a strike; this is explained more thoroughly in chapter 9.

Another situation where fly entry can make a difference is with fish that are hiding near bushes or trees that overhang a bank. Two species come immediately to my mind: bass and snook. If you use a Bend-Back-style fly you can often fool a wary bass or snook. Toss this fly (which is nearly weedless) into the brush, then slowly tease it out of the branches so it gently plops in front of a bass or snook. You now have a good chance of getting into a fight with that fish.

Before making that first cast, always consider how you'll hook the fish, how you'll fight it—and how you'll land it. I've sometimes successfully cast to and hooked big fish in a rush. But when it came to landing them, I was in such a position that I couldn't.

Along with entry, consider another factor. So many anglers make a cast to a fish, realize they're not satisfied with it, and so make another—and sometimes another cast. All this disturbance will frequently put down the fish. In freshwater situations it usually pays to fish out a cast—even if you feel it's not a good one. *But when you're fishing saltwater flats and make a poor cast to a fish moving away, ask yourself this: "Is there a possibility that the fish might see my fly?" If not, recast immediately.* The difference is that in most freshwater situations the water is moving and the fish are still. In salt water, though, generally the fish are moving and the water is relatively static.

Many poorly placed casts can be avoided if you practice accuracy casting at home. (The water is not the place to learn it.) You can make a game out of it. *One tool I often use when doing conducting casting seminars is a mousetrap.* This delights my students. Buy a mousetrap and place it on your lawn, set so that it will go off if it's hit by a fly. Tie on the end of your leader an old weighted fly or popping bug with the bend and point removed. Begin casting at about 20 feet, working your way farther back as your skills progress. You'll be astounded how difficult it is to spring the mousetrap. Even top-drawer fly fishermen may have to make a dozen or more casts at 25 or 30 feet before the trap is sprung. But keep practicing; in a short time your fly will be landing within inches of the trap. This will improve your accuracy while you have fun.

Try tripping a mousetrap with your weighted fly to better your casting accuracy—it's fun!

3

TACKLE

A trip to a fly shop can easily convince you that there's a huge number of rods, reels, lines, and flies available. Choosing improper tackle for your fishing situation can be disastrous. Using a light trout rod to subdue a giant tarpon is a sure path to failure. Likewise, a tarpon rod is worthless on a trout stream.

The wise angler will first choose his flies, then a line to cast the flies, followed by a rod to handle this line, and, finally, a reel to accommodate all his chosen tackle. While this is the correct procedure, I'm going to begin by addressing fly rods.

Fly Rods

There's a host of fly rods to choose from, ranging in length from 5 to 16 feet. These can accommodate lines as light as size 1 and as heavy as 15—and even lead-core lines. There are slow tapers, medium tapers, and fast tapers—and choosing the correct taper for your fishing conditions is vital to success.

Let me first say that very short rods have their place in fly fishing. These are rods from 5 to 7 feet in length. When you're fishing in what I refer to as tunnels—small creeks overhung with brush—a short rod will allow you to cast, while a longer rod would be useless. In almost all fly-fishing situations, however, I recommend that you use a rod of at least 7½ feet. In many cases a longer rod (up to 9 feet) will serve you better. Some people claim that shorter rods are more sporting. Actually, it's just the opposite: A short rod gives you a shorter lever to use against the fish. No experienced offshore tuna fishermen would use a long big-game rod—it would give too great an advantage to the fish during a fight. Longer fly rods offer many advantages over shorter rods, as well; in fact, I once listed 17 reasons why a long rod is better than a short one. Some of these advantages, all vital to better presentation, are: During the drift, you can guide or manipulate your fly better; roll-casting is easier, as is the pickup for your backcast; you can strike better; it's easier to keep your line above the surface or background bushes on the backcast; mending the line is much more effective with a long rod—and so on, and so on.

So how do you select the correct rod for your fishing purposes? First, unless you fish in only one place for one species, you need more than one rod. (Even then you may need several rods.) Fortunately, in almost all fishing conditions except offshore, you can get by with only three rods. But of course no fly fisherman will stop at that. The three rods that will do you for almost all fishing situations are matched to a 6-weight, an 8-weight, and a 10-weight line. The smaller 6-weight rod will work for most trout fishing situations where you're casting small flies. The 8-weight is the most versatile of the three. It will handle fairly heavy streamers, conehead streamers, weighted Woolly Buggers, bass popping bugs, Clouser Minnows, and similar heavy freshwater flies, as well as the sinking-tip or sinking lines needed to fish these flies properly. It's the perfect rod for small and largemouth bass, as well as many salmon situations—both West Coast and Atlantic species—and I enjoy it for most steelhead fishing situations, too. There never has been a better redfish, snook, or bonefish rod. The 10-weight rod will do for heavier freshwater fishing, such as when throwing heavy flies to northern pike or largemouth bass. It's also the most utilitarian rod for general saltwater work; only when you go for big tarpon or offshore species will you need a rod heavier than size 10. *Almost any rod made in the last decade will handle three sizes of line well: one size lighter than recommended, the suggested line, and one size heavier.*

A little-understood reason for using heavy, powerful rods for giant tarpon, sailfish, amberjacks, and other strong species is that *you need to eventually lift them to the boat.* A 100-pound billfish, or a powerful amberjack or cobia that digs deep for the safety of a wreck, must be physically lifted to the boat with the rod. While this book doesn't get into fish-fighting tactics, presenting the fly to the fish with the correct tackle is important. There are some powerhouse rods that handle lines from 12- to 16-weight. They're long rods, and have very slow tapers. They usually have stiff tips and don't cast well. The best all-around extra-powerful fly rod has a relatively soft tip—which makes casting lines easy. But its lower third is extremely strong. You can cast even lighter lines with such a rod. Still, long rods put you at a disadvantage during the fight. The shorter the rod, the shorter its lever, and as long as it's strong enough it will allow you to fight fish more efficiently.

A simple experiment may help you understand why longer rods work against you during a fish fight. Hold a 12-inch ruler by one end and have someone push down on the other. Of course you can't support the ruler. Now slide your hand up until only 6 inches of ruler extend from it. Have someone push down again and you'll find you can fully support the ruler.

So it is with longer and shorter rods when you're fighting big fish—the longer the rod, the more the fish has the advantage.

The hardware on your fly rod is also an important part of presentation. Your reel seat should be sturdy. Some trout fishermen prefer small, delicate rings that weigh virtually nothing to hold the reel on the cork. Under hard use, however, such rings often cause the cork of the grip to take a set where the reel is fastened in position. This may lessen the security of the fit. The weight difference between these tiny rings and a lightweight aluminum seat that offers security is minimal; I suggest the aluminum seat. Any reel seat should offer rings that don't loosen after firm tightening.

There are two popular types of reel seats: downlocking and uplocking. Downlocking reel seats tighten toward the back of the rod; with an uplocking seat, the rings move away from the bottom of the rod as the reel is secured. Downlocking seats often place the reel at the very end of the rod butt, while uplocking seats give you a short butt extension that you can rest against your stomach when fighting a fish. Most people prefer uplocking reel seats.

Your most important hardware, however, is your guides. While most people don't consider guides important, they can be a factor in good presentation. The first guide is called the stripping or butt guide, and it's the largest on any fly rod. It "funnels" the line on the cast. If the stripping guide is too small, the line chokes as it travels through the smaller-diameter rings. Many experienced anglers are now aware that on larger rods (sizes 8 and above), a large guide is required to shoot line efficiently. It should be a minimum of 16 millimeters; actually, on rods size 8 or bigger, I prefer at least a 20-millimeter guide. The problem is that such guides look outlandishly large, making it hard to sell them. So rod manufacturers usually don't put them on most rods. Cosmetics do count when selling a rod. Almost any fly shop can replace your smaller butt guide with one of 20 millimeters or more.

What many trout fishermen don't consider is that a large butt guide may be even more important on a trout rod. Generally, when trout fishing you're casting the leader along with less than 20 feet of line. In fact many times the leader is longer than the line outside the guides. So when you need to shoot a little line, you're asking that small amount of fly line outside your rod tip to drag maybe twice as much line through the guides to the target. *I urge all of you using trout tackle to install a 16-millimeter butt guide on your trout rods—those used with line sizes 3 to 7. You'll be amazed at how much better the line shoots through this larger ring.*

There are many types of guides for fly rods. For your stripper (butt) guide, you need what's called the bridge type. This is what you see on plug-casting tackle—a guide supported by a stout brace or bridge. For cosmetic reasons the lower half of a fly rod is usually equipped with two such guides. Actually, after the fly line enters the first one it's traveling straight; no further bridge guides are needed.

The remainder of the rod is usually supplied with snake guides. There are other acceptable types of guides, but hard chrome-plated snake guides

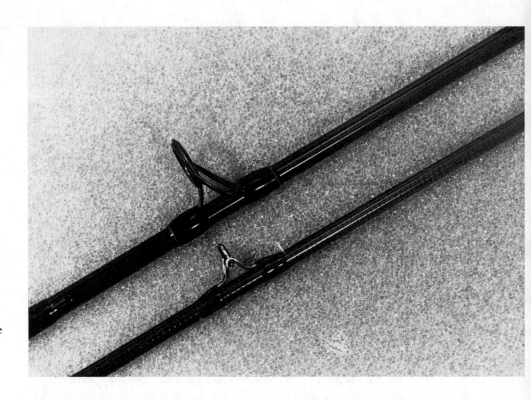

Large butt guides let line flow through easily. Small ones, like the lower guide, create undue friction and restrict shooting line on the cast.

are still preferred by almost all experienced anglers. *What's important is the size of these snake guides. They should be as large as possible without affecting the rod's action.* Very small guides (which are often mounted on trout rods) have two distinct disadvantages. First, they throttle the line that passes through them, decreasing your ability to shoot line. Second, when you hook a fish, the line that the fish pulls through the guides as it tries to escape tends to knot. *If your guides are very small, the line will almost surely snarl in one of them and break your leader. If you have larger snake guides, though, you need only turn your rod upside down before the knotted portion of the line enters the guides: it will generally travel through safely.*

Your tiptop is also important. A light, hard chrome-plated tiptop is the universal choice of almost all experienced fly fishermen. Most other tips are too heavy—although some of the new ceramic tiptops are fairly acceptable. What's important is the size of the tiptop. As with guides, the larger the tiptop (without affecting rod action), the better. Some rod companies now offer hard chrome-plated tiptops that are very large, but also very light. Remember, the larger the tiptop, the easier the line will glide through it when you shoot—and the easier knots will pass through, too.

Fly-rod handles need to be considered as part of presentation. The type of handle you use will often affect how well you cast. There are three basic fly-rod handle shapes. One is called a cigar; it tapers, at least at the front end, to the shape of a cigar or cone. Such handles are generally found on fly rods used for trout fishing—those handling lines from sizes 1 through 7.

Three basic handle shapes (from left to right): the cigar; a half wells, which swells at the top; and a full wells, with swelling at the top and bottom.

This is an impractical shape, although *with lighter rods* it does work fairly well. Because it presents to a potential buyer a sleek-looking, streamlined handle, manufacturers continue to make it. But if you want a handle better designed to be gripped during casting, choose either a full or a half Wells. A full Wells has a swelling at each end of the handle, a half Wells only at the very forward end of the handle. The thumb can be placed against this swelling to apply pressure during the cast. Because distance is not a problem in most trout fishing, the cigar shape will work. But you'll find that a

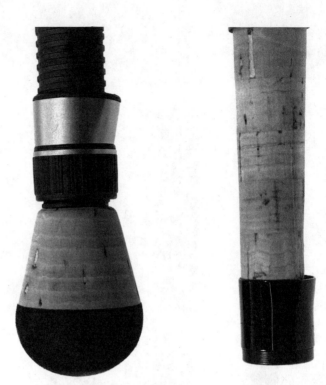

The round butt extension on the left is much more comfortable when fighting big fish.

full or half Wells, or a variation of these, is more comfortable and efficient on almost all rods that throw a line heavier than size 7.

On the bottom of rods that toss bigger lines and fight large fish (8-weight and heavier) is what's called an extension butt. This can range from a very short stub to several inches in length. An extension butt allows you to place the butt of the rod against your stomach during a fish fight. *A butt extension more than 2 inches long, however, will often snag the fly line when you shoot it—and cause a missed opportunity.* If you'll be pressing the butt extension firmly against your belly during a fish fight, the shape of that extension is important. You'll need one that's well rounded so it's comfortable. Sharp-edged butt extensions can be painful when you fight a fish, and often leave bruises.

Poor presentation can result from a slippery rod handle. You often have to handle fish when releasing them—transferring some of their slime to the rod handle. Later, this may affect how firmly you handle the rod. *It pays to occasionally clean your rod. One of the easiest methods is to use a rough rag or fine steel wool. Saturate the rod handle with warm, soapy water and then scrub it clean.*

Another presentation problem that has plagued fly fishermen (and other casters, too) is a rod tip that suddenly leaps from the rod. Usually, this is caused by improperly putting the rod together. When we used bamboo rods we were told to align the guides on the two sections, then shove the rod together in a straight line. That's exactly what you shouldn't do

To prevent your rod from coming apart during a presentation, coat the ferrules with a candle.

with fiberglass, boron, or graphite rods. *Instead, hold the tip section so that the guides are at a 90-degree angle from the rear section. Holding the forward section between the two fingers and your thumb, rotate it 90 degrees as you bring the two sections together. Even with the two fingers and thumb, if you rotate 90 degrees the rod will remain securely in place and you'll eliminate the problem.*

Occasionally the male portion of a fiberglass, boron, or graphite rod will become very dry, and even a 90-degree seating will not keep the rod parts together. What you need to do then is lubricate only the male end. Do this by stroking the end of the section with a candle. Beeswax works, but it's sticky and collects grit that can eventually create wear on the rod. Paraffin is also used, but it doesn't hold well on the blank and requires frequent applications. What works best for me is a candle, which has some oil and wax and remains on the blank for a considerable time.

Fly Reels

The type of reel you use should be tailored to the type of fishing you do. If you fish trout streams so small that a trout's longest run is 30 feet, then you don't need a reel with a large line capacity. Conversely, if you fish steelhead or Atlantic salmon, which usually head toward the sea the moment they're hooked, you do need a fairly large capacity, as well as a light, smooth drag. And of course if you fish in salt water, the requirements again will vary. *Few inshore saltwater fish (with the exception of giant tarpon and possibly some albacore or tuna) require a reel with a backing capacity of more than 200 yards.* But if you tangle with billfish, wahoo, and the many other fast-running offshore species, you'll need a lot of backing. For bigger billfish and wahoo, even 400 yards is sometimes not enough.

Let's begin our consideration of the proper reels for different kinds of fishing at the small end of the scale. Many trout reels, especially for lines from sizes 1 through 4, are minuscule gadgets, sometimes only a little more than 2 inches in diameter. In the store and in the hand, these little "jewels" seem delightful. On the water they aren't. Several problems occur when you use reels that have very small-diameter spools. First, when you pull line from them, it comes off in tiny coils. Fly lines, especially floating lines, tend to remain in the condition in which they were stored. With a small reel this means in very tight coils, which are hard to eliminate when you strip off the line for use. Another problem is that if you try to wind line on quickly, you must make many turns with such a small spool. Also, because reels with small spools have to be wide—so that you can get all the line on them—you have to use more care to level-wind recovered line. If you don't some messy tangles can occur, followed by lost fish. Finally, if the escaping trout does get to the end of the line that you've pulled from the spool, the narrowness of the line that remains on the spool makes it very difficult for the fish to pull off any more. In short, if you like these little jewels and insist on using them, know that a reel with a larger diameter (such as the loop style) would serve you better. If you *still* prefer the small reels—then have at it. The reason we fly fish is for fun.

In my opinion, if you fish for trout in streams where long casts aren't possible and long runs aren't expected of the fish, you need a very narrow-spooled reel that has a large diameter—approximately 3 inches in width. Such a reel will reduce the coiling problem and allow you to level-wind the line more easily. Because of the large diameter, additional line is easily pulled from the spool. Best of all, you can recover line much faster.

Narrow-spooled trout reels, like the one on the left, are inefficient. It's better to use a reel that has a much larger diameter, like the one on the right.

Where long runs are not encountered, such as on spring creeks, eastern trout rivers, and similar waters, a trout reel requires enough spool capacity for the fly line and no more than 75 feet of backing. Such a reel should be light and rather durable. Some of the best of these relatively inexpensive reels are made of graphite or very light aluminum.

If you expect the fish to make frequent and longer runs—such as steelhead, Atlantic salmon, bonefish, albacore, or striped bass—you need a reel of no more than 200 yards capacity. But it should have a smooth drag. Many people recommend more capacity than this, but it really isn't necessary. I've caught more than 1,000 bonefish since I started fishing them in the late 1950s. Only one bonefish has ever run off more than 150 yards of backing. What you really need is a smooth drag.

Confusion reigns among many fly fishermen concerning their reel drag and how to adjust it. I've read many different recommendations from outdoor writers as to the proper drag setting—from 10 to 40 percent of the strength of the leader tippet. If you don't understand the function of a fly-reel drag, you may well wonder just how to set it.

Before I address this, let's look at drags on fly reels. The drag on any reel is simply a mechanical brake. Some reel manufacturers use magazine ads to boast about their revolutionary drag materials (airplane wheel brake-shoe material, space-age plastics, and so on). But if you talk to experienced, saltwater fly fishermen who've used reels made from a variety of drag materials, you'll find that they've had the most trouble-free years from

A sampling of saltwater reels. Top row, left to right: Scientific Anglers Mastery Series, Abel Model 3, Penn International, and Billy Pate. Bottom, left to right: Lamson LP-3.5, Islander, and Tibor Riptide.

that old standby, a cork drag. There may be some rare materials used today, but cork has served us exceedingly well for generations. The old saying, "If it ain't broke, don't fix it," is certainly true here.

A drag has two slipping speeds. The **starting drag** is the amount of pull required for the drag to begin to slip or give line to an escaping fish. The other, **running drag,** is the amount of energy required to keep the drag slipping once you're beyond the starting drag phase. *A low starting drag is vital to prevent fish from breaking off.* Many reels have a high starting drag, but once set in motion have a smooth release. Well-designed reels have two important built-in factors to help you control a fish you're fighting: Their starting drag is low and their running drag is very smooth.

What breaks most leader tippets in fish fights is not steady pull, but sudden jerks to the leader. You can easily prove this. Take a length of 6-pound-test monofilament and grasp the two ends in your hands about a foot apart. Slowly spread your hands; you'll be surprised how difficult it is to break 6-pound line. Now take another length of line from the same spool and, again, grasp it firmly between your hands. Give a quick jerk; the line will snap easily. I like to say that it's the jerk on the wrong end that breaks the leader.

What this test demonstrates is that a steady pull will usually restrain the fish, but jerk suddenly on the leader and you'll see the end of the battle. If you can prevent that sudden jerk as you fight the fish, you stand a good chance of landing it.

Again, the drag is simply a mechanical brake. To fight a fish solely with your drag is a mistake. You may adjust your drag so that in the beginning it slips at 2 pounds of pull—but other factors will effect changes in that drag setting during a fish fight. If you adjusted the drag with a straight pull, and then the rod bends as you fight the fish, you'll incur more drag. Friction from the line dragging through the guides will add more pounds to the drag. As a fish pulls line from the reel, spool capacity is reduced. Once the line on the spool diminishes, it takes more pounds of pull to keep the drag slipping than what you first established. For example, when a spool is reduced to half its capacity, it may take three times as much pull to keep the drag slipping.

All of this emphasizes that depending upon a mechanical drag during a fish fight can mean the loss of a trophy. *To meet the various and changing conditions required of a drag when fighting fish, you need to be able to make instantaneous adjustments.* This is only possible if you first establish a very light mechanical drag, *and then use your hands to apply additional pressure.*

The better you become at fighting fish, the less mechanical drag you'll use, and the more you'll rely upon your fingers to restrain the fish. To accomplish this, you need rarely set a drag for more than 1 pound of straight pull. Here's my favorite way to set a drag for most species: I first make sure my lips are very dry. Then, grasping the fly line as firmly as I can between my lips close to the reel, I pull line from it. *When I've just exceeded my ability to pull line off with my lips, I've reached what I feel is the correct drag setting.*

The author demonstrates his favorite method for setting the drag on fast-running fish. Adjust the tension until you can no longer pull off line through your compressed lips.

Once your drag is set, you can then use your fingers to control the line during a battle, making instant adjustments. Also, the line from the reel to the first guide should travel between two fingers of your rod-holding hand. For fighting high-speed running fish offshore, many of us use a glove to keep fingers from getting friction burns. Inshore and in fresh water, this glove is rarely needed. To restrain the fish you simply tighten the line against the rod blank with your fingers. Apply your fingertips to the inside of the reel spool to add pressure. If your reel has a rim control you can place your palm against the spool for even more pressure.

With a light drag setting established your starting and running drags will be very low, and you can apply as much pressure as you wish. You can release it instantly by releasing your fingers. This is the key to how experienced anglers battle big, fast-running fish. Thus, as you prepare for a presentation, it's important that you select the right drag for your purpose.

If you have a rim-control reel, you can make a simple device that will give you an exceptionally smooth drag. Cut from an old leather belt the shape of a Ping-Pong paddle, but no larger than a dime. The "handle" should be no more than ½ inch long. Lash the leather handle to the reel brace so that the "paddle" lies over the rim (see the photo below). If a fish runs, just push on the smooth leather paddle to apply pressure that gives a wonderfully smooth drag. This is an excellent way to install a fine drag on an inexpensive rim-control reel.

Unless you have a lot of experience in fighting big fish, don't try to readjust the mechanical drag after you've hooked a big fish. Instead, learn to use your fingers. When you finally hook that trophy of a lifetime, you'll be rewarded with a catch.

It's possible to crank a reel with either your left or your right hand. Nearly all saltwater fly fishermen use their dominant hand to wind with. (Your *dominant* hand is the one you use most—if you're right-handed, for example, your dominant hand is your right one.) The majority of fly fishermen who are right-handed and wind with their left hand are trout fishermen, who haven't had to do a lot of winding when battling their quarry. The age-old concept is that if you're right-handed, you have more power in your right arm to fight a fish. You also don't have to switch hands to wind in line.

But the problem when a strong fish (an Atlantic salmon, steelhead, or saltwater species) runs off a lot of line is not having enough power in your arm to fight it. Instead, it's getting all that line back on the reel. This means some fast and continuous winding. For some of my seminars, I bring along two identical reels loaded with exactly the same amount of line. Inevitably, a student will claim he can reel just as fast with either hand. So I have him

A small leather tab on a rim-control reel makes a fine drag.

pull the same amount of fly line and backing off both reels. Then, with the second hand of my watch, I time how fast he can reel in the line. No one as yet has been able to wind faster with his nondominant hand. This in spite of the fact that he may have been winding with his nondominant hand for years!

Some righthanders will try to prove that they can wind their fly reel well with their left hand by telling you that if a right-handed fly fisherman uses spinning tackle, he'll wind with his left hand. But if that same person also has plug-casting tackle, he'll almost always have a plug reel that he winds with his dominant hand—despite the fact that he must switch hands at the end of the cast to retrieve line. Why is this so? The reason is simple. The spinning reel travels in large circles—one turn of a spinning-reel handle means at least four or five turns of the spool. This is easy to do with either hand. But a plug-casting reel's handle revolves in tight circles; one turn with the handle gives just a single revolution of the spool. *It's far easier and less tiring to crank a small handle in tight circles with your dominant hand. To be ready to hook a fish and fight it when you present a fly, use a reel that you wind with your dominant hand.*

Before presenting a fly your tackle should be in top form. Fortunately, reels don't require much maintenance. For most freshwater reels, an occasional lubrication of the spool shaft and the screw holding the handle will keep things turning freely. It's the drag that will almost always give problems. A jerky drag or one that won't slip as it should can cost you fish. *For fly-reel drags that have one or more soft washers—which rub against metal washers or the inner face of the spool—it's vital that you remove all drag adjustment at the end of each fishing trip. This is probably the greatest abuse that drags suffer. What occurs is this: When the adjustment screw is tightened, it compresses the softer washer or washers against the harder ones. This allows the drag to slip when a fish escapes. But if the drag adjustment remains under tension during reel storage or for long periods of time, the softness is slowly squeezed from the washers, and the drag will no longer function properly.*

Soft drag washers need to be lubricated so they'll slip. For many years the cork drags used in saltwater fly reels were lubricated with neat's-foot oil. These days, however, some manufacturers use special lubricating compounds on the cork or on the softer washers. Since these are specially formulated, I suggest you write to your reel manufacturer and ask for a small supply. Don't overlubricate the washers. Generally, just a smooth film over the softer washers is enough.

Here's another reel-storage tip. The tippet, the thinnest leader section, can be almost impossible to locate when you arrive at a fishing scene. There are two simple tricks that will help you do so. At the end of a fishing trip, don't wind in all of your leader; instead, leave about 6 inches of the tippet outside the reel. If you have holes in your reel spool, insert the line through one of them. On your next trip you simply push the tippet end out of the hole and you're ready to string up the leader and line. The other trick is just as simple, and it works even if you wound all of your leader

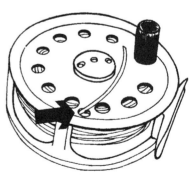

To locate the leader end on your next trip, store it in one of the reel spool's holes. When needed, simply push it back through the hole.

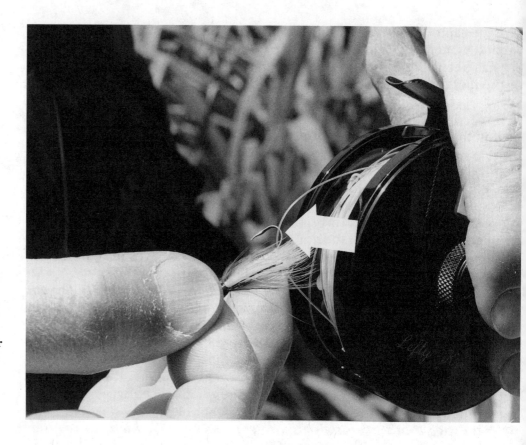

Another trick to locating the leader end is to find the thinner part of the leader—the tippet—slip a hook under only one strand, and start winding. The leader will chase around the hook until the end appears.

onto your reel spool. Look closely at the leader on the spool. Locate the tippet—the thinnest piece of the leader. Slip a hook under it. Be sure that you only snag one line; this won't work if you get two pieces of the tippet on the hook. Once you've captured a piece of the tippet with your hook, simply wind slowly. The leader will chase around as the spool revolves, and soon the end of the tippet will appear. This trick is much like holding a rope in your hand somewhere along its length, then pulling it in until you arrive at the end of the rope.

Backing

Many great fish are lost because of what you might consider an unimportant part of tackle. In fact, probably no piece of fly-fishing gear is so ignored as the backing on the reel. And this doesn't apply just to saltwater situations. Steelheaders often watch in dismay as a fish escapes downstream, where they can't follow, only to see the end of their backing—and the fight. Atlantic salmon fishermen are often called upon to give more line than they want to a battling fish. Even on very light gear, a good trout hooked in heavy water may run off more than 90 feet of fly line.

Fly lines are rarely longer than 105 feet, which is a very short run for some freshwater, and certainly many saltwater, species. To permit the fish you hook to be landed, there has to be enough backing on the reel for it to make long runs and exhaust itself. But not just any old backing will do. The kind of backing you use, how much you use, its color, and even the combination of backings you use, can all be important factors in catching fish.

A number of line types are used for backing. First, nylon monofilament is rarely used. Monofilament stretches when pulled tautly. If you're fighting a strong fish with mono backing and you recover it on the reel, the mono may be in a stretched condition. If you then pile more loose line on top, you may be creating a critical problem. If the fish makes another long run, comes to the stretched portion (which is now thinner mono that has dug into the bed of line), and jerks—it usually will snap your leader. Monofilament has long been considered a poor material for backing.

The most popular backing is Dacron, available in most tackle shops, or a very similar material called Micron, manufactured by the Cortland Line Company. These two materials owe their popularity to the fact that they stretch very little under stress and lie flat on the spool. For many years experienced fly fishermen used squidding line—a braided nylon that also lies flat on the spool and works well. It's now difficult to obtain, though.

The new braided casting lines might appear to be a breakthrough in fly-reel backing, but they have some drawbacks. DuPont manufactures one from Kevlar; others use various braiding systems and materials. These are not like any other lines—Dacron, Micron, braided nylon, or nylon. They have one outstanding characteristic: a thin diameter for their strength. For example, the average new braided casting line of 30-pound test has the diameter of about a 10-pound nylon monofilament line.

Fly fishermen immediately said, "Great—now I can put two or three times as much backing on my reel." But it's not that simple. First, I believe if you use any braided line that tests *less than 30 pounds* for backing you may encounter troubles. Such lines are so thin that they tend to dig into the backing, causing the same kind of problem associated with nylon monofilament. And many of these lines are very thin and very slick. If you fail to *very carefully* level-wind the line back onto your reel spool as you recover it while fighting a fish, and it piles higher on one side of the spool, it has a tendency to tumble down into a disastrous mess. You also need special knots to tie most of the braided casting lines. *Conventional monofilament knots are usually poor performers with these lines.*

If you do use these new braided lines for backing on your fly reel, the most important factor in getting good performance is how you place it on the spool. Even with 30-pound-test line, the diameter is so thin that you must make sure to put on all the backing as firmly as possible. *I use a glove to put tension on the line as I reel it onto the spool. If you fail to do this, even 30-pound test may dig into the bedding and lose you a fish.*

Still, these new braided lines (of approximately 30-pound test or stronger) have two advantages. For small freshwater trout reels whose spools are almost filled with fly line, a thin-diameter backing is helpful. It will permit you to easily add 20 or so yards of backing—almost always enough. And in salt water, the angler who *carefully* installs this backing on his spool can add about 50 percent more of it than he could Dacron or Micron. This in turn offers two benefits: If you prefer a smaller saltwater reel—for example, when bonefishing—you can now fish with the proper fly line and adequate backing. And if you seek long-running fish, such as billfish, you'll be able to put considerably more line on your reel.

Realize that when backing causes lost fish, it's usually because it was installed improperly. Regardless of whether you're using Dacron, Micron, squidding line, or a new braided casting line, it's extremely important to place the backing on your spool under pressure. This way your bedding will be firm and won't allow a line to dig into it.

The two most often-used backing lines are 20- and 30-pound-test Dacron or Micron. Factors that determine which test you should use are how large your reel spool is (if it's small you can't get much 30-pound-test line onto it), and how strong your leader tippet is. Obviously, you don't want to use backing that tests less than your tippet—or you may lose leader, line, and fish.

Many fly fishermen who seek sea trout, bonefish, redfish, and other species that don't require a heavy leader tippet—and who prefer light, small reels—select 20-pound-test Dacron or Micron. However, I use 30-pound Dacron or Micron for almost all my backing needs. If you want to make an illuminating test, take a 2-foot strand of 20- and another of 30-pound-test Dacron or Micron. Have someone hold a fly rod firmly in front of you. Insert one end of the 20-pound strand in the butt or stripping guide. Grasp the two ends and saw the line rapidly back and forth about 30 or 40 times. Then do this with the 30-pound piece. Now look at both strands (you may need a magnifying glass). It might surprise you to see that the lines—especially the 20-pound test—will resemble a barbed-wire fence. This test tells me that Dacron and Micron do abrade. My experience has led me to believe that you'll fairly often need to check 20-pound braided Dacron or Micron for wear, but 30-pound will last for years.

A major reason for backing on fly reels is to have enough line to let the fish make an escape run. For years, however, outdoor writers and fly fishermen have vastly overrated the distance that many fish will run. Bluefish and stripers will *rarely* run off more than 125 yards of backing (plus 30 yards of fly line). I've caught some large stripers and bluefish—none ever hit 100 yards of backing plus the fly line.

Bonefish are legendary; they're supposed to run 250 yards. I'm not sure how many bonefish I've caught of more than 10 pounds, but it has been quite a few. None ever ran off more than a fly line and 150 yards of backing. That's nearly two football fields away! Many fly fishermen who seek snook, redfish, sea trout, and similar species carry reels loaded with 250 to 300 yards of backing—which will never be needed.

There *are* some fishing situations where a lot of backing is demanded. You'll need at least 300 to 400 yards for billfish and some of the offshore speedsters, such as wahoo, tuna, and mackerel exceeding 40 pounds, to mention a few. Giant tarpon can pull a lot of backing from a reel, especially if you're fighting from a staked or anchored boat. *But with these few exceptions, a fly fisherman whose reel is loaded with 150 yards of backing, plus a fly line will almost never in his lifetime hook a fish that will run it all off.*

Some Backing Tricks

Anglers have devised several backing techniques that you may want to try.

1. Some anglers use fly line and backing of the same color, or very close. This is not a good idea! I prefer to connect a backing markedly different in color from the rear of my fly line. It gives me a better idea where the end of the fly line is.
2. It's often advantageous to know just how much line has been pulled from your reel. For example, if you're on a saltwater flat with a marker or channel buoy 200 yards away, knowing how much line a fish has pulled out could have a major bearing on how you fight it. Backing comes in many colors, ranging from fluorescent to dull reddish brown. Some anglers use various lengths of different colors to tip them off. For example, you might connect 100 feet of bright chartreuse backing to your fly line; to that you'd connect 100 feet of a much different color; and so on. To connect the line, use loops. Bimini twists can be made in both ends of each color of backing, then looped together. Many fly shops can also build spliced loops in your backing for you if you don't know how. The loops will flow through the guides; if you ever want to add or remove a color link, simply unloop it.
3. Some billfishermen and tarpon fishermen place about 100 feet of monofilament between the rear of the fly line and the front of the backing. They believe that this acts like bungee cord, absorbing the shock of a leaping fish, which helps them subdue fish they may not otherwise have taken. Actually, a fly line itself has a great deal of stretch. I once laid a size 9-weight-forward line out on a lawn, straight, but not taut, with one end secured. Then I picked up the other end. I walked 12 feet before I felt the line was about to break. Nevertheless, there are big-game fishermen who prefer a shock absorber between the fly line and backing. Any fish that jumps with great frequency and ferocity, such as a billfish or tarpon, lunges against the leader and can break it. Here's a way to build a shock absorber into your backing that will reduce the chance of a leaping fish breaking your leader: Connect 100 feet of 25-pound *brightly colored* nylon monofilament to the rear of your fly line with a Bimini twist loop, and then connect the other end of the nylon monofilament to your backing with a loop-to-loop system. If a fish

jumps when you have the fly line and monofilament outside your rod tip, the mono will stretch like a giant rubber band, often preventing the leader from snapping. *Use brightly colored monofilament so that a boat operator can see it during the battle and not run over it—which has happened to me.*

4. There's an advantage in building a whipped loop in the rear of your fly line, and using a Bimini twist loop in the backing: You can loop-to-loop the fly line to the backing. Loops never hang in the guides during a fish fight; they also enable you to change lines on your spool with ease.

    Remember, backing is often ignored when fly tackle is considered, but it forms a vital link between you and a trophy fish and deserves your attention.

5. Although modern saltwater fly reels require little maintenance, backing does, yet it's an item that almost never receives attention. If you fight a fish that runs well into your backing, that line will soak up a lot of salt water. Most anglers just spool the line on; later, when they get home, they clean the reel surfaces but leave the salt-encrusted backing. What I recommend instead is that upon returning home, you fill a sink with *warm, soapy water* and place the backing in it. Wash your spool's sides with the same soapy water and wipe it clean. Drain the soapy water, flush the backing line with clear water, and replace it firmly on the spool.

Hooks

Selection of the right hook is vital to good fly fishing. For years saltwater fly fishermen were limited to a very few models. Now, however, there's a profusion of terrific hooks for both fresh- and saltwater anglers. And in many ways they're vastly superior to those manufactured just a few years ago.

Before we examine which hooks should be used for different species or fishing conditions, it might be worthwhile to look at the various parts of a hook. Each has a function that can be a liability or can help you catch more fish.

Of course, every hook has an eye. There are ring eyes, turned-down eyes, and turned-up eyes. For most fishing, other than trout, a standard ring eye is probably your best choice. Turned-up eyes are often used for dry flies. The turned-up eye is certainly recommended for dry flies on a hook size of 18 or smaller; turned-down eyes reduce the gap clearance on small flies, making it difficult to hook fish. Turned-up eyes are also fine if you want to snell on a bite or shock tippet, but I can think of no other reason for using them in salt water. Turned-down eyes—those whose eye is tilted downward—do offer a slight advantage for some patterns and fishing conditions. They're most commonly used on trout flies of size 16 or larger. When I'm tying a Bend-Back-style fly, I prefer a turned-down eye. This fly is tied reverse style—the wing is tied on the point side of the hook. This causes the hook to ride under water with the point away from the bottom. The turned-up eye forces the fly to ride more in a reversed position. In my view one reverse-style fly, the Clouser Deep Minnow, is the most important underwater fly to come along in a decade or more. This fly has lead eyes attached to the hook; these cause the hook to ride with its point up or reversed. And while a ring eye does a nice job, I think the turned-down eye (which, when tied reverse style, actually rides up) does a better one. When the fly is crawling along the bottom, each twitch on the line causes the upward bend at the hook eye to lift the fly off the bottom.

The shank is the straight portion of a fly. You can now buy commercially made bendback hooks; these have a short, straight portion just in back of the hook eye, and then the shank is bent so you can tie a Bend-Back fly. Such a bend should be only slight—barely detectable. In my view, the commercial models that I've seen were bent way too much. On a good Bend-Back pattern the wing hides the hook shank. If the body of the shank falls well below the wing, it's not properly tied, and while it is rather weedless the fish seem less attracted to it.

The diameter of the shank is important, too. Hooks with a very thin diameter (providing the steel is well tempered) are excellent for getting better penetration in a tough-mouthed fish, such as a tarpon. Thin hook shanks also permit you to tie flies that will sink more slowly than would the same pattern tied on a larger-diameter model. Trout fishermen use thin-shanked hooks to get a higher float from dry flies, and thicker shanks are used to cause nymphs and streamers to sink faster. All hooks are categorized as either normal or "X." An "X" designation tells you that this isn't a regular shank. Thus a 2XL is a hook slightly longer than normal, and a 5XL longer still. A hook with a 2XS label would be slightly shorter than normal length.

The barb is what's supposed to hold a hooked fish. For years relatively huge barbs were constructed; many hooks still have them. Today most experienced fly fishermen prefer only the "suggestion" of a barb, or none at all. I've been hooked by eight people during my fishing career and am here to tell you that a little bit of barb holds a hell of a lot of meat. You simply don't need much barb to hold a fish. For more than 20 years I've crushed the barb from all my hooks, except those for serious jumpers such as big tarpon and billfish. For these fish, I file away *almost* all the barb. The major reason for removing or reducing the size of the barb is to help in penetration. The smaller the barb, the less meat the hook has to penetrate—and the easier it is to release the fish, as well. A mistake made by many who crush the barb on a highly tempered hook (such as most trout hooks) is to clamp down the pliers at right angles to the hook. Instead, slide the point of your pliers past the barb and then close them firmly (see the photo on page 40). This will support the hook; rarely will one break. The trend among modern hook makers is to reduce the barb to a very small one—and I think this is a move in the right direction.

Most experts agree that the biggest fault of anglers, whether we fish for tiny trout or throw our flies to sailfish, is that too often we use hooks that aren't sharp enough. Maybe it's because we assume a fish's mouth is simi-

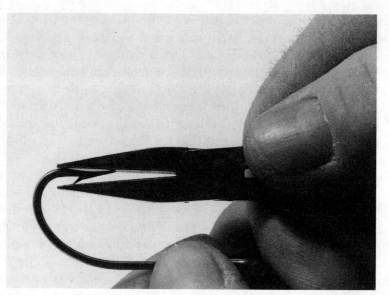

Crimp a barb in this manner and you'll never break another hook.

lar to ours. It isn't. A fish has to grab a crab with tough claws or a baitfish with upraised spines on its back. It takes little imagination to consider what would happen to the inside of the mouth of a human who did this! A fish's mouth has to be rubber-tire tough. If hooks are to quickly penetrate that tough inner lining, then, their points have to be very sharp.

Most hooks are manufactured by feeding a soft wire into a machine. A miniature hatchet strikes the soft wire, raising the barb. Then the point is ground, or a stamp pounds the end to a point. Following this, the hook is bent to shape, then heat-tempered to harden it. The sharpness of the point is determined by how well the grinding or stamping operation works. A dozen hooks examined from the same box will often show varying degrees of sharpness. Some modern hooks are "chemically" sharpened. This is done by agitating the hooks in an acid bath that eats their metal. By withdrawing the hooks at precisely the right time, they're left with a sharp point.

But any point can be dulled during fishing, so it pays to check and resharpen when needed. If I miss two strikes, I'm careful to check my point. There's an easy way to do this: Press the point gently against your thumbnail, then drag it across the nail's surface. If the point doesn't dig in immediately, it's time to resharpen. Hooks that are sharp can be dulled in many ways. The bone in the mouth of a fish can turn the point. The point can hit something during your backcast (this happens a lot when dry-fly fishing), or get dulled when it's pulled free from a snag. Whenever you miss two strikes you think you should have connected on, make it a habit to check your hook point.

I believe that the most inefficient hook point is one that's perfectly round. Not that this won't work—it will—but it's really more of a punctur-

Sharp hooks are essential. The best way to check them is to drag the point across your fingernail under only slight pressure. If the hook doesn't dig in, it needs sharpening.

ing tool. Since the process of chemically sharpening hooks has been developed, however, you can now get round points that are very sharp. There are experienced tarpon guides in the Keys who've told me they prefer this new chemically sharpened round point. They claim that it's more than sharp enough for penetration, so it needs no presharpening; in addition, a round hook tends to leave the smallest hole in the fish's mouth during the battle. Still, the most efficient point for me is one that has sharp cutting edges and a well-supported point that won't curl when you strike a fish. Even on a size 10/0 saltwater hook, I sharpen just the very tip.

There are many ways to sharpen a hook. Any one of them is better than doing nothing. With the exception of some of the hard ceramic models, most experts feel that sharpening stones are not the most efficient tools for shaping hook points. A stone soon grooves. Files or tools that resemble files, on the other hand, have flat surfaces; this is what you need to get the desired sharp cutting edges.

For trout fishing, one of the best tools is a fingernail file, available at most drugstore and cosmetic counters. They're often called diamond dust files, but they're usually made with silicone carbide. This file is a flat aluminum strip with a handle. On one side of the strip is a coating of very fine material that will sharpen even a size 24 hook. The other side is a bit coarser and will sharpen hooks as large as a size 2. If you're going to sharpen hooks of size 2 or bigger, I suggest buying a different file—a *6-inch-long Nicholson Smooth.* It can be found in many hardware stores.

Files have a tendency to rust, but I've developed a simple method to prevent this. Take a discarded man's belt. Cut two strips from the belt almost as long as your file. Lay them on waxed paper or aluminum foil so that the rough side of the leather faces up. Then saturate the leather a number of times with WD-40 or a similar compound. When you think that the leather has absorbed all the WD-40 it can, place the file between the two treated surfaces and wrap the leather with tape to form a file holster. With this gadget I've been able to carry my file around salt water for two years without rust occurring.

To create a point that's well supported (so that it doesn't curl when striking a fish) and has cutting edges, make what I call a diamond point. For me this is the best of all sharpening methods. *First, it's important to understand that if you sharpen a hook with a file by stroking from the bend toward the point, you'll finish with a burr on the point. To properly sharpen a hook with a file*, always *stroke from the point toward the bend of the hook.*

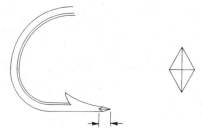

Sharpen the hook into a diamond shape for the best results.

Here's how to make a diamond point. I think everyone knows what a pup tent looks like—a triangular shape. What you're going to do is create an upside-down pup tent shape on the inside of the hook point, and a normal pup tent shape on the outside. Hold the hook so the point is toward you. Angle your file to the side and make several strokes near the point. This forms one side of an upside-down pup tent. Then angle the file against the other inside surface and make several strokes. This forms the complete upside-down pup tent, with a sharp end on the bottom. Now angle your file on one outside edge, stroking toward the bend. This will form half a pup tent, as well as another sharp edge. Angle the file on the other side of the point, stroking toward the bend, to form the other side of the pup tent. You've now given a diamond shape to the point—four cutting edges that end in a sharp, well-supported point. *One other important idea: Only sharpen the back a short distance.* For example, on a 3/0 hook I would never sharpen more than 1/16 inch of the point. You want a very short, sharp, and well-supported point.

Hooks used in saltwater fly fishing today are basically made from either carbon steel or stainless steel. Some anglers avoid stainless; they feel it remains in an escaped fish's mouth for long periods. But I've been told by several biologists that fish form a festering sore around any hook, and can get rid of a stainless hook about as quickly as one of carbon steel.

The final and perhaps most important factor in hook construction is the temper of the steel. One of the most popular stainless hooks in the world is too soft. The disadvantages of a softer metal are that the hook's point will curl on the strike, or won't hold up when you hook hard-mouthed fish (this is another reason why you should sharpen only the tip of the point). Also, on the strike the hook might be crushed closed, or during the fight the bend might open enough to permit a fish to escape. Fortunately, the stainless hooks that have been developed in the past three or four years are almost all of high-grade steel and resist bending. These newer models are as different from the old as a simple box camera is different from a modern computerized camera. You can now purchase stainless hooks that are about as hard-tempered as the old-fashioned carbon steel ones.

Hooks are important in freshwater fly fishing, too. Obviously, the lighter the wire (so long as it's strong enough), the higher a dry fly will float. But you need different lengths of hooks, as well as hook diameters. A caddis nymph is usually best tied on a hook with a curl in its shank. Many stonefly imitations are best tied on longer-shanked hooks. *Bend-Back flies for salt or fresh water should always be tied on longer-shanked hooks for better hookups.* When you need to get flies deeper in the water column, hooks with a larger-than-normal diameter are recommended.

How do you select hooks for your purposes? Several factors influence hook selection. If you're fishing very shallow water, a lightweight hook is obviously desirable; look for a thin-wire hook when you're dry-fly fishing, seeking trout or bass in skinny water, or on the flats after redfish, bonefish, or flounder. If you're trying to get down deep over a wreck or reef, on the other hand, then a heavier shank is desirable. The power of the fish and the strength of your tippet are also vital in selecting the right hooks. If you're after a world record on very light tippet material, you simply won't be able to drive a large-diameter hook through the fish's flesh on the strike. With normal gear, a very light-wire hook will be useless if you're trying to keep a fish from heavy cover. With soft-mouthed fish such as sea trout or shad, a very thin-diameter hook tends to cut through the flesh, opening a hole that the hook may fall from during the battle.

Hook color has some influence on the pattern you tie, too. For example, sand eels are important in fly fishing the waters of the Northeast. These bait are sleek and silvery. Bass seek minnows that are basically silvery in color. When I'm tying streamer flies to imitate these baitfish, then, I much prefer a light wire-plated or stainless hook. A fly tied with a dark-colored hook looks unnatural. Conversely, I wouldn't use a silver-plated hook for a Woolly Bugger pattern.

Hook size is also important. Most tiers use a size 16 hook for a normal size 16 fly, but if you tie flies smaller than size 18, they're sometimes best tied on a hook 1 size larger than recommended—providing that hook is made of light wire. This results in better hookups. In salt water, however, bonito and often tuna will feed on very small baitfish—sometimes no more than 2 inches long. Snook do the same with glass minnows. Dress these patterns on a large hook and you reduce your chances for a strike. *If there's a trend among saltwater fly fishermen regarding hooks, it's that they almost always use hooks much bigger than is required.* Not too many seasons ago the two most popular hook sizes when fishing for tarpon in the 60- to 150-pound class were 4/0 and 5/0. Experienced fishermen have since found that using a smaller hook makes a fly that's easier to cast and penetrates better, and so most tarpon patterns today are tied on 2/0 or 3/0 hooks. I expect the trend toward using smaller hooks for many saltwater species to continue.

Let me suggest that it is important to think about what hooks you'll use for various species and fishing conditions. And I'd like to recommend that you look at some of the most modern models of hooks, too; perhaps you'll find among them several new types that fit your needs exactly.

Leaders

Every fly fisherman has to use a leader, so it pays to understand the functions of this important piece of tackle. (I'll go into more detail in part 2 about leaders for specific situations or species.) There are four basic types of leaders, each different from the others. Those used to catch trout are perhaps the most complex. (I'll delve much deeper into this subject in chapter 10.) These leaders have to control drag and allow the fly to float naturally with the currents. They must also allow a very quiet entry. For much general fishing we have a basic tapered leader, which is used for salt water, salmon, bass, and a host of other species. This leader can be composed of either several strands of different diameters of monofilament knotted together, or a single strand tapered from a large to a small diameter. Such leaders must turn over the fly easily at the end of the cast. *They also allow you to manipulate the fly.* Level leaders are made up of a single strand of monofilament of the same diameter, and have special applications. The final leader is one with a bite tippet on the end, which can be of wire or heavy monofilament. This leader is built so that sharp-toothed fish, such as pike, muskies, barracudas, wahoo, and other species, can't sever the connection to the fly.

Fly fishermen have developed some terminology involving leaders. It might be worthwhile to examine some of these terms:

Butt Section This is the thickest part of a leader and is connected in some manner to the fly-line end.

Midsection The part of the leader between the butt section and the tippet.

Tippet The thinnest or weakest section in a tapered leader.

Bite Tippet Sometimes called a shock tippet or shock leader, this is a piece of wire or a heavy monofilament attached to the front of the tippet and connected to the fly. It's used to prevent sharp-toothed fish from cutting off the fly.

Class Tippet The International Game Fish Association has established special requirements in order for an angler to be awarded a world record. It has divided the tippet strength into various classes. A class tippet is usually referred to as a specific strength tippet that would qualify for a world-record catch.

Butt Section   Midsection   Tippet   Bite or

Shock Tippet

Parts of a leader

X   This designates the strength of the tippet. For example, a leader may be referred to as a "12-foot 6X." Trout fishermen tend to complicate things—it makes it more mysterious and fun for those who enjoy the sport. So instead of just listing the strength of the tippet, they describe it as an X factor. What the devil does *X* mean? The following is not totally accurate, but it's close enough for you to know how strong a tippet is. If you subtract the number in front of the X from 9, you get the approximate strength of the tippet. Let me give two examples. If the leader is a 7½-foot 5X, subtract 5 from 9 and the tippet is approximately 4 pounds in strength. One more example: A 9½-foot 3X is a tippet testing 6 pounds. Because many companies manufacture monofilament with slightly different processes, the pound test can vary slightly—but it's rarely more than a pound off this formula.

Diameter   For many years if you wanted to know the diameter of a leader, you simply subtracted the X factor in thousandths of an inch from .011. For example, with a tippet of 5X, subtract .005 from .011. A 5X leader would then be .006 inch in diameter. A 6X leader would be .005 inch, or $\frac{1}{1,000}$ inch thinner. The newer monofilaments throw this arithmetic off a little, but the rule is still valid enough to be useful.

Materials

Leaders are made from a number of materials. There's monofilament, which can vary in its degree of limpness (more about this later). Some leaders (mainly the butt section) are made from very thin strands of monofilament that are braided. A rather new product is fluorocarbon, which resembles nylon monofilament. This material is slightly larger in diameter than the same-strength monofilament. The advantage of fluorocarbon, though, is that it possesses the same light reflective index as water—which means that fish are less likely to see it. It also has specific density approximately 1.8 times that of water, which means it will sink slowly. For extra-clear waters (such as some lakes) and for exceptionally sharp-eyed fish (such as the tuna family), fluorocarbon *tippets* may offer some real advantages. I don't believe that using a tapered leader made entirely from the more expensive fluorocarbon offers much of an advantage; I suggest using it only in the tippet connected to the fly. Leaders also come in various colors, from clear to brilliant orange and yellow. Some tapered leaders have a metallic core; these are designed to sink quickly when you're fishing for trout with nymphs and streamers. There's also a special material that you can add to your leaders to give them some shock absorbency. This material is often called Power Gum or Shock Gum; one manufacturer calls it Bunjeebutt. You may want to take a look at this. I'll explain its purpose a little later.

The reasons for using a leader need to be understood. Perhaps the most important function of a leader is generally not appreciated. If you fish calmer water for trout or bonefish, for example, you know that you need a longer leader. But most people don't know why the leader needs to be lengthened. *The main reason is to get the impact of the fly line farther away from the fish.* It's the crashing of a fly line to the water that alerts the fish. That's why the most popular trout lines are 3- to 5-weight—especially for dry-fly fishing and delicate work. The calmer the water, the more difficult or wary the fish, the longer the leader must be. This applies to fly fishing worldwide. For instance, on a spring creek where wise fish reside, a 16-foot leader is not unusual. And in late spring or early summer, when giant tarpon have been cast to many times, they move to the white sand flats on the ocean side of the Keys. If you use a short leader here, you'll only spook fish. It's not unusual under such conditions for experienced tarpon fishermen to employ a leader of 16 feet. When I bonefish I find that most of the time, a 12-foot leader is the shortest I want—unless the wind is really puffing. But on a calm day I quickly lengthen my leader to 16 feet. Such long leaders—if properly tapered and matched to the rod and fly—will turn over well.

Another important function of leaders is to present a near invisible connection between the fly and the fly line. Obviously, if you were to tie your fly directly to the line, few fish would ever strike.

A leader also has the function of either creating a drag-free drift, or allowing you to manipulate the fly. The difference between these two leaders is substantial and I'll address it shortly. It's important that the tippet not be too large in diameter, lest the fish see it and not strike. But larger-diameter leaders can spoil the action of the fly. The tippet must thus be supple enough to allow the fly a natural freedom of movement on the surface or beneath it.

Another factor in good leader design is the ability to unroll properly, but allow the fly to come to the water rather quietly. This is where using the correct materials and building the proper tapers is important.

Remember, too, that you can attach a bite tippet to the front of your leader to prevent cuts or fish with rough mouths from abrading through the connection to the fly.

Finally, a careless act by many fishermen has caused the deaths of many birds. If you clip off a piece of leader material and throw it away, a bird may pick it up for use as a nesting material. But they can get tangled in it when flying. Take it home and discard it or burn it. But don't throw leader material away.

Let's examine the different kinds of leaders more closely.

Tapered Leaders for Trout

Almost all trout leaders are tapered. Trout are sharp eyed and wary, and they live in a relatively small environment, even when you consider a fair-sized river. Otters eat them, cormorants gobble them down when they're small, raccoons harass them, ospreys and eagles pluck them from the water—and fishermen are always bothering them. In hard-fished waters many trout have been deceived a number of times by what looked like a tasty fly, only to find they were hooked to an angler. No wonder they're wary! For this reason the insect imitations that we offer trout must float or drift to them in a natural manner. While even the novice dry-fly fisherman knows that his fly must float without drag, many long-time trout anglers don't understand that nymphs fished in the water column should also come to the trout in a natural manner. Drag occurs under water just as it does on the surface—and trout are very much aware of this. Correctly tapered leaders are called for whenever you're fishing trout.

Let me say a few words about what I think is important in building any kind of tapered leader. *For years we've been told that we should use stiff material in the butt section. I believe this to be totally wrong.* When your rod sweeps forward and stops, the line behind you begins unrolling from the tip. Gradually the line unrolls until it arrives at the leader—which must also unroll to deliver the fly. *Common sense should tell you that if a supple fly line unrolls and arrives at the leader, a stiff butt section is going to resist unrolling.* What you really need is enough **supple weight** in the butt section to cause the leader to continue to unroll. *You need a flexible butt section, but one heavy enough to let the inertia from the line continue to unroll the remainder of the leader. I repeat—you don't want a butt section that's stiff and unyielding. Instead, you want a butt section that's heavy enough to carry the energy to the end of the cast yet also very flexible, so it will unroll easily.*

I believe that the best tapered leaders (for any kind of fly fishing) should have a butt section that's limp, but heavy. For most trout dry-fly leaders I like a butt section of *at least* .023 inch in diameter. **This butt section should comprise nearly 50 percent of the total leader length.** It should then taper rapidly from the butt section to the tippet.

Tapered Leaders for General Fresh- and Saltwater Use

With the exception of trout fishing, tapered leaders generally fall into a single category. The same principle applies: You need a butt section that's flexible yet heavy enough to transfer the energy of the cast through the line and leader to properly deliver the fly.

It's a little difficult to buy the exact tapered leader you need for every fishing situation, although companies are now responding to the need. Still, I think it's best for fly fishermen to know how to build their own tapered leaders. And in some cases you may want to modify an existing leader for a changing situation. It's really easy to do.

You'll have to construct your tapered leaders from various diameters of monofilament. It's helpful to know that you can join two sections of monofilament more easily if they're of the same apparent limpness. *If you use monofilaments that are all the same brand, you'll find that your knots form and close better.* For example, you could use all Ande, or all

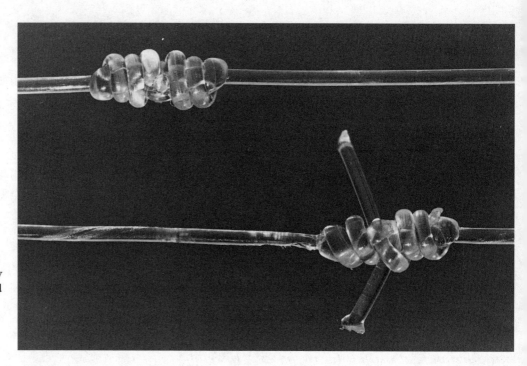

If knots are closed correctly, they won't slip. Therefore they should be closely trimmed, as shown above. Protruding stubs, like those below, catch the leader, grass, and other materials.

DuPont Super-Tough—any of the premium-brand spinning lines will work well. Spinning and plug-casting lines are usually limp, but not too limp, and have high knot strength.

Incidentally, when you're finishing a leader, after all knots have been closed firmly be sure to trim them close. If not, they may cause you trouble when you start casting and fishing. Also, never use rubber or a similar material to remove coils from a leader. This will cause small ruptures in the leader that will easily break. Instead, firmly grasp a portion of the leader in your hands then run the leader several times through your clenched fist. The friction heat built up by running it through your hands will eliminate almost all coiling—and do the leader no damage.

You need only one knot to build tapered leaders—either a surgeon's knot or a blood (sometimes called a barrel) knot will do. *The surgeon's knot usually doesn't tie well in lines testing more than 40 pounds. I prefer using a blood knot down to 30-pound test. With lines testing less than 30 pounds, I generally use a surgeon's—it's quick and just as strong.* If you use a surgeon's knot on a line that tests less than 10 pounds, make it a triple surgeon's rather than the conventional double. If you use the blood knot, I recommend that on a line testing more than 25 pounds, you make only three turns with both tag ends to join the strands. On diameters smaller than this, make one more turn with the lighter test than with the stronger. For example, on 20-pound test you'll make four turns, but on 15-pound you'll make five turns.

Because you'll be casting different sizes of flies with medium to powerful rods—and may be encountering wind—your tapered leaders will vary

Never remove the coils from a leader by pulling it through a piece of rubber. This often nicks the line and may seriously weaken the monofilament. Instead, grip the line securely in one hand and pull the leader through your other, tightly clasped hand. The small amount of heat and the tension you exert in the clasped hand will cause the leader to straighten—and without any damage.

slightly from situation to situation, but the procedure for tying them is the same.

When fishing with lines from sizes 9 through 12, and throwing flies that are difficult to turn over (crab patterns, large Lefty's Deceivers, Clouser Minnows, Whistlers, and similar patterns), I recommend that you use a butt section of 60-pound test. If your rod is 7 through 9 in size and you're throwing smaller flies, I recommend using 50- or no smaller than 40-pound test for the butt section. For 5 and 6 rods, try a 30-pound butt section. *One of the most important factors in building good tapered leaders is to begin with a heavy, flexible butt section.*

Here's how to build a basic tapered leader: Start with a butt section that's half the length of the total leader. If you begin with a 10-foot leader, make the next section 1 foot in length. *The 30- and 20-pound sections will remain 1 foot in length for all tapered leaders.* If you increase the leader to 12 feet, increase the length of the next section to 2 feet. If you make a 14-foot leader, increase the second section by another foot (up to 3 feet); for a 16-foot leader, increase the second section an additional foot (to 4 feet). Add approximately 2 feet of tippet (of 15-, 12-, or 10-pound test) and you have a simple formula for making a great tapered leader for most fresh- and saltwater fishing situations. (This formula does not apply to trout fishing, however; see chapter 10.) Don't worry about being too exact. If you're off by a few inches with any of your strands, it won't make a difference. Unlike some tapered leaders, you won't need a micrometer to build these. Finally, add your tippet.

If these directions sound difficult when you read them, look at the chart below; I think you'll agree this is a very simple way to build leaders. And while this may seem like an outrageous formula to most fly fishermen, try casting such a leader against any other. I think you'll be convinced.

I remember telling Bob Clouser about this concept. Bob guides smallmouth bass fishermen for most of the summer on the Susquehanna River near his home and shop. Many of his clients are not good casters and Bob, of course, likes to fish his lead-head Clouser Minnows. Soon after I showed him this formula, he called me. "I can't believe how well my clients are turning over their flies," he said. "This formula works on short or long casts and even into the wind."

Here are six formulas for making different lengths of leader, all with 50-pound test butt sections, *if you're using a fly rod of 8-weight or larger.*

Length	50 lb.	40 lb.	30 lb.	20 lb.	15, 12, or 10 lb.
8'	4'	1'	6"	6"	1½–2'
9'	4½'	1'	1'	6"	1½–2'
10'	5'	1'	1'	1'	2'
12'	6'	2'	1'	1'	2'
14'	7'	3'	1'	1'	2'
16'	8'	4'	1'	1'	2'

Remember, all the monofilament you use should be from the same manufacturer.

Level Leaders

Tapered leaders are not necessary in many fly-fishing situations. Indeed, in many cases they don't serve as well as level leaders. A level leader is one composed of a single, uniform strand of monofilament. Generally, you'll need it whenever you can let your line and leader fall to the surface without fear of frightening the fish. A typical situation in which a level leader is best is fishing in lily-pad-choked waters. The bass are not going to see your leader; nor will it have any impact on the surface, which is covered by the pads. A tapered leader, with strands connected by knots, can create problems here: The knots will pick up bits of grass, or snag in the lily pad leaves or stems. In such a situation a level leader of 15- or 20-pound test, connected to the fly line and the fly, is ideal. Such a leader usually need only be about 6 or 7 feet long. It will turn over beautifully and eliminate the problems that a tapered leader would incur.

A level leader is best fished where there's floating grass or the surface is choked with vegetation, such as in many largemouth bass and pike environments. The same applies in saltwater areas where grass has been distributed on the surface by the tide. Floating grass can snag on the knots used to build the tapers, spoiling your retrieve. Furthermore, this grass disguises the line and leader's impact on the water anyway, so that a tapered leader is neither desirable or necessary.

When you're throwing a fly under low, overhanging brush, a short, level leader will do the job better than a tapered one. A tapered leader often slows the cast down at the end, opening the loop. A short, level leader, however, will let you throw a tight loop under the branches. For some species you may have to add a short shock leader. Snook fishing in such situations is best done with a 4- to 5-foot leader of 15- to 20-pound test. It should have a 1-foot section of 30- or 40-pound mono between it and the fly to avoid cutoffs.

Another situation in which I prefer a level leader is when I'm using a sinking-tip line and have removed half (5 feet) of the sinking front portion. This gives me a floating line with a 5-foot sinking tip—a great line to use with a popping bug or Dahlberg Diver for snook in the backcountry. A short level leader is attached, usually 4 to 6 feet of 15-pound test. If I throw the bug or Diver into a hot spot and start an immediate retrieve, the fly will move noisily along the surface. If the retrieve is delayed, though, the short line will cause the fly to be dragged a few inches under the surface. Then, when I start my retrieve, the fly will swim back to the surface and begin gurgling; it'll keep making noise so long as I continue the retrieve. If I stop, the bug will sink below the surface again. A level leader is by far the best one to use with such an outfit.

For some years experienced fly fishermen have recognized that they don't want to use a long leader when fishing a sinking fly line. The line sinks quickly and the long leader goes down slowly. This forces the fly to ride to high above the line in the water column. Short leaders—rarely longer than 4 feet, and often shorter—are the ticket. There's no need to taper very short leaders; simply attach a level length of monofilament to the end of the sinking line, tie on your fly, and start fishing.

While you may or may not be interested in this, I enjoy taking photos of jumping tarpon, and a level leader helps me get good shots. Instead of using a conventional tarpon leader, take a short level section of 25- or 30-pound-test monofilament and attach it to a shock leader of 80- or 100-

pound mono. Have someone use this rig to cast to and hook a tarpon. Then tell the angler to lock the drag and not let the fish run. The tarpon will rarely be able to take line or break it. Instead it jumps all around the boat at close range, where you can often get some dandy photos.

As you've seen, then, there are many areas of fly fishing where a level leader is more desirable and practical than a tapered one. But both level and tapered leaders can be complex. I will get much more specific as to their design and use in part 2.

Fly Lines

The number of fly lines available today boggles the mind of even an experienced fly fisherman. I believe that the Cortland Line Company alone makes more than 350 different lines, if you count line weights, tapers, sink rates, and colors. And I've heard that Scientific Anglers makes even more. From this huge inventory, how do you select lines for your special fishing requirements?

First, let's examine basic fly lines, of which there are four types.

Weight-Forward Lines

The most popular design in both salt and fresh water is the weight-forward. This is a line with a front taper; behind this is a heavier belly section, and behind that some long, thin running line. By holding the front taper and heavy head outside of the guides on your forward cast, you can obtain distance when shooting line. The thin rear line is easily pulled through the guides when the heavy forward section is released on the shoot.

There are many different weight-forward line designs. The conventional weight-forward taper has about 10 feet of front taper, a level belly section of from 28 to a little more than 30 feet in length, followed by approximately a 5-foot back taper that meets the level line behind. A good trend I've seen recently among line companies is matching the weight-forward head length to the approximate fishing conditions of each line. Thus, a 3- or 4-weight line would have a belly section of maybe 28 feet, while a heavier line used for distance casting (such as in steelheading) might have a belly section exceeding 40 feet.

Other weight-forward line types are available. If you fish for bass along shorelines you may make short casts, retrieve line close to you, then pick up and shoot back into the target area without many false casts. In this case a weight-forward line that has a shorter belly section would be desirable. The same holds true if you're standing on a flat's bow waiting for incoming tarpon, permit, or bonefish. The fish is relatively close and you have little time to ready your cast, so a weight-forward line that has a short, heavy belly section and shorter front and back taper is helpful. In situations *where most of your casts are not long* and you want to reduce false-casting, specialty lines have been developed. These are called bass bug tapers, saltwater tapers, or a name referring to a specific target fish—tarpon tapers, bonefish tapers, and so on.

Short-bellied tapers are not the best lines for distance casting. If you're attempting a long cast, you'll hold considerable line outside the guides during false casting. The thinner running line at the rear of a short-bellied taper will have trouble turning over the heavy head well outside the rod tip, though; faulty casting usually results. *Short heads are usually for short casts. Lines with a longer front and back taper and belly section lend themselves better to distance casting.*

Weight-forward lines with short heads have another disadvantage. Because the front and back tapers are rather short and the belly section is thick and heavy, the weight is concentrated in a shorter length. *The increased weight and diameter make the line more air resistant—but also cause it to come to the water with a heavier splashdown.* In calm waters this can alert fish and ruin your chances. However, some manufacturers have become aware of this shortcoming; they're now making lines for bonefish and tarpon with a slightly longer taper, which allows for a more delicate presentation and easier distance casting. Check the specs on a fly line: If it measures at least 40 feet from the front of the line to the rear of the back taper, you've got good all-around line for flats fishing.

If you're a fairly good caster, conventional weight-forward lines will usually deliver a quieter presentation and land you more fish.

Weight-forward lines come in all sink rates, from floaters to rapid sinkers. I've found that lines with a designated sink rate of IV or V don't cast well *if the entire line is a sinker. The level portion to the rear is heavy and limp, and doesn't shoot through the guides well.* If you try to make a high-speed cast and shoot such a line through the guides, frequent tangles will result. In these cases a shooting head is much superior to a full fast-sinking line.

Clear or nearly clear weight-forward lines are available. Because a limp, level line doesn't shoot well through the guides, especially in warmer climates, manufacturers now make lines with a braided core of many fine strands of monofilament. This helps the line shoot better. Examples of such lines include bonefish and tarpon tapers. *It's important to realize that a fly line designed for bonefish or tarpon is intended for use in the Tropics.* It may thus work poorly in colder climates. It can become so stiff that it's a pain to use. Conversely, both Cortland and Scientific Anglers manufacture pike lines, which of course work well in colder climates—but can become limp and unmanageable in the Tropics. This is not the fault of the manufacturer; it's poor line selection on the part of the fly fisherman.

All modern fly lines have a core (usually a braided material) over which a tapered coating is applied. Most floating lines have a braided nylon core,

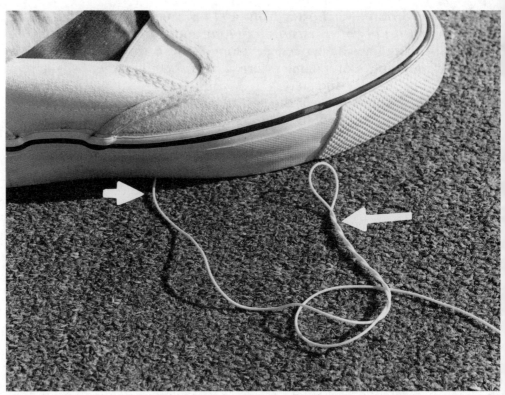

One of the most common mistakes that damage your line is to roll it under your foot on a boat deck. This puts a series of twists in the line that can't be removed.

while most sinking lines use Dacron, which sinks a little faster than monofilament. Dacron doesn't retain much coiling after it's been stored on the reel, but when you pull a floating line off your spool, it needs to be straightened. One of the quickest ways to do so is to have a companion firmly grasp one end, while you take the other. Then give one steady pull. This will generally remove all coils. If you're in a boat or by yourself, another fast way is to place a loop under your foot while you hold the loop's two ends. This amounts to about 8 or 9 feet of line. Grasping the line in both hands firmly, give a good pull to remove coiling. Repeat with more line and in a minute or so you can remove the coils from all the line you need for casting.

Some fly lines have a braided Kevlar core. Manufacturers say that this reduces elasticity in the line, resulting in a better hookset on the strike. But I think a little forgiveness on the strike may help you avoid breakoffs on the hookset. I've tried several Kevlar-core fly lines, and I'm not pleased with them. While Kevlar has less of a tendency to coil than monofilament, every Kevlar line I've used did display some curling effect. Because you can't stretch a Kevlar line, you're unable to remove those bothersome curls. I suggest avoiding braided-Kevlar-core fly lines.

But there's one weight-forward fly line I've fallen in love with, and I use it a great deal. It's manufactured by Scientific Anglers and called the Stillwater Taper. It's designed like a conventional weight-forward line, but several things make it unique and help me catch difficult fish. First, it has a fairly long belly and front and back tapers. This allows a gentle presentation of the fly. Second, it's perfectly clear—as clear as any monofilament spinning line! Third, it was designed for cold-water lakes, but I find that it isn't too limp when used in the Tropics. Because of these three characteristics, it's a fabulous line for fishing clear waters (such as in lakes), where wary fish are often put off by a conventional fly line. In effect, you have a leader from the fly to the backing! I've taken smallmouth bass and trout with this line at times, when I'm convinced I wouldn't have on a conventional fly line. I also like the Stillwater Taper's sink rate, which is a bit faster than an intermediate sinking line. And on a shoot for distance, this slick monofilament line moves like a scalded dog. You can average longer casts than you can with conventional fly lines. Airflo makes a similar line, as does Monic; Royal Wulff Products sells a triangle-taper clear mono line. I urge you to try one of these lines if it fits your fishing conditions. So far as I know, clear fly lines don't work well with a nail knot to fasten the leader; I recommend a whipped loop.

Some weight-forward sinking lines now have the same continuous color throughout their length. For example, a full-sinking line may be all gray or all brown. Some tarpon and bonefish tapers are also the same color throughout. The clear monofilament lines are perfectly clear throughout their length. "So what's wrong with that?" you may ask—if you've never used these lines. With any sinking line, you'll find that you can't lift much of it from beneath the surface to make your backcast. Instead you need to retrieve the line until you can make a roll cast, which will lift the line from beneath the water and allow you to make the backcast. The problem with a line uniform in color, then, is that you never know how much line is still below the surface. You'll frequently retrieve too much line, necessitating extra false casts to get back to the target. Or you'll attempt a backcast but never get the line out of the water.

There's a simple solution to this. Go to a local pond or stream and make a series of casts. Determine just how much line you can have out to make a good roll cast, lift the line from below the surface, and make a good backcast. Mark the spot on the line with a permanent marking pen. When you get home, make a tube nail knot of at least 10 turns with 6-pound-test monofilament on the mark. Make sure you pull both ends of the nail knot firmly. Then carefully clip the ends tight against the coils. Add a little Plio-bond, Ultra-Flex, Aquaseal, or similar glue to the nail knot. *The next time you retrieve this line you'll feel the nail knot as it moves across your stripping finger and know that it's time to make your roll cast, in order to set up a good backcast. This works during the retrieve even after dark.* In fact, most of the time you can hear the nail knot scraping over the rod guides. The knot is so small, however, that it doesn't interfere with casting.

Sinking-Tip Lines

There's a specialty line available called a sinking-tip line; brand names include Wet Tip and Sink Tip. Usually this is a weight-forward line; the front portion of the line sinks, while the rest of it floats. The tip portion comes in various sink rates, from very slow to very fast. It's important to understand how the sink rate of the tip can affect both casting and fishing success. To aid anglers, the sinking tips of such lines are often a different color than the rest of the fly line. Also, some manufacturers color-code the tips to indicate the sink rate. These colors make it easier for you to select from the many sinking tips which one you need for existing fishing conditions.

Sinking-tips are useful in some situations, but before looking at the advantages, let's examine some of the drawbacks to using this design. *Perhaps no other line is more difficult to cast and make a soft and easy presentation.* The sinking portion of the line is usually the same diameter throughout. As the floating line unrolls forward smoothly, it encounters the short, weighted portion and has some difficulty making this heavier tip continue to unroll. This casting problem is compounded when the tip is heavier (its sink rate is faster). Sinking-tips are not for delicate presentations or lazy casters. While a tight loop is often desirable when you cast a floating line, not so with a sinking-tip. If your loop is too tight, frequent leader tangles will result. You want to throw a slightly open loop to keep the weighted tip from collapsing in front of the line and leader. If you develop too much line speed, the weighted tip will unroll and tuck under. This, of course, again spoils presentation. At this writing, the only manufacturer I know that has attacked this casting and presentation problem is Scientific Anglers. Its Mastery Series Wet Tip lines have a design different from most others: The tip section varies in length according to the weight of the line. The lighter the line, the shorter the sinking portion; where the floating section joins the weighted part, their weights are nearly the same. Most important, the forward end of the sinking section attached to the leader is tapered. If you've cast conventional sinking-tip lines and then fish with a Mastery Series, I think you will agree that it's much superior.

In chapter 8, "Casting," I'll demonstrate how to make casts with weighted fly lines.

Another drawback of sinking-tip lines is that the front portion sinks, while the rest of the line floats. They're designed this way so that you can pick up the floating section and then lift the sinking portion from the water more easily for your backcast. The problem, however, comes when you begin a retrieve. The floating portion is drawn toward you; *this causes the sinking part of the line to loft toward the surface.* Unless you make a fairly long pause between strips, the tip continues to move upward in the water column. And during fast retrieves, the sinking portion will actually be pulled to the surface.

What this means, of course, is that while you're using a sinking-tip because you want the fly to swim under water, it won't swim at a consistent depth; it'll be pulled upward every time you strip in line.

Also, if you make a long cast with a sinking-tip line onto water that's choppy or wavy, the waves will affect your retrieve. The sinking portion of the line will be below the surface but the floating portion will be bobbing up and down on the waves, causing the fly to move when you're not manipulating it.

Having read all of this, you may wonder why anyone would want to use a line with a sinking tip. There are some special purposes for which it excels. One is fishing largemouth bass in a lake whose surface is coated in vegetation, but features small open pockets in the grass or lily pads. A similar situation occurs when you fish snook that are holding in sand holes or pockets of water that are slightly deeper than the flats surrounding the hole.

If you use an underwater fly and floating line to cast to such pockets, you'll have difficulty getting the fly deep in the water. And with a full-sinking line, the portion of line between you and the hole in the weeds will sink into the vegetation; this will severely interfere with your backcast.

This is one place where a sinking-tip line excels. You can move near the open hole in the weeds and cast so that your fly falls to the far end of the opening. The sinking-tip will take the fly deep into the water. Then start your retrieve and, as the sinking portion approaches the near edge of the hole, strip faster. This will cause the fly to loft upward and will allow you to lift the line out of the hole for an easy, trouble-free backcast, without worrying about catching the vegetation. No other line works so well in this situation.

When you're making short casts, want the line to get down quickly, and aren't making long retrieves—such as in trout and Pacific salmon fishing—a sinking-tip is often the perfect line.

And there's another situation in which the sinking-tip will do something no other fly line can. For this you need a sinking-tip with a slow sink rate, or one that has only a 5-foot sinking section. If you have a conventional sinking-tip with a 10-foot sinking portion, you can cut off the first 5 feet. This gives you a floating line with a 5-foot sinking tip.

Using either of these sinking-tips, attach a long leader—at least 9 feet—and to this secure either a popping bug or a Dahlberg Diver. Make a cast into cover where a snook, bass, or other fish is likely to be hanging out. If you begin retrieving the moment the bug hits the water, the short sinking section will remain on the surface, and you can work the popper or Diver exactly as you would with a floating line. Then stop retrieving and wait a bit. The sinking portion will slowly drag the popper or Diver below the surface.

After a long pause, begin retrieving again. This will cause the bug or Diver to swim under the water for a brief period then emerge on the top, where it will again act like a popping bug or Diver. This procedure—swimming the bug then manipulating it on top—can be repeated again and

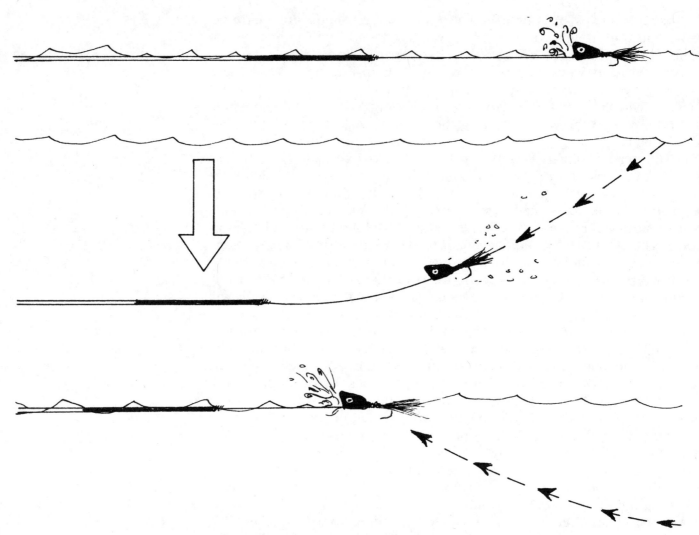

Fishing a popping bug with a sinking-tip.

again. It will only work with sinking-tip lines and at times can be devastating to many species, especially snook and largemouth bass.

Sinking-Head or -Belly Lines

Another version of the weight-forward line is the sinking-head or -belly line. Here the first 20 to 30 feet of the front of the line sinks, while the remainder of the line is rather thin, but floats. Actually, these lines are modified shooting heads, which I'll examine next. The advantage of a sinking-head or -belly over a sinking-tip is that the entire head sinks, which means the fly will go deeper. And because a considerable length of the line sinks, the fly will track at the same depth as the sinking portion of the line; during the retrieve it will stay at the same level in the water column. This is a decided advantage over a sinking-tip, whose floating portion will cause the fly to rise on every strip of your retrieve.

Your casting technique needs to be modified slightly with a sinking-tip or -head. I'll go into more detail on this in chapter 8, "Casting." But basically, because a sinking-head or -belly is thin and heavy, this line will transport flies better and farther with less effort than a floating line can. On a windy day, then, a sinking-head can really help you get distance.

Most weight-forward sinking lines have a front taper, which doesn't sink as fast as the heavier belly. This causes the fly to ride well above the belly portion. Jim Teeny, a superb northwestern steelhead fisherman, revolutionized sinking lines when he developed his Teeny lines. The head portion of these lines is level, then all of the sinking portion descends at the same rate—dragging the fly deeper than would a conventionally tapered sinking line. Almost all experienced anglers today, especially in salt water, have a Teeny line in their possession. The front portion sinks, but the rear of the line is a different color, and floats. This allows the line to shoot better than if the rear portion was sinking. It also tells you when to make the roll pickup for your backcast: When the colored line arrives at the tiptop, it's time to make a roll cast, lift the line from the water, and backcast. Next to a conventional floating weight-forward line, I consider one of these Teeny lines a second choice for many fishing situations. They're coded with a number that explains what the head portion weighs; a Teeny 300, for instance, is a line whose head weighs 300 grains. Such a line will work well on a 7-, 8-, or 9-weight rod and is perhaps the most useful Teeny line for bass, steelhead, salmon, and general saltwater fishing. Trout fishermen using a 6-weight rod will like the Teeny 200, which will let them get their flies well down in the water column. Remember one thing about casting any weighted lines: *For some reason I don't understand, a rod can handle a weighted line that's 1 or 2 sizes heavier than the floating line it could cast.* A standard size 6 line is 160 grains; you will thus have no trouble with a Teeny 200 on a 6-weight rod.

Shooting Heads

One of the challenges in much of fly fishing is being able to swim the fly through enough water. The ability to make longer casts and thus accomplish an extended retrieve can make a considerable difference in whether or not we score.

Coupled with this problem is that we're confronted by the wind nearly all the time. There are few fishing situations in which God allows us cast downwind. More often we have to throw into it. This is especially true for those who wade and fish open water, such as on big lakes, or in salt water, where a breeze blowing toward the land is the normal pattern. Another frequent problem is getting the fly deep enough in the water column. In many situations just swimming the fly a few feet deeper can mean more hookups.

Conventional weight-forward lines are fine for casting to 60 or so feet. But if repetitive casting at more than 70 feet is called for, it takes a strong and experienced fly fisherman to keep at it for any length of time with this line. Also, weight-forward lines have a rear section that is rather large in diameter. When you're fishing deep, this increased diameter reduces your ability to shoot the fly to the target. It also impedes the descent of a sinking line.

Tournament casters realized many years ago that by attaching some extra-thin line behind the heavy forward portion at the front of the fly line, they could obtain greater distance. These are called shooting heads by most anglers, although the correct designation is shooting taper, and when you're purchasing a commercial shooting head it'll be referred to as *ST*. Thus, an 8-weight line that floats a 30-foot shooting head would be labeled *ST8F* (Shooting Taper size 8 Floating). To buy a commercial shooting head, you need to purchase the head separately and attach it to some thinner line, called shooting line. Line manufacturers sell both the shooting heads and the shooting lines. Commercial shooting lines are simply level lines. For most freshwater fishing a shooting line of .027 inch is adequate. But for saltwater fly fishing you need to know that shooting lines with a diameter of less than .030 inch may test less than 15 pounds. In salt water, a shooting line that measures .035 inch or slightly larger is safest, since smaller-diameter shooting lines are often weaker than the leader tippet. If you put enough strain on the tackle handling a shooting line of .030 or smaller during a fish fight, the shooting line may break, losing you both shooting head and fish.

Fly fishermen use a number of materials for shooting lines, ranging from monofilament (usually 25 to 40 pounds in test) to braided leader butt material and commercial shooting lines. If you want to obtain the most distance and greatest depth with a shooting head, then monofilament is supreme. Many people, however, feel that this light line blows around too much in a breeze, and tends to tangle. The braided leader butt line is okay, and it shoots exceptionally well. But it's very rough on the hands; with repeated use it can cut through your skin. Most anglers attach commercial shooting line to the shooting head.

Commercial shooting heads are generally 30 feet in length. You can make your own shooting heads that will cast farther than most commercial ones—and it's easy to do. Buy a double-taper line that's *1 size larger than the rod calls for.* For example, if you're using a 9-weight rod, buy a 10-weight double-taper. You can make two shooting heads from a single double-taper line. The midsection of a double-taper line is level, and it tapers exactly the same way at each end. Measure back from one end of the line and cut it off. How far you measure depends on how good a caster you are. If you can easily throw 70 feet with a weight-forward line, then cut off 38 feet of the double-taper. This will give you a shooting head that's 8 feet longer than a commercial 30-footer. *Any fly line, once it unrolls or straightens, will fall to the water.* Yours will unroll a longer distance toward the target before it begins falling. Later, if you determine that 38 feet is too much for you to handle, you can shorten it.

If you've purchased a commercial shooting line, you'll need to connect it to the back of the shooting head. There are several methods. You can use whipped loops in both lines, joining them by looping one to the other. This gives you the advantage of having a shooting line on your reel; you can then loop on the type of shooting head you need for existing fishing conditions. The disadvantage is that loops tend to catch in the guides, and I find this bothersome.

Another method is to strip the finish from the last 1½ inches of the shooting head then, using size A thread and a fine needle, sew the two ends together. Put in at least a dozen stitches and the connection will be stronger than the lines. You'll have to whip over the stitches.

Perhaps the quickest and easiest method, however, is to obtain an inexpensive spool of Cortland 30- to 50-pound Braided Mono Running Line, then join the shooting head and shooting line by inserting the two line ends into a 4-inch section of it. Whip or seal the ends of the braided butt material.

If you purchase a commercial floating shooting head, I suggest getting it 1 line size larger than your rod calls for. And if it's a weighted commercial shooting head, I prefer it 2 sizes larger than the rod calls for. The reason for this is that when you make a longer cast with a weight-forward line, you always extend more than 30 feet of line outside the rod tip. Using a floating shooting head 1 size larger, or a sinking head 2 sizes larger, will permit you to shoot that line over a longer distance.

If you're not currently using shooting lines to obtain great distance or depth when fishing, you may find them of considerable help.

There will be occasions when your fly line is damaged or cut, and you'd like to repair it. Or you might want to modify it, such as by making your own shooting head. Most fly fishermen have little idea how to do this. Fortunately, it's a simple trick. What are some situations in which you might want to know this uncomplicated technique? Many anglers are now using Teeny lines, such as the most popular of all, the Teeny 300. The forward portion of this line sinks rapidly; the remainder is a floating shooting type. The trick when fishing these is to stop your retrieve when the rear of the sinking portion arrives at the rod tip, then make a roll cast to lift the line from the water for your backcast. But because you're stopping nearly all your retrieves at this point, the line just inside the tiptop receives the most wear. Many fishermen will discard the entire line once this part of the floating line is badly worn. But it's a simple matter to cut off the used area and reattach the sinking head to the newer part of the floating line.

Another example is when a fly line is cut in two. It might be severed on contact with a sharp object, or perhaps you stepped on it and it was cut. Regardless of how this happens, a simple procedure will reconnect the two parts and make the line as good as new.

Also, if you enjoy using shooting heads, one of the most practical ways to get the heads you want to use is to buy a double-taper line. Cut from each end the amount of line you wish to make a head. You can then either permanently attach the head to the shooting line or form detachable

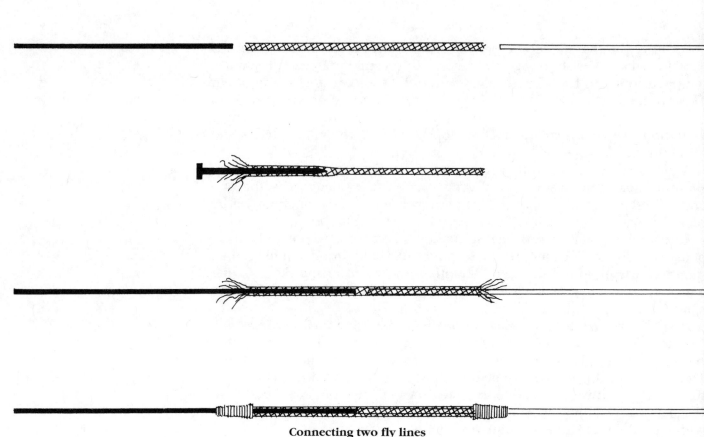

Connecting two fly lines

loops, so that you can exchange different heads while using the same shooting line.

What makes all of the above possible is the aforementioned Cortland Braided Mono Running Line. This comes on a 100-foot spool—enough for you and your friends for a lifetime of fly fishing. The cost for the spool is roughly $10. Any fly shop that handles Cortland products can get it for you. It can be purchased in 30- or 50-pound test, *but the 50-pound is useful for all purposes and I recommend buying only it.* The 30-pound is okay for working with smaller trout lines, but if you work with line sizes 8 or larger, the 50-pound makes these projects so much easier—and it *will* function on smaller lines.

Study the drawings above to see how you can connect two sections of fly line, or make a loop. After either project there will be a number of frayed strands at the end of the braid. Trim these loose strands with sharp scissors; you'll then need to secure the ends so the braid doesn't unravel. There are several ways to do this. You can secure them with Krazy Glue or Zap-A-Gap. But I don't recommend this. You can also use thin monofilament and make a nail knot over the frayed ends—which is okay. The last method is the one that I prefer—using a fly-tying bobbin to make a whipped loop (see chapter 5 for directions on making a whipped loop).

For either the nail-knot or the whipped-loop method, it's necessary to coat only the whipped finish with Aquaseal, Pliobond, Flexament, or a similar glue. No glue should be placed on the braided portion; it would act like a Chinese finger. Study the drawings and practice on some old fly line. You should be able to learn the technique after only one or two attempts.

Fly-Line Color

There has been a lot of discussion about what color line is best. Except for a few special situations, I find that line color has little effect on fishing—but a major effect on accuracy during presentation. In very clear waters (salt or fresh) a bright-colored line, unless accompanied by an extra-long leader, will often cause fish to refuse your offering. One example of this is when tarpon are swimming over ocean flats of white sand. These fish are spookier than a cat in a dog pound and a bright-colored line—even with a long leader—will often flush them. This same applies when you're fishing the flats of the Northeast for cruising striped bass in water less than 6 feet deep. If a school of stripers is moving down the flat and several fish run across a bright-colored line, they'll often flee—causing all the nearby fish to panic, too. Smallmouth bass and trout feeding in the air-clear waters of lakes, tailwaters, and larger, very clear rivers definitely seem to be aware of bright-colored lines—although when the streams are narrow the problem doesn't seem to be as worrisome.

On the North Island of New Zealand, the guides are positively convinced that bright lines spook trout and insist on fishermen casting dull-colored line and leaders as long as 18 feet. What's interesting is that not too far south on the same island, and in essentially the same fishing conditions, guides don't think line color is a problem. First, let me caution you about fishing with a guide who insists that you have to use certain gear or do things his way. If you don't do exactly as he says, and you don't catch fish—you know who's going to get the blame! But back to the North Island trout-fishing guides. Most of these fish are caught in rather small streams. Some are spring creeks, where the guides are even more persistent about using subdued lines. Of course, if you cast with your rod in a vertical position the fly line will be traveling overhead—anywhere from 12 to 16 feet above the water. I agree that in this case, trout will see the line. But most keen trout fishermen wouldn't do this; we'd make a low side cast. Think about it: If the cast is low to the side and you're using an 18-foot leader, how in the world is the trout ever going to see the fly line? I've successfully demonstrated this low-cast technique on several occasions to these New Zealand guides, who still wouldn't agree.

Here's the lesson to be learned from this situation. Anytime you're casting to spooky fish in very clear water on small streams or in the shallows (such as bonefish), avoid overhead casting. Try keeping your cast as low to the water as possible. If you'll make your retrieve in shal-

low water, however—where a portion of a school of fish may see the line—then a neutral line color is your best choice.

What's critical to remember about trout fishing—or casting to any other wary fish in shallow water—*is that the darker or muted-color fly lines often spoil your accuracy.* Casting is a visual sport. Whether you realize it or not, most fly fishermen are monitoring the cast as it unrolls in front of them. To prove this, try two experiments. First, make a forward cast while looking at your target; as the rod stops, close your eyes. After the cast has fallen to the water, open your eyes. Try this several times. Then make several casts with your eyes on the target the entire time. Another way to prove that you actually monitor your cast while it's in flight is to make several cast with a long-billed hat, then several with a short-billed. *Because the long bill interferes with your ability to see your forward cast, you'll find that accuracy improves when you wear a short-billed hat that allows you to see the line throughout its forward flight.*

For most casting, where accuracy is essential, I believe the fisherman is best served by a bright-colored line that's easy to see. If you're seeking wary fish in a fairly large body of unusually clear water (a lake or large stream or river), then a dull-colored line is necessary—but realize that your accuracy will suffer. When fishing smaller streams and shallow water, I think it's a disadvantage to use muted-color fly lines.

Still, all rules have exceptions. The clear (transparent) fly lines now available can be useful when you seek especially hard-fished and wary species, such as bonefish in the Florida Keys. These bones are among the toughest in the world to fool—they are pursued daily. A transparent or clear line will give you an edge when you're after them. Also, when schools of fish are moving through super-clear water toward your fly, a clear line can be helpful; a bright-colored one might cause the school to flare. (This is especially true with albacore and bonito.) And in some trout-fishing situations a transparent line will offer an advantage.

But most of the time, in most of the places you fish, a bright-colored line will let you cast more accurately. If your leaders are long enough and your casts suit existing conditions, you will probably catch more fish with them.

4

FLIES

This chapter is an overview of flies used to catch fish. Throughout this book I'll be more specific when I discuss flies for special species or fishing situations. And because trout flies are the most complex of all patterns, I'll discuss them only in chapter 10, "Trout." For now, let me present many of the types of flies offered to fish.

Basically, flies can be divided into several categories. There are those that imitate a food that predatory fish feed upon, be it mayfly or saltwater baitfish. Other flies resemble nothing in nature but are often effective in drawing strikes; these are referred to as attractor patterns. Some flies are designed to be fished on the surface—dry flies and popping bugs are examples—while others, such as terrestrials and emergers, are fished in the surface film. There are flies designed to be fished within the water column, and others tied to be retrieved right on the bottom. Part of being a successful fly fisherman is understanding how all these various patterns are to be fished.

Let me give you an example. A major food for many trout is the sculpin, a spiny little minnow somewhat resembling a catfish that lives in abundance in many trout waters. Sculpins are basically nocturnal—they prefer to move around either at night or when light levels are low. They also have no swim bladders. When they stop swimming, they sink to the bottom. If you know all these characteristics of the sculpin, you'll realize that you should fish imitations of them early and late in the day, or at night, generally retrieving close to the bottom. Fishing this pattern during midday or high in the water column wouldn't be nearly as effective. The point I'm trying to make here is that it's necessary to understand as much as possible about the pattern you're using. Dragonfly nymphs are a choice food for trout in lakes. They move in short, quick bursts of speed. Therefore, the best retrieve when using an imitation of this insect is not a steady one. Sand lances or sand eels are skinny baitfish that inhabit the salt waters off New England. Sometime in June they hatch in incredible numbers, growing to full length by the end of summer. When striped bass are gorging on them, they'll often refuse any fly that's not sleek enough to imitate this favorite food. You need extremely sleek, silvery sand lance imitations.

The following are some basic characteristics of flies. Not all features are found in every fly pattern. But here are some of the most important traits to look for when considering your fly selections:

Shape

This may be one of the two the most important factors in selecting your fly. Shape is important in freshwater trout fishing as well as in salt water. When freshwater trout are feeding on insects, it's important to know if they're mayflies, terrestrials, or caddisflies. While all fish are opportunistic, when a heavy hatch occurs trout will often key on a specific insect to the disregard of all others. This means you must duplicate, to some degree, the shape of that insect. Or if striped bass are feeding on a baitfish with a deep body, such as an alewife, it's best to have a fly pattern that to some degree also has a deep profile. In salt water you can often identify the shape of baitfish in the area by looking for dead ones that have been swept by the tide to the beach or into eddies.

Size

The shape and the size are perhaps the two most vital characteristics of the flies you offer fish. If trout are feeding on size 20 hatching mayflies, most of the time a well-presented mayfly imitation of the same size is best. Yes, there are times when an outlandishly sized fly will draw strikes, *but day in and day out the best procedure is to offer a fly roughly the shape and size of the hatching insects or predominant bait.* Size can be figured into all fly fishing. For example, if you use a teaser of 10 inches to lure a billfish to your boat, removing the teaser and offering a 5-inch fly would not be as effective in drawing a strike as would a fly closer to the size of the teaser. Another example is a bonefish fly. A 10-pound bonefish has a very small mouth. To use a large fly to entice this fish would be ridiculous. That's why most bonefish flies range from ½ inch to less than 3 inches in length. Size can also be influenced by the size of the fish you want to catch. I know people who fish the Potomac River near my home for smallmouth bass. They cast flies 1 to 3 inches long and wonder why they don't catch larger bass. I take a number of smallmouth bass of better than 2 pounds (a few may even top 4 pounds) each year from these waters—but I use flies that average 3 to 5 inches in length. *Elephants eat peanuts, but they don't make a living off them!* If you want to entice a large fish into striking, be it bonefish, snook, brown trout, or northern pike, your chances improve when you cast a larger fly.

Sink Rate

The sink rate of an underwater fly is critical to fishing success, yet it's often one of the most disregarded factors in getting fish to take your offering. You may have used the correct pattern, cast the right distance, and retrieved at the proper speed, but if your fly is at the wrong depth in the water column all your efforts may be in vain.

It's important when considering the sink rate of a fly to understand how the fish we seek catch their prey. Fish that feed on the bottom are said to have inferior mouths—located near the bottom of the head. While they'll occasionally take food in the water column, their mouths are designed to catch prey on or very close to the bottom. Examples of species with inferior mouths are redfish (channel bass), suckers, bonefish, and carp. The opposite is true of tarpon, smallmouth and largemouth bass, trout, northern pike, striped bass, and many others—these have mouths located in the middle of the head. These fish are better adapted to catching their food either in the water column or on the surface. Bottom feeders rarely take anything from the surface. When you're seeking bottom feeders, then, weight your fly so that on the retrieve it will descend quickly to or near the bottom. *More important to realize is that fish that aren't bottom feeders will rarely descend in the water column to take your fly. They'll rise to it but almost never drop down to get it.* This, of course, means that sink rate is critical—the fly should ride in the water column either at the cruise level of the fish or higher.

Many factors go into selecting a fly with the correct sink rate. Let's examine some of them. Obviously you can add weight to a fly to make it sink. However, the type of weight, how much is secured to the fly, the shape of the weight added, and its location on the hook are all important in how the fly sinks. For years the most common method of sinking a fly line has been the use of lead fuse wire wrapped on the hook shank. Lead wire can be obtained in four sizes—½, 1, 2, and 3—from many fly shops. While the wires vary a little, size ½ has an approximate diameter of .008 inch, while the larger size 3 fuse has an approximate diameter of .030 inch. By wrapping the same fly pattern with different sizes of lead wire or varying the turns of the fuse wire on the hook shank, you can alter the sink rate. *Many tiers don't realize that a hook rides with its point down because of the weight of the bend.* **If the lead wire you wrap around the hook shank weighs more than the portion of the hook that is its bend, then the point will ride up because the shank is now heavier than the bend. This permits you to tie fly patterns on a straight hook that you can crawl on the bottom to reduce snagging.**

The Wapsi Fly Company revolutionized the tying of sinking flies when a few years ago it introduced lead eyes. They're made from lead, dumbbell shaped, and sold in six popular weights: 1/100 ounce, 1/50 ounce, 1/36 ounce, 1/24 ounce, 7/32 ounce, and 8/32 ounce. Some people object to introducing lead into the environment, so manufacturers now make metallic eyes from nontoxic brass or from a combination of antimony and tin. Such eyes weigh approximately 65 percent as much as lead eyes of a similar diameter.

The past several years trout fishermen (and some bass anglers) have been profiting from a technique developed in Europe a decade or more ago: the use of brass or other metallic beads or cones tied in usually immediately behind the hook eye. Nymph, streamer, and Woolly Bugger patterns that use the beadheads or coneheads have become a part of the arsenal of most experienced trout fishermen. While some claim that the bead- or conehead resembles an air bubble attached to a nymph, I believe it's the *weight* of the bead that's most responsible for this fly's success. Most free-drifting nymphs ride the water column down deep or close to the bottom, so these heads get the fly down to where fish expect to see their prey.

Before we had lead eyes, metallic cones, or beads we used bead chain, which is made in several diameters. Less heavy than lead or metal, bead eyes still have their uses in situations where you want a fly to sink, but not too quickly. Bead chain can be purchased in fly shops and many hardware stores.

THE IMPORTANCE OF POSITIONING THE WEIGHT

Obviously, the heavier the weight, the faster the fly will sink. But *where* the weight is positioned on the hook shank is vital to how the fly sinks and is retrieved. When a fly is placed in the tying vise in the normal manner and lead eyes attached on top of the hook, the pattern will ride upside down, or with its hook point up. If the weight is concentrated at the rear of the hook, however, the rear of the fly will sink faster. For example, to make a good crayfish fly you may want to put the lead wire or lead eyes at the very rear of the shank. If you want the fly to dip and dive headfirst anytime slack is entered into your retrieve, then put the weight at the front of the hook shank. One reason that the Crazy Charlie and its host of imitations have become the standard for bonefish is that the pattern dives for the bottom upon entering the water—with the hook riding up. The same can be said of the Clouser Minnow.

During the past few seasons bass and trout fishermen who revere the Woolly Bugger fly pattern have discovered that when tied with either lead eyes or a bead- or conehead, this fly is often more effective. As so often happens in fly fishing, the British discovered such a weighted Woolly Bugger fly many years ago: Soon after the Woolly Bugger came out, they added bead-chain eyes (later metal-bead or lead eyes) to it and called it the Dog Nobbler. More than a decade later U.S. fishermen "discovered" the value of these weights on Woolly Buggers, too. Some anglers get an even faster sink rate by installing a metal conehead at the front of a Woolly Bugger.

Aside from using weights, there are other techniques for getting your flies to the proper depth. During the late 1950s sinking lines began to appear on the market; prior to this floating lines were the only choice available. For decades fly fishermen had used leaders of 9 feet or longer for salt and fresh water. When sinking lines came along, though, anglers soon realized that while the line went down, the fly rode well above it in the water column. The problem was that we were using a sinking line with that long, buoyant leader. *Even today many fly fishermen use leaders on sinking lines that are too long and never get their flies down where they want them.* With a sinking line, most of the time it's better to use a short leader. It should rarely be as long as 6 feet. *Unless the water is exceptionally clear, when I'm using a sinking line I prefer a leader of no more than 4 feet. I've caught many fish with leaders as short as 6 inches.* Underwater fish don't seem too aware of the leader unless it's exceptionally large or interferes with the action of the fly.

The following paragraph may seem to contradict what I have just written. But when you're using a **floating line** you can get a *weighted* fly down to reasonable depths—if you use a *long* leader. There are many fly-fishing situations that require using a floating line in rather shallow water, but with a fly that must be fished on the bottom. You can do this by using a long leader, which will permit a weighted fly to drop quickly. One of the best situations I know of for this technique is fishing for trout in water no deeper than 3 feet where sculpins exist. I use a floating line and at least a 10-foot leader. Years ago Dave Whitlock gave me a fly he'd developed and said, "You can use this fly, but don't ever write about it." I've followed his advice, but now Dave sells this fly through Umpqua Feather Merchants and it's available in hundreds of fly shops. You wouldn't normally buy this ugly-looking fly, but Dave's Near Nuff Sculpin is terrific on smallmouths and trout. The fly is heavily weighted with wrapped lead fuse wire, so it sinks fast and rides with the hook point up. Sculpins live on the bottom and, with no air bladders, will sink when they're not swimming. So Dave's fly should be fished *slowly* on the bottom. To do this correctly attach the fly to a long leader on a floating fly line. Make your cast and let the fly rest on the bottom. Then make only *1-inch-long* strips, letting the fly rest between them. This is one of the deadliest flies in my fly box and has taken many larger trout and smallmouths for me.

Another method of getting flies down—mostly in trout fishing—is the use of weight attached to a leader. Leaders have been constructed to sink. Most come from Europe; they're effective, but they haven't become popular in this country. You can also hide the weight within the fly when you tie it. Most fly fishermen use wraparound lead strips, molded weight, or split shot. All are standard methods of getting the fly down in the water column, where it's needed. I discovered for myself in New Zealand and Chile, where the waters are the clearest that I've ever seen, that when fishing such clear streams or lakes it's often best not to attach the weight to the leader. In such waters you can observe the trout. And when a leader with nymphs and weight attached comes into the fish's range, it will often move to one side to permit the rig to pass. In such situations I find that a nymph with the weight hidden under its dressing is more effective. Many times I will also place split shot against the head of the nymph or streamer. This aids in casting and gets the fly down faster. If you do add split shot to the leader, you may want to try this: Make a blood, surgeon's, or similar knot in the leader. Clip off one tag end, but trim the other tag end very short. Then crimp split shot on the latter tag end. It can be removed easily and will never damage the leader—which sometimes happens when the split shot is pinched on. If the split shot snags on the bottom, you can often pull hard enough for the split shot to slip off the tag end, too.

Still another method of adjusting the sink rate of the fly is to select the proper fly line. Manufacturers now offer lines in five different sink rates. By carrying several lines with you, and flies tied with various amounts of weight (including none), you can fish almost all water down to 30 feet deep.

Many fish hold at a specific level in the current, so it's vital to swim your fly at that level. Indeed, the sink rate of the fly during the retrieve is one of the most important factors in whether or not fish accept your offerings. (This is especially true of steelhead.) Be aware of this factor, and adjust your lines and patterns to swim your flies at the desired depth.

Color

The color of the fly pattern is also important. It's often vital to use a mayfly imitation close in color to the hatching insects. I don't believe that you have to blend many colors of materials to get an *exact* coloration, however. You don't need a dry fly whose body is made from the underarm fur of a gorilla from Africa mixed with Australian possum—but you do need to have a close color. Much more about this when I discuss trout fishing with dry flies (see chapter 10).

Certainly when you're fishing for bottom-feeding species such as bonefish and redfish, it pays to start the day with fly patterns that are approximately the color of the bottom. For example, if the bottom is covered in rich, olive turtle grass, then a fly that's basically olive is called for. Conversely, if the bottom is white sand or marl, such as in much of the Bahamas and Christmas Island, then a light pink, white, cream, or light tan would be a good color to start with. It makes sense when you figure that creatures that didn't blend well with the bottom were probably eaten up a long time ago. To survive they had to match the color of the bottom.

My experience indicates that when fishing popping bugs, color is unimportant. All such bugs are silhouetted against the sky, so they appear mostly black to the fish. However, it's often important for you to see the bug during the retrieve. For this reason I prefer a bright yellow bug. If you feel that a particular color is important, I suggest that you at least paint the face of the bug a color you can see clearly. The face of the bug won't show to the fish—just to you.

Mike Laptew is an incredible diver-scientist who has spent hundreds of hours under water studying both fish and flies. He's made some fascinating observations. For instance, he once told me that when the light level is very low in the morning and evening, all flies have a definite yellow cast to them. This may explain why yellow bucktail jigs and flies are often so deadly. Also, I know that black Lefty's Deceivers are often effective in drawing strikes, but not until Mike told me of his observations did I understand why. He said that when he views most flies the way a fish would *with the sun behind them,* such flies appear black. This makes sense when you think about it: They're silhouetted against the sun. Mike is developing a film about his observations under water, which should be a real eye opener for fishermen everywhere.

One thing experience has taught me is that when you tie flies that incorporate red and white, you can do it either right or very wrong. I've proved this by deliberately tying flies in two different ways and monitoring the results. If you tie the fly with the red in its back, or along the length of the fly, and the white in front, it won't be effective. But when the fly is mostly white in color *with a small amount of red at its front,* it will produce much better. I'm guessing, but I think the reason is that as a predatory fish approaches this fly from the rear, it sees a long white belly and short, red gills.

Flash

The flash built into many underwater flies can be extremely important. When Mylar first came onto the fishing scene (I found out about it in the mid-1960s), fishermen immediately realized that the flashes it emitted could be attractive to fish. After briefly experimenting with Mylar, I figured that if a little of it was good, a whole lot would be much better. So I constructed flies solely from Mylar—and they were dismal failures. While there are a few species and situations where a fly constructed completely of Mylar is effective, most of the time that's not true.

Most flash used in flies comes from a Mylar source, including familiar trade names like Krystal Flash, Flashabou, and Cactus Chenille. The first two are strips of Mylar ranging from ultrathin to as wide as ⅛ inch. Some strip Mylar has a holographic feature built in that increases its reflectiveness. It's manufactured in flat strips (Flashabou) or twisted (Krystal Flash). Cactus Chenille (which is also called by other names) is made by twisting extremely short strands of Mylar into a fuzzy chenille that's highly reflective. It's mainly used for building fly bodies. One popular example of its use is in the Woolly Bugger that substitutes Cactus Chenille for regular chenille.

Strip Mylar (Flashabou, Krystal Flash, and so on) can be bought not only in different widths but also in a multitude of colors. *I find that I often get more strikes if I blend several colors. I can further enhance the striking ability of the pattern by using a combination of flat strips and twisted strips—for example, by combining Flashabou and Krystal Flash.*

Earlier I mentioned Mike Laptew, the scientist who has made studies of flies under water. Several fly tiers I know, including myself and Bob Clouser, have for some years been letting a few strands of Mylar extend ½ to 1 inch beyond the hook on our flies. Dan Blanton has most prominently promoted this idea, and has helped many fly anglers catch more fish because of it. The past several years I've been tying almost all my underwater streamer-type flies with what Dan appropriately calls a flashtail. And Mike Laptew recently made some comments to me that reinforce the idea of using the flashtail technique to tie your flies. Mike explained that under water, the tiny baitfish twist and turn in the current, their silvery sides giving off what he described as stroboscopic flashes of light. He and I feel that these brief flashes of light, somewhat like those emitted from an airport beacon, attract the attention of gamefish, luring them to the bait.

Mike added that when a fly fisherman is retrieving a Clouser Minnow, similar stroboscopic flashes are emitted. The Clouser Minnow has a weighted head. Here's what happens. As the retrieve stops, the weighted eyes at the front of the fly cause the pattern to dip forward as it sinks. But when the angler strips line again, the weighted front rises, causing the back of the fly to whip downward—somewhat like the end person on a crack-the-whip line of skaters. This whipping motion at the rear of the fly causes that flashtail to imitate the baitfish's flash. And since this works with a Clouser Minnow, any fly that has weight in the front and a flashtail should produce the same desirable flash. Dan Blanton's Whistler fly, for instance, has a weighted head and flashtail—and it gives off those seductive flashes. Incidentally, if you put a flashtail of Flashabou (it doesn't work with twisted Mylar such as Krystal Flash) on your streamers, try *gently* pulling the protruding ends between your thumb and first finger, much like you would score a ribbon with scissors to place on a Christmas package. Just use tender care. It looks like a bass lure; the plastic curly tail jigs, and I think this improves the action of a flashtail.

Almost all swimming fish give off some flash. The coloration may differ with different species. Generally those in stained water, such as snook and redfish, will give off a subtler tone—a sort of gold or copper flash. Those in clearer water tend to give off a brighter or more silvery flash. *These factors should be considered when tying patterns to entice the fish you seek.*

Earlier I mentioned that a red-and-white fly should have the short length of red at the front. I believe that placing red gills on many streamer patterns will draw more strikes. For this reason I try to place gills on most of my streamer flies. After much experimenting with calf tail, bucktail, and feathers to represent the gills, I've switched over to Mylar. I now use exclusively either Flashabou or Krystal Flash for gills.

Another tip for using flash materials is never to cut all the Flashabou, Krystal Flash, or whatever at the same length. This would cause most of the reflection to come from the very end of the material. Instead, try tying a series of flies with the flash trimmed at different lengths along the wing. When you fish these you'll see that little sparkles of light will appear along the length of the bait, rather than just at the end.

Sound

Building sound into a fly can be important. I'm not talking about rattlers and similar noisemaking devices, but about how the fly is constructed. Let me first address the rattlers or sound chambers that some fishermen use. If you believe in them, continue to use them. I've experimented with every rattler I could get my hands on, however, and I can't see that they make a difference in the number of strikes I get. I've tried rattlers made of glass, metal, and plastic. I've tried them with smaller and larger balls inside. Some have had one large ball inside, others two or even three. There's no doubt that in some crankbaits used with plug- or spin-casting gear, rattlers are at times very effective. But crankbaits wobble sideways as they're retrieved; flies move in straight line back toward the angler. I think that very little sound occurs when a fly with a built-in rattler moves not back and forth, but in a straight line. Still, having confidence in your flies is half the formula for successful fishing. If you feel rattlers are getting you more hookups, keep using them. And if I find a new rattler, I'm still going to test it.

As I mentioned, when discussing flies with built-in sound *I think about how the fly is constructed.* Most fly fishermen are aware that fish locate the creatures they feed on with two different sound sensors. One is located in the head; the other is the lateral line—a sound-sensing organ that runs along each side of the fish. Using these two sensors, fish are able to locate their food even in muddy water or at night. Most freshwater fly fishermen know that big trout feed more at night than during the day—as do many saltwater species, such as snook.

There are times when having a fly that produces vibrations or sound waves under water during the retrieve is essential. I'll be more specific when I deal with individual fish species in part 2 of this book. For now, remember that when you're fishing after dark or waters that are roiled, cloudy, or just plain dirty, a bulky fly that produces sound waves when retrieved will draw more strikes. A good example of this is fishing tarpon in such places as the rivers of northeastern Costa Rica. The tarpon here have grown up feeding in muddy water, and a sleek tarpon fly will draw virtually no strikes. But one with large eyes of either bead chain or lead that has a heavily dressed wing will produce. When you need to make more vibrations or noise to attract predatory fish, the body and wing of your fly must "push" water on the is retrieve. Sleek flies just won't cut it.

Translucence

Translucence isn't always important, but it can be. This is especially true when you're fishing in clear water where the baitfish are translucent. An opaque imitation of such baitfish will often serve you poorly. Fish like albacore and tuna have incredibly good eyesight and when they're feeding on bay anchovies, silversides, and similar baitfish, a fly dressed with translucent materials will often outfish other patterns. Also, when you're fishing clear lakes for trout or bass with minnow imitations, translucence can make a world of difference. Here a fly with synthetic, transparent wing will outfish one of bucktail or natural hair.

How do you get translucent flies? Mainly through the wing material. For years we used polar bear hair—but this bear is now a protected species. Polar bear was translucent. In fact, it was similar to a fiber optic: It actually allowed light to travel through it. Fortunately, plastic has come of age for us, and we now have many types of translucent materials that can be used to construct fly patterns with beautiful, translucent wings, including Ocean Hair, Super Hair, and my personal favorite, Kinky Fibre—superb stuff for streamer wings. These materials resemble ultrathin strands of monofilament (although many aren't nylon) and are usually crimped throughout their length. This improves their effectiveness as wings. Of course, they come in a huge array of colors, from black to fluorescent.

Don't overlook the value of dressing some of your streamer flies with these translucent materials—it can make a difference in the stories you tell following your fishing trips.

Eyes

Many underwater fly patterns are tied without any type of eye. But for many fishing situations, eyes can make the difference between having fish strike or ignore your offering. There are some baitfish in the sea that have developed a false eye pattern on the rear of their bodies. This is just coloration, but it appears to be a huge eye. If such a baitfish is facing south and a predator moves in for the capture, it will think the baitfish is going to flee northward because of this false eye. Instead, the baitfish flees south.

There's no doubt in my mind that just before striking a smaller species, gamefish often concentrate on the eye of the prey. It's like a target or bull's-eye to the predator. Repeated experiments have convinced me that in clear water it's often not only the fly patterns with eyes, but those with *enlarged eyes,* that will draw more interest and strikes from predatory fish. For instance, I've tied two similar flies—but with different-sized eyes—and fished them during the same tidal phase. Almost always the fly with the larger eyes will draw more strikes.

It's a simple matter to attach eyes to your flies, even if you don't know how to tie. Today, most fly shops sell packets of Mylar eyes in different sizes and color combinations. These eyes have a sticky glue on the back; you just press them onto your fly pattern. These come in size ranging from ⅛ to ½ inch in diameter. Because the eyes are printed on brilliant Mylar and often in highly contrasting colors, they really stand out on a pattern. If you want to position them on flies you already have, press them in place, then coat with either several applications of head cement or a thin layer of five-minute epoxy.

There are many other kinds of eyes. One that has gained much popularity in the past few years is the lead eye, which looks much like a dumbbell. Lead eyes come in six sizes, as listed in the following table:

Weight	Diameter
$\frac{1}{100}$ OZ.	$\frac{4}{32}''$
$\frac{1}{50}$ OZ.	$\frac{5}{32}''$
$\frac{1}{36}$ OZ.	$\frac{3}{16}''$
$\frac{1}{24}$ OZ.	$\frac{7}{32}''$
$\frac{1}{18}$ OZ.	$\frac{1}{4}''$
$\frac{1}{10}$ OZ.	$\frac{9}{32}''$

For bonefish and almost all freshwater fishing, I generally prefer the $\frac{1}{50}$- or $\frac{1}{36}$-ounce lead eyes. For trout fishing, either the $\frac{1}{100}$- or $\frac{1}{50}$-ounce type is usually best, although for sinking heavy nymphs and Woolly Buggers, many anglers prefer the $\frac{1}{36}$- or $\frac{1}{24}$-ounce. For permit, and when I'm bonefishing in water more than 2 feet deep, I use the $\frac{1}{24}$-ounce lead eyes. For most inshore fishing, such as seeking barramundi, striped bass, snook, sea trout, or threadfin salmon along a mangrove-lined shoreline, I suggest the $\frac{1}{36}$- or $\frac{1}{24}$-ounce lead eyes. The $\frac{1}{18}$- and $\frac{1}{10}$-ounce are heavy and require the use of a 9-weight or heavier rod to cast easily. These two eyes, the heaviest manufactured, are superb when you want to drive a fly deep in the water column, such as in channels or when fishing a reef. They're also effective when you're offshore and need to get your fly down quickly, before the fish leave the area.

Some fishermen are now using metallic eyes instead of lead. Brass and most of the metals weigh about 65 percent as much as the same-sized lead eye. While they won't sink as quickly for the same size, this isn't necessarily a liability. Brass eyes are larger in diameter than lead eyes for the same weight, so you can place larger eyes on your fly and still not have too much weight. In shallow water brass eyes can often be a better choice than lead of the same diameter.

Bead-chain eyes are used on many flies. These were the first weighted eyes used on flies. They won't sink a fly as quickly as lead or brass will, but they permit you to attach rather large eyes that really aren't very heavy. Bead chain is manufactured in four sizes:

Size	Diameter
3	$\frac{3}{32}''$
6	$\frac{1}{8}''$
10	$\frac{3}{16}''$
13	$\frac{1}{4}''$

Bead chain can be purchased in a brass or a silver finish, and a few fly shops now offer it in stainless steel.

One of the advantages of eyes is that they enable the fly to create more sound waves in the water. When waters are dirty from mud or silt, or the light level is low such as near or after dark, large eyes may draw more strikes. Larger protruding eyes will, when the fly is retrieved, create sound waves that radiate out from the head, alerting nearby fish to the fly's movement. This is particularly an advantage of bead-chain eyes: A very large bead chain will create considerable sound waves yet not sink too rapidly in the water column.

Of course, the main reason for using lead, brass, or bead-chain eyes is to make the fly sink faster. And the faster the fly needs to sink, the heavier the eyes you need, with lead eyes the best choice for this. The major reason that Crazy Charlies and Clouser Minnows work so well is that they dive fast, permitting you to fish deeper in the water column. Another reason why weighted eyes are often productive is their ability to affect the action of a fly. If the eyes are located near the head of the pattern, each time you stop your retrieve they'll cause the fly to dip downward. This gives an up-and-down motion to the fly, much like that of the lead head jig used on spinning tackle.

Popping Bugs

There are some fly types and patterns that I think deserve special attention. I'll begin my discussion of those I feel all fly fishermen should understand with the popping bug. This is one of the best flies you can carry in your box. Just about every fish except trout and bottom feeders will eagerly strike a popping bug, often called just a popper. It's one of the oldest of patterns cast with a fly line, and still one of the best. A serious fresh- or saltwater fly fisherman should never be without a few of these; they'll catch you everything from bluegills to billfish.

The popping bug has several advantages over other flies. Because it doesn't sink, you can leave it floating while a wary fish examines it. You can also throw it ahead of a cruising fish and wait until the proper moment to begin your retrieve. A popper can make a lot of noise or very little; just how much noise is created depends upon its design, and your retrieve. Other flies are rather silent; when fish are deep or hidden from view, a streamer fly might swim by unseen, and even rattler flies produce very little noise. But a noisy popper on the surface will attract fish from fairly deep water for a strike.

One of the great advantages of a popping bug is that it can create so much disturbance that fish seem to believe it's a bigger creature than it actually is. It's this deception that allows us to catch trophy-sized fish on poppers. For example, larger amberjacks, cobia, and other saltwater species will rarely strike a streamer fly, no matter how big it is, but they will take poppers. Smallmouth bass of chest-beating size will frequently take a rather small popper actively worked on the surface. Northern pike in excess of 20 pounds will take fairly small bugs. Smaller bugs are much easier to cast than large streamers—and, I think, will trigger strikes that streamers won't.

Finally, predators of any kind, from grizzly bears to striped bass, will seek out crippled or easy-to-kill prey. They concentrate their efforts on what will give them the highest yield of food for the least effort. That's where the popping bug is supreme. It can be moved slowly and erratically, creating the impression of a weak, struggling creature on the surface.

But even if they didn't effectively draw strikes, popping bugs would still offer you the added thrill of seeing fish actually break the surface and crash on your bug. It is a rare angler who would rather experience an underwater strike than one on the surface. That's why dry-fly fishing is far more popular among trout anglers than fishing under water.

Good popping bugs have certain characteristics. Poorly designed ones have a lot of air resistance and are difficult to cast. Properly designed poppers cast vastly better. Many bugs perform poorly on the water because they're dressed with too many or the wrong materials. The way a bug sits on the water is important. Bugs with a body that sits parallel to the surface don't hook fish as well as bugs whose hook bend hangs well below the surface. Rarely considered but vital to good hookups is a sharp hook point. *Popping bugs must carry sharper hooks than other kinds of flies.* A bug is buoyant and sits on the surface. As the fish attempts to grab it, the buoyant bug tends to move away. A sharp point immensely increases your chances of getting a hookup. Finally, a well-designed popping bug will lift easily and quietly from the water on the backcast. Bugs that dig into the water and come out making loud noises will often spook interested fish. These are some of the criteria to look for in any good popper, be it for panfish or offshore species.

A variation of the popping bug is the slider. While not used as much as it should be, it can work exceptionally well under calm conditions, when fish are a bit wary of a noisy popping bug. The slider is simply a popping bug whose front end is shaped like a cone. This means it doesn't pop when retrieved; instead it darts about erratically, closely resembling a crippled baitfish. There are many times when a slider will outperform any other fly you can cast; if you use popping bugs, sliders should be in your arsenal, too.

Many people who fish bugs claim that certain colors are important. I've been fishing popping bugs on all types of water since 1947, and it's my belief that the bug's color means almost nothing. Instead it's the shape, size, and manipulation of the bug on the water that count. Most of us make our own bugs and place eyes on their bodies. If you think about it, the eyes are almost always located above the water; the fish are never going to see them. But we like them, so we put them there to please ourselves.

Materials for Popping Bugs

Popping bug bodies are usually made from cork, but they can also be constructed from balsa wood, various types of plastics, and even from deer hair spun on a hook and trimmed to shape. Let's look at each material and its advantages and disadvantages.

Cork This material is light, easy to cast for its size, and very buoyant. For many years it was the premier material for popping bug bodies. It can be shaped easily and accepts paint well. In small sizes it's rather durable. But there are disadvantages. It's hard to build a large body from cork—you just can't get it large enough. Longer cork bodies are rather brittle. And there's the biggest drawback: It's difficult to obtain high-grade cork today. The best cork has no pits or holes. The wine industry, which is vast and expanding, uses the finest cork to stopper bottles. Fly-rod manufacturers, too, consume a great deal of the better cork in handles. It's thus getting increasingly more difficult to obtain good cork for popper bodies. You can, however, use ground cork and glue as a filler. This does a reasonable job, but it's not as satisfactory as a bug body made from high-grade cork.

Still, for panfish and smallmouth bass poppers, cork is probably as good a material as any, and many experienced anglers will fish with nothing else.

Balsa Wood This is another material that's been in use for decades. It has the advantage of being available in a huge variety of sizes; it can also be shaped to your wishes. It's light, tougher than cork, and accepts paint well. Its disadvantages are that you have to shape balsa poppers yourself, and in larger sizes it's a little more air resistant than cork on the cast, because it's slightly heavier. It's also less buoyant than cork and some plastic foam materials.

Plastics Many modern popping bug bodies are being constructed of some type of plastic that's buoyant enough to float. The range of such plastic materials available is vast. They fall into two basic categories: hard foam bodies and softer foam bodies.

The hard foam bodies are usually molded to shape and in a specific color. You can buy bodies preshaped and often with the hook already secured in place. Such bodies create the most durable of all popping bugs, and you need only attach whatever materials are needed to the hook shank and the bugs are ready to fish. These bugs, however, are usually heavier, more air resistant, and more difficult to cast than cork or balsa wood.

Softer foam bodies are made from closed-cell foam and come in two different categories, both softer than hard foam. Many bugs are made from such materials as beach sandal soles. These bodies are extremely tough; you can catch many fish on a well-constructed popper from this material. But it's also rather heavy and difficult to cast—more so than almost any other popper body material. And the popper sits lower in the water than most, because it lacks the lightness of other materials. Then there are the softer-yet closed-cell foam bodies. You can squeeze this material between your fingers and feel it compress— but it returns to shape as soon as you release the pressure. The best such material that I've found (and I've searched for years) is Ethafoam, made by Dow Corning. It's not durable—sometimes Ethafoam bugs last only long enough to catch one or two fish. And you need to test whatever glues you'll use to secure the hook; some glues will dissolve the plastic. I prefer five-minute epoxy for getting the hook to hold well. To offset such problems, though, Ethafoam bodies offer advantages that no other bug material does. The material is fairly cheap. It can be shaped easily with a razor blade. And the most outstanding characteristic of this material is that it's almost weightless; you can make very large popper bodies that weigh virtually nothing. This means you can cast them well. These huge poppers attract bigger fish, such as some of the offshore species—amberjacks, cobia, and similar fish that demand a big offering.

Deer Hair Finally, popping bug bodies can be made by spinning deer hair on the hook and then trimming it to shape. Deer hair is cheap, readily available in many colors, lightweight when first cast, and easy to shape to fit your desires. Bugs made from it are generally used for bass fishing. *In fact, one major use of the deer hair bug body is fishing lakes that have boat docks*—favorite hideouts for bass. A good trick is to drop the popping bug on the dock then pull it gently into the water. A balsa, cork, or plastic bug would clunk down on the dock and alert the wary bass, but a deer hair body lands gently. It can be dropped and teased into the water in silence. The disadvantages of deer hair bodies are few—but to me, they're serious. Deer hair bodies cast and work very well when first fished. Gradually, however, they soak up water, along with fish slime if you're catching fish. This increases their weight, making them more difficult to cast and less buoyant on the water, which in turn affects their action. I've about given up using deer hair for popper bodies. It's been my experience that the people who enjoy using deer popping bugs the most are fly tiers. They relish making these beautiful creations and fishing them. Of course, there's nothing wrong with this! For me, though, I want a bug that casts and acts the same from the time I tie it on until I clip it off—deer hair bugs don't do that.

Popping Bug Shape and Design

Popping bugs come in many shapes and designs, and there are good reasons behind each. But if you buy your popping bugs, you should know that many commercial ones are not well designed—and often don't fish well.

Let's look at bug design. To get a bug to hook a fish you have to cast it. That means the bug should have little weight and a minimum of air resistance. During its flight the materials on the body should not tangle, which would ruin the presentation. Once on the water it should be buoyant, lively on the retrieve, and appealing to the fish. A well-designed bug will also lift from the water easily on the backcast; a poorly designed one will

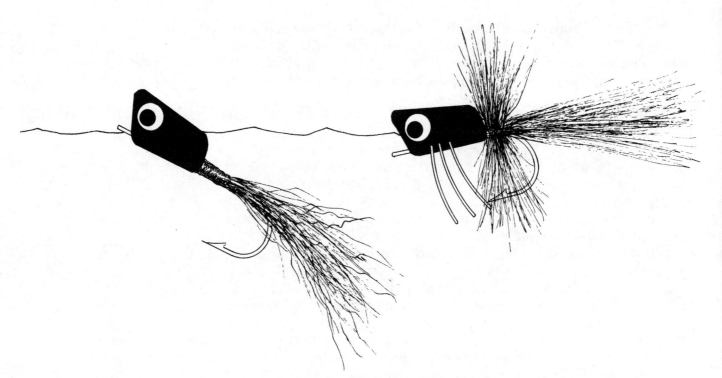

On the right is a poorly designed popper; the left is correct.

dive and make a great deal of noise as it leaves the surface. Finally, the bug must also efficiently hook the fish that accepts your offering.

Look at the average popping bug in a fishing tackle shop. It has a cupped face, and the hook eye is usually positioned near the center of this face. Bushy feathers extend well beyond the body. Between the tail feathers and the bug body is densely palmered hackle. This is a poorly designed bug. The cupped face will often "gulp" water as you make your backcast, scaring any nearby fish. The long, trailing feathers are air resistant and also force the body of the bug to sit almost flush with the surface. The wound hackle between the rear feathers and the body radically increases air resistance, further forces the body to sit flat on the surface, and restricts action on the retrieve. Many poppers also have a short hook shank that positions the point under the body.

There are more reasons why all this is bad, too. The cup face makes noise. The hook eye positioned in the center of the bug face tends to drown the bug on the pickup for your backcast. The feathers contribute to tangling and making casting more difficult. The body sitting flush on the water means the hook isn't pointing downward. And the short-shanked hook means the fish has to grab the entire bug before the hook point will impale.

Now let's examine what I believe is a well-designed popping bug. *The hook eye is positioned flush with the base of the body.* This causes all of the body to sit above the water, permitting a quiet, easy backcast. Better bugs don't need cupped faces to make noise, either. Plenty of surface disturbance can be generated (if desired) if the face of the bug body slants just a little forward when at rest. *There are no feathers radiating around the hook shank. Instead, a sleek tail is tied on that offers little air resistance. The hook shank is long, with the hook point located well to the rear of the popper body.*

This is a good popping bug. It will cast well. Because the bug has a slanted face, the hook eye sits on the surface and the long shank causes the entire popper to be tilted up slightly; thus the bug lifts quietly and easily from the water. The hook hanging downward and well away from the body means that the first thing a striking fish contacts is the hook point—resulting in better hookups.

This design can be used for almost any freshwater and many saltwater fishing situations. The only difference is that for the salt, you should use a plated or stainless hook instead of a bronzed one.

The shapes of popper bodies are also interesting, and each has its purpose.

Pencil Popper   This is a sleek bug that gets its name from the fact that the rear of the balsa wood body is shaped with a pencil sharpener. This bug casts exceedingly well and offers a superb imitation of a crippled minnow. It's best used on fresh water; large pencil poppers don't seem to work as well as other poppers in salt water. One situation in which the pencil popper is great is fishing in lily pads and similar aquatic vegetation. *The narrow diameter of the body lets it slither through pads and weeds where a wider body would almost certainly hang up more frequently.* Adding a weed guard to a pencil popper lets it fish through even heavier aquatic vegetation.

Marabou Gerbubble Bug   The original Gerbubble Bug was designed decades ago; its balsa wood body had chicken neck feathers extending out from the sides and rear. The marabou version is vastly more effective. Indeed, replacing the conventional sparse feathers with soft, fluffy marabou changes this popper into the best largemouth bass popping bug I've ever used. Largemouths in stillwater (lakes, ponds, tanks, and so on) frequently move up to bug that's being worked on the surface. They often lie there—watching it. The marabou Gerbubble Bug is superior because long after the last twitch of the bug, the marabou continues to softly undulate. This is often more than a bass can resist. Also, when this bug is lifted from the water, its marabou feathers fold into a slim shape that offers virtually no air resistance.

Weedless Popper   Weeds on the surface can often ruin your freshwater fishing. By shaping a hook with pliers, as you would to make a Bend-Back fly, and tying it in upside down (point up on the body), you can make a bug that rarely snags in the weeds.

Dahlberg Diver   This is one of the few really new flies to come along in decades. It's a combination popping bug and streamer. The shape of the trimmed deer hair head of this fly makes it pop and dive when line is retrieved. I find that the Diver works best if, before fishing it, you place some paste flotant on the cone portion of the head—this helps waterproof it. This popper is effective for just about all freshwater species and a host of inshore saltwater fish.

Slider   This a specialty popping bug with a pointed face. When retrieved it makes very little noise—but neither does almost any naturally crippled baitfish. *There are times when a silent retrieve with this bug will outfish any other fly.* One situation is in water that's very calm and rather shallow, where fish are easily spooked.

In salt water there are several effective popper patterns that vary slightly from the ones above.

Gallasch Popper   The basic popping bug that for decades has been used more in salt water than any other is what is generally referred to as the Gallasch Popper—in honor of Bill Gallasch, who popularized it. This bug, usually dressed on a long-shanked hook in sizes from 1 to 3/0, is effective all over the world. It cast well, fish like it, and it hooks well. Enough said.

Bob's Banger   This is another great bug in salt water, and many other people have put their names on it. The Banger makes a lot of noise—although in most saltwater situations an increase in noise usually doesn't frighten fish. It's also sometimes a little difficult to lift from the water, because the hook is centered in the body. The Banger is constructed a bit differently from most other popping bugs. Long bucktail is usually attached to the hook, then the remainder of the shank is wrapped with Cactus Chenille or plain chenille. A hole is made in a closed-cell foam rod by heating a wire and searing a smooth hole through. While not necessary, the outer part of the foam body can be wrapped with colored, reflective tape. The hook is inserted through the body and the fly tied on. Through different body diameters, body colors, and tail colors, you can vary the noise and appearance of this bug.

Offshore Popper   This is a very large bug—including the feathers or hair, the bug may be as long as 7 inches, with a face diameter of an inch or more. It's generally made from Ethafoam and so rather easy to cast on a 10-weight or heavier rod. The size, bulk, and noise of this bug cause it to attract large striped bass, cobia, dolphinfish, and a host of other saltwater species that don't want a sample; they need "groceries."

Billfish Popper   This is a specialty fly designed to catch billfish, although it will interest many offshore species. Construct a large streamer fly, usually a big Lefty's Deceiver type. Then make a soft foam head about ¾ inch in diameter the way you would the body of a Bob's Banger. Force the foam head over the streamer fly. Experience in billfishing has taught me that you must secure the foam head to the

A good assortment of freshwater popping bugs

streamer. *When a fish grabs the fly and runs, a foam head that's not tied in will slide up the leader during the fish fight. Twice I've had smaller, sharp-toothed fish bite the foam head and leader—losing me a catch.*

Quick-Change Popper Heads

Many times a quick-change popper head can cause fish that have been ignoring your offerings to strike. Once a friend of mine was fishing a grass-covered basin for sea trout. Several fish had flashed at his streamer, but none struck it. They seemed half interested, but varying retrieves and depths didn't change their minds. Clipping off the fly, my friend inserted his leader through a quick-change popper head and reattached the streamer. He made a cast. The fly dropped to the surface and the wet streamer dangled downward in the water, buoyed by the popper head. He

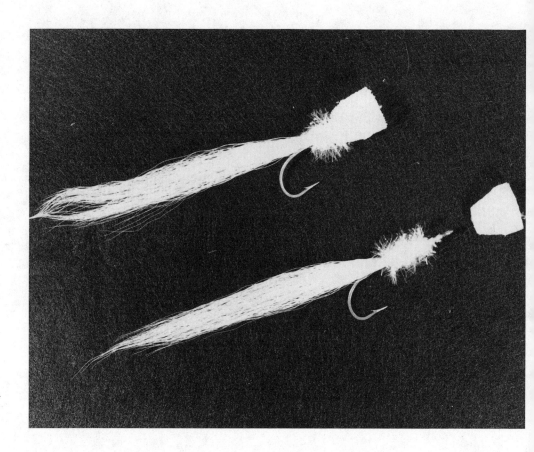

On the top is a quick-change popper ready to fish. The components are separated on the bottom.

began a typical popping bug retrieve, *pop-pop*-stop, then *pop* again. Two sea trout rushed the fly and, as expected, the smaller of the two grabbed it. During the next half hour my friend caught five more.

Bear in mind he was using the same streamer that the trout had already refused—it was the addition of a noisemaking head that turned the trick. Converting from a silent streamer to something that makes noise can often produce. Many anglers have caught a billfish on a fly, experienced billfishers almost all agree that impaling a slip-on, soft popper head on the hook at the head of a streamer will usually draw more and faster strikes. There are many other saltwater fishing situations in which a quick-change popper will increase your hookups, too.

Quick-change popper heads are not a new idea—they just haven't caught on yet. Maybe it's because they look like a popping bug that was haphazardly thrown together. Whatever the reason, you can often catch more fish by using one. In most cases you simply shove it onto the nose of a streamer fly you have in your box. There's no need to make special flies—just the heads.

Some basic guidelines, however, may be helpful.

If you tie streamers that you think you might use with a quick-change head, it's a good idea to locate the head of the fly (which normally rests against the hook eye) about ¼ inch back from the eye. This will allow you to slip a popper head over the hook shank. It also gives the head better support than simply pushing it over the eye would, so it tends to stay in position better when you fish. For this reason standard-length or extra-long-shanked hooks are often best suited. Wright and McGill model 66SS or Mustad 34011 hooks work well. Remember, too, that all surface lures tend to be knocked away when a fish strikes; popping bugs should thus have hooks as sharp as possible. I find it best to presharpen the hooks before I tie the flies. Also, tie the heads so that they taper to the hook shank. I usually tie the streamer at the rear of the hook, and fill the shank with Cactus Chenille. This allows me to slide the head over the shank much more easily.

All sorts of materials have been used for quick-change heads. The original versions were constructed from cork, and many still are. But cork is relatively heavy, and it fractures easily when the strike occurs. Balsa wood is another common material that has the same inherent disadvantages as cork. Deer hair heads have been spun on tubes, too; the tube is then jammed against the hook eye. This works, but the deer hair tends to soak up water after being fished. This diminishes the head's action and makes it more difficult to cast. Styrofoam is also used. It's very light, easy to work with, and easy to cast, but it's more brittle than cork. Generally you can catch one or two fish, then you have to replace it.

By far the best material I've used is Ethafoam. It's a closed-cell foam, meaning that it won't absorb water. Soak it for a week and it still won't absorb a drop. It will float high and stay light as long as it's fished. It's very tough for a plastic foam and will take abuse. Push your finger against it, release the pressure, and the foam will return its original shape. It's also so light that you can make extra-large popper heads from it that weigh virtually nothing.

Ethafoam is made by the Dow Chemical Company, which has regional offices located all across the country. You can call information to get the local number. Generally, however, you don't have to go to this much trouble. Ethafoam is considered one of the finest materials for packaging fragile items. Many computers, word processors, and other delicate instruments are supported by a few blocks of it during shipment. Visit a local computer store, RadioShack, or similar outlet and chances are there'll be some Ethafoam in the dumpster. The material is very light and granular in appearance; if you're not sure it's Ethafoam, shove your thumb into the material and hold it a few seconds, then release the pressure. If it's the right stuff, it will immediately return to its original shape. Few other foam materials will do that.

You may want to make several sizes of popper heads for the same streamers. Certainly large streamers, such as those used for amberjacks, cobia, or billfish, call for larger heads. I rarely use a quick-change head smaller than ½ inch across the face; for sailfish I use one with about a 1-inch diameter. Cobia, larger striped bass, and amberjacks like a *lot* of noise, so I sometimes make those heads 1¼ to 1½ inches across the face. For most fishing in fresh or salt water, a face diameter of ½ to ¾ inch is all you'll need—and these cast fairly well. You can make the head too short. If you do, you'll find that there isn't enough material to prevent it from breaking up. Rarely do you need a head more than 1⅛ inches in length, and generally one of ¾ to 1 inch is ideal.

You can cut them to any shape, but generally a round tube of Ethafoam is preferred for quick-change heads. You'll need a simple tool that requires only a few minutes to make. Go to a local plumbing shop and purchase 1 foot of thin-walled copper tubing that has whatever inner diameter you desire. (I buy several different diameters.) You only need about 4 or 5 inches of tubing, but plumbing shops aren't going to sell it in that length. Cut off about 5 inches of the tubing. Sharpen the *inner* edge of one end. Don't sharpen the outer edge. Slice a piece of Ethafoam with a sharp knife to the length you want your head to be—usually ¾ to 1 inch thick. Lay the foam on a piece of cardboard and rotate the sharp end of the tubing against the foam until it punches through.

You now have a rod of Ethafoam the size of your tubing's inner diameter. You'll need to make a hole in the center so that you can pass the leader through it and impale the head on the hook. The best method I know to make the hole is to use a piece of wire about the size of that in a conventional coat hanger. Heat the wire with a match or candle; when it's warm to the touch, carefully force it through the center of the rod. If you overheat the wire, you may ruin the head by melting too large a hole. I find that a match or candle works well. Also, by making the hole with a warm wire, you'll sear the inside of the hole to a smooth finish, allowing the leader to pass easily through. If you punch a jagged hole through the foam, though, it often snags the leader and makes it difficult to insert.

You can also make quick-change slider heads. Punch out a rod of Ethafoam, then carefully taper its front end with a double-edged razor to form a bullet shape. Such heads are often better for striped bass, sea trout, snook, and redfish in shallow water. In very thin water a popper makes so much noise that it often frightens the fish—but a slider head quietly twitches about on the surface, much like a struggling baitfish, and can draw strikes when a streamer or a popper head won't.

You can color the Ethafoam with permanent marking pens. Some people like to two-tone the heads. Most of the time, just plain white suits me.

With larger flies, such as those used for billfish, after a fish strikes it will make a swift, long run. This may cause the quick-change head to slip up the shock leader and onto the tippet. It's happened to me. Then a bonito or similar sharp-toothed fish saw the attractive white thing and grabbed it—severing my tippet and me losing my billfish. For such large fish I now install the head at the front of the fly. Then I tie it with Dacron or a similar line.

Another advantage to quick-change heads is that if you're fishing with them and decide they aren't working, you can get rid of them quickly. Just strip them off. Keep a number of quick-change heads of different shapes and sizes in your fly box and you may find that on those days when the fish won't hit anything—they will!

The Clouser Minnow

No fisherman would want to be limited to a single fly for the rest of his life. And if you'd been forced to make that choice a few years ago, it would have been even more difficult. Today, though, whether you fish for trout, large or smallmouth bass, walleyes, bonefish, barracudas, or offshore for dolphinfish, there is one fly pattern that will work incredibly well.

It's good enough that in the last several years I've caught 83 species of fish in salt and fresh water with it, ranging from a 5-ounce brook trout to a 6-foot shark. After more than five decades of chasing fish around the world I can tell you that *this is the single most effective underwater fly I've ever fished.* Best of all, it's one of the easiest patterns to tie.

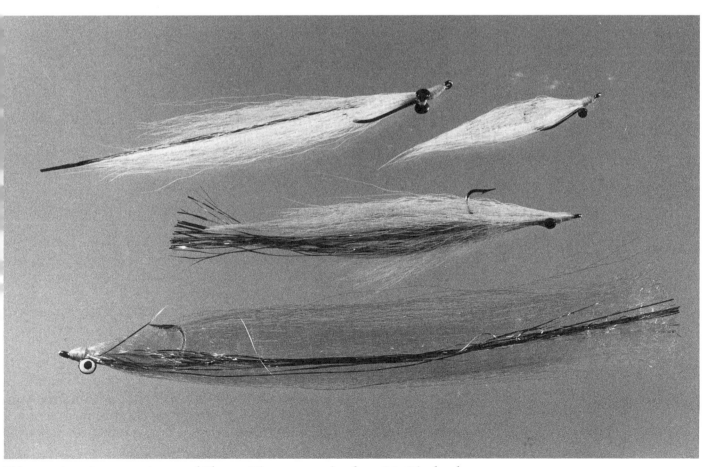

This assortment represents several Clouser Minnows ranging from 3 to 9 inches long, with different colors and materials in the wing.

The pattern is the Clouser Deep Minnow, often referred to as simply the Clouser Minnow or just—Clouser. In 1989 I walked into Bob Clouser's Fly Shop in Middletown, Pennsylvania, less than 2 miles from Three Mile Island. Though Bob services trout fishermen in the region, the huge Susquehanna River less than a mile from his shop is also one of the best places in the country to try fly fishing for the coveted smallmouth bass.

While we talked, Bob handed me several crude-looking flies that at first glance I thought were unfinished. "Lefty, I fished these yesterday and they really knocked the bass," he said. "Give 'em a try while you're out there today."

I must confess that I thought they were a pretty lousy-looking patterns and shoved them in my pocket. The day was a bit slow, though, so by mid-morning I withdrew them from my pocket and tied one on the leader. Despite the lead eyes, I found that it cast exceedingly well. Watching the fly as I retrieved it, I realized that it did look a lot like a minnow—and on my third cast a smallmouth hit it. I spent the rest of the day working with the flies Bob had given me and came away convinced that with some work, this pattern would be dynamite, not only on the bass Bob had designed it for but also for just about any predatory fish.

Bob and I talked about the fly. He thought it was already pretty good, but after our discussion of its latent possibilities he became really enthused. Between us we worked on the pattern. During the next month or so we resolved a number of problems and I said to him, "I'm going to tell the world about this, Bob. You really have something."

"Okay, but what are we going to call it?"

"Let's call it the Clouser Deep Minnow, since it represents a minnow and it sure can go deep." Bob agreed. As the fly gained popularity around the world, the name was shortened to the Clouser Minnow—and as I said, many now call it the Clouser.

One of the most important qualities of this unique pattern is that it does a superb job of representing a baitfish. If you think about it, when you look at a baitfish in the water, you don't see the gills, all the side markings, or any great detail. *Instead you see a "suggestion" of a baitfish, and often you see the eye.* That's exactly what a Clouser Deep Minnow shows you—if you tie it properly. It's important not to overdress the pattern. What you want is a fly that looks a bit unfinished, so that when it's brought back under water it'll offer that suggestion of a baitfish, and also accentuate the lead eyes. The minimal dressing permits the fly to get down deeper, too.

Of course, one of its other assets is that unlike many baitfish imitations, which are made of buoyant materials such as wool and deer hair, this fly sinks like an anvil in a swamp. It goes down—and fast. One of the major problems with flies that sink is that frequently you can't get them to sink deep enough. But even with a floating fly line, if you add a long, tapered leader you'll be able to fish the Clouser Deep Minnow much deeper than most conventional patterns.

Yet another asset is that when retrieved, the Clouser's hook rides up. Many fish, especially trout, spend most of their lives close to the bottom.

Flies fished in this part of the water column are almost always more effective. The Clouser Deep Minnow can also be tied on a bendback hook, or with a monofilament or wire weed guard—I prefer the latter, using number 5 (.014-inch diameter) stainless-steel trolling wire for small flies. For medium-sized flies (such a Lefty's Deceiver for striped bass, redfish, snook, and largemouth bass) I prefer number 6 wire (.016-inch diameter); for big critters that have crushing jaws and live in heavy cover (such as Nuigini bass, large snook, or large barramundi number 7 wire (.018-inch diameter) seems to be best.

Dressing the Clouser Minnow

One of the key ingredients in this pattern is its lead eyes, located at the front. These eyes turn the fly over well in the wind; they also cause it to sink quickly and ride with the hook up. Lately, some organizations and anglers have decided not to use lead eyes, believing there's an environmental risk. If you prefer not to use lead, there are now metallic substitutes.

The wing on a Clouser Minnow can be made of many materials. The most popular is dyed deer bucktail in various colors. However, Arctic fox and calf tail are often used on smaller flies—sizes 6 through 12. If I need flies with translucent wings or wings of 6 to 12 inches in length, my two favorite materials are the synthetic Super Hair and Kinky Fibre.

Add either Krystal Flash or Flashabou to the wings to give sparkle. On small flies I prefer Krystal Flash; on large flies, since Flashabou is limper and undulates easier, that's my choice. A combination of two or more flashy colors often works much better than a single color. Also, combining Krystal Flash and Flashabou can give a unique appearance to the fly that fish find exciting. **Don't forget to use a flashtail.**

It's important to understand that when you tie this fly, you're not always tying it the same length; nor are you limited to a specific color combination such as you would be when tying a Black Ghost or a Mickey Finn pattern. The pattern is similar to a Lefty's Deceiver in that it is a way of putting materials on the hook; you can change size and color combinations to suit existing conditions.

The original Clouser Minnow was tied with the lower half of its wing on the bottom of the hook. But I find that tying all the wing materials on the top of the fly (as it swims through the water) gives a more realistic appearance. Either way seems to work, though. Bob agrees that when you use synthetic materials, such as Kinky Fibre or Super Hair, in the wing, the fly will appear more realistic in the water if you tie all materials on one side of the hook.

One of the most popular Clouser Minnows is the chartreuse-and-white; this has been one of the hottest striper flies the past several seasons in the Northeast. Some guides I know say, "If it ain't chartreuse, it ain't no use." I'll use it as an example of how you tie the Clouser.

Place the hook in your tying vise in the normal manner and secure a pair of lead or metal eyes about 3/16 to 1/4 inch behind the hook eye. Then turn the hook over in the vise so that the lead eyes are on the bottom. Attach just forward of these eyes the desired amount of either white bucktail or white synthetic hair. On top of this add 8 to 20 strands of either pearl Krystal Flash, pearl Flashabou, or a combination of the two. Secure on top of that fluorescent-chartreuse-colored bucktail or synthetic hair. Cement the head and the fly is finished.

This chartreuse-and-white Clouser is the single best big bonefish fly I've used; I'd choose it if I was limited to a single pattern for this species. If I had a second choice, it would be another Clouser tied the same way but substituting light tan for the chartreuse upper wing. For bonefish I generally use 1/50-ounce lead eyes on a size 2 hook. I make the wing of bucktail and about the length of a man's small finger. The total diameter of the wing, when pinched, would be about the size of a wooden barn-burner match. For striped bass I step up to a size 1/0 or (no more than) a size 2/0 hook and make the wing length about 4 to 6 inches, depending upon whether I'm fishing schoolies or large stripers.

My favorite Clouser Minnow for most trout in water less than 3 feet deep is on a size 8 hook, with lead eyes weighing 1/100 ounce. A wisp of yellow calf tail forms the bottom half of the wing; just two strands of copper Flashabou separate it from a light tan calf tail upper wing. The entire fly ranges from 3/4 to 1 1/2 inches in length. Worked on a long, thin tapered leader along the bottom, it makes a superb tiny crayfish or sculpin imitation. Conversely, if I'm seeking dolphinfish or many other offshore species such as barracudas, I'll try to imitate the basic baitfish they feed on, which has a white belly and either a blue or green back. A Clouser Deep Minnow dressed on a size 3/0 hook, with lead eyes of either 1/18 or 1/10 ounce and a wing of synthetic hair ranging from 6 to 12 inches long, is deadly.

I've given these examples only to show you how versatile this fly can be. If you're longing to carry fewer underwater flies but want to be well prepared for many fishing situations, you could never make a better choice than a variety of sizes and color combinations of the Clouser Deep Minnow.

Lefty's Deceiver

The Lefty's Deceiver is perhaps the most popular saltwater fly pattern in the world—and it's also used a great deal in fresh water. I developed this fly in the late 1950s to catch striped bass in the Chesapeake Bay. A good underwater fly needs several characteristics to score well. One—it should be easy to cast long distances and into the wind. Two—it should have a baitfish shape and appeal to predator fish. Three—its materials shouldn't foul during the cast. I think that the Lefty's Deceiver meets all of these criteria; that's why it has become so popular. But many people tie it improperly.

Like the Clouser Minnow, it really isn't a precise pattern; instead it's a style or method of tying a fly. It can consist of many colors, vary in length, and be tied on many different sizes of hooks. The fly is routinely dressed and used in lengths from 2½ inches to more than a foot. But unless you follow the proper procedure when you tie it, the fly loses some of its fish-catching appeal.

The four most commonly made mistakes are:

1. Using saddle hackles that are too thin when a wide profile is required. Wide saddles or neck hackles will generally work better.
2. Not using enough saddle hackles. A *minimum* of six (three pairs to a side) is usually called for, unless a very thin pattern is needed. With larger flies (size 1/0 and bigger) four or even five pairs of saddles should be used—a total of 8 or 10 saddles.

This assortment shows the many ways you can tie the Lefty's Deceiver. Top left: Deceiver with weed guards; top right: a Tiny Deceiver; middle left: a Deceiver heavily weighted with lead wire on the shank and called a "Grocery Fly"; bottom: a Magnum Deceiver, approximately 10 inches long.

3. Many people tie the fly so that the saddles flare out from the hook shank. The original Deceiver was supposed to represent a baitfish, not a swimming frog. The neck feathers or saddles on each side are intended to flare inward; this more exactly represents the motion of a swimming baitfish. If the feathers are tied so that they flare outward, however, the fly has a frog's kicking, swimming motion, which fish often find irresistible. I tie it both ways, depending on what I want the fly to do. So tying feathers that flare in or outward is your choice. But whichever way you choose, a correctly tied Lefty's Deceiver lifted from the water for the backcast will travel through the air like a sleek knife blade.

4. The collar of bucktail (or whatever substitute is used) *should extend behind the hook bend.* Too many tiers make this collar too short, which gives the fly the outline of a squid and can allow the wing to foul on the hook during a cast. If the collar is carried well in back of the bend, though, when under water the fly has the shape of a baitfish. The collar also forms little currents as the fly is retrieved; these "mini eddies" roll off that collar and move back along the saddles, giving the fly a swimming motion. Finally, the collar prevents the wing from underwrapping the hook on your cast.

Tying Method

Step 1 Select three to five hackles that all curve to the left when the glossy side is laid on the table. If a grizzly hackle (dyed or natural color) is to be used on either side to create a scalelike pattern, select one that curves to the left and another that curves to the right. Adjust the tip ends of all the hackles that curve the same way so that they're together. Once all are in this position, dip the feathers in water and stroke them so they'll stick together. Lay these hackles down *so that the butts extend over the table edge.* Select a similar number of hackles that curve the opposite way. Again, once they're together dip them in water and stroke. Place both units of feathers together; if you dip the combined sides in water and stroke the feathers, they'll all remain together. Now you can tie all the hackles in at one time.

Step 2 After securing the feathers, add to each side 6 to 10 strands of Krystal Flash or Flashabou. On small flies—up to size 3/0—I prefer Krystal Flash. But because Flashabou is more supple than Krystal Flash, on larger flies I prefer Flashabou. A mistake common among tiers who use Krystal Flash or Flashabou on streamers, I believe, is clipping all the flashy material at one spot. I feel it's much better to clip the material at varying lengths along the wing. This gives more realistic flash along the length of the fly, rather than generating most of it at the point of clipping. Also, if I build several colors into the wing of a fly, I like to add just a few strands of comparably colored Flashabou or Krystal Flash into the various wing materials. Thus, if a wing is white, yellow, and blue, I'd add pearl into the white material, gold into the yellow, and blue into the blue. Don't forget to leave a few strands of Mylar trailing behind to create a flashtail.

Step 3 After you've positioned the hackles and flash material at the rear of the hook, wind the thread forward to within ³⁄₁₆ to ¼ inch of the hook eye. At this point the collar is put on. *It should be put on in two stages.* Select bucktail, calf tail, or another material—although most of the time bucktail is best—and position it on the far side of the hook. Put an equal amount on the near side of the hook—but don't place any on the top or underside of the hook.

Step 4 Turn the hook upside down and put on 10 to 15 strands of bright red Flashabou or Krystal Flash to represent the gills or beard. *But don't allow this to extend as far as the hook point, or it could tangle in the point and you could miss a strike.*

Step 5 Return the hook to the normal tying position. To give the fly coloring on the back I use either peacock herl, synthetic hair, or dyed bucktail. This should reach three-quarters of the length of the fly; it represents the darker back of a baitfish. Tie this material on top as an elongated collar. Three of my favorite colors for topping are medium gray, light green, and blue.

The fly is now complete, except for coating the head with protective cement. I favor placing eyes on the head; I feel they help draw strikes. But thousands of fish have been caught on Lefty's Deceivers with no eyes. The easiest way to apply eyes is to use the glue-on Mylar eyes made by Witch-craft and available in most fly shops. You can coat them with head cement, but many tiers prefer to cover the head with five-minute epoxy. A Deceiver with an epoxy-coated head has a different action than one without.

The photo on page 91 shows some of the different lengths and color combinations you can tie this fly in. It can also be bulky or sleek, depending on what you want to do with it.

Learn to tie and fish the Deceiver and you will surely catch more fish in salt water.

The Half & Half

This fly combines the attributes of the Clouser and the Deceiver. Tie on a wing at the rear, as you would for a Deceiver, but then add a Clouser on the front. You'll have an easy-to-cast fly with a longer profile.

The Bend-Back

The Bend-Back was developed in the last century for freshwater bass fishing, but it's still extremely useful in all areas of fly fishing. If I was limited to a dozen saltwater patterns, one of the first I'd select would be a

Bend-Back. In this pattern the hook shank is slightly bent, and the wing is tied reverse style—so that the hook point rides up instead of down on the retrieve. So far as I can tell, the Bend-Back was first used in the Mid-South before the turn of the century. Bass fishermen there were plagued by the dense thickets of lily pads in which largemouth bass roamed. Conventional patterns didn't work well simply because the hook point hung down and was too often snagged. This reverse-tied fly with a bent hook was the answer. During the late 1950s the Potomac River, where I lived and fished for smallmouths, was choked for several years with yellow star grass. This aquatic weed made it impossible to fish conventional flies. Again, the Bend-Back was the answer. It could be cast up on weeds that protruded above the surface, dragged across them, and dropped into the open pockets where bass were simply not used to seeing a fly. It's also deadly when dressed as a sculpin pattern and dragged along the bottom of a trout stream. One great advantage of the Bend-Back is that it doesn't require a weed guard. *It's important when tying a Bend-Back to use a hook shank slightly longer than regular. I like a 2X- or 3X-long hook. Some anglers complain that the longer-shanked hooks don't hook fish as well as the conventional. But they do hook fish very well.*

Since the late 1960s the Bend-Back fly has really gained popularity, especially in salt water. Because the hook rides up, I find that it's very effective on just about all species except larger tarpon and billfish. The upper inside of a bigger tarpon or billfish's mouth is hard—it's mostly bone. Because the Bend-Back rides point up, I've missed many strikes on larger tarpon and billfish with it, so I no longer use it for these fish. But for just about every other species that will strike a streamer fly in fresh or salt water, I think the Bend-Back is superb.

One of the best situations in which to use a Bend-Back is working a mangrove shoreline casting to snook, redfish, snappers, and other species that lurk back among the branches. At Barra Base Lodge on Bathurst Island in Australia, for example, threadfin salmon and barramundi will cruise in among the mangrove roots during high tides. The roots of these trees may extend out more than 50 yards from the bank, and fish can be seen deep inside searching for food. Tides of 6 to 8 feet rush in and out, roiling the water with sediment. A favorite fly for these waters is a black Lefty's Deceiver. The trouble is that even if you have the guts to cast way back under the mangrove roots, you're invariably going to snag and ruin a lot of presentations. So on my second trip to Barra Base I took along Lefty's Deceivers tied Bend-Back style. I was able to throw these flies among the mangroves with only rare snags in the spiderlike roots.

There are many other places where the Bend-Back fly comes in handy: ponds carpeted with lily pads, for one, as well as floating grass—whether it's loose freshwater bay grass or sargassum weed that's well offshore. Floating grass tends to shuttle down your line and snag your fly. Many species of predatory fish roam sargassum weed lines offshore, knowing that these are one of the few places small fish can hide in the open sea.

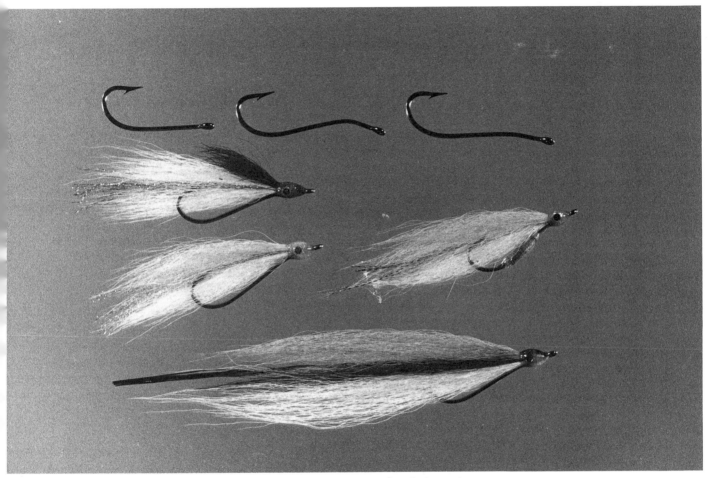

Top row, left to right: a regular-shanked hook, which is too short; a hook that is bent too much; a hook bent correctly before dressing. The rest are examples of various Bend-Backs.

Barjacks, dolphinfish, blue runners, rainbow runners, cobia, and many other species will feed among the loosely packed sargassum weeds. You need a weedless fly for such work, and while weed guards work fairly well, the Bend-Back is much more efficient.

Inshore fishing in the Northeast, where you either wade the surf (where grass collects as the waves carry it to the beach) or work from a boat close to shore, is plagued with floating strands of grass. Again, the Bend-Back will permit you to fish virtually free from snags. Striper fishermen who work these waters at night often don't realize that their fly has fouled from weeds, and few fish ever strike a fly with weeds dangling from it. Thus at night, a Bend-Back ensures a snag-free retrieve.

There are other places where I use the Bend-Back to great advantage. One is any steep bank, rather free of debris, that drops rapidly into deeper water. The bank can either be dry or have some water on it. Using a fast-sinking line and a long leader (at least 12 feet), I cast my fly and most of my leader up on the bank. I allow time for the sinking line to reach the bottom in the deeper water. Then I begin a slow retrieve. If it's slow enough, my leader and line will crawl across the dry or wet bank and enter the water. As I continue the retrieve my leader drags the fly down along the side of the steep bank, then follows the path of the sinking line lying on the bottom. Many times a fish that sees a fly crawling down the underwater bank and then across the bottom can't resist—and a strike follows.

Another place I enjoy using a Bend-Back is wherever largemouth or smallmouth bass, snook, barramundi, redfish, threadfin salmon, tarpon, snappers, or other species are lying under an overhanging branch but are very spooky. If I drop a fly here at the end of my cast, the resultant splash will often frighten the fish. *So using a Bend-Back streamer, I deliberately throw the fly into the branches above the fish.* If I jerk on the line at this point, it will often snag. But if I tease the line slowly while I retrieve, the Bend-Back will almost always crawl over the branches and finally drop into the water with a minimal splash. I've seen several fish actually watch the fly crawling through the branches; when it fell to the surface they instantly grabbed it.

My favorite form of fly fishing is for bonefish. But there's one place where Crazy Charlies, Clouser Deep Minnows, and other similarly tied patterns are difficult to fish: in the dense beds of turtle grass that are prime feeding locations for bonefish. What's needed to effectively fish here is a Bend-Back, which can be drawn through thick strands of turtle grass with little fear of snagging. I also use the Bend-Back on bonefish cruising a very shallow flat that's covered with fly-catching coral. The Bend-Back is by far the best pattern for such an area.

In Alaska millions of salmon spawn in the freshwater rivers, and they can bunch up in incredibly dense schools. When retrieved here a standard pattern will often snag the fish. Some anglers use a weed guard, but this often becomes deformed after a few casts, and a new fly must be attached. Not so with a Bend-Back. You can drag it through and over the bodies of the salmon without a hangup—yet when a fish takes, it's yours. A prime technique for many species of fish is to swim your fly around docks or rotten underwater pilings. Again, the Bend-Back is an ideal tool for such situations.

Tying Instructions

The Bend-Back is an easy fly to tie, but there are a few simple rules you must follow to make it effective. If the wing is tied too sparsely, the fly will sometimes fail to travel with its hook up. *You need a moderately full wing for this fly to ride properly on the retrieve. The biggest mistake made by most tiers is to bend the hook too much. If too great a bend is made in the hook, the part of the fly tied on the hook shank will dangle below the wing. Fish will often refuse such a fly; also, a hook bent too deeply often won't hook the fish on the take.* If the Bend-Back is correctly tied, the wing hides most of the hook, including the point. *Another important point is that Bend-Back flies tied on regular-length hooks don't hook fish as well as those on longer-shanked hooks. I tie all my Bend-Backs on 2X- or 3X-long hooks.*

To tie the Bend-Back, hold the hook upside down (point up). With a pair of pliers, grip the hook ⅛ to ⅜ inch behind the eye (depending on size of the hook). Bend the hook downward. *When you feel the hook start to bend, that's enough!* Dress the shank as you would any standard streamer. *The wing is tied on the part of the hook shank behind that eye that was not bent. Don't tie any materials on the hook shank—to be most efficient, this fly should consist of just a wing.* That's it. The Bend-Back is a method of tying; you can make these flies on hooks as small as size 6 for bonefish and as large as 5/0 for offshore species.

Weedless Flies

Many gamefish ambush their prey from a place of concealment. Like a hungry snake, curled and ready, they lie in wait. And when the hapless prey comes within range—they strike! Only if they can be hidden from their victims do many predatory fish have a chance of catching enough food. There are many different environments that predators use to hide in: under boat docks, sunken logs, grass, and rocks, to mention a few.

Fly anglers are forced to fish such waters if we expect to catch many of these predators. But our chances are often spoiled by the inability to work our flies through such hazards as sunken logs, underwater tree limbs, and grass. Fortunately some ingenious tiers have developed a number of methods of making flies that allow us to swim flies in the toughest of cover.

Most of these methods depend upon a guard of some sort to protect the hook point and prevent snagging. All such flies are referred to as weedless-style ties—although they can certainly be fished where there are no weeds.

There are a few basic points to remember when you fish a weedless fly. Most important is that once the fly is in the hazard area and may become entangled, never pull sharply on the line. *This quick, jerking motion will often force the weed guard to collapse, or else drive the hook into the very thing you want to avoid.* Instead, tease the fly very gently through the menacing area before continuing your retrieve.

Monofilament has become the standard material for weed guards. The rule regarding what size of mono to use is to look for a rather stiff monofilament that's about the same diameter as your hook shank. But mono deforms badly after only a few fish are caught, so I prefer the more durable stainless-steel trolling wire to protect my hooks. For smaller flies (sizes 6 through about 1/0) I use number 5 trolling wire; for heavier flies (sizes 2/0 through 5/0), number 7 trolling wire seems right. It doesn't make any difference if the wire is bright stainless or coffee colored. Such

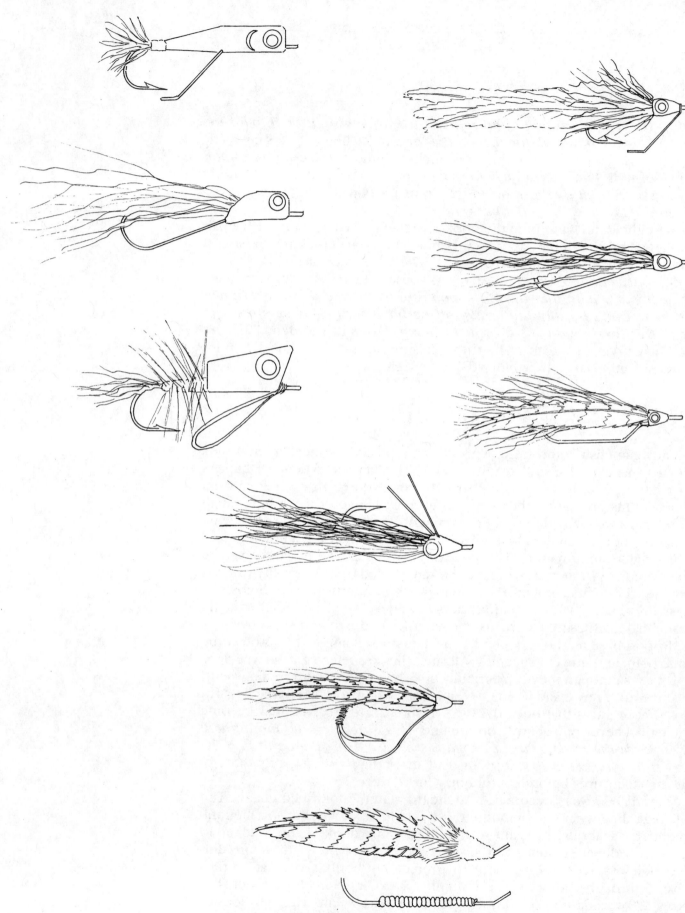

An assortment of weedless fly variations

wire can be obtained from any catalog or store that serves the offshore fishing fraternity.

If you do use a single strand of a stiff monofilament for a hook guard, a simple trick will help it collapse easier on the strike while keeping it just as effective for fishing through obstructions. A stiff stub of mono protruding from the fly body tends to push the fly away as the fish mouths it. So instead, make the mono guard a bit longer than normal. Then, using a *double-edged razor blade,* slice the very end of the monofilament several times. A double-edged blade will trim the end down to the thickness of a human hair, and this will cause the stub to collapse quickly on the strike. Just make sure the trimmed area is beyond the hook point—the guard works as effectively as an untrimmed one in protecting the hook.

Weedless flies can also be fished out of the water. It sounds crazy, but what I'm suggesting is that deliberately throwing your fly into a brush pile, a boat dock, an overhanging limb, or up on a bank is often a good idea. No more silent entry can be made into a quiet pocket holding a fish than by the use of this technique. For example, if you see a fish lying in inches of clear water under a bush, by casting your fly into the limbs and then teasing it until it gently falls in front of the fish, your chances for a strike are enhanced. You can do the same thing on a boat dock in a clear lake. Seeing something that appears good to eat fall silently from the dock to the surface will often draw a strike from a hesitant bass. Drawing a weedless fly across lily pads and plopping it into a hole often draws a good strike, too.

There's another good out-of-the-water place to work a fly: wherever a bank falls steeply into the water. If fish are holding close to or just off that steep bank, a weedless fly combined with a sinking line can mean more hookups. Cast your fly up on the bank. Give the sinking line time to fall to the bottom. Begin a *slow* retrieve. The sunken line will drag the weedless fly across the dry bank, down the vertical wall to the bottom, and across the bottom for some distance. A fish that sees a fly enter the water, slither down the bank wall, and start crawling the bottom is very likely to strike it.

I offer these ideas as only two of the many ways that you can use weedless flies to catch more fish.

The drawing on page 98 shows a number of methods of tying weedless flies. From this wide choice, you should find something that fits your fishing.

Rabbit Fur Flies

A relatively new series of flies popular with many fishermen are those made with rabbit fur. Actually, this an old technique; New Zealanders were using rabbit fur strips on streamer hooks before World War II. Rabbits were foreign to that country, and when they were imported from England they went wild. The habitat was perfect. There were so many that I guess fishermen decided to use them in their fly patterns.

Rabbit fur has many of the characteristics of marabou. It undulates in the water under the slightest manipulation by the angler or the currents. When used in short lengths it can be very tough. It can be spiraled around a hook shank, tied on top in a strip form, or left to dangle off the back, creating a snakelike swimming motion when it's retrieved. Of course, it can be dyed a variety of colors—but some of the natural colors are also very effective. Rabbit fur varies in length, depending upon the variety of rabbit the hide was taken from. Angora rabbits furnish some of the longest hair—as long as 1¾ inches. The wild rabbit that so many hunters shoot has some of the shortest hair fibers.

A disadvantage of using rabbit fur is that when thoroughly wet it holds a lot of water and becomes more difficult to cast. Another drawback to using rabbit hair as a long extension behind the hook is that during false casting, the hide can break and the tail fall off. Rabbit can be toughened, however, without interfering too much with the action. After you tie the fly, add only to the hide immediately behind the hook either a small amount of Pliobond (a rubber-based glue) or just a touch of thin Goop (a glue available in tackle shops and hardware stores). Both of these glues are very tough and flexible; they'll make the leather that hinges behind the hook during casting fairly durable. Some people also form a hoop of monofilament at the rear of the hook shank to prevent the tail from underwrapping the hook and fouling the cast.

Rabbit fur strips can be purchased in many fly shops, in case you don't want to cut your own. If you decide to cut your own, you can't just place the hide on a surface and cut strips from it; you'd slice through the hair on the underside of the hide. You must instead support the rabbit skin in the air while you make the slices. A simple way to do this is to clamp one end of the hide to a table, then stretch the hide taut and clamp the other end. Then, holding the lower portion of the hide, make slits of the desired width with a sharp razor blade. You can make a number of strips at once by bolting several single-edged razor blades together, spaced the proper distance apart with washers. If the fur is to be used lengthwise along the hook shank (as on a wing), make your cuts from the front of the hide to the rear. If the fur is to be wrapped in a circular manner around the hook shank, cut the strips across or sideways on the hide.

While rabbit fur was probably first used on freshwater flies for trout, a few years ago U.S. bass fishermen starting using this material to make a number of flies for a variety of species. One of the first was an eel-like worm that imitates a plastic worm. This generally consisted of a long, tapering strip of rabbit fur (usually dark in color) tied at the back of a long-shanked hook. Then the body was built up of either dubbed fur or chenille, with a soft hackle spiraled the length of the body. Sometimes the rabbit fur was wrapped along the hook shank to increase bulk. Such flies were rather buoyant in the water and sank slowly. But they were intended to be fished deep, so weight was added in the form of bead-chain eyes, lead eyes, or lead wire wrapped underneath the dubbed-fur or chenille body. A monofilament weed guard was added. Today this remains one of the best largemouth bass flies to fish around pilings, cypress stumps, boat docks, and similar structures, where a slow-moving, undulating fly will draw strikes.

Leeches form a large portion of many fish's diets, and perhaps no material does a better job of imitating a leech than dyed rabbit fur. A short strip is tied on at the back of the hook for a tail, then the fur is spiraled forward to the hook eye. The best leech patterns either add a thin body of chenille or dubbed fur, or have the rabbit strip widely spiraled forward. Don't wind the fur close together as you move forward on the hook or you'll get too much fur on the fly, and it will sink poorly.

An old and proven pattern for surface-feeding largemouth bass is the Gerbubble Bug. This bug usually is tied with a hackle feather radiating from each side, but substituting a strip of rabbit fur for the hackle feathers gives it considerably more action. However, it's much more difficult to cast than marabou used for the same purpose.

One of the best freshwater fly patterns—it's also very effective in shallow waters inshore—is the Dahlberg Diver. The substitution of a rabbit fur strip for the conventional tail will make this fly even more appealing on the retrieve to snook and tarpon.

Saltwater anglers are using rabbit fur strips on their flies for tarpon and bonefish. These are often referred to as Tarpon Bunnies, or Bonefish Bunnies. The wing of a Tarpon Bunny is often a combination of a strip of rabbit fur and saddle or neck feathers; usually the extended wing behind the fly is made of rabbit. For tarpon, a fly that doesn't sink too fast but rather suspends or slowly sinks in the water column is often desirable. The Tarpon Bunny can be thrown on a floating or slow-sinking fly line well in front of an oncoming tarpon, and because of the fly's slow sink rate you can delay your retrieve until the fish is near your offering. This is a very effective technique.

The wing of a Bonefish Bunny is almost always made entirely of rabbit fur. Generally a little weight has to be added in order for the fly to sink quickly. Some anglers will wrap the shank with size 1 (.013-inch) lead fuse wire to sink it. Others use 1/50-ounce lead eyes to drive the fly quickly to the bottom.

Since rabbit fur flies undulate very well at slow speeds, it's important not to hurry your retrieve. In almost all situations, if you want to get the most action from rabbit fur flies, a slow retrieve is best.

5

ESSENTIAL KNOTS

F ly fishermen are fascinated with knots. This is especially true among those who fish in salt water, where it's soon evident that strong knots are vital to success. Unfortunately, most freshwater fishermen don't realize the value of good knots until they hook a trophy—and then lose it.

There are hundreds of knots. And while they can be fascinating, you only need about nine to cover just about every fly-fishing situation in fresh and salt water, from taking a wary brown trout sipping size 22 dry flies from the surface to landing a northern pike, sailfish, or giant tarpon.

The most important rule to remember in good knot building is that no knot breaks until it slips. This rule includes all lines, from the 2-inch hawser rope used to secure a steamship to the dock to a fragile 6X tippet attached to a fly. It's vital that knots be drawn securely. If the knot is lubricated (dipped in the water or moistened with saliva), it will draw down better.

Knots that are properly drawn tight don't need Krazy Glue or other additives. Tying overhand knots in the tag end of knots or adding glue to them is an indication either that you're not using a good knot or that you're not drawing it tight enough to keep it from slipping. While silicone and other super lubricants help you draw a knot tight, these lubricants are extra slippery, and unless extreme care is taken they sometimes slip under tension. *Laboratory tests have shown that it's impossible to completely close any knot with your bare hands in monofilament larger than 15-pound test.*

It's extremely important to follow instructions carefully when you tie the knots that follow. *Especially critical is the number of turns you make around the standing line.* The improved clinch knot, for example, should have five turns around the main line for lines testing roughly 8X to 6 pounds; four turns for 8 to 12 pounds. For most monofilaments of larger than 12-pound test, the improved clinch knot is difficult to close, and I don't recommend it.

If you use 6-pound line or less to tie this knot and make only four turns, you won't have enough turns around the standing line to keep the knot from slipping. And if you make six turns (I recommend five), you'll have too many turns to draw the knot properly tight to keep it from slipping. All this is said to impress upon you that instructions on how to tie a knot are developed through considerable testing on machines. These tests determine the best way to tie it. Only after such testing are knot instructions published.

After tying thousands of knots for testing on my machine, I finally realized that there's a better way to close clinch-type knots. First, let me emphasize that most fishing knots are variations on either the clinch, nail, or overhand knot. Clinch-type knots include, for example, the blood knot, improved clinch knot, and uniknot. How many times have you tried tying a blood or clinch knot (or another variation of a clinch) and had it come down so far, and then fail to close properly? Here's my suggestion: *Once you've formed the knot and it's ready to be closed, pull on the tag end*

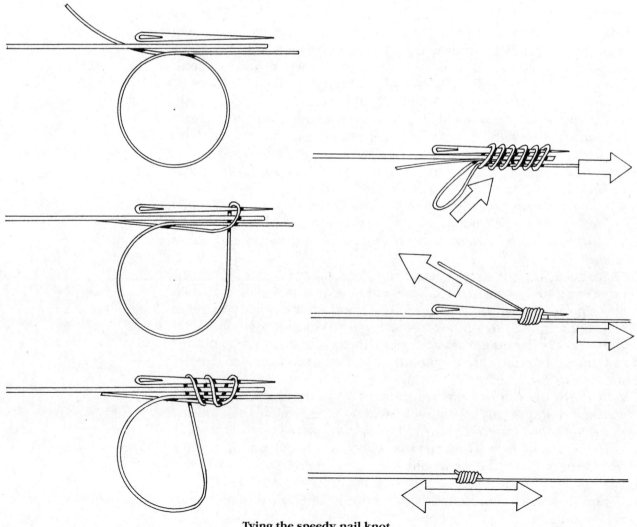

Tying the speedy nail knot

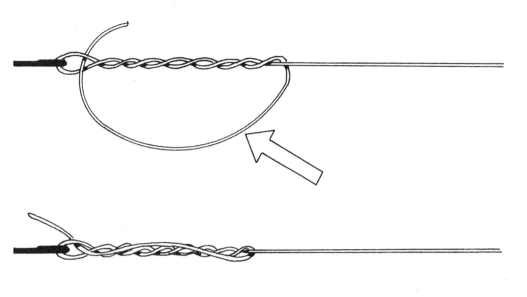

How to properly close a clinch knot

(or ends, for a blood knot) until it lies flush against the spirals or twists around the main line. Once it lies flush, wet it and pull the knot closed. You should have no further trouble closing clinch knots easily and firmly.

There's another important point to remember if you're connecting two different sizes of monofilament: *The knot will close much better if you use similar monofilaments.* If, instead, you use two monofilament strands with different degrees of stiffness, you'll find it more difficult to close the knot properly.

To develop good knot technique, learn to use knots that have a high line strength, *then practice tying them at home.* Correctly tied and closed tightly, they'll serve you well.

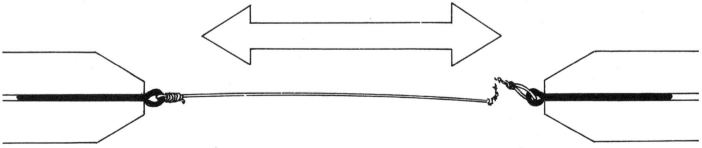

To test any knot, use a single strand of line to tie the two different knots on identical hooks. Then, grip the hooks with pliers and jerk repeatedly until one of the knots breaks. Test ten times.

Whipped Loop

This is my preferred way to attach either backing or the leader to my fly line. *Some fly lines, such as those with a Kevlar core or with monofilament laid down over a solid core, don't work well with a nail knot, which can slip off.* For these, the whipped loop works very well. Always test a completed whipped loop for strength by holding a nail or thin rod inside the loop and pulling on the main line. *When properly tied, this loop is stronger than the main line.* The loops don't hang up in the guides because of their rounded ends. And when properly constructed, they never pull out during battle. I use a whipped loop in both ends of my fly line; by adding a loop to the backing, I can exchange fly lines anytime. This is an outstanding advantage. Loops also allow you to substitute another leader quickly—a vital factor in coping with different fishing conditions. I consider the nail knot a disadvantage in this regard. Be sure to wrap thread around bobbin foot four times before you start to whip, and coat the threads when finished.

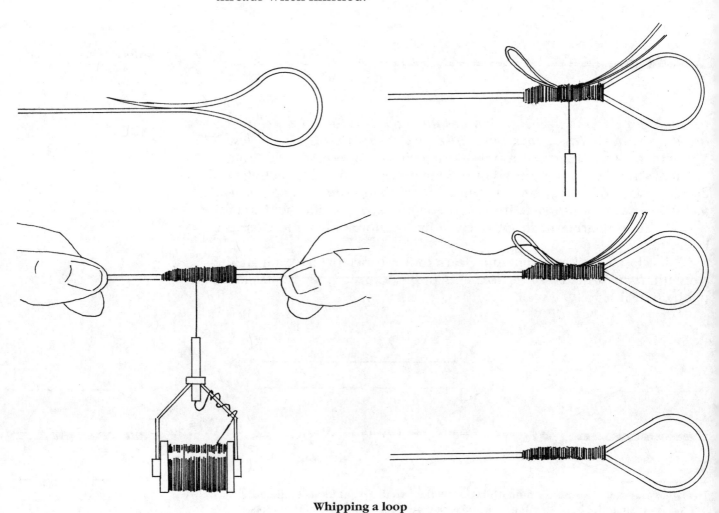

Whipping a loop

Surgeon's Knot

There are many situations in which you must connect two different diameters of monofilament together; in some cases, too, you need to connect braided wire to monofilament. The surgeon's knot makes these connections quite well in monofilament lines up to 60-pound test in strength, or braided steel wire to 40-pound test. The most important factor in constructing a good surgeon's knot is that once you've tied it, you must pull all four ends very tight or a weak knot can result. For building tapered leaders, the surgeon's knot is almost always stronger than a blood knot, and it's much quicker to tie. It allows you, for example, to quickly join 6-pound-test leader material to 40-pound-test.

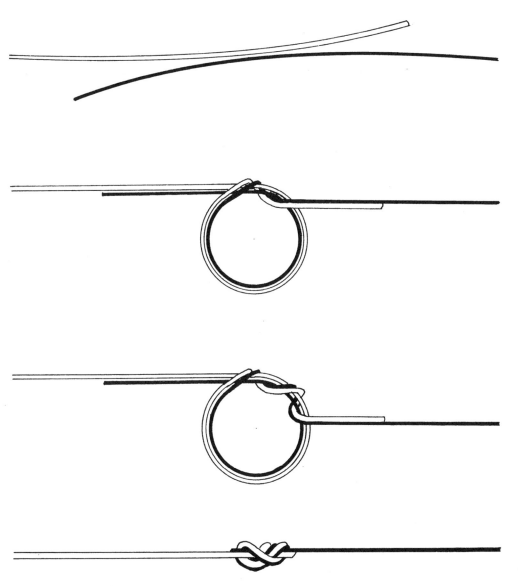

Surgeon's knot

Bimini Twist

This is the single most important knot a saltwater fly fisherman can learn—and it has great importance to freshwater fishermen who want to tackle large, powerful fish on light tippets. Most knots result in a connection that's weaker than the line they're tied with. The Bimini twist, however, will never slip—so it never breaks. When you build a Bimini twist, you end up with a doubled line or loop extending from the knot. This is where

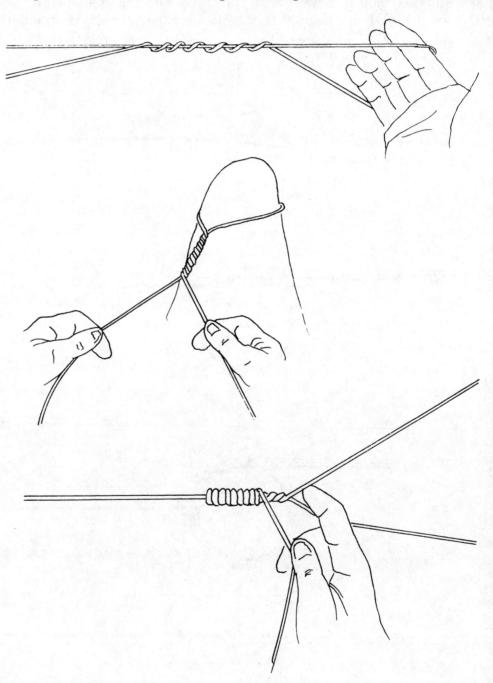

Bimini twist

the value of the Bimini lies. For example, if your tippet is 12-pound test and you want to join it to a shock leader of 100 pounds, almost all connections will result in a knot of less than 12 pounds. *But when you make a Bimini (which is stronger than the line) beyond the knot, you have two pieces of 12-pound line—24 pounds—with which to attach the hook or other line.* Almost any knot you now tie will be stronger than one made with the single-strand 12-pound. The Bimini is the one knot serious saltwater fishermen should use (fly, plug, and spin casters, as well as trollers)—but freshwater fishermen should use it, too.

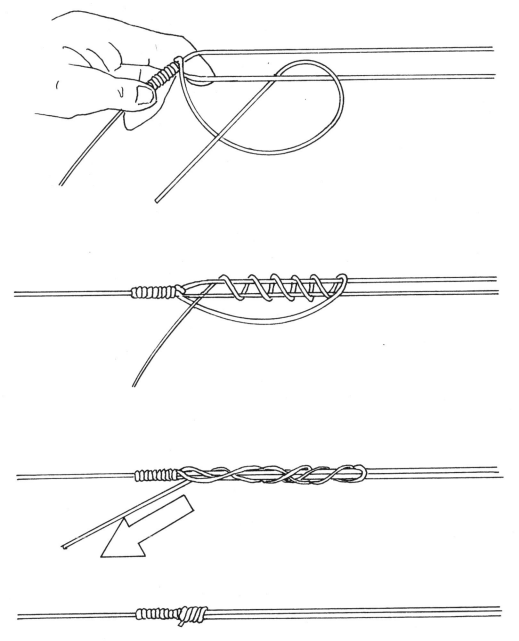

Bimini twist (*continued*)

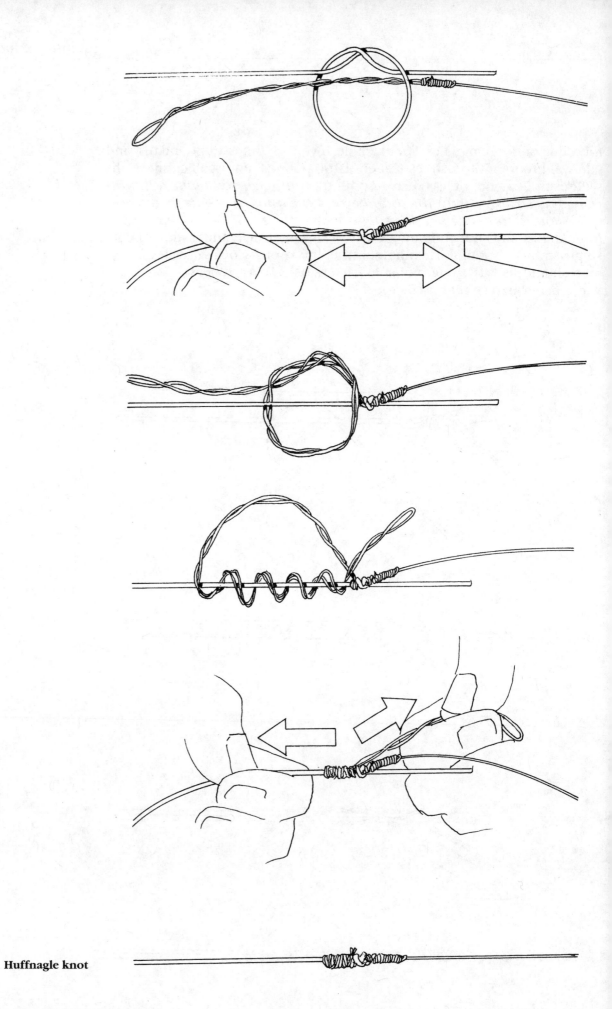

Huffnagle knot

Huffnagle Knot

This knot has a number of names, but Huffnagle seems to be the most common. Although slight variations on the knot are possible, the drawing at 110 shows one basic method that works very well. The Huffnagle knot is superb for joining very large-diameter monofilament (such as that used as a shock leader in saltwater fly fishing) to a thin monofilament tippet or a tippet constructed with a Bimini twist. An advantage of this knot is that it forms one of the smallest connections when large (80- to 120-pound, for example) monofilament is joined to a small strand. The knot lies straight once it is complete, giving your fly improved action on retrieve.

Albright Knot

Of all the knots used for connecting different diameters of line together, my personal favorite is the Albright. Because this knot is very old (it was developed in the early 1950s) some feel that it isn't as good as a "new" knot. But the Albright is a superior knot when properly tied and has served me well for decades. Not only does it connect different diameters of monofilament, but it can also be used to connect braided or solid wire to monofilament. It has been used to connect backing to fly line and even monofilament leaders to some types of fly lines. The most important factor in tying this knot is to be sure that none of the wraps overlap each other as you close it. If you overlap the monofilament, it will sometimes break at that point.

Nonslip Loop

With the exception of the George Harvey dry-fly knot (see page 116), my favorite knot for attaching flies to the leader is the nonslip loop. If this knot is tied correctly, it remains at the full strength of the monofilament. A loop knot offers advantages. Most important is that it allows the fly greater freedom of movement. A nymph can swim more freely, a popping bug can gurgle and pop better, Clouser Minnows and other weighted flies will dip and dive more. If you're forced to attach your fly to a heavier-than-normal tippet, the loop knot will still allow the fly to swim or move naturally. Once you begin using good loop knots, you won't consider any other.

The most popular loop knot is the Uniknot, formerly called the Duncan loop. This knot isn't as strong as the tippet with which it's tied. The nonslip loop is, however, and it can be tied in ½-pound-test monofilament to 120-pound test. It may look complicated but it really isn't. Study the drawing on page 113 and think of it this way: You make an overhand knot, take

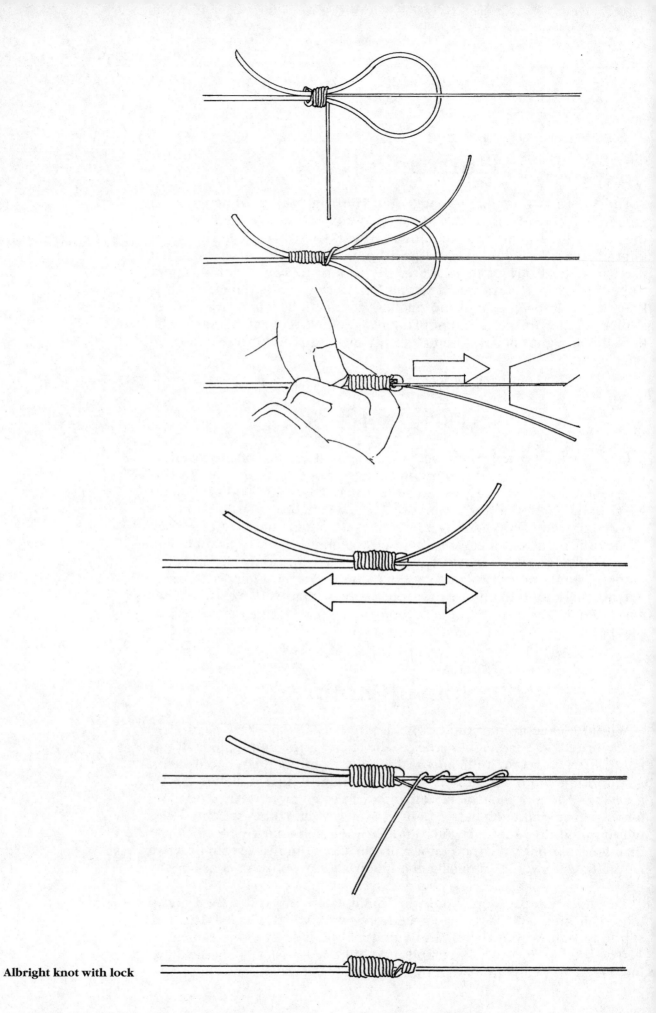

Albright knot with lock

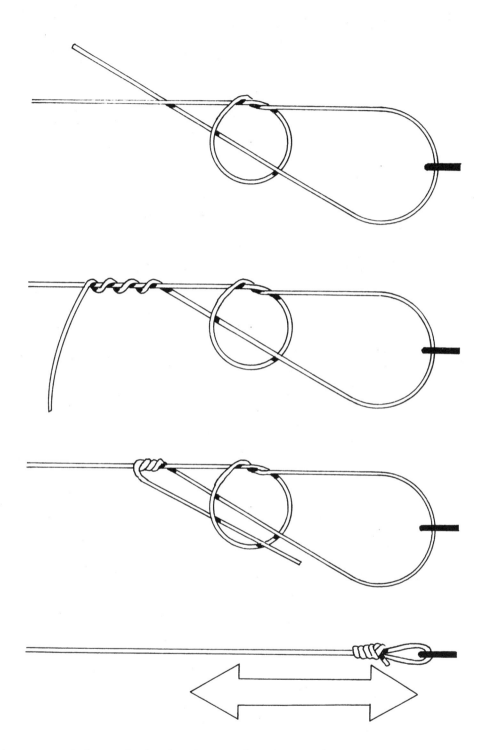

Nonslip loop

the tag end through the hook eye, then bring this tag end back through the overhand knot the same way the tag end came out. If you don't do this, the knot will be weaker. Then make a certain number of turns with the tag end around the main line and again insert the tag through the overhand knot, being sure to again go through the overhand just as you did in the beginning. To make the loop smaller, try this: Before the tag end makes the prescribed wraps, pull gently on the main line to make the overhand

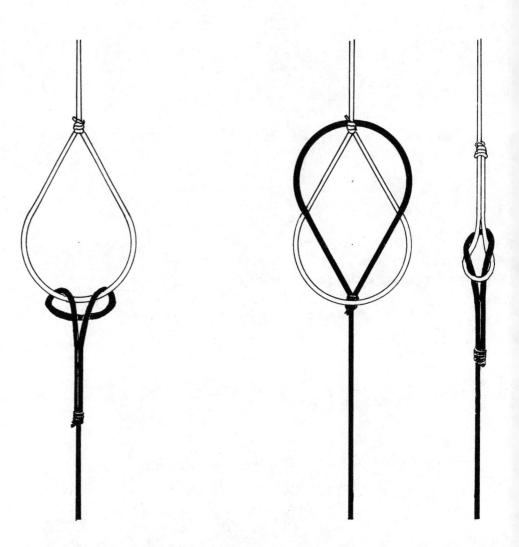

The correct (right) and incorrect (left) way to loop-to-loop

smaller, then pull lightly on the tag end. This will cause the overhand to slide down to the hook eye, permitting you to make a smaller loop.

Here's the most important aspect of building a nonslip loop for full line strength. You must make the recommended number of turns with the tag end around to get full strength. Learn the following: For lines testing from ½ to 6 pounds, make seven turns. For lines testing 8 to 12 pounds, make five turns; for 15 to 40 pounds, make four turns; make three turns for lines from 50- to 60-pound test. Only one turn is needed on lines testing more than 60 pounds.

Trilene Knot

While most people use the improved clinch knot to attach their tippet to the hook eye, a much stronger knot—it usually breaks at or near 100 percent of line strength—is the Trilene knot. It's very easy to tie; with practice it's quicker and easier than the improved clinch. *It's important that you don't "improve" the Trilene knot, as you do the clinch knot.* Improv-

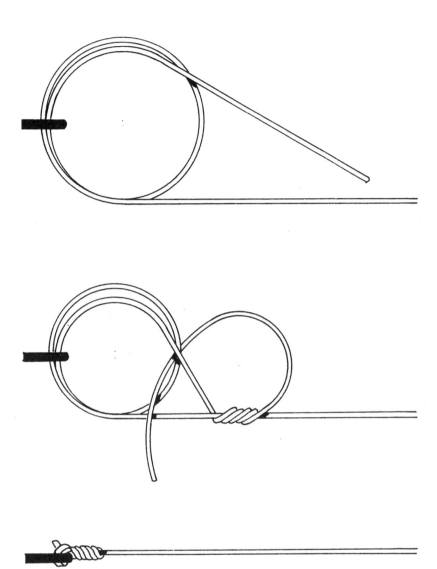

Trilene knot

ing the Trilene knot actually *weakens* it; it can't be drawn tight enough to keep it from slipping when the improvement is added.

Maximum strength from a Trilene knot is obtained when lines testing from 8X to 6 pounds are given with five turns around the main line. With 8- to 12-pound test, I recommend four turns; three turns are best with 15 or 20 pounds. I don't recommend using the Trilene knot with lines stronger than 20 pounds.

Figure-8 Knot

When you're using braided wire for fish with sharp teeth, I recommend the figure-8 knot. I don't think any instructions are needed, if you study the

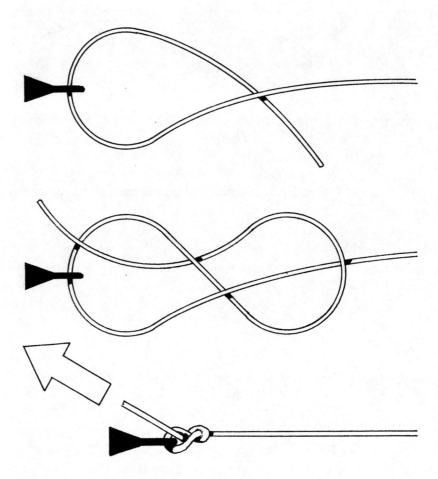

Figure-8 knot

drawing. *There is one caution. When you draw the knot tight, be sure to draw only on the tag end. If you pull tightly on the main line, you'll pull some of the kinked braided wire in front of the hook, which will cause the fly to swim unnaturally in the water.*

George Harvey Dry-Fly Knot

This is my all-time favorite knot for attaching dry flies to the tippet. It has great strength, and it also holds the dry fly so that it never tilts to one side during the drift. It may look confusing, but it's really simple and easy to tie.

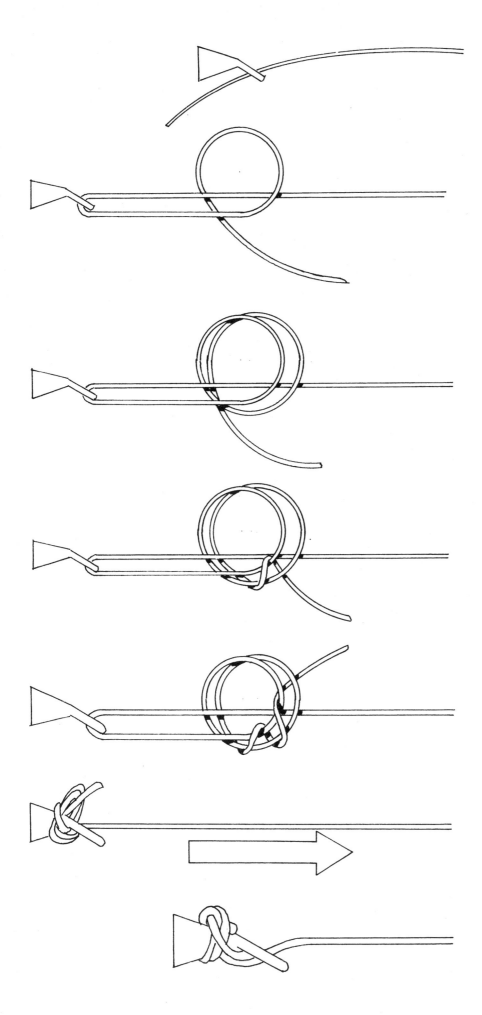

George Harvey dry-fly knot

6

SEEING FISH

The ability to see a fish before you make a cast is a great advantage, and in many cases essential to success. This is true in both fresh water and the salt. Three natural conditions help defeat you from seeing your quarry. One is wind. Another is rain that muddies a stream or waves that stir the bottom. Waters that have been roiled with sediment or stirred by the wind, and surfaces so distorted that you can't see beneath them, are factors you can do little about. But a third factor is too much or too little light on the water. Too much light often produces glare, and too little light doesn't allow your vision to penetrate the water. You can do a lot about reducing glare. In fact, one of the first things a fisherman learns is that polarized glasses will reduce glare considerably, improving his chances of seeing fish.

There are two basic types of polarized glasses. One is simply a polarizing screen sandwiched between two pieces of soft and rather inexpensive clear plastic. This is the least expensive type of polarized glasses, and so long as they remain in good condition, they work well. They do scratch easily, however, and most fishermen go through many pairs of these before they elect to buy the second, improved type—those glasses whose polarizing portion is sandwiched between either two clear pieces of optical glass or two pieces of *scratch-resistant* plastic.

If you use prescription glasses, you also have two options. You can purchase clip-ons. These are simply polarized lenses without a frame that attach to your regular glasses. I've never found any clip-ons that were totally satisfactory. All I've tried are the soft plastic type—which scratch easily. Also, when traveling in a fast-running boat I've had the wind blow them off. Most fishermen who are serious about their sport will eventually purchase a pair of the much more expensive prescription-ground polarized glasses. Once you use these, you'll never go back to clip-ons.

If you see poorly up close but your distance vision is good, you may want to purchase an inexpensive pair of the glasses that have a tiny magnifier in the bottom of each lens. The rest of the lens is polarized. These are available in many places.

A few tricks will let you use polarized glasses more efficiently and get better service from them. First, there are three popular tints of glasses: blue-gray, brown-amber, and yellow. Many people believe that when fishing offshore, the blue-gray kind let them see better under the surface. These certainly perform best for me. But on the flats and in the shallows, the brown-amber color (years ago called Cosmotan) seems to be the best. It's certainly the most popular choice by a wide margin. There is, however, a third pair of glasses that I find extremely helpful when light conditions are bad: On dark, overcast days when rains may threaten, for example, yellow-tinted glasses are superb. Not all optical outlets sell these. The only company I know of at this writing that does is Hobie—but I suspect many more will in the future. The yellow builds contrast and helps you separate the objects you view, much as shooting glasses will under poor light conditions. On rainy, overcast days or when fishing in the woods for trout I find the yellow glasses superior to all others—although on sunlit days they create a considerable amount of eyestrain for me, so I avoid using them under bright-light conditions. I've experimented with clear polarized glasses and found them very disappointing. I think it's because they lack contrast.

Keeping glasses clean is essential, and there are some tricks to doing so. Obviously, you'll want to store soft plastic polarized glasses in a soft protective case and use care when you put them down to avoid scratching. Many such glasses develop scratches because they're laid down with the

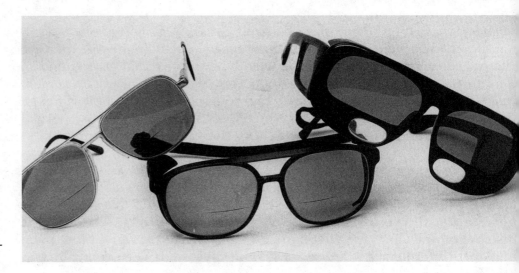

The author uses three different tints of polarized glasses to suit different fishing and light conditions.

front of the lens contacting a surface. Glasses also need to be cleaned, and a common cause of scratches on softer lenses is permitting some salt spray to collect on them then, after it dries into crystals, wiping them with a napkin or cloth. The hardened salt crystals will often scratch the lenses. Instead use a little water to soften the crystals. Fresh water is usually obtainable from the onboard cooler in the form of melted ice. Dip your glasses into the ice water and then clean them. Almost any optical store sells small, easy-to-carry bottles of lens cleaner, which works well. You can also carry a small bottle filled with a commercial household window cleaner, such as Windex. But the best cleaner for glasses is one I discovered from a doctor, who handed me what looked like the miniature envelopes that hand wipes come in. At the time I thanked him, but I really didn't understand how valuable these little items would be. Called **alcohol swabs** or **alcohol wipes,** they're 1-inch-square pads saturated with alcohol. I urge you to try them; I don't how I ever got along without these. They cost less than three cents each. I use them for a variety of purposes—anytime I want to clean a small surface—but one of their best uses is to clean saltwater spray that's dried on your glasses. Dab an alcohol swab on the salt crystals and they disappear. Wipe the glasses dry and they'll sparkle. I now carry these in my sunglass case, fly box, tackle bag, and fishing vest.

But you'll be better off if you never need these swabs—indeed, I have a fetish about keeping my glasses clean when fishing. If a drop of salt spray gets on them, I want to wipe it off before it dries. The best thing I know to wipe water off glasses is a good, dry paper napkin. Trouble is, if you carry napkins in your pockets and it rains, salt spray gets to them. Or you might fall in, or start sweating, and the napkins will become useless. For this reason I carry several napkins in my shirt pockets inside a small plastic bag. One of the first things I do when I prepare for a trip is place a good supply of napkins in a medium-sized Zip-Loc bag and store them in my tackle bag or box.

Another vision problem frequently presents itself, especially when you're landing a fish. The fish is finally brought to the boat, you bend over, and, just as you pick it up, the fish beats the surface wildly with its tail. This causes water to splash on your glasses, and it never seems to drain off quickly enough. But there's a cure for this, too. It's a product that, when applied to a clean car windshield, will cause water to bead up and run off the glass. In all but a heavy rain, this material will flush water so quickly from the car windshield that you really don't need your wipers. It works on eyeglasses, too. The brand I use is called Rain-X, although I'm sure similar products are sold under different names. It's inexpensive, a bottle will last a lifetime, and it's obtainable from many auto parts stores.

I have been told that this material will ruin some types of plastic sunglasses. I've been using it for years with no problem, but take warning. To use it, clean your polarized glasses, then put a little Rain-X on a piece of napkin or cloth and apply it to the lenses. It virtually disappears from eye-

Paper napkins can be kept clean and dry in a small Zip-Loc bag.

Water splashing on your glasses can inhibit your sight. Use a coating of Rain-X—available in auto parts stores—which causes water to immediately run off the glasses.

sight within seconds. It will last for several days of hard fishing, unless you clean your lenses frequently.

One manufacturer applies a Teflon coating to its sunglass lenses to discourage dirt from accumulating. This company says that Rain-X will eventually remove the Teflon coating. But on all the other glasses I've worn, Rain-X has worked wonders for me.

Manufacturers design polarized glasses for what they consider average viewing situations—which doesn't always apply to fishing. If you're looking into the water and find there's some bothersome glare, try this trick: Tilt your head to one side and then the other. Not always, but often, tilting the head will change the angle of the polarized glasses and eliminate some additional glare.

When you're wading or moving forward in a boat seeking fish in shallow water, it's best to have the sun either behind you or at least off to the side behind you. This will eliminate much surface glare. But side shields attached to your eyeglass frames prevent glare from striking the inside portion of the lenses. *These side shields are almost a necessity when you're flats fishing.* You can make your own from a variety of products, but several companies now sell super-tough side shields that fit most frames. Other companies have built side shields into their frames—a commendable idea.

Almost any angler who fishes in warmer climates and wears glasses has experienced one constant problem: The glasses are forever slipping down on the nose. This is not only bothersome but can also interfere with vision. There are devices you can attach to the rear of the frames that will keep your glasses tight against your head. I find these are uncomfortable, however, so I've come up with a simple device that allows me to establish exactly where on my nose I want the glasses to sit. Once the adjustment is made, the glasses stay there. They can also be quickly readjusted to another position.

Eliminate glare by pointing toward the fish.

Attach a short length of string (I use old fly line) to the earpiece of each frame. Then sew on a loop of Velcro—the looped part on one string and the hook part on the other. Position your glasses where you want them, then simply engage the Velcro sections to hold the glasses firmly in placed.

Light is polarized at 88 degrees from the sun. This means that if you look into the water with the sun at that angle you'll experience little or no glare. This trick only works if the sun is not overhead, however, and re-membering the 88 degrees may be difficult. So here's another trick to help you see under water without polarized glasses: Point your thumb at the sun; where your first finger points, there will be no glare (see the drawing above).

Chuck Edgehill demonstrates that small field glasses can be used to locate fish, determine what's hatching, and—best of all—figure out what your friend is using to catch those fish.

A good pair of field glasses will help any fly fisherman see more fish. Small and easy to carry, these glasses will let a trout fisherman see what's hatching and where fish are located. Saltwater fly fishermen can observe distant birds breaking on fish, search for snook under a mangrove, and so on. There's a host of situations where these glasses will aid you.

7

APPROACHING

Approaching fish without alarming them is a learned art. The two things that alert fish to danger more than any others are motion and sound. Motion is perhaps even worse than sound.

Motion

Predatory fish like herons and ospreys have fed on fish for eons. A stalking heron or swooping osprey or bald eagle is a life-threatening event to a fish. So it behooves the fly fisherman to make as little motion visible to the fish as possible. If you can approach from behind brush, a rock, or any structure that prevents fish from seeing your movement, the chances of your catching one improve. And approaching fish while highlighted against the sky is not nearly as effective as having a solid background behind you. There will be times when it's best to crawl to a spot. I remember fishing with John Goddard and Nick Lyons on a private Montana trout stream that's perhaps one of the best for dry-fly fishing in the nation—and maybe the world. The stream is rather small, but the fish are big: Many 22-inch and bigger trout cruise this spring creek. There's no brush to speak of along the banks. It's grazed by cattle and the grass is only inches high. To make a good approach to these exceptionally wary fish you must crawl to a spot, keeping as low as possible. Then you slide down over the bank. Stand up and the game is over. Once you're over the bank, your profile isn't outlined against the sky—but vertical casting will leave your rod swishing through the air. Thus the best casts are made here by keeping your rod low, so it's not outlined against the sky. Many people don't realize that a high rod is often visible to fish—whether you're on a spring creek, such as this one, or a bonefish flat. The motion of that rod working back and forth will often cause panic among nearby fish.

Standing up straight near the water means that the trout are going to see you, which reduces your chances of getting them to take.

Wearing the proper clothing can also be critical to success. For example, trout streams in the East usually have green foliage along their borders. Wearing a brightly colored shirt here is like carrying a beacon. The fish are going to quickly see any movement you make in clothing bright enough to contrast with the background vegetation. In vogue among many fly fishermen these days is the wearing of flashy hats—some even made of bright fluorescent materials. I watched a fly fisherman sneak down a Pennsylvania stream a few years ago. He stalked quietly and appeared to be aware of the need for a cautious approach. He caught nothing during the time I observed him. I think the reason was that he was wearing proper green clothing—but a hat of brilliant fluorescent yellow. I'm sure all the trout saw him long before he got close.

The background is what you want to match. On a western U.S. stream, where the vegetation is often brownish or tan in color, a light tan fly-fishing vest and clothes would blend in well. The dark green clothing that worked so nicely on the eastern streams may do poorly out West—and vice versa. Many saltwater fly fishermen work from boats. The guide poles the boat across a flat and the angler stands either in the bow or on a small

Crouching low like this will help you score better.

platform. This added height helps the angler see the fish—but it also makes it easier for the fish to see the angler, particularly if his clothing contrasts with the background sky. For such fishing, it's best to wear white, pale blue, or some other shade that blends with the sky and clouds. Dark colors would create a silhouette, warning the fish.

Experienced trout fishermen know that wearing highly reflective items while fishing can also give them away to the trout. For example, the hemostats used to remove hooks are generally chrome plated. So are the zingers—small retractable devices that hold clippers and other small tools. This chrome plating gives off flashes of light as you move around. Fortunately, some manufacturers now offer these tools in a dull black finish. If you already have such chrome-plated tools, keep them inside your jacket or paint them a dull color. Some anglers also buff the fine finish on their fly rods to dull any reflective flash made while casting. Frankly, I don't think this is a problem; I can't recall a time when I believed a reflection from my rod caused me to lose an opportunity.

An eddy is water traveling in a circle. Eddies occur in streams, rivers, along channels in salt water, and even on the open ocean, although these

Wearing bright clothing and casting in the bright sunlight means trout will see you.

By wearing clothing that blends with the background, and by standing in the shade, this angler will be less visible to trout.

When you're using a long rod in a tight corner with little space to cast, you can often slide your rod hand up near the butt guide and shorten the rod by as much as 18 inches. After the cast, hold the handle as you normally would to fish.

are often not as noticeable. For many years fishermen have been claiming that fish, especially trout or salmon holding the current, are facing upstream. But this isn't true. *Fish do not face upstream. They face into the current.* This is a very important factor to consider both when you approach fish and when you present the fly. If there's an eddy along a bank, the fish at its outside edge may be facing downstream. *As the water turns in the eddy, its fish will be facing into the current.* Some will be looking directly downstream, others either looking toward the near or far bank.

This knowledge can help you approach your quarry while remaining unseen, and help you place your fly so that it comes to the fish in a natural manner.

Most fly fishermen use a rod 8½ to 9 feet in length. With such a long rod, you may find that on some streams the bank on the far side is too close; your long rod will prevent you making a good cast. A simple trick that often works is to slide your hand up the rod to just below the butt or stripping guide. You'll have no trouble making a tight-quarters cast. When the cast is finished, return your rod hand to the handle.

Here's another problem during the approach that can cause a lost fish, but is easily remedied: If you wear hip boots, they're often supported by straps attached to your belt. The ends of the straps dangle down outside your boots. During a cast, and sometimes when fighting a fish, your line can tangle in this dangling strap. This is an easy problem to solve. Simply remove the strap from the boot. Reverse the position of the buckle so that the top is at the bottom. Insert the strap again, and the end will go inside your boot instead of dangling on the outside.

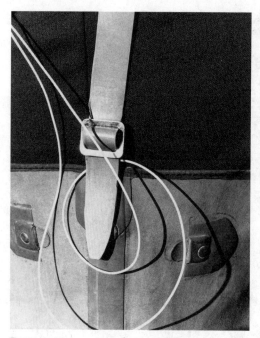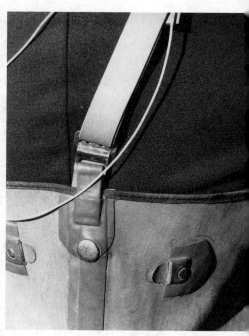

Boot straps can tangle your line.
Remove the strap and reverse the buckle, causing the strap to lie inside the boot.

Sound

Sound is the other factor that alerts fish. It's not quite as important as motion, but it can surely doom your chances. Crunching your boots on gravel, tumbling debris before you as you crawl down a rocky bank, or roaring into a location in a boat—all will alert and frighten your quarry.

A simple example can explain the basic problem. Many streams are bordered by fences that you have to climb to reach the water. I've watched some fly fishermen carefully climb the fence—then jump to the ground on the other side. If you do this with a fence close to the stream, be assured that every trout nearby will hear you contact the ground, and know there's danger present.

I prefer to walk on a bank of grass or soft dirt as I approach a trout stream, rather than treading on a gravelly one, which crunches underfoot, sending signals to the fish. If you use a wading staff—and it's a good idea—I recommend a wooden one, which doesn't clang against the bottom like a metal one (it also floats). When moving from one location to another, don't let the wading staff drag on the ground behind you. Once, on the Delaware River, I was fishing with another outdoor writer. I never had to wonder where he was. He allowed his wading staff, which was an aluminum ski pole, to drag on the ground as he walked. I could trace all of his movements as the pole clattered over the gravel bars. I'm sure trout a long distance away knew that he was approaching.

Water transmits sound about four and a half times faster than air does. Salt water transmits sound slightly faster than fresh water. *This is a very important factor in making a good approach.* Whether you're wading a bonefish flat or a calm pool on a small trout stream, always be aware that water will send any sounds you make quickly to the fish. *For this reason, never wade when you don't have to.* Too many anglers fishing small streams will get into the water to make the cast. That can be a mistake. *Only when you can't make the right presentation otherwise should you consider stepping into a stream.* Your feet grinding on gravel, slipping off rock, and making other warning sounds will often defeat your efforts.

When wading I like to think of the water in front of me as something like a balloon. If you hold up a balloon full of water and poke against one side, all of the other side of the balloon will surge away from you. This is exactly what happens when you wade, *especially if the water is calm.* (The noise you make is reduced when the water is moving swiftly.) As you wade notice the small waves moving out from your legs during your forward strides. For some reason many anglers seem to think that this is only a surface disturbance. It isn't! Just like when you poked the balloon and the water surged away, the entire water column directly in front of you is affected. Waves are moving outward from top to bottom because of your disturbance. The lateral line on a fish tells it someone is approaching. The calmer the water, the slower you must move if you hope to get close to wary fish. This is true both on a redfish flat and when fishing a calm spring creek for brown trout.

Walking with your rod held out behind you in the woods is much better than having it out in front of you.

When you wade on calmer waters, if you see small waves radiating out more than 18 inches from your legs, you're wading too fast! *When I'm approaching wary trout in a calm pool, I move my forward foot so slowly that it may take several minutes to progress just a few yards.* I've spent 10 minutes wading slowly just to get into position to cast. If you are going to wade, consider speed. Make it on the slower side. This is an important concept many fishermen disregard.

A long time ago I learned about which direction to wade when fishing meadow streams for bass, bluegills, and other warm-water species. In Maryland, where I've lived most of my life, many small streams meander through the lush countryside. Many of my most pleasant fishing trips have involved grabbing a 3- or 4-weight fly rod, a floating line, a small box of flies, and a companion, then driving a few miles from home to one of these streams. It's not high-profile fishing, and a minimum of gear is needed. Long ago I switched from tennis shoes to regular wading shoes. But since I only fish this way during the warm months, the water temperature is in the 80s and very comfortable. All you need is a rigged rod, a small popper, streamer, or wet fly, and a pair of wading shoes.

At first we would drive to a bridge and park the car; one angler would go downstream while the other went up. Such streams should produce about the same number of strikes in either direction, unless the character of the water is very different. But I soon realized that one of us would always catch more fish than the other, unless there was a great difference in our skills with the tackle. Who caught the most? *Invariably it was the fly fisherman who waded upstream.* I'm not sure why; my friends and I had learned to wade cautiously and make a good approach. The only reason we could figure out is that the mud and debris kicked up by wading always traveled downstream. In front of the downstream wader, this apparently alerts the fish.

Such meadow streams have bridge crossings every 2 or 3 miles, so we eventually altered our method of fishing them. I would drive my friend to a bridge, dropping him off with an extra key to the car. I'd then drive to the next upstream bridge, park the car, and wade upstream. My friend, upon reaching the car, would drive to the next upstream bridge to pick me up. This is a great sport for two fly fishermen to enjoy.

I'm continually amazed at the serious bass fishermen, some considered professionals, who will in a high-speed modern bass boat roar into a cove they plan to fish. Then they chop the motor. These heavy boats, which run almost out of the water when at high speed, on the stop will suddenly sink deep in the water. This causes huge waves to radiate outward from the boat. The waves race to the shore, washing debris back into it, and often muddying the area near the bank. Saltwater fishermen are also guilty of this action. Aside from dropping dynamite overboard, I can't think of a more effective way to disturb the peace and silence of a cove or any water you plan to fish. I have an aluminum 17-foot jon boat, rigged with a 60-horsepower jet engine. It's a dream boat for getting around on the rocky rivers of the Mid-Atlantic where I fish. When I approach a favorite fishing location, I shut off the big jet engine a good distance away. Then using ei-

Flip Pallot wades upstream when fishing smaller meadow creeks; wading downstream reduces your catching chances.

ther the electric motor or a pole, I quietly move into my fishing spot. I'm positive this delivers more hookups for me.

If you fish on saltwater flats with experienced guides nearby you will soon—*very soon*—learn that running motors in shallow water close to other anglers can start a fight. One of the quickest ways to get into an argument on a tarpon or bonefish flat is to operate your motor at high speed near someone who's fishing. Experienced guides know that this puts down local fish, and they won't tolerate it. The same ethics apply when you're leaving an area where others are fishing. On occasion I've been tarpon fishing, especially in the Florida Keys, at spots where there were a number of guides either staked out waiting for moving fish, or poling quietly along. I've watched good guides leave an area by poling more than ½ mile away from other anglers before starting their engines. It's an indication of how seriously these guides take engine noise.

Again, fish survive by the danger indicators that come to them. While they aren't brilliant, anything that's out of the normal pattern of their lives they regard as a threat until they're satisfied that it isn't. Motion and noise are two factors that fish use to alert them to danger. We need to constantly keep this in mind. Let me cite a good example. One well-known outdoor writer, when fly casting, rocks his body back and forth in a most pleasing manner; it looks so smooth. Several times when we fished together, though, I felt his beautiful casting motion was detrimental. If you're in shallow water, such as the backcountry of the Ten Thousand Islands, the bottom is soft and mushy. Step out and your foot will sink a foot or more before it contacts solid turf. I've watched this great caster rocking back and forth while false casting, and in turn the boat rocked with him. If I looked carefully, I could see the small waves radiating outward from the boat. Even the bottom nearby would become stirred. I'm certain fish feel the pressure created by a boat as it rocks back and forth like this—or when you push it too fast through the shallows. I believe that when you're in a boat in the shallows, the slower the boat progresses and the less it rocks, the better.

Another factor is important when fishing from boats: *The boat is like a giant drum, resonating any noise made within.* Remember how much faster water transmits sound than air does? A slight noise made in a boat sitting on the water is communicated rapidly to the fish. If you want to prove this to yourself, snorkel with your head under water and have someone make noise within a nearby boat. You'll be amazed how well you hear it—and the fish will certainly hear it better than you do. In deep water you can get away with some boat noise. *But in shallow water all noises are detrimental to fishing success.*

There are a number of things you can do to reduce or eliminate this problem. The most important is to be constantly aware of the noise factor. Anything you do to avoid it will help. Don't jump from the boat platform to the bottom of the boat. Try not to drop anything on the deck, and when you're moving around in a boat, plan how you'll do it without making noise. Take care to store things so you can move around freely. If you carry tackle boxes, or other containers, glue a section of outdoor carpet on the bottom. In a boat, I prefer to carry most items in soft bags. I also place a section of outdoor carpet between the mount on my electric motor and the boat. This padding further reduces any vibrations that are sent to the fish.

Years ago I was told by experienced fly fishermen that loud talking didn't bother fish in the shallows. From my own experience I know that this isn't true. When fishing in shallow water keep your voice low—or you'll suffer the consequences. You can easily test this. Locate some fish in very shallow, calm water. Then make a loud shout. Even if the fish don't scatter, they'll definitely change their attitude, and you'll know they've been alerted.

8

CASTING

Casting skill is the most important tool the fly fisherman can possess. If you can't get your fly to the fish, you can't catch it. I've fished with some great fly casters who were poor fishermen. They could throw a fly into the next zip code, *but they lacked the expertise to throw it correctly for the existing fishing situation.* Then there are some poor casters who are terrific fishermen. They know where to put the fly to interest the fish. Because they catch a lot of fish, they often argue that they don't have to be better casters. Unfortunately, that's simply not true. *The better you understand casting principles and the more different casts you can master, the more opportunities you're going to have.*

It's important to understand that casting involves more than just holding a rod in a vertical position and moving the line back and forth over short distance with a small fly attached. Good casters are accurate; they're also able to throw a long distance and, to a large degree, defeat the wind—which is a constant enemy in many types of fly fishing. There will be times when you need to throw a high backcast or into a hole in the brush to ensure that you don't snag the background. Being able to throw a curve cast can bring rewards. *Almost every fly fisherman throws an inefficient roll cast*—perhaps the second most important cast of all. And there are variations of the roll casts that should be mastered as well. I could go on, but I'm hoping that what I've said so far will stimulate you into wanting to become a better caster.

I've developed a few rules or principles over the years that I believe help explain just what fly casting is and how you can become a better caster.

I'd like to emphasize that there are two basic missions that casters need to accomplish. First in importance is accuracy. If you can't make an accurate cast, then you aren't going to catch many fish. But in much of fly fishing (aside from seeking trout) you need both accuracy and the ability to deliver a line over a long distance. There are occasions, too, when speed is essential. Often the wind is blowing, or you're using wind-resistant flies. So your second mission as a caster is to develop line speed.

Most fly fishermen experience some casting problems unless they're casting small flies a short distance. If you're only going to fish for trout with short-range casts, then the traditional casting method of bringing the fly rod up to the vertical position—about 1 o'clock on a clock face—on your backcast will suffice for many situations. **However, as I hope you'll see later in this chapter, bringing a rod to a vertical position on the backcast will not allow you to make many of the special presentations that could result in more hookups for you.**

Instead, learning to bring your rod from the 9 o'clock to 1 o'clock positions will let you deliver a very accurate short-range cast. For this reason you should learn the method. It is possible to make long casts using this method, but you'd need to polish your double-haul and exert far more energy than is necessary. Casting all day long with this method can be very tiring for all but the young and strong.

Fly casting is not a magician with a magic wand. *Instead it's nothing more than basic high school physics.* You bend or flex the lever (the rod), accelerate the tip, and then stop it. The flexed rod causes the long line to unroll back and forth, delivering the fly. *Think of the fly line as a long sinker that unrolls beginning at the rod tip; when it finally unrolls completely, it falls to the water. To be a good caster, you'll need to direct the energy of the unrolling line in the direction of your target. Spending any energy delivering the line in any other direction means you must expend more effort to get to your target. This is essentially what fly casting is all about.*

Here are the rules that I have developed to help me teach casting and to improve my own casting.

Rule 1   The rod is a lever. The longer you move the rod through the casting plane, back or forth, the more it aids in your cast.

Many people have misinterpreted this rule. I'm not suggesting that you move the rod through a long distance when you're only throwing a small, easy-to-cast fly a short distance. For example, if you're tossing a small dry fly to a sipping trout no more than 30 feet away, the rod only needs to move through a short distance on the back and forward strokes. But if you need to push a big bass bug into the breeze, or deliver an air-resistant fly to a distant target, then bringing your rod back a longer distance will immeasurably help you do so. *What's important is to understand that the more help you need, the longer you should move your rod back and forward during casting.* With an extremely difficult or long cast, the rod should be nearly parallel to the water behind you.

Rule 2   You can't make any cast until *you* have the line end moving. And you should lift all of the line from the water before making a backcast.

You have to get the end of the line moving before you can cast. That doesn't mean the line end is drifting on the current; *you have to get it moving.* A good analogy is someone dragging a water hose over a lawn. The sprinkler on the other end isn't going to move until the end of the hose does. Likewise, you can't cast your fly until you have the end of the line moving. I believe that one of the greatest faults of fly fishermen is to start the backcast with the rod held high. It's possible to make a decent short cast this way. But when a longer cast is required and you hold the rod high, the line end doesn't get moving until the rod has passed the vertical. Then, because the rod is now descending down and back behind you, a large sag develops in your backcast. *Since you can't make a forward cast until you get the line end moving, most of your forward cast is wasted just removing slack or slag from the line. What little forward rod motion is left often can't deliver an efficient cast.*

The second part of Rule 2 is important to catching fish as well as making a better backcast. Surface tension grips the line as it lies on the water. *Perhaps one of the main reasons why many fly fishermen don't catch trout with dry flies, or connect with bonefish and tarpon, is that the backcast is made while some of the line is still on the water.* Even if only a few inches of line lies on the water when you make a backcast, you must rip it free of the water. *The noise made as the surface tension releases the line frightens or alerts any nearby fish.* An important technique in making a good presentation to wary fish in calm water is making sure all of your line is elevated above the water before you make your first backcast.

A major reason why many anglers can't lift a long fly line from the water is that they don't get all their line off the water before making the backcast. If any line remains on the water when you make your final backcast, the surface tension gripping the line will cause you to waste casting energy just to get it loose from the water.

Rule 3   The line will go in the direction that the rod tip speeds up and stops during the final moments of the cast.

All casting strokes, whether short or long, can be divided into two parts. The first portion is relatively long; it gets the line moving and the rod bending. *Then, at the last instant in a cast, the rod tip is accelerated rapidly and stopped. I call this portion of the stroke the **speedup and stop.** It's vital to understand what the speedup and stop does to your casts—for it has a major influence on direction and distance.*

Many instructors use a clock face to explain when to perform certain casting functions. I believe this to be misleading. The position on a clock face where a function is made has nothing to do with the direction in which the fly and line will ultimately travel. Let me give you an example. Make a paper airplane from a sheet of typewriter paper. Throw the airplane three times, but concentrating on what would be 11 o'clock on a clock. First, holding the airplane in your hand, bring it forward at a climbing angle and then release it at 11 o'clock. Of course, the plane will soar upward. Repeat the experiment by moving your hand straight ahead and then releasing the plane—and it will travel straight ahead. Now hold your hand above your shoulder, bring the airplane forward and downward, and let it go. The plane will soar down into the ground. All three airplanes were released at 11 o'clock, yet all three planes traveled in a different direction.

Eleven o'clock had nothing to with where the planes traveled. It was the direction in which you stopped and released the plane that determined its direction. The same is true with a fly rod. If you stop the rod tip while going straight ahead, the line will go straight ahead. If you stop the rod (at any hour on a clock face) while going forward and down, then the line will travel forward and down. A major reason why most people have a big sag in the backcast is that the rod tip stopped while going back and down, hence the line went back and down. *If you want to throw a straight backcast that travels in a slightly upward plane, you must stop the rod tip at an upward angle, speeding up and stopping while going away from the target.*

As we discuss various casts, try to remember that the line is going in the direction at which you speed up and stop the rod tip at the end of the cast. Every efficient backcast should travel in the *opposite* direction from the target. For example, when fly fishermen make a cast across a stream then allow the fly to drift downstream, most have to make a series of backcasts before they can place the fly back upstream. The reason for the series of backcasts is to work the fly line around during each false cast *so that eventually the backcast is traveling in the opposite direction from the target.* When this occurs, the angler directs the final forward cast at the target. *It's important to understand that if the backcast is in a direct line opposite the target, the forward cast is more efficient.*

To accomplish this, follow a simple rule. At the end of your backcast and again at the end of your forward cast, *your thumb should be positioned behind the cork handle from your target.* On your backcast, for example, if you stop and see that your thumb is not behind the handle from the target but off at an angle, then the fly line will travel at an angle that isn't straight away from the target. The same is true on the forward cast. If your thumb on the stop has rotated slightly to the left, the line will rotate to the left at the end of your cast. But if your thumb is positioned directly behind the cork from the target, you'll deliver the fly and line straight at the target. This is true with a vertical, slanted, or side cast. I can't emphasize too strongly how much this simple trick can help you obtain a more efficient and accurate cast.

It's also important to understand that a minor movement of your rod hand on the handle results in a major movement of the rod tip. Try a simple experiment: Hold the rod parallel to the ground. Brace your upper arm against your body and rock the rod back and forth with just your hand. Look at the label immediately in front of the rod handle (Sage, Orvis,

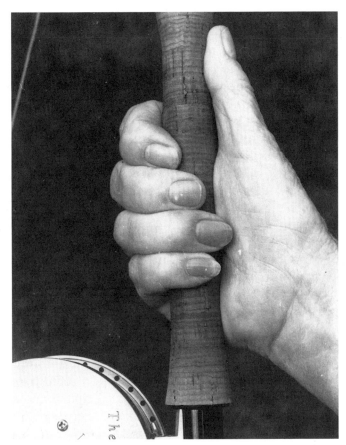

The importance of the thumb in casting is not often fully appreciated. At the end of both the back and forward casts, the thumb should be positioned directly behind the cork from the target.

Loomis, whatever). You'll notice that this label is moving maybe 2 inches. Now look at the rod tip—you'll see that it's probably moving 8 to 12 feet. *What this means is that any motion made with your rod hand will be greatly magnified at the tip.* Failing to understand this principle can result in not throwing the line straight behind you, opening your loops too much, and many other casting errors.

> **Rule 4 The size of your loop is determined by the distance that your rod tip speeds up and stops at the end of the cast. The shorter your speedup and stop, the smaller will be your loop. And the faster you move the rod tip through that distance, and the more suddenly you stop it, the faster and farther your line will travel.**

It's necessary that you understand why a large loop doesn't go far. For decades we've heard it said that large loops don't go anywhere because of air resistance. While air resistance is a *minor* factor, it's not the main reason. A large loop means you're throwing the fly line around a big arc or curve. The energy of your cast is being directed around a circle. *A tight loop means that most of your energy is directed at the target.*

As I mentioned, all casting strokes are divided into two parts—a relatively long motion and then a short speedup and stop (often called a power stroke). When you make the speedup and stop, your rod tip actually travels in a very slight arc. It begins at the top of the arc and moves slightly downward. The farther the speedup-and-stop stroke travels, the more the rod drops in this arc. *The distance that your fly rod descends from the beginning to the end of the speedup and stop determines your loop size.* For example, if you make a long speedup and stop—one in which the tip drops 3 feet from the start to the end of the stroke—you'll have a 3-foot loop. If your stroke is incredibly short and your tip only drops 4 inches, your loop will be 4 inches in size. This often seems to be difficult for people to understand, but it's true.

Why do most people make large and inefficient loops? Because they move their wrist too much during the casting motion. *The more the wrist moves during the cast, the larger the loop will be.* This is especially true during the speedup and stop. Worse, large loops direct energy around a curve, and the final part of the cast down toward the water. Remember, the line goes in the direction the tip stops at the end of the cast. You can easily test the big loop–small loop concept as related to wrist movement. Make several false casts, allowing your wrist to move a lot during each. Note how large your loops are. Now try making the cast *with your forearm only* (not your whole arm, which would cause you to move in a greater arc). *Use no wrist motion, or as little as you possible can.* Your loops will diminish immediately. Forearm-only casting reduces the distance that your tip speeds up and stops, so if you stop the tip going at some upward angle behind you on your backcast, and toward the target (not down at the water) on your forward cast, you'll improve your cast immediately.

How far your cast will go is determined by four things. *You need to stop the tip going in some upward direction on your backcast, and ahead of you on your forward cast. You also need to make the shortest speedup and stop that you can.* Add two more factors and distance will increase: *The faster you speed up, and the more abruptly you stop the tip over that short speedup-and-stop distance, the faster the line will travel—and the farther you'll be able to cast.* I can't emphasize too strongly how important it is for efficient casting to stop quickly. The lower portion of your loop is coming out of the tip of your rod. If you stop the cast and immediately lower the rod, you'll tear apart any loop you were creating. *Instead, stop while going toward the target and then mentally count to three before you lower your rod.*

To understand how important it is to stop quickly, use the analogy of a brush loaded with paint. If you sweep forward in a long motion, little paint will be thrown directly ahead from your brush. But if you move forward and then suddenly, over a short distance, speed up rapidly and stop abruptly, much more paint will be thrown from the brush—and straight ahead! The same is true with a fly rod. Speed up rapidly over a short dis-

Becky Giles holds a hula hoop as Larry Kreh practices casting through it. This is an excellent way to improve your loop size and control.

tance at the end of your cast, then stop abruptly, and you'll throw more of the cast's energy toward the target.

Remember, for years we have called the final portion of a cast a power stroke. *It is not a power stroke. It is a speed stroke, coupled with an abrupt stop.*

> **Rule 5   To make a backcast directly away from your target, your rod tip and hand must also travel in a straight line at some upward angle in a straight line away from the target. More important, *the speedup and stop of the backcast must also be directed in a straight line away from the target and stop in some upward direction.***

Rule 1 explains why you want to move the rod through a longer distance on the cast when you throw heavy flies, make longer casts, or need more help on any cast. *If you hold the rod in a normal manner, with the thumb pointing up or vertically, moving the rod behind you in a straight line with the tip stopping at an upward angle is very difficult; it takes long hours of practice.* People who hold the rod handle with the thumb up and then move the rod well behind them usually cause the tip to travel down and back behind them. This causes the line to go down and back (remember, the line goes in the direction that the tip speeds up and stops).

To move the rod well behind your body, *and still travel in a straight line away from the target throughout the cast, is easy.* Lower the rod until *the tip* is below your belt. You can't make this cast if the rod tip is held high before starting. Turn the rod so you can make a side cast. **Use only your forearm**—*never use your whole arm to make the backcast or the tip will travel in an arc!* Move the rod tip as far back as you want, *while traveling at some upward angle and straight away from your target.* The motion is similar to hitchhiking. To help you do this correctly, *make sure that the rod tip is below your head during all of the backcast.* This will ensure a better backcast. Allowing the rod tip to go back well above your head will often put a deep and undesirable sag in your backcast—which you'll have to remove before you can make a forward cast.

You can then come forward and make either a side cast or a vertical cast. But keeping the rod tip well below your head enables you to travel in a straight line and speed up and stop going away from the target—ending with the rod tip as far back as you desire.

Special Casts That You'll Need

If you're going to make good presentations, you need many special casts. Mastering these casts will enable you to catch many more fish. Just remember that the five casting rules outlined above will allow you to make every cast that's possible with a fly rod.

The Roll Cast

Next to the conventional overhead cast, the roll cast is used more than any other. There are hosts of fishing situations where this cast is beneficial; in some cases it's downright necessary. Its most frequent application is in spots where there's little or no room for a backcast. Another case would be when you need to lift a dry fly silently from the water. In yet another situation, your fly is snagged on something. Making a roll cast, allowing your leader and a small amount of the line to roll beyond the snag, and then making a backcast will often free the fly. If you're fishing with a fast-sinking line or lead-core shooting head, you need the roll cast to lift your line from the water so you can make a backcast. There are vertical roll casts, and side roll casts, and so many situations for using both that I could write a whole chapter in this book just about the roll cast.

The shame is that almost no fly fishermen I see make an efficient roll cast. Even worse, some instructors teach what I regard as poor technique, which only complicates the problem of learning what really is an easy cast to master.

To deliver a good roll cast, consider several important but easy-to-understand points:

Point 1 The most important factor to realize is that you're modifying only the backcast. *Instead, most fly fishermen modify the entire cast.* If you already know how to make a good forward cast, don't change this when you roll-cast—*only your backcast is modified.* I'll explain this in a little more detail later.

Point 2 The line on any cast will go in the direction in which the rod tip stops at the end of what most people refer to as the power stroke, but I call the speedup and stop of the rod tip. This is an extremely important point, which I'll explain in more detail a little later.

Point 3 The *size of the line loop as it unrolls on the cast* is determined by only one factor: the distance the rod tip moves during the final part of the cast, which I refer to as the speedup and stop. After the rod moves forward, the speedup and stop occurs. The rod tip is traveling in a slight arc or curved path (it's very difficult to make the tip travel straight ahead during the whole speedup-and-stop motion). The distance that the rod tip drops from the beginning to the end of the speedup and stop (or arc) is exactly the size that the loop will be. For example, if your rod tip drops 2 feet on the speedup and stop, your loop will be 2 feet in size.

Point 4 The longer the rod moves through the cast, the more it helps with that cast. Watch great casters: In some manner or another they manage to get the rod well in back of them. This is true even if they stop the rod in an elevated position. They have learned that the farther that the rod tip moves during the cast, the farther and easier the fly and line go.

WHY MOST PEOPLE HAVE TROUBLE ROLL-CASTING

Here's how the typical fly fisherman makes the roll cast (if you study the photos on pages 144 and 145, you'll see what I mean): The rod is brought up until it's nearly vertical. Then it's swept forward and downward. Reexamine the four important points made above and you'll see that this roll cast violates all of them.

Let's examine them point by point. Point 1 says that you shouldn't modify your forward cast. If you can make a good forward cast, there's no reason to alter that. *Try something to prove this point.* Make several conventional false casts. Then make your forward cast by sweeping the rod forward and downward—the way most people roll-cast. This will drive the line down in front, causing a piled mess in the fly line and leader—just as it does when most people roll-cast. *There's no need to modify the forward cast you've already mastered. This experiment should convince you that when roll-casting, make your forward cast just as you would a conventional forward cast.* To monitor this technique, observe your forward cast.

The inefficient method of roll-casting is to position the fly rod as shown here. This allows a minimum of rod movement to aid in your cast.

If it travels in large circular loop, you're not casting it efficiently. If the loop is rather oval in shape, you're doing it right.

Point 2 indicates that the line and fly go into the direction you stop the rod tip. Most people end a roll cast by driving the tip toward the water. That's one reason why the line usually falls in a heap on the surface in front of them. *At the end of the speedup and stop the rod tip should be traveling forward, not downward.* Point 3 explains that the size of your loop is determined by the distance you speed up and stop the rod tip at the end of the cast. Most people begin a roll cast with the rod tip held vertically, then sweep forward and downward in one continuous motion. This forces the rod to throw the largest loop possible, which means the angler is throwing the energy of the cast around the largest circle possible. Your rod's movement will be vastly restricted if you hold it vertically at the beginning of the cast.

ROLL-CASTING THE EFFICIENT WAY

Improving your roll cast is really very easy. Here are the steps to accomplish it: Slowly bring the rod back as far as you can. *The best results for longer roll casts occur when the rod tip is behind you and pointing directly away from your target—parallel to the water.* The longer you move the rod tip behind you, the more the rod helps in the cast. When you need

The line follows the direction of the rod tip, speeds up, and stops. Loop size is determined by the length of the speedup-and-stop stroke. By driving the rod tip downward, as shown by the arrow, you throw the largest loop possible and direct the cast down toward the surface. This is why so many roll casts pile up.

additional help, move your rod and hand back as far as fishing conditions allow. *It's very important that during all of the backward movement, your rod hand doesn't rise above your shoulder. Indeed, for longer roll casts, if you can bring back your rod hand at about the belt level—that's even better. The rod should be parallel to the water.* It's vital that at this point, you stop. If the line in front of you doesn't stop, you won't make a good roll cast. What happens when you stop (and you only have to pause for a heartbeat) is that surface tension grips the line. Your rod can then load or flex against this tension when you sweep forward.

There's no need to hurry at this point. After the line stops, make a normal forward cast. Study the photo at the top of page 147. Throughout this forward cast you should keep your rod hand at the same height as when you started. If your hand travels at a downward or upward angle, a poorer cast will result. *But if you make a normal forward cast with your rod hand moving straight ahead, you'll be directing almost all the energy of your cast at your target.*

At the final moment in the cast, the shorter the distance of your speedup and the faster your rod tip stops, the tighter will be your line loop and the farther it will go. The same happens when you make any good forward cast.

The efficient way to roll-cast. First, realize that you only want to modify the backcast; make a normal forward cast. The longer you can move the rod on the forward cast, the more the rod will help you cast. Position the rod *as far behind you as possible.* When in a tight corner, try to still move the rod back as far as you can. Most important is that the rod hand be *below* the shoulder, as shown. The rod is *parallel* to the water.

In summary, remember that you need to do only a few things to make a good roll cast:

1. Move the rod back until the tip points directly away from the target behind you.
2. Stop the line end so that surface tension can grab the line, allowing you to load the rod.

Bring the rod forward in a *straight* path with your rod hand. It's vital to travel straight ahead. If your hand travels downward on the forward stroke, you'll increase the loop size and throw some of the cast down toward the surface.

When ready, make a *normal* forward cast—stopping the rod going straight ahead.

3. Make sure your rod hand stays at the same elevation during the entire forward cast and is directed straight ahead.
4. The shorter and faster your speedup and stop, and the more completely you stop the rod tip, the easier and farther your roll cast will travel.

If you desire a tighter forward loop and a longer cast, do what you'd do to make a normal forward cast. However, make your speedup and stop faster and shorter, and stop quicker. Note this loop is smaller than in the previous photo.

There are several situations in which a modified roll cast can be extremely helpful. One is when you need to make a forward cast that stays very close to the surface and has to travel back under overhanging brush. Here, bring your rod back to a vertical position and then, just before the start of your forward roll cast, drop the rod over so that you can make a *side roll cast.* Make the stroke as you would a normal, vertical roll cast— but moving the rod tip parallel to the water, even during the speedup and stop. *If you want your cast to remain parallel to the water, then your speedup and stop must be made parallel to the water.* Otherwise your line and fly will end up in the brush. For example, if you begin the speedup-and-stop stroke with the tip 12 inches off the surface, *the tip must travel at 12 inches off the surface and stop that high above the water.* It's also important to make a very brief speedup and stop; a long one would create a large loop that might not go back under the brush.

Another situation in which a variation of the roll cast can be helpful is when you've impaled your hook in a log or other obstruction. Make a roll cast with a large loop—so large that it will unroll and go beyond the spot where the hook is impaled. *As soon as the loop passes beyond the fly, make a hard backcast.* The line in the air that has passed beyond the fly will usually pull the fly free.

The roll cast is also handy when you're fishing a short line and want to change direction. Make a roll cast roughly in the direction you want to throw the fly. If you then make a backcast opposite your target, it'll be easy for you to throw the fly to the target. And you can often get a wonderful drag-free drift by using a modified roll cast. Try this: Make a downward roll cast *with the rod tip directed at the water where you want your fly to drift.* What you're doing is deliberately causing the leader and front portion of the fly line not to straighten out, but to collapse. This, of course, produces a great deal of slack in your leader and the front of your line— which allows you to obtain a long, drag-free drift.

The roll cast can lift a popping bug or other fly from the surface with minimal disturbance, too. Make a roll cast that's angled upward and your line will roll out and lift the bug or fly almost vertically from the surface. As soon as the fly leaves the water, make a normal backcast. The result is a lift and backcast with almost no surface disturbance. I use this cast constantly when I want to pick up a dry fly and without frightening the fish. The same technique can be used to lift a sinking line from the water so a backcast can be made.

You can also use a roll cast to free almost any grass that snags on the fly. Near the end of a retrieve, make a roll cast directed upward. This will lift your line above the water. Now watch carefully: *When all of the line is above the water, but the fly is still under water, make a hard backcast.* In fact, make an extra-hard backcast. Use a single-haul if you know how, to generate additional line speed. What occurs is that the water grips the fly loaded with grass, creating enough resistance on the vegetation that the hook acts like a shear. *Remember that the backcast must be made while the line is in the air but the fly is under water.* About 90 percent of the time this frees the grass and you can continue to fish.

The Aerial Roll Cast

The aerial roll cast is used only for short-range work in spots where almost any other cast with a fly would be impossible. It's especially useful for trout fishing on small streams. Here's the common problem: You want to deliver your fly to a target—but there's no room for a back- or roll cast. Worse, there may be overhead obstructions, too. The aerial roll is effective to about 15 or 20 feet, but works better at slightly shorter distances. I haven't included photos since I feel it's easy to understand this useful cast.

Extend your leader and approximately 6 to 10 feet of fly line outside your rod tip. Hold the fly in your hand. *Be sure to hold the hook by the end so that the point won't impale you.* Lower your rod tip to the water so that it points at your target. *It's vital to begin with the rod tip inches above the water and the tip directed at the target!* Sweep the rod tip swiftly up *and directly away from the target.* Keep a firm but not-too-tight grip on the fly. How high you bring the rod tip before making a forward cast is dependent upon any overhead obstructions. Ideally, if you can sweep the rod tip at least up to a vertical position, the cast is easier to make. However, you can cast at least 15 feet if you bring the rod just past 45 degrees from the surface.

Quickly bring your rod as high as conditions will allow, keeping your grip on the hook bend. The instant it has reached its highest point the rod tip is *immediately* swept forward. Don't make any stop between your back and forward casts! It's vital that you change the rod's direction without a stop. This keeps your line and leader in a tight loop. Up to this point you should be holding the hook firmly enough that it won't slip out of your fingers. This permits you to load your rod with the line and leader that are sweeping through the air. *The instant that the rod begins to sweep forward, reduce your grip on the fly,* but allow the tight, fast-moving leader and line to pull the fly from your grip.

On the stop in your forward cast be sure to direct the rod tip well above your target. This will cause the leader and line to unroll in the air in the target's direction. If you drive the rod tip downward at this stop, you'll throw the line down and short of the target. After the stop, lower your rod to fishing position. If you sped up and stopped your rod tip above and in the direction of the target, the line will unroll and the fly will drop exactly where you want it.

Casting Angle

A lot of you must be confused about the angle at which you should direct your forward casts. Some instructors teach that you should throw directly at your target; others say the cast should be directed at about eye level; and some instructors really don't define the direction. Yet the angle at which you direct your forward cast is critical to successful presentation. Here's the real story: When you're fly fishing, no one casting angle is correct all the time. You need to consider what you're trying to do: where you want the fly to go, what you want the line to do while it's in flight, the direction of your line and fly, and how the fish will take your offering. This may seem complicated, but it really isn't. It's also vital to understand that some types of casts simply can't be made unless you direct both your back- and forward casts at a specific angle. Thus, it's imperative that you know when to throw a cast toward the water, when to direct it at eye level, and when to angle it slightly upward.

The Slightly Climbing Forward Cast

The average *forward cast is probably best directed it at about eye level. Perhaps 70 percent or more of your forward casts should be thrown in this direction, for optimum fishing results.* There are a number of advantages to throwing the fly and line at eye level. One of the most important is that at the end of such a cast the line's energy is expended straight ahead. Also, when the line completes its forward motion, the fly falls softly to the surface. Another major reason for making most casts at eye level is that the line, traveling well above the surface, can be trapped at any time with your line hand. This stops forward progress and permits you to accurately stop the fly so that it falls gently on the target. It's much like a spin caster trapping the line when his lure is over the target, or a plug caster using his thumb to drop the plug at the desired spot.

A cast directed above eye level is very useful and, in some cases, absolutely necessary. For distance casting this is the way you should direct your fly. If you shoot a bullet from a rifle aimed at the ground in front of you, that's where the bullet will go. But if you point the gun upward and pull the trigger, there's no telling how far the bullet will travel. The same thing occurs with a fly line. A fly line travels forward as the loop unrolls. *When the loop unrolls or the line straightens fully, all of the line and the fly fall to the water.* To delay this impact with the water, make the cast at a climbing angle that allows the line to fully unroll as far away as the cast will go. If you put enough energy into a cast to throw the line 100 feet, but direct the cast downward at a target 60 feet away—it will travel only 60 feet. *An exaggerated upward cast is essential when throwing a lead-core or heavily weighted shooting taper a long distance.* These weighted lines begin falling almost as soon as the rod stops. By throwing an elevated cast, though, you can often greatly increase its distance. And remember that while the elevated cast is moving through the air, you can trap the line with your line hand so that it falls on the target. This is how best to obtain an accurate cast, especially at a longer distance.

In many casts, after the rod's forward motion is stopped and the line is in flight toward the target, you can do something to improve your fishing situation. *Remember, once the rod tip stops you can't alter cast direction. But you can make some changes in the line between your rod and leader.* For example, in a reach cast you throw across a wide current flow

Larry Kreh is throwing a slightly elevated cast. This permits him to stop the line in flight over his target and deliver a softer presentation than a cast aimed down at the surface.

to get a drag-free drift for your fly. This is a very effective cast for trout fishing and can sometimes be used in salt water, too. In a regular cast, fly line falls in a straight line to the surface. The swift current will then push on the line's midportion in the water and cause it to bow. This creates a snap-the-whip effect, greatly accelerating the fly's drift—and fish will rarely take such an offering. A reach cast, however, allows you to place the line between you and the fly, *upstream* of the fly. This way drag doesn't occur until the midportion of the line is pushed downstream from the fly. But it's impossible to make a reach cast if you throw at a downward angle or even at eye level. *What's necessary is a high, slow cast. Then, while the line is unrolling toward the target area, the height of the line above the water gives you enough time to lay your rod and line over in an upstream direction.* An eye-level or downward cast would hit the water before you could move your rod very far. Only if you cast high and slow will you have time to lay your line over. It's also vital that you allow slack line to slide through your line hand. If you hold on to the line as you lay it over, you'll pull back on the front end and spoil a part of your cast.

To place your line and leader upstream of the fly to get a drag-free drift, cast a slow, high cast well above the water. The slow, high cast gives you time to lay your line over.

As soon as the forward cast stops, lay the rod well upstream, as the arrow indicates. It's very important that you allow slack to feed through your line hand; otherwise you'll cause the line to fall in a bad cast.

If you cast slow and high and allow line to feed through your line hand as you lay the line upstream, your cast will fall with slack in the leader.

Wind is the enemy of the fly caster—so many think. But it can also be your friend. You can use the wind to help you make a longer cast if it's blowing from behind you. *To do this throw a low backcast, then come forward with a much higher climbing angle than normal.* A line tossed high in the air and downwind will act somewhat like a kite: The wind will catch the line. When you do this properly, you'll be able to throw more line than you can buy.

The major problem with throwing a fly at too high a climbing angle into the wind is that once the loop unrolls and the line is fully extended, it will fall with too much slack in the front of the line and leader. Also, throwing high into a wind will cause the line to be a blown back a considerable distance, thus shortening your cast. Of course, if you want to put slack in a dry-fly leader, throwing an elevated cast will do so. More about this later.

The Downward Cast

There are rare times when throwing the line in a slanting downward angle—directly toward the target—is advantageous. *Of the three angles at which you can direct any cast, the downward angle should be used the least.*

A major reason for throwing a line down and straight at the target is that it allows you to drive your fly under overhanging bushes, boat docks, a bridge, or other obstructions. By throwing a fast, high-speed cast, you can rifle your fly or popping bug back under the brush or trees.

Another time this cast is effective is when you want to attract the attention of a fish. This is often a very good cast to get a shark's attention, for instance. It results in the fly slapping onto the water, causing the shark to come investigate. I've sometimes used this method effectively with northern pike, too. Most of the time, however, throwing a line that crashes the fly to the surface will frighten or alert the fish.

And try this cast when you're throwing into the wind. A major problem with this is that at the end of your cast, the breeze blows the fly back toward you—reducing distance, spoiling accuracy, and allowing unwanted slack to accumulate in the forward end of your leader and line. To deliver the fly to your target without slack in the line, the trick is to throw the cast at a downward angle with enough force so that it speeds to the target. *As soon as the loop unrolls, the fly is thrown into the water—thus no blowback of the leader or line occurs.*

There are disadvantages to throwing at the surface. As I noted above, a slanting downward cast causes your fly or bug to turn over fast; its hard splashdown will in most situations actually alert the fish. If there's a general rule to fly presentation, it's that you should avoid alarming the fish or putting them on guard. The more naturally a fly approaches a fish, the more likely the fish is to take it. The greater the disturbance created by the cast, the less likely the fish is to take the fly—except in those few cases that require a noisy presentation.

Another problem with the downslanted cast is that unless it's perfectly thrown (which is rare), the belly of the line will strike the water first. And once the belly contacts the surface, the rest of the line can only unroll toward the target. There's no chance for the cast to go any farther. A cast made at eye level or slightly climbing can be stopped over the target; one aimed at the surface must be thrown perfectly.

The Side Cast

In some situations a side cast, with the line traveling parallel to the water, is best. Where there are overhanging obstructions such as boat docks, trees along the shoreline, or bridges and you want to get your fly well back under them, a properly thrown side cast will do so better than a vertical. Also, when you want to throw a wide curve to the left or right, a side cast will throw a larger curve than any other method. When I'm casting to spooky trout, bonefish, tarpon, snook, redfish, permit, or other species, whenever possible I'll use a side cast. There are two advantages to it. One is that the line remains low and is unlikely to be seen by the fish. The other is that at the end of the cast, the fly falls from just above the surface. *An overhead cast would drop the fly from a height of at least several feet, and often more. The line crashing to the water usually scares a fish more than the impact of the fly itself.*

While perhaps the best angle to throw the fly on most casts is eye level, realize that if you're to fish effectively you'll have to adjust your casts' direction to accommodate the existing fishing situation.

Properly Controlling Line on the Shoot

Failing to properly control your line when you shoot it on the final forward cast can result in inaccurate casts, missed strikes, and other problems. This control is especially important when you're shooting a great deal of line—but it's also essential when fishing dry flies, nymphs, and other patterns that are generally cast a short distance.

What almost all fly fishermen do on their last forward cast is release the line after the speedup and stop. This means that control of both the cast and the retrieve is lost until the line can again be trapped in the hand.

To achieve accuracy, a spin fisherman will overcast the lure toward the target, then feather the line with his forefinger to slow it down: When the lure is over the target, the finger traps the line, stopping the flight and dropping the lure. A plug caster does the same thing, but instead of the forefinger he presses his thumb against the revolving spool to stop the lure at the desired distance. Fly fishermen have the same option—but not if they release the line at the end of the forward cast, which takes away their control of the line's flight.

Just as bad is that when the line is released like this and the fly falls to the water, it will be nearly impossible to hook any fish that might strike. When you're targeting difficult-to-see fish that are rapidly moving (such as bonefish and tarpon), you always want your line hand to be in control. What drives a good guide on a tropical flat crazy is to see his client cast, release the line, and, at the end of the cast, look down to find his line. Only after he grasps it in his hand does the angler look up to locate the fish. But because these fish are difficult to see, he frequently has no idea where that might be. This usually means a lost chance. Only when extreme distance is necessary and you don't expect the fish to strike immediately should you even consider letting go of the line in your hand. *For almost all fly-fishing situations, a better presentation can be made if on the shoot, the line remains under the control of your hand.*

Study the four photos on pages 156 and 157; these illustrate the right and wrong ways to shoot line. Learn to funnel the line through your hand on the shoot and you'll cast more accurately, and hook up more often.

When you're fly fishing for diffi-cult-to-see fish such as bonefish, a major fault is releasing the line on the shoot, as shown here.

Instead, when you shoot the line toward the target, form an O-ring with your thumb and first finger, allowing the line to flow through.

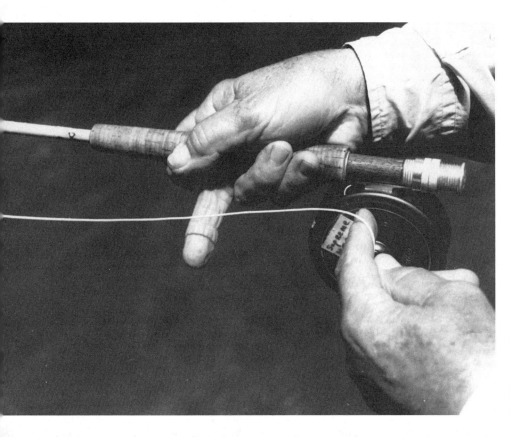

Observe your fly in flight. When it's over the target, trap the line flowing through your O-ring fingers, then move the line over to your index finger holding the rod.

This caster has kept his concentration on the fly and never looked down. As his index finger gathers in the line he lowers the rod, and when the fly touches the water the retrieve can begin.

Casting Sinking Lines, Heavy Flies, and Weighted Leaders

Many fly fishermen believe that casting sinking lines, lead-core shooting heads, heavily weighted flies, or a long leader to which is attached split shot, maybe a nymph indicator, and several flies is something to be avoided whenever possible. But once you understand the problem, fly casting sinking lines and weighted flies is no longer dangerous or even a chore.

Let's look at a typical situation—an angler using the very popular Teeny 300 line. Nearly 30 feet of the front end of this line sinks rapidly, while the remainder of the line is thin and floats. In essence, it's the same as using an improved sinking shooting head. The angler casts the line and retrieves it. Let's assume he's casting in a northerly direction. To make the most efficient backcast, the line should travel directly away from the target. Because he's casting to the north, his backcast should be directed due south.

On any backcast, a floating line tends to decrease in speed rather rapidly. *But a weighted line or a floating line with a heavily weighted fly on the leader tends to continue to travel at a very high rate of speed throughout the backcast.* **Therein lies the problem!**

Our angler's Teeny 300 is thus traveling rapidly southward on his backcast. And now a northward forward cast has to be made. This means that a line and fly that are flying south at a very high rate of speed must suddenly and very abruptly change direction. *It's this abrupt change of direction that creates the problems casters have when throwing weighted fly lines or flies!* The problem is further complicated if our angler is fishing a long leader with split shot, an indicator, and several flies attached. All of these contain weight; when an abrupt change of direction occurs, serious tangles in the leader can result.

Once you understand that the solution is to avoid a quick change in direction at the end of the backcast, then everything else falls into place. Actually, fly casting a sinking line—even a lead-core shooting head—can be easier than casting a floater. You can use the weight and speed of the line to your advantage once you know how to eliminate that abrupt change in the direction of your cast.

How to Do It

To eliminate this abrupt change of cast direction you must know two things. *First, with sinking lines or long leaders with indicators, split shot, and/or several flies attached, your backcast should be as slow as possible. Second, you can't make your forward cast to obtain a tight loop, as you would with a floating line.* For sinking lines and weighted flies, what you want instead is just the opposite. It's the tight loop traveling rapidly in one direction and then reversing that causes most problems. *You want to create a wide loop at the end of your backcast that travels lowly to the rear.* This causes the leader to travel around a curve. Think of the leader and fly as a boat trailer attached to your car: When the car goes around a curve, the trailer smoothly follows behind. When a wide loop is made on the backcast, the leader and fly don't make an abrupt change of direction. Instead, they trail smoothly around the curve. Once the leader and fly have rounded the curve and your line is heading toward the target, you can make a normal forward cast.

So how do you create a wide loop with a sinking line? You need to employ the water haul—a variation of the roll cast. At the end of a retrieve, roll-cast so that the sinking line outside your rod tip is laid out straight on the surface. Now watch the end of your fly line! *When the front end of the line unrolls and contacts the water, begin a low and gentle drawing back of the rod. Then make the slowest backcast possible that will still carry the fly all the way to the rear. Don't make a rapid backcast! The main purpose of the water haul is better rod loading; it is to allow you to get your sinking line or fly out of the water and then lay them back on the surface so you can make a* slow *backcast.* To make a water haul with a floating line, follow the same procedures, except you won't have to make a roll cast to lift your line from below the surface.

You also want the line to travel in a curving arc or well-rounded loop to the rear. Begin the backcast as if you were making a *low* side cast, with your hand low. Your rod hand should travel to the rear in a horseshoe or U shape, until the fly has been brought back and the forward cast is started. *This will require that you a keep* constant *pulling pressure on the rod throughout the backcast.* When explaining this important technique I ask my students to imagine that the rod tip is inside a horseshoe, and it must have constant pressure on it all the way around the inside of the horseshoe. If that's accomplished, a round backcast results. The ability to apply constant, circular pressure throughout the backcast is difficult for some casters; there's a tendency to throw the line back rather straight, as you would a floating line. A simple exercise will teach you to apply the required constant pressure, though: Extend about 12 feet of line outside your rod tip. Hold the rod parallel to the ground and at belt level. Rotate your wrist clockwise, much as if you were winding in line. Watch the line; you want to make sure that the rod tip and the line travel in a circle, *not in an oval.* If you were winding in line, the reel handle would travel in a perfect circle. Try to make your wrist rotate the same way during this exercise. Then, when you have the line swirling in a circular movement as your hand rotates to the right, and when the rod tip is at the top of the circle you're making—begin a forward cast!

If you've been rotating your hand properly and make your forward cast as the tip rides to the top of the circle, you'll find that the line drives well forward. This exercise will help you master the necessary slow, circular backcast. Now you can make a complete cast with a weighted line, weighted fly, or a leader with several items attached. Complete the retrieve, then make a roll cast to begin the water haul. Lower your rod as the line and leader unroll in front of you. When the front end of the line contacts the surface, begin a slow, constant, circular rod motion to make the

The proper casting of weighted flies, sinking lines, or trout leaders with several flies, split shot, and an indicator will eliminate leader tangles. Details explaining this special cast are in the text.

If you're using a heavily weighted fly or sinking line, retrieve until you can make a roll cast. When the line fully extends in front of you and the fly touches down, you're ready for the backcast.

Keep your rod tip just above the surface. This is important. Draw the rod back until the tip is nearly at a right angle to you. *At this point you need to pull continuously so that the rod tip goes around a large arc.* Don't make a regular backcast; you want to make a large unrolling loop behind you. Continue to pull on the rod tip so that you form a large loop, as shown here. This will cause the leader, heavy line, and fly to turn smoothly around, instead of making a quick change of direction from back to forward cast.

Once the fly has rounded the corner, you can make a normal forward cast, as you would with any line. By aiming well above you, as the arrow indicates, you eliminate any chance of the heavy line or fly hitting you on the forward cast.

backcast. Make the slowest backcast you can, using the method you just learned in the exercise. Be sure that your rod hand starts low—at about belt level—and travels rearward in that circular motion. Once your rod hand rounds the circle and starts forward, you can make your regular forward cast.

Mastering this cast will allow you to throw weighted lines and flies—without tangles.

There's one more important point. *Never false-cast sinking lines, weighted flies, or a leader with several items attached.* False-casting requires that you throw the line rather rapidly, with a quick change in direction at the end of each forward and backcast. But with weighted flies and lines, it's important to throw the *slowest* backcast you can, resulting in a very wide loop that causes the fly and leader not to make an abrupt change of direction. *If you make a water haul and a poor backcast is the result, don't false-cast. Instead, if another backcast is needed, make a gentle forward cast and drop the line to the surface in front of you. As soon as the line end falls to the surface, make another water haul.*

With these methods you will never again want to avoid throwing weighted lines.

The Double-Haul

Next to the proper casting stroke, the double-haul is the single most important tool you can possess. It will permit you to throw a longer line—even against the wind—and to toss heavier flies and lines with less effort. Once you've mastered it, you'll use it to some degree on almost every cast.

I've observed thousands of fly fishermen in my lifetime of fly fishing. *With rare exceptions it's my belief that every caster uses the double-haul incorrectly, or at least inefficiently—and this includes many of the great casters I've been lucky enough to fish with.*

Before discussing my concept of proper double-hauling, it's important that we review casting fundamentals. While it may seem redundant, reviewing these casting rules will help you better understand double-hauling—one of the most important facets of fly casting and fishing. *All casting strokes are divided into two parts: the relatively long motion in which the rod is gradually accelerated, ending with the much shorter, faster speedup and stop of the tip.* The speedup and stop is often referred to as a power stroke. Of course, it isn't a power stroke, it's a speed stroke, and it's important when learning double-hauling to think about speed.

Rule 1 The shorter the distance the rod tip travels at the end of the cast during the speedup and stop, the tighter the loop will be.
Rule 2 The faster you accelerate the rod tip over that final short distance *and the quicker you make the stop*, the greater the speed the rod tip will deliver to the line.

Rule 3 Many fishermen don't realize that once the fly line straightens, it will begin to fall. The line obtains distance by unrolling. *When it has completely unrolled, it will go no farther.* To obtain distance you must get the line to travel as far as desired before the loop opens. *To make a distance cast you must make the line arrive at the target before it unrolls or opens. The only way to do this is to both increase the acceleration of your rod tip over a short distance and make an abrupt stop.*

To appreciate these fundamentals, you can conduct your own interesting experiment: Make several false casts, sweep your rod forward *near the end of the casting stroke* in a relatively long speedup and stop. You'll see a large loop develop. Then repeat this experiment, but making a much shorter stroke at the end. The loop size will diminish. Now make another cast. This time, make a short speedup-and-stop stroke (to form a small loop) *but during this speedup and stop, move the rod tip rather slowly* and *don't stop quickly.* You'll see a small loop form, which doesn't go far. Repeat the casting stroke, but this time move very rapidly over that *short distance* at the end of the cast, and make the rod tip stop as abruptly as possible. *You'll observe that the loop will be smaller, and the swiftness of your stroke and abruptness of your stop will cause the line to travel much farther.*

It's vital to understand that the smaller the loop is (so that most of your cast's energy is directed toward the target), the swifter your rod tip moves through that very short final distance, and the quicker your stop is—the farther your cast will unroll before it begins to fall. If you understand these three factors, you'll quickly grasp why a single- or double-haul permits you to make longer casts.

Just what is a haul? A single-haul is a downward pull on the line during the cast. A double-haul is a downward pull on the backcast and again on the forward cast. And just what does the haul do?

When you pull swiftly on the line in your hand, you cause the rod tip to flex. Toss a short cast out in front of you and then hold the rod parallel to the ground. With the rod still, yank downward on the line in your hand. The rod tip will flex rapidly and cause the line to leap upward. **When you make a haul, all you do is move your rod tip faster. This is the most important factor to understand about hauling—single or double.**

Most fly casters are taught to make a long downward pull during the backcast and again when coming forward. In my view this is an inefficient use of the double-haul.

First, realize that you when you make a haul, you flex the rod tip. It's important to good casting to make a very small loop. The angler who makes long and continuous hauls causes the rod tip to flex over a greater distance than the fly fisherman who makes a shorter haul. *Remember, the shorter the haul, the shorter the distance the rod tip will flex, and the tighter the loop. Long hauls will develop wider and less efficient loops.*

Second, the faster you stop the rod tip at the end of your cast, the more the energy of the cast will be catapulted toward the target. Since hauling causes the tip to flex, it's vital to efficient casting to stop the haul with the speedup and stop. Ideally, the haul should begin when the speedup starts and it should end when your rod hand stops. **Your rod hand's speedup and stop and your line hand's haul should be simultaneous—both starting and stopping at the same time.**

For example, if your rod hand moves 3 inches at the end of the cast for the speedup and stop, your haul should be no longer than 3 inches. There are fishing situations where you may have to draw your line hand well away from your rod hand, to remove slack or help flex the rod. *But the actual, brief haul should occur only during the speedup and stop.*

Long downward pulls on the backcast cause several problems. The rod flexes deeper, so the loop is larger. Pulling on the line after your rod hand stops causes some of the cast's energy to be directed downward instead of directly away from the target. Fishermen who make long hauls on the backcast frequently find that on the forward cast, the line has become wrapped around the rod butt. This won't happen with the shorter haul strokes I recommend. Finally, if you make a long downward pull, your line hand then must rise toward the reel so that you can make another haul. And unless you've developed great line speed on the backcast, as your rod hand begins to move forward and your line hand travels toward it, slack will be pushed into the system. *This slack will have to be removed before the forward cast can proceed.*

To make the most efficient double-haul, the hand holding the line should follow the reel on the backcast. *Try to keep your hands close together—no more than 12 inches apart.* Watch the line end on the water; after this has been lifted from the surface, you can make the haul. **Make the speedup-and-stop motion with your rod hand and the haul at the same time, beginning and stopping simultaneously.**

During the forward cast your line hand should travel in front of the reel, staying at the same distance from your rod hand. Then make both the haul and the speedup-and-stop motion again, together. Make sure that your rod and line hands stop together as the cast ends.

There may be times when, as you lift the rod for the backcast, your line hand must move downward to eliminate unwanted slack or to flex the rod. If this is necessary, your line hand may be well below your belt when you make the speedup and stop with your rod hand. Make the brief haul from this position. *Do not* raise your line hand toward the rod. *Maintain the same distance between your rod and line hands as you sweep forward and no slack will occur. When the rod hand makes the speedup and stop, the line hand (down by your hip) makes that brief haul.*

Of course to make a good backcast, especially a long one, remember that the lower you position your rod before beginning the backcast, the more efficient this cast will be.

To summarize, a line falls when it opens. To reach a target the line must get there before it opens or unrolls. And the *only* way you can accomplish this is to form a small loop, and to make the rod tip move faster and stop quicker.

Learning the Double-Haul in 15 Minutes

Because there are so many motions involving both hands in the double-haul, it's very difficult to learn while casting. *The method I've developed to teach the double-haul has the average caster learning the technique within 15 minutes.* Some have learned it in five.

I want to emphasize that the slower you do this exercise, the faster you'll learn the double-haul. The faster you do it, the longer it will take. Here's the method: On a lawn, work out about 20 feet of line. *It's important that you make side casts low to the ground, not vertical casts, during this exercise.* With the line stretched out on the lawn in front of you, begin to *slowly* move the rod back to the side. *Make sure that your line hand follows the reel and that your two hands are no more than 12 inches apart.* Make a normal side backcast with your rod hand. *At the same time you complete the speedup and stop, give a fast* **1-inch** *tug on the line with your line hand.* Try not to tug more than 1 inch, and concentrate on making your rod and line hands move through the casting and haul motions at the same time. If you've made the moves correctly, the line will zip back behind you. As it falls to the grass, your hands should still be 12 inches or less apart.

Here's the important part: Don't make your forward cast immediately; stop and think about what you did. Because the line is on the grass behind you, you can also take time to analyze what you're going to do on the forward cast. Bring the rod forward *slowly*—with your line hand leading in front of the reel and close to it. Then make a forward side cast and, at the same time, a 1-inch haul with your line hand. I'll warn you that most people have trouble coordinating the forward cast with the haul. Stick with it and it'll soon come. Continue this exercise until you see you're hauling correctly. It's vital that during this learning session you move ever-so-slowly back and forth prior to making the haul and the speedup and stop. Within five minutes most people—*if they're making the motions slowly and allowing the line to lie on the grass after each cast*—will have the technique pretty well down. Once you feel you have it, try false-casting using the double-haul. As soon as something goes wrong, stop and resort to the grass exercise again.

To further improve your double-haul, try using a half rod. By working with a short rod, any casting flaws will be more evident. As you learn to make the brief stroke and haul simultaneously, you'll find that your casting improves.

Making Your Double-Haul Better

Watch 100 fly casters use the double-haul under different fishing conditions. Rarely will you see one change the speed of his line hand on the haul. When you haul with your line hand, you accelerate the rod tip. The faster the tip accelerates and stops, the farther the line will travel. *Yet once a fly fisherman learns the double-haul, he too often makes all subsequent hauls at the same speed.*

When you want to make a longer cast, the tendency is to put additional power into your rod hand. This opens the loop, shocks the rod, and creates a poor cast. *If you want to make a longer-than-normal cast, try this. False-cast until you have a fair amount of line out, but your rod hand is still controlling a nice loop and no shock waves appear in the line. Now don't use any more force with your rod hand. Instead, increase the speed of your double-haul. Don't make the haul longer—only faster. When I ask good casters to back off on the power in their rod hands like this, they've immediately picked up 10 feet on their casts.* **Think of the double-haul as a gear shift.** When you need more speed, change gears and increase the speed with your haul. *Never increase the length of the haul*—just the swiftness. And don't try to obtain additional distance by putting more power or speed into your rod hand.

The Curve Cast

It was a dead-calm morning in the Florida Keys. The surface was like oiled glass—not a ripple anywhere. The sun had just risen. Laid-up tarpon were resting in the deep-water basin, their big bodies suspended just below the surface. Here and there I could see just the tip of a tail or dorsal fin, pinpointing their locations. Such fish are as spooky as a pickpocket at a police convention. My guide quietly, very quietly, pushed the boat ahead. At the same moment we both saw a nice tarpon facing toward us, maybe 25 feet away. Invariably, under such conditions, if a cast is made to the fish and it follows only a short distance, it sees the boat and flees.

A curve cast is the answer here. I made the cast. The fly landed 6 feet to the right of the fish and slightly in front, with the leader gently falling to the surface. The line had fallen so that the end had curved and lay 6 feet to the left of the tarpon. I started my retrieve; the fly swam from the tarpon's right, past its head, and then off to the left. But it never got a chance to follow the curve in the line: The tarpon swished its tail, moved forward, and inhaled the fly. Ten minutes later the hook fell free on a jump and we went looking for another fish. But it was the curve cast that had been responsible for that hookup.

There are two ways to make a curve cast. One way is to bring your rod forward into a vertical position, permitting a curve to the left or right. I find this is the most difficult of all the casts I teach. Explaining and demonstrating it to students is tough; and I've never been able to clearly describe the vertical curve cast in writing, either. However, if you're right-handed, it's easy to understand and master making a curve to the left. Of course, the reverse is true for a left-hander. While this limits you to curving the line in one direction only, the ability to make even this cast offers many advantages when fishing.

The curve cast gives you a tool that can do several jobs. On numerous occasions I've used it to drop my fly or popping bug on the other side of a rock, a tree standing in the water, a boat dock, or another obstruction. I then began my retrieve but hooked the fish while it was still behind the obstruction.

The curve cast can also be invaluable on a trout stream or saltwater flat. Here, of course, fish will be looking either away from you or toward you (as my laid-up tarpon were). If you cast in a straight line to drop your fly in front of a fish looking away from you, then retrieve the fly, the fish will often refuse your offering. The reason is that a fly that swims directly toward a fish is unnatural. Predator fish expect to chase their prey, not have it approach in the attack mode. On the other hand, if the fish is facing toward you and only a short distance away, as it follows the fly on the retrieve it'll all too often see you, and the game is over.

The basic problem here is to avoid "attacking" the fish with your fly. Instead, you want to make a cast that will permit the fish to follow your fly a long enough distance to become interested in striking—but not see you. A properly presented curve cast will allow a fish to track the fly for at least 6 to 10 feet without drawing it any closer to you. I can't emphasize how important this is when a fish is close to you.

There's another situation in which the curve cast is helpful: when you want to swim a fly parallel to a shoreline or some fish-hiding structure. The general method is to make a cast to the shoreline and retrieve the fly more or less right back to you. But a fish along the shoreline will see your fly much the way you would see a knife pointed at you lengthwise. You wouldn't see much. Make a curve cast, however, and your fly will swim parallel to the shoreline, giving the fish a side view of it—much more effective. Along a saltwater shoreline bordered by mangroves, for example, you might want to retrieve your fly parallel to the roots. The curve cast is very effective at this. Rather than throwing your fly to the root-lined shore and retrieving it directly away, use this cast to make it to swim along the roots. Then that fish gets a look at the wide profile of the fly. You can do the same thing when fishing a trout stream, or the shoreline of a lake. Once you master the curve cast, you'll find many practical uses for it in your fly fishing.

Before I tell you how to make the curve cast, let me explain again that every cast, back- and forward, is made up of two basic parts. There's a relatively long motion, and near the end of the cast there's a brief speedup and stop of the rod tip. *The line and the fly will go in the direction in which you speed up and stop the rod tip.* To understand and master the curve cast you must understand these two casting principles.

Since you want your fly line to travel parallel to the water, and to end in a curve, *your rod tip must travel parallel to the surface during the speedup and stop.* This will cause the rod tip to curve or hook at the very end of the cast.

Here's how you accomplish this. The backcast should be a *low side cast,* so that at the beginning of the forward cast your rod comes forward low and parallel to the water. If you make a conventional vertical backcast, the curve cast will be very difficult to make. You need to make a low side backcast! Then on the forward cast your speedup and stop must be very swift, and *the rod tip must stop dead!* This high-speed motion, coupled with the dead stop, causes the rod tip to flex into a curve to the left (if you're right-handed). The rod tip moves in a sharp bend or curve to the left and parallel to the surface, so the leader and line end will do the same—because, again, the line, leader, and fly go in the direction that the rod tip speeds up and stops. The faster (not harder) you move the rod tip during the brief speedup, and the more abruptly you stop it, the greater will be the resulting curve in your line and leader. You can increase the curve in your line even more if you use a haul on the forward cast to increase tip speed. Of

A very low side backcast must be made to set up the curve cast.

course, if your rod tip travels downward (rather than parallel to the water) on the speedup and stop, you'll throw the line downward into the water and no curve will appear. *It's absolutely necessary that during the speedup and stop, your rod tip travel parallel to the surface.*

Facing the target, when you come low and forward to the side stop your rod quickly at about 45 degrees from the target you face. The faster you stop your rod, the deeper the curve that results.

Once you've mastered making the curve cast, getting extreme accuracy with it is easy. Face your target. During the forward cast, if you sweep your rod parallel to the surface *and make your stop 45 degrees from the fish,* the curve in the line will land in front of you. Face the target and complete the above operation and your curve casts will be accurate. Study the photos on pages 168 and 169 to see how the cast is made and some typical fishing situations it can be used for.

The Stack Cast

This is one of the oldest of all casts. It's used primarily for those situations in trout fishing where you want to create slack in the leader and forward portion of your fly line, enabling your fly to drift drag-free. Every decade or so someone renames it. I've heard it called a pile cast, a puddle cast, a stack cast, and many other names. Regardless of the name, today it's one of the most important casts a trout fisherman can learn.

I used to trout fish with a certain outdoor writer. He threw one of the biggest, ugliest forward-cast loops imaginable; you could've ridden a bicycle through his loop. Yet with dry flies he often outperformed far better casters. It was some time before I realized why. His loop was huge and when it turned over, the leader and forward end of his fly line collapsed into a pile—allowing his fly to drift a long way free of drag.

The purpose of the stack cast is to get a lot of small waves into the leader, and often in the front of the line. Only when the leader directly in front of the fly straightens will drag occur. It's vital to understand that if you want a drag-free drift, the tippet immediately in front of your fly must have some waves or slack in it.

The stack cast is one of the easiest of all casts to master. It requires only that you understand four simple things:

1. The cast must be made slowly. If you cast at high speed, nothing will be accomplished!
2. The lower you take your rod on the backcast, the easier it'll be to perform the stack cast.
3. The cast must be aimed high in front of you. The higher the cast is aimed, the more slack will accumulate in your leader. You may have to make several casts in a particular fishing situation to obtain the angle you need.
4. *As soon as the cast ends, you must drop the rod.* If you leave your rod tip elevated at the end of the cast, the line hanging from the tip to the surface will begin to slowly sag back toward you. As the line creeps backward, it will draw most of the slack out of your line and leader. *Many people who make a check or stack cast fail to realize that by not dropping the rod immediately*

at the end of the cast will pull out the very slack they worked to put in.

This cast is so easy to understand that I didn't supply photos of it.

The Change-of-Direction Cast

The change-of-direction cast is invaluable. It works best when you have less than 35 feet of line and leader outside your rod tip. It can be made with additional line outside the tip, but it becomes more difficult.

Here are three typical situations in which this cast is useful. You're standing in the front of a bonefish boat retrieving your fly. Suddenly, the guide tells you to change direction *fast* and cast to an incoming fish. If you make a series of false casts, your fly won't get to the newcomer in time. The same thing can happen in trout fishing: You're fishing over a trout rising to dry flies. Out of the corner of your eye you see another, larger fish take a fly from the surface. You don't have time for a series of false casts; what you need is a single back-and-forward cast that'll drop the fly right on target.

Here's an even more common situation. You've made a cast upstream and allowed the line to drift through a good-looking hole. Now you want to return the fly to that same upstream starting point. Most people do this with a series of false casts: They make a backcast, then turn slightly upstream on the forward cast. Another backcast is made and, as the rod is brought forward the cast is directed even farther upstream. Another backcast is made, and the final cast is directed at the target.

If you understand why anglers make series of false casts, it'll be easy for you to learn how to change direction with one back and one forward cast. *The most efficient backcast is one that travels in a direct line (180 degrees) away from the target. The reason for series of false casts is to allow the angler to slowly work the backcast around until it's directly opposite the upstream target.*

Once you grasp this, you can make a change-of-direction cast. Here's how: Your fly has drifted downstream and you're ready to cast it back to the starting point. Move your rod tip rapidly until it points at the target, *making sure that you keep the tip very close to the water.* Remember the rule that you can't make a cast until you have the line end moving? As you move the rod tip toward the target don't stop, or the line end will stop, and you'll have to get it moving again before you can make a backcast. When the rod tip is aimed at the target, make a strong backcast in the direction *opposite* the target. Often, a single-haul on this backcast will help you make a good forward cast. Now come forward and drop the fly on your target.

Here's a summary of the important points: Lower your rod, then move it quickly and low to the water until it points at the target. Don't stop! Make a backcast opposite the target, and then a forward cast to the target.

Ed Russell shows that the change-of-direction cast is helpful in almost any fly-fishing situation. It allows you at a relatively short range to make a rapid (one-backcast) change in direction. Ed's line is downstream. To throw upstream quickly, he keeps the rod tip just above the surface and sweeps the rod to the right toward the target—still keeping the rod low.

Once the rod tip points at the target, a backcast is made with some speed *opposite the target,* as shown here.

The left arrow indicates the backcast's direction—180 degrees from the target. The long arrow at right points to the target area.

The Right-Angled Cast

There are times when you're fishing with little or no room behind you and a roll cast would be difficult. Here's a typical example: You're on a stream with a high bank behind you. You've made a cast out from the bank, and your fly has drifted downstream. You'd like to make another cast at right angles to the bank out in the stream, but you have little room for a backcast. It would be tough to roll-cast in this situation, but a right-angled cast will do nicely. It works well to about 30 feet; beyond this it becomes much more difficult.

Here's how you accomplish a right-angled cast. Make a backcast, being sure to take your rod and hand well behind you. The farther back you take the rod, the easier this cast is to make. As the backcast nears its end, bring your rod hand swiftly forward until it's even with your body. You now have the line end moving. Remember casting rule 3? The line always goes in the direction in which you stop. As your hand becomes even with your body, use your rod hand to make a fast speedup and stop at a right angle to the backcast and ending toward the target. If you make the speedup and stop at a right angle and stop when pointing toward the target, your line will sweep forward, make a right-angled turn, and speed in the direction of the target. If you encounter difficulty in making this cast, remember three things:

1. **Move your rod and hand well behind your body.**
2. **Bring them forward rather swiftly.**
3. **If you don't make a right-angled turn during the speedup and stop, you won't be able to perform this very valuable cast.**

With the bank beside you make a backcast, allowing the rod to go well back behind you. Then move it forward until your hand is even with your body.

If during the speedup and stop your rod hand makes a sharp right-angled turn toward the target, the line will sweep forward and make the same turn.

The Long-Line Pickup Cast

There are times when you need to pick a long line from the water to make a backcast. You may, for example, have made a long cast and suddenly see a fish rise in another direction. Or you may have made a long cast to a cruising fish, which didn't take. Before the fish gets away, you need to make another cast—one that requires lifting a lot of line from the water for a quick backcast. These are just two of many situations when a long pickup is needed.

If you can cast a fairly long distance but have trouble picking a long line from the water, it'll help to know why you're having this difficulty. For almost all casters, lifting a long line from the water is difficult *because they never get all the line off the water before making the cast.* Remember rule 2? You need to get the line off the water before making a backcast. When considerable line is on the water, surface tension grips it firmly, resisting your every attempt to release it from the water so you can make a backcast. Once you understand that *all* line should be lifted from the water before you make the backcast, a long-line pickup becomes easier. With practice a good caster should easily be able to lift at least 65 feet of line off the water; a really good caster can lift even more line and make a good backcast.

Here's the way you do it. Touch your rod tip to the surface so that you can get maximum lift with it. Remove all slack, making sure the rod tip remains on the water. Extend the first finger of your rod hand and place it on the first guide (the butt guide). Once you master the cast you won't have to do this, but as you learn, placing your finger on the butt guide will help.

You're now ready to lift the line from the water. You must realize that lifting the rod will only remove a certain amount of the line. Some of it will still be on the surface, and it must be released before a good backcast can be made. That's why you must keep your fingertip on the butt guide. Once you've lifted as much line with your rod tip as possible, a quick drawing down of your line hand should get the rest of it off. In the beginning, if you don't place your fingertip against the guide, you'll naturally bring your line hand down as the rod starts to lift line. If you're a normal person, and I assume you are, you must be careful not to let your fingertip off the guide until the rod has lifted as much line as possible. Now that you know the importance of starting low (with the rod tip in the water) and keeping your fingertip on the guide until the rod has done its job, let's proceed with the cast.

The rod tip is touching the surface. *Do not lift the rod vertically.* If you do, before you've lifted all the line from the water the rod tip will be traveling down and back. The speedup and stop will then be down and back, developing a sag in your line that you'll have to remove before a forward cast begins. *Instead, make a side cast that travels up and back.* If you keep the rod tip below your head as it travels back and up on the side cast, you'll be able to lift the maximum amount of line. The more vertically the rod travels, the more likely a poor backcast will result. As you bring the rod back to the side *keep your fingertip firmly on the butt guide.* Keep watching the line. When you feel that you've lifted as much line with the rod as you can, draw swiftly down with your line hand until the remainder of the line is off the water—then make your backcast. A single haul can assist on this backcast.

One word of caution: You must lift the rod rather quickly. I don't mean you have to jerk the line from the water. But if you lift the rod slowly, the line between the rod tip and the water will sag down, making it nearly impossible for you to pick up a long line.

This may sound like a difficult cast to master, but if you remember the basics—place your rod tip in the water, move it swiftly back to the side keeping the tip below your head, and draw down with your line hand when needed—you'll find that you can do it effortlessly.

The Back-Forward Cast

There are many times when throwing a forward cast to the rear, then making a conventional forward cast in front of you, serves you better than the standard back-and-forward cast. For example, there may be trees or brush behind you. But when you turn around and examine the obstacles, you see a hole in the brush into which you can deliver a backcast. Most fly fishermen who attempt a conventional backcast into that hole will meet with disaster. They look at the hole then face forward and throw a normal backcast, hoping that it goes into the safe area. Usually it doesn't. Making a cast like this is like shooting a gun with your eyes closed. Instead, you need to turn around and look at the target area, throw a forward cast into it, and, at the end of the cast, turn around and throw a regular forward cast.

Another excellent use for this cast is when you need to make an immediate backcast to a fish. If, for example, you're standing in a boat fishing for tarpon and suddenly the guide yells that a fish is approaching from behind, the back-forward cast is a much more accurate way to cast to this newcomer than a backcast would be. Here's how you do it:

Photo 1   Look in the direction of the hole in the trees—or whatever target area you need to throw the line into. Then lower your rod until the tip touches the water. It's important that you begin this cast with a very low rod. As you raise the rod, move your body so that your weight shifts to your back foot; also, *before starting the cast, turn your hand so that your thumb is behind or underneath the rod handle from the target hole in the brush.* If you don't start with the thumb in this position, you'll throw a poorer cast! Continue to move your hand toward the rear, as shown in the photo. This is one of the few casts for which I recommend that your rod hand be higher than your shoulder on the speedup and stop.

Photo 2   As soon as your hand passes beyond your head, make a speedup-and-stop action with the rod toward the target. Don't make this speedup and stop too soon; wait until your rod hand has passed well beyond your head! Because you're looking at the hole in the brush and can see the line as it travels backward, you know where you're delivering the cast. As the line loop enters the hole, turn your

To throw a fly into a hole behind you, place your thumb underneath the rod handle and keep the reel upright, as shown. The rod tip should nearly touch the water. Face the target so you can see where you're going to cast.

With your thumb behind the rod handle opposite the target, you can now throw an accurate cast into the hole. Then reverse your hand so you can throw a normal forward cast.

hand around and face the water; your thumb is now in the normal position to make a conventional forward cast. Make the regular forward cast to your target in front of you.

The extra-high backcast is useful in many situations. Face the target; the lower the rod tip to the water, the better. Be sure that your thumb is underneath the rod handle before you make the backcast. Turn your head and face the obstructions behind you.

The Extra-High Backcast

Many fishing situations require an extra-high backcast. Steelheaders know this, as do trout fishermen and surf casters who've had a high wall of sand behind them. Almost every fly fisherman has at some point been frustrated because he must make a very high backcast. But within limits, there's a cast that will do this. With 50 feet of line it's very difficult, but with less than that, the following cast will produce remarkable results. It's a back-forward cast with a slight modification. Beginning with your rod tip in the water, follow the directions for the back-forward cast. Here's the difference: You know, of course, that the direction in which you speed up and stop the rod tip determines the direction of your cast. So here, once the rod passes beyond your head, make the speedup and stop in the direction in which you want the line to travel. That's it.

The angle at which you stop the rod tip determines the direction of the cast. Here the arrow shows that the author has aimed the cast very high. As soon as the backcast ends, turn your rod hand around.

Once your hand turns around, make a normal forward cast.

The Tuck Cast

The tuck cast is one of the most useful for anglers who fish in the current and offer underwater flies. This cast causes the leader and line to "tuck" back under the forward portion of your fly line. The fly begins to sink upon contact with the water as the slack you've placed in the cast drifts downstream. The result is that the fly can sink deeper than it would following a straight-line cast. Tuck casting is generally regarded as a technique used when nymph fishing, but it works with any underwater fly that you want to drift naturally and deeper in the current. Almost everyone familiar with the tuck cast regards it as a method of tucking the leader and fly *directly underneath* the line as it falls to the water—but you can modify it to obtain curves to the right or left. The curve tuck cast will often catch more fish than a cast in a vertical plane.

The tuck cast is made exactly like the curve cast I described earlier, except that it's made in a vertical, not a side, position.

Make a high vertical cast. *The important factor here is that the line attain a very high speed. In fact, you want enough speed to make a cast that would travel two or three times farther than the amount of line you're casting. Without excessive speed, the tuck cast won't work!* It helps to use a single-haul on your forward cast. Then stop the rod **at just past the vertical position.** The more vertically the rod is stopped—and the greater the line speed—the more of your leader and fly will tuck on the cast. *The lower the elevation of the rod on the forward stop, the less tuck can occur.* Also, the rod must be stopped dead at the end of the cast. *It's vital to hold the rod* motionless *until after the tuck—any movement, back or front, will detract from the amount of leader that gets tucked under. The stationary rod and great line speed are the two most important factors in a good tuck cast.*

Begin the tuck cast by making a very fast and high cast. You must develop good line speed to do this, so a haul on the forward cast helps.

If you've made a cast with great line speed, stop the rod high and straight ahead. The weighted fly will cause the rod to flex forward and then it will flip back, causing the leader and fly to tuck under the line.

If you hold the rod perfectly motionless at the vertical angle, the force of your high-speed forward cast will straighten the line and bend the rod. Then your rod tip will recoil. *It's this recoiling of the rod tip that creates the tuck cast—providing the rod is held motionless at this stage.* The line falls to the water with the leader and some of its own forward portion of the line tucked back under. Drop the rod tip as the line begins to fall to the water. The more tuck you desire, the greater the line speed you need on the forward cast. The fly will begin to sink as your line begins drifting downstream. Because of the slack, the fly is able to dive deeper before you start your own retrieve.

The Tuck Cast with a Curve to the Left or Right

You can also make a tuck cast so that the line tucks with a curve to your left or right. This is advantageous in many fishing situations. For example, if you're wading with the stream bank on your left and you'd like to get a nymph or streamer deeper on its downstream drift, use the tuck-to-the-left cast. To do this, make a conventional tuck cast, with one exception: During he speedup and stop lean the tip slightly to the right. This will cause the uck to occur, but will also whip the nymph around so that it curves left; he fly will then precede the leader during the drift. Curve to the right at he end of the tuck cast to get a left-hand curve.

The Skip Cast

Sometimes you'll want to cast a fly well back under a dock, overhanging rush, or the like, and a normal cast won't do it. The skip cast is the an-wer. Remember, when you were young, throwing a flat stone so that it kipped several times on the water before ending its flight? Keep that in mind when you make a skip cast. Have enough line outside the rod tip to each your target. You must make a very low backcast—so low that the ine is just above the surface. (Remember how you kept your arm low when you made the stone skip?) On the forward cast you must aim at a pot on the water well in front of your target. The cast won't work unless ou develop a lot of line speed, so a line haul helps here. (If you threw the tone back then with little force it wouldn't skip; neither will the line skip now unless you get it moving fast.) The line will strike the water well in ront of the target, then skip low and forward and under the dock or over-hanging trees. Once you've mastered it, you'll find many uses for this cast.

The skip cast is a great one to drive a fly well back under overhanging brush, a bridge, a boat dock, or similar structure. Use the same concept you did when you were a child and skipped a stone across the water: You never threw the stone at the target. Instead, you threw the stone so it struck the surface well in front of the target. You should do the same with this cast.

To deliver such a cast it's essential that you make a very low backcast. The skip cast can't be made well if the rod is brought back in a vertical position. Make a low side backcast and bring the rod forward angled very slightly downward. Note how far above the water the rod is kept. Aim the fly so it strikes the water not too far in front of you. Note where the fly has struck the water. The cast must be made with extra speed, since you want the fly and line to skip forward after striking the water. As with the stone, the faster you throw your cast, the farther it will skip.

Depending on the angle of impact, the line and fly will skip and sail low to the water and back under the brush, as shown here.

Casting and Wind

Wind is perhaps the greatest enemy of the fly caster in salt water. Because there's almost always a difference in temperature between a land mass the nearby sea, there's usually a continual flow of air from one to the other. On creeks and lakes there are wind breaks in the form of high banks or trees—a luxury not afforded the saltwater fly fisherman. This, plus cold fronts, means that if you're going to fish the salt you have to know how to handle a breeze. Also, many freshwater situations require only a short cast. But to be successful in salt water an angler often needs to throw a longer distance. There are thus two special demands placed on a fly fisherman in salt water: He must cast accurately, and often quickly at a target that will soon disappear; and he faces almost constant casting into the wind. Most freshwater fishermen are appalled at the winds they must fish against when they come to the salt and are often unprepared for them. It sometimes leads to discouragement and an avoidance of fishing salt water.

Using the Wind to Your Advantage

Actually, an experienced angler can often use the wind to his advantage. For example, on some flats, coves, and bays, when there's no breeze the water is so calm that presenting your offering without alerting the fish can be very difficult. The approach of the boat and motor, or the crashing of the fly line and fly to the placid surface, can often frighten fish. Under such conditions the wise angler waits until these areas are slightly rippled, allowing him to make a better presentation.

Another situation in which wind can help is when you fish shallow basins or bays that feature a narrow opening through which the tide flows to fill and drain the pool. Knowledge of wind direction and its effect on the tides in such a basin is vital, for when a strong wind blows from a specific direction it empties the basin on an outgoing tide. At such times the tide forces most of the fish to escape through the basin's outlet—concentrating them for your cast.

If there's a stiff wind at your back you can actually throw more fly line than you can buy. Throw the backcast low behind you then, as you come forward, attempt to make a much higher-than-normal cast toward your target. This elevated line is caught by the breeze, which turns it into a kite, carrying it along for a great distance. Under such conditions anglers who can throw a tight backcast will find that they use the wind to extend their cast and search more water with their fly.

Casting into the Wind

The exact opposite type of cast is used to throw into the wind. The problems here are compounded: For one thing, the air resistance of both the fly and the line makes obtaining any distance a problem. And a major concern comes at the end of the cast—as soon as the line is fully extended or unrolls—when the breeze can blow the fly, the leader, and part of the line back toward you. To prevent this, aim directly at the spot you want the fly to land and try to drive the fly down and at the surface. If this is properly executed the line will unroll and, as soon as the leader and fly are fully extended, the fly will be in the water, without blowback.

There are some basic rules to observe if you're casting into the wind. The major mistake anglers make when the wind increases is to use the same rod with a larger or heavier line. For example, if a WF9 line is being cast and the wind comes up, many sportsmen will substitute a WF10 line on the same rod. That's exactly the opposite of what you should do. The size 10 line is much larger in diameter, so it is has more wind resistance. And another factor enters, too—rod action. You need to throw tighter loops into the wind. The size of a loop is, of course, determined by the distance that the tip rod moves through an arc at the end of the forward cast. If you use a 10 line on a 9 rod, the heavier line causes the rod to bend more deeply during your casting motions—causing you to throw a loop much larger than normal.

What you should do is substitute a line *1 size lighter or smaller than your rod calls for.* In this case it would be a size 8. *But—and this is important—you need to extend more than the normal amount of line. By having a little more than the usual amount of line outside the guides, the 8 line will weigh as much as a 9 and cause the rod to bend as if you were casting a 9. Tight loops will then be possible.* Because more line is outside the guides with the 8, it has a thinner diameter and will encounter less air resistance. Also, the increased amount of line held aloft during the false cast means less line has to be shot to the target. This is a lesson that most fly fishermen haven't learned, but every serious tournament angler (who measures his casts with a ruler) knows and uses this trick.

A common mistake of anglers drifting and fly casting when the wind is blowing is to cast with the wind; this results in the fly falling downwind of the boat. Because the boat is being pushed along by the wind, it tends to override the fly and spoils the retrieve: Either you have difficulty retrieving fast enough to get the desired action, or the length of your retrieve is shortened. Under such conditions you should cast down and across the wind. The fly will land off to one side, but the wind will help carry it to the target. This results in a long retrieve and little effort when tossing the fly.

When you're approaching a school of fish or a target area in a boat, if you're right-handed have the boat operator approach from upwind. Stand in the right rear (left front) corner of the boat, where you can make your backcast over the water, then use the wind to help you make a cast at an angle sideways to it. A left-hander would approach *from* upwind and stand on the left rear corner of the boat.

With a stiff breeze blowing, it's best under most fishing conditions not to use a floating fly line, which has the largest diameter of any fly line of comparable weight. Thinner lines allow you to cast into the breeze more easily. If you must fish shallow, use at least an intermediate line. If possible, a high-density or similar sinking line—which has a greater mass for a thinner diameter—will allow you to throw farther with less effort.

The double-haul technique is vital for casting into a breeze. As I've described, this is a casting technique in which you pull down at the end of both back- and forward casts, causing the line to greatly accelerate. All fly lines stop their forward motion and begin falling as soon as the loop unrolls. A double-haul does only one thing: It makes your line travel faster. Thus, if you make a loop that's relatively large—it opens after, say, two seconds to deliver your fly at 40 feet—and by using a double-haul you can double your line speed, with this technique you could throw the line 80 feet. Every serious saltwater fly fisherman uses the double-haul.

Loop size has a great impact on how well you can cast into the breeze. Smaller loops concentrate your energy in the target direction, while large loops tend to throw your effort over a wider circle; they also encounter more air resistance. Thus, if you can throw smaller loops you can be more efficient by concentrating your energy toward the target and decreasing air resistance. *The size of your forward casting loop is totally determined by the distance you move your wrist (or rod tip—same thing) at the end of the cast.* Learn to load the rod and then, at the last moment in your forward cast, make the smallest wrist motion to form a tight loop. You'll drastically improve your distance against the wind.

Another way to obtain more distance on windy days is to use shooting-taper-style lines (often called shooting heads). Such a line has a conventional heavy forward portion, usually with a double or weight-forward taper. But instead of the relatively large running line behind this head (which the head must drag to the target), a shooting taper has a very thin line, which permits the head to travel a far greater distance. While many people use monofilament for the shooting line behind the head, anglers experienced in the wind prefer commercial shooting line, which is an ultra-thin level fly line. There are two problems with the monofilament. Since it's so thin, it tends to tangle and kink—and such kinks are often impossible to remove. But the major problem is that when the head is released, the light mono lying at your feet is often picked up in a mass and carried toward the stripping guide—resulting in a snarled mess.

Another trick to obtain more distance in the wind is to use smaller or lightly weighted flies. Admittedly, some species and conditions call for a fly that's larger, sinks faster, or is bulkier. But if you're going to get your offering to your target, a smaller, less wind-resistant, or lightly weighted fly may better let you do so.

9

RETRIEVING

Accuracy

Fly fishermen considering how to retrieve a fly often fail to think about accuracy. *Many anglers practice casting for greater distance, when they should first consider accuracy.* No matter how well or far you can cast, if you don't hit the target, you've missed your opportunity. Many trout rise to a fly and then refuse it, simply because the cast was inaccurate. It wasn't that you had the wrong fly—just that your cast wasn't accurate. (I'll explain this in greater detail in chapter 10.) Set a mousetrap on your lawn that's ready to go off, then try hitting it with a weighted fly to improve your accuracy. I can't emphasize too strongly how important it is to place the fly on target. This applies equally to casting a dry fly to a sipping trout and a huge streamer to a sailfish that has been teased to the transom. Accurate casting is something you never get too good at.

But accuracy is more than making your fly hit the target. Because we're human, we frequently make casts that don't go exactly where we want them to. But remember, a fly rod is a long tool, and it can help you change the path of a retrieve. In many situations it permits you to alter your retrieve in several directions as the fly progresses through the water.

Sometimes even if you could do it, dropping your fly right on the nose of a fish might not be a good idea. It could frighten the fish. But if you could carefully guide the fly from its first impact, you could have a strike.

When you see a cruising fish, you must cast just as accurately as you would to a bass lying beside a rock. The difference is that the fish is swimming, so you have to anticipate where you can make your retrieve. If your cast is a little off target, you can sometimes use the rod to manipulate your line to track the fly close enough to the fish for a strike.

One of the greatest mistakes made by all fishermen casting to cruising fish is to look at it during the cast. If you look at the fish you'll proba-

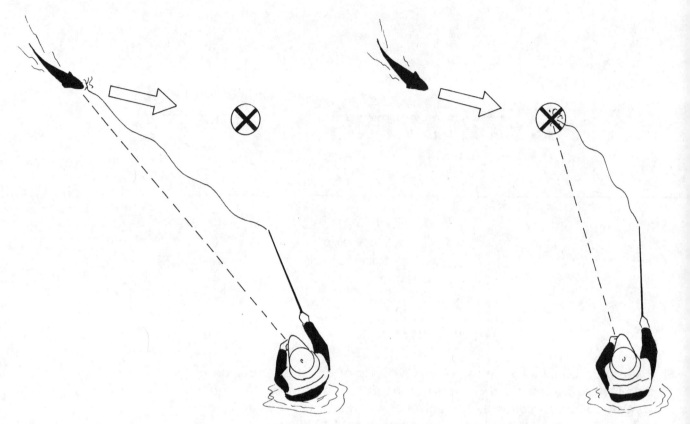

Look at the target, not the fish.

bly throw your fly at the fish. I taught shotgunning years ago. I instructed my students to look intently at the target, bring the gun properly to the shoulder, and, while still looking at the target, pull the trigger. The body instinctively aims at what it looks at. *Thus, if you look at a cruising trout, bonefish, or whatever, you'll probably hit it. Instead, you must keep the fish in your side vision but look at the spot where you want the fly to land. This is an important part of presentation and retrieve that even few experienced anglers realize.*

Line Manipulation

While casting accuracy is vital to getting a lot of hookups, the ability to manipulate the fly line with the fly rod once your retrieve begins can make a huge difference in how many fish accept your fly. The most common example is mending line during a drift when you're trout, salmon, or steelhead fishing. You want the fly to drift naturally with the current. If you cast across the water, the current will act more strongly on the center of your line, causing it to sag downstream. This will pull on the fly, making it drift unnaturally. To offset this sag, make a mend in the line. A mend is simply a curve you put into the line.

When a downstream sag occurs in the line, as shown, it causes the dry fly to drag unnaturally, in turn causing trout to refuse the fly.

If you roll the rod tip up and over, an upstream curve (or mend) develops, allowing the fly to drift naturally again.

Let me give you some examples that I hope illustrate how you can control the path of your retrieve in almost all fly-casting situations. Say you're a trout fisherman standing in the stream, and you believe that directly below you lies a nice trout. You have the option of throwing your fly to one side of and upstream from the fish, then allowing it to drift downstream and sweep across in front of the fish as your leader straightens. This retrieve gives the fish one opportunity to look at your fly. But if after your fly sweeps to the side of the fish, you roll the rod over (mending the line), the fly will sweep back across in front of the fish. When your leader straightens again, repeat the mending process by rolling the rod tip back in the opposite direction. The fly will again sweep back in front of the fish. I've used this technique many times to tease or irritate a fish until it took the fly.

Here's another example of how you can use the rod to manipulate the fly. Incidentally, it's easier to alter the direction of a retrieve with a floating than a sinking line. However, you can make some change in direction even with a lead-core line. Say you're fishing along a saltwater dock. You make a cast along the dock. As you retrieve the fly, you note that there's an indentation in the dock. If you sweep your rod in a mending motion by rolling the top over in the direction of this indentation, your line will lift out of the water and fall toward the cavity. Continue to retrieve and the fly tends to follow the path of the line. When the fly nears the end of the cavity in the dock, roll the rod tip in the opposite direction; the line will lift up and fall away from the hollow, and the fly will follow the line. By mending the line with the rod, you can frequently retrieve a fly in several different directions on the same cast. You can use this cast to move your fly along a weed bed, a rock ledge, or another structure. This is a technique many fly fishermen fail to use to advantage.

With an underwater fly, presentation is the most crucial part of getting a fish to strike. Naturally you want your fly to land so that it doesn't spook the fish, yet is within sight of the predator. But just as important a part of presentation—and maybe even more vital—is the retrieve.

First, there are few ironclad rules for correctly retrieving an underwater fly. To some degree your retrieve must be matched to local fishing conditions, the species of fish you're seeking, and the type of creature your fly is intended to imitate.

But a number of retrieve techniques apply to almost all fishing situations. *One of the most common mistakes is to make your cast then release the line.* The fly falls to the water, and you're too distracted by trying to recover the line to begin your retrieve. Never throw the line away. Keep the line flowing through your curled fingers and when the fly touches down, you are in control—now!

If you direct your cast at eye level or slightly above, you can track its progress through the air. This allows you to trap the line and drop your fly on target.

There are times when you'll catch more fish if you begin your retrieve the moment the fly gets wet. A fly that hits the water in front of a fish and then streaks away appears to be fleeing, and the fish often strikes instincively. Other times, though, the exact opposite situation is true. I find that with redfish and snook, splashing the fly down gently then slowly moving a few inches only is frequently deadly. *One thing you almost never want to do is throw a fly close to a fish then let it slowly tumble or sink, void of any life or action.*

For several decades now outdoor writer Charley Waterman and I have been preaching, writing, and urging fly fishermen that for good technique when retrieving almost any underwater fly, they need to keep the rod low—so low that in fact the tip can often touch the water, in the direction of the fish. Still, there are many fly fishermen who flip the rod tip up and down to manipulate a bug or streamer.

There are problems with a high rod. *First, a popping bug or streamer gets little chance to pause or stop during the retrieve. Stopping the bug's movement often draws strikes.* Here's why: With the rod elevated and twitched to manipulate the fly or bug, the line straightens with each flip of the tip, and the fly or bug moves forward. When you pause, the line sags toward the water immediately in front of the rod tip, and this sagging motion continues to pull on the fly or bug—so that it never does stop. *To ensure definite pauses during your retrieve, place the rod tip nearly at the surface and, with your line hand, make long, short, fast, or slow pulls on the line—which will affect the fly or bug. But once you stop the line retrieval, because your tip is low and your line straight, the fly pauses.*

Two other factors justify a low fly rod during the retrieve. If a strong wind is blowing and your rod is elevated, the breeze pushes against the line between the rod tip and the water, and—like the sagging line—it will cause your fly or bug to be dragged. Another reason for keeping the rod tip in or near the surface when retrieving is to improve your strike ratio. With the rod held high, when a fish takes your offering your sweep of the rod must first remove the slack between the rod tip and the water before you can begin to tighten the line to bury the hook. In some cases this can mean a lost fish. But if you hold the rod tip low or in the water on the retrieve, the line is taut between the tip and the fly, and any motion on your part begins to set the hook.

There are a few exceptions to this in salt water. When you're trying to tempt a big jack crevalle or trevally to hit a popping bug, or often when you're fishing king mackerel, making a sudden, long sweeping movement with your rod can give the fly a tremendously fast leap through the water—turning a reluctant fish into one that will smash your offering. But most of the time this special technique will simply defeat your purpose.

Another major mistake made by fly fishermen—particularly on rivers, or where a strong tidal current occurs—comes when they make a cast across the flow to where a fish may be holding. Here the tendency is to leave the rod pointing in the direction that the cast was made while the line and fly drift downstream. This creates a belly in the line. As the current enlarges the belly, it acts on the fly much the way it would on a row of ice skaters on a rink. If the inside skater stops and the line begins to swing, the outside skater soon will be going considerably faster. So it is on a retrieve. The

By flipping the tip upward to work an underwater fly, you place unwanted slack in the line.

By pointing the rod low and at the fly, you avoid slack, and a better chance of hooking the fish is ensured.

belly in the line begins to accelerate the fly on the end of the leader, and soon the fly is traveling at an unnaturally high speed—and will usually be ignored by fish.

To get the kind of natural drift from your fly that you need to draw strikes, you must alter the direction of your rod during the drift. As soon as you make a cast, watch the current flow and begin moving your rod along with it. Try to keep the line between the rod tip and the fly as straight as possible. A reach cast and mending line upstream can also improve your presentation. Two things are accomplished: First, a more natural drift occurs, which will draw more strikes. Second, because the line is drifting straight and free of slack, you can strike more efficiently. If possible, watch your fly—especially when the fish nears it. It's usually easy to watch both when the fish is near. Use the fish's actions to determine if you need to alter your retrieve. One of the myths in fly fishing is that you should wait until a stalking tarpon grabs your fly and turns before you strike. The problem is that often a tarpon will take the fly and continue straight ahead. If you can see the fly, *wait until the tarpon closes its mouth, and then strike.*

Certainly there are two rules of retrieving an underwater fly that I believe are vital to all situations. One is that *if a fish follows your fly for 6 to 8 feet and doesn't take it—change your retrieve! Often a good trick is to make two or three quick line pulls, to make the fly look like it's in trouble and trying to flee. Then return to your normal retrieve.* This will usually draw a strike. *The second rule of retrieving an underwater fly is that there's only one situation in which letting your fly stop dead, devoid of any movement, will induce a strike. This is when you're fishing permit with a crab imitation. With every other species I'm familiar with, keeping your fly in motion—however slight—once it hits the water will increase your hookups. Even if the fly is staying in a small area, give it at least a tiny bit of lifelike action.*

With popping bugs, however, the reverse is often true. By retrieving and giving the bug a lot of action you frequently can induce fish to strike. Still, there are many times when a noisy retrieve is disastrous. Larger fish cruising the shallows are easily frightened by a loud popping bug. Enter a backcountry mangrove cove or creek where the water is slick and calm, and many times a splashy retrieve with a bug will draw a zero. Instead, start fishing with a very gentle retrieve—the bug should barely disturb the surface. Even better under such conditions is to use a slider (a popping bug with a bullet-shaped head). This can be retrieved so that it creates a small wake on the surface but makes no audible noise. When you're seeking largemouths on calm lakes, a bug that's teased slowly is often better than one that lies there motionless. Work a Marabou Gerbubble Bug with this technique and more strikes will result. (For more information on this, see "Bass" in chapter 11.)

One reason that the Dahlberg Diver is often so deadly in shallow saltwater fishing situations is that it can be popped loudly, popped quietly, made to move like a slider—and even pulled underneath the surface to swim like a fish. If you fly fish and haven't use Dahlbergs on largemouth and smallmouth bass, snook, and redfish, you have a treat in store for you.

Sink Rate

The sink rate of an underwater fly is critical to fishing success. It's often one of the most disregarded factors in getting fish to take your offering. You may have used the correct pattern, cast the right distance, and retrieved at the proper speed. But if your fly is at the wrong depth in the water column, your efforts may have been in vain.

When considering the sink rate of a fly, it's important to understand how the fish we seek catch their prey. I think it's so important that I'm going to repeat some information I discussed in chapter 4. Fish that feed on the bottom are said to have inferior mouths—located near the bottom of the head. While they'll occasionally take food in the water column, their mouths are designed to catch prey on or very close to the bottom. Examples of species with inferior mouths are redfish (channel bass), suckers, bonefish, and carp. The opposite is true of tarpon, smallmouth and largemouth bass, trout, northern pike, striped bass, and many others—these have mouths located in the middle of the head. These fish are better adapted to catching their food either in the water column or on the surface. Bottom feeders rarely take anything from the surface. When you're seeking bottom feeders, then, weight your fly so that on the retrieve it will descend quickly to or near the bottom. *More important is to realize that fish that are not bottom feeders will rarely descend in the water column to take your fly. They will rise to it, but almost never drop down to get it.* This, of course, means that sink rate is critical—the fly should ride in the water column either at the cruise level of the fish or higher.

Many factors go into selecting a fly with the correct sink rate. Let's examine some of them. Obviously you can add weight to a fly to make it sink. However, the type of weight, how much is secured to the fly, the shape of the weight added, and its location on the hook are all important in how the fly sinks. For years the most common method of sinking a fly has been the use of lead fuse wire, which can be obtained in four sizes (½, 1, 2, and 3) from many fly shops. By wrapping the same fly pattern with different sizes of lead wire or varying the turns of the fuse wire on the hook shank, you can alter the sink rate. Many tiers don't realize that a hook rides with its point down because of the weight of the bend. If the lead wire you wrap around the hook shank weighs more than the portion of the hook that is its bend, then the point will ride up because the shank is now heavier than the bend. This permits you to tie fly patterns on a straight hook that you can crawl on the bottom to reduce snagging.

The Wapsi Fly Company revolutionized the tying of sinking flies when a few years ago it introduced lead eyes. Manufacturers now make metallic eyes from nontoxic brass or from a combination of antimony and tin; these weigh approximately 65 percent as much as lead eyes of a similar diameter.

The past several years trout fishermen (and some bass anglers) have been profiting from a technique developed in Europe a decade or more ago; the use of brass or other metallic beads or cones tied in usually immediately behind the hook eye. Nymphs and Woolly Bugger patterns that use beadheads or coneheads have become a part of most experienced trout fishermen's arsenal. While some claim that the bead- or conehead resembles an air bubble attached to the fly, I believe that it's the *weight* of the bead that's most responsible for this fly's success. Most free-drifting nymphs ride the water column down deep or close to the bottom, so these metallic heads get the fly down to where fish expect to see their prey.

Obviously, the heavier the weight, the faster the fly will sink. But *where* the weight is positioned on the hook shank is vital to how the fly sinks and is retrieved. When a fly is placed in the tying vise in the normal manner and lead eyes attached on top of the hook, the pattern will ride upside down, or with its hook point up. If the weight is concentrated at the rear of the hook, however, the rear of the fly will sink faster. For example, to make a good crayfish fly you may want to put the lead wire or lead eyes at the very rear of the shank. If you want the fly to dip and dive anytime you enter slack into your retrieve, then put the weight at the front of the hook shank.

Aside from using weights, there are other techniques for getting your flies to the proper depth. During the late 1950s sinking lines began to appear on the market; prior to this floating lines were the only choice available. For decades fly fishermen had used leaders of 9 feet or longer for salt and fresh water. When sinking lines came along, though, anglers soon realized that while the line went down, the fly rode well above it in the water column. The problem was that we were using a sinking line with that long, buoyant leader. Even today many fly fishermen use leaders on sinking lines that are too long and never get their flies down where they want them. With a sinking line,

For most species you need a very short leader with a sinking line to ensure that the fly gets down where the line is. An 8-inch leader was used to catch this nice bluegill.

most of the time it's better to use a short leader. It should rarely be as long as 6 feet. Unless the water is exceptionally clear, when I'm using a sinking line I prefer a leader of no more than 4 feet. I've caught many fish with leaders as short as 6 inches. Underwater fish don't seem too aware of the leader unless it's exceptionally large or interferes with the action of the fly.

The following paragraph may seem to be a contradiction of what I've just written. But when you're using a floating line you can get a *weighted* fly down to reasonable depths—if you use a *long* leader. There are many fly-fishing situations that require using a floating line in rather shallow water, but with a fly that must be fished on the bottom. You can do this by using a long leader, which will permit a weighted fly to drop quickly. One of the best situations I know of for this technique is fishing for trout in water no deeper than 3 feet where sculpins exist. I use a floating line and at least a 10-foot leader. Years ago Dave Whitlock gave me a fly he'd developed and said, "You can use this fly, but don't ever write about it." I've followed his advice, but now Dave sells this fly through Umpqua Feather Merchants and it's available in hundreds of fly shops. You wouldn't normally buy this ugly-looking fly, but Dave's Near Nuff Sculpin is terrific on smallmouths and trout. The fly is heavily weighted with wrapped lead fuse wire, so it sinks fast and rides with the hook point up. Sculpins live on the bottom and, with no air bladders, will sink when they're not swimming. So Dave's fly should be fished *slowly* on the bottom. To do this correctly, attach the fly to a long leader on a floating fly line. Make your cast and let the fly rest on the bottom. Then make only *1-inch-long* strips, letting the fly rest between them. This is one of the deadliest flies in my fly box and has taken many larger trout and smallmouths for me.

Another method of getting flies down—mostly in trout fishing—is the use of weight attached to a leader. The weight can be wraparound lead strips, molded weight, or split shot. All three are standard methods of getting the fly down in the water column, where it's needed. I discovered for myself in New Zealand and Chile, where waters are air clear, that when fishing such clear streams or lakes it's often best not to attach the weight to the leader. In such waters you can observe the trout. And when a leader with nymphs and weight attached comes into the fish's range, it will often move to one side to permit the rig to pass. *When waters are especially clear and fish enjoy great visibility, I believe that a nymph tied with the weight hidden under its dressing is more effective.* Many times I'll also place split shot against the head of the nymph or streamer. This aids in casting and gets the fly down faster. If you do add split shot somewhere on the leader, you may want to try this: Make a blood, surgeon's, or similar knot in the leader. Clip off one tag end, but trim the other tag end very short. Then crimp split shot on the latter tag end. It can be removed easily and will never damage the leader—which sometimes happens when you pinch the split shot on.

A final method of adjusting the sink rate of the fly is to select the proper fly line. Manufacturers now offer lines in five different sink rates. By carrying several lines with you, and flies tied with various amounts of weight (including none), you can fish almost all waters down to 30 feet deep.

Many fish hold at a specific level in the current, so it's vital to swim your fly at that level. Indeed, the sink rate of the fly during the retrieve is one of the most important factors in whether or not fish accept your offerings. (This is especially true when seeking steelhead.) Be aware of this factor, and adjust your lines and patterns to swim your flies at the desired depth.

The Downstream "Retrieve"

Fly fishing is bound by tradition, which is a good thing, but sometimes it pays to break the rules. With trout, there are a number of fishing situations in which it's either impossible or inadvisable to cast upstream and allow the dry fly to drift back with the current, something many consider the only way to fish a dry. For example, if there's a fallen tree in a bend of the river, with current sweeping toward that tree, it would be impossible to cast from a downstream position. In this case you should be upstream from the tree and allow your fly to float downstream, feeding slack into the line so it drifts naturally. On some smooth waters where the trout are unusually shy, drifting the fly downstream to a trout will draw more strikes. More anglers are beginning to recognize that casting upstream and retrieving as the dry fly floats back down isn't always the best method. This also applies to fishing nymphs. There are some situations in which floating a nymph downstream, rather than retrieving it from the conventional upstream position, is much preferred.

Retrieve Speed

For some fish a slow, deliberate retrieve will work better than a quick one. Northern pike seem to explode on a fly that's slowly teased along. And tarpon generally strike flies that are slowly retrieved, rather than very rapidly. Permit usually require no retrieve. Drop a crab pattern as close to the nose of a fish as possible and allow it to sink to the bottom. If the crab fly is retrieved, the permit almost always runs away.

There are some exceptions, but after more than 50 years of hard fishing for freshwater bass I've come to the conclusion that most of the time in most places, a popping bug that's kept in continuous motion coming back to you will draw more strikes than one popped, paused until all the circles disappear, then popped again. Occasionally, on lakes or where there's little current, a slow stop-and-go retrieve will do well for you. But generally, I have better luck if I keep my bug always in motion. This is especially true for smallmouth bass. I'm also convinced that when you're retrieving a tarpon fly and a tarpon is tracking your offering, the worst thing you can do is stop all fly motion. It almost always results in disinterest by the tarpon, which moves away. No matter how little motion you use, your fly needs to have some movement all the time. *There are few times when a perfectly dead or motionless fly is a preferred retrieve in fresh or salt water.*

Crappies and walleyes definitely want a slow-moving fly. Bluegills will actually run away from a fast-moving one. Because they're so small, when they approach a possible food source and it begins zipping through the water, they apparently aren't sure if they can eat it—or it will eat them. The trick on all three of these species is to create movement with your fly, but keep it slow. That's why soft hackles, rabbit fur, and similar materials that undulate with the slightest twitch of the rod are good for crappies, walleyes, and bluegills.

A proper backcast should be made after the fly line is lifted free of the surface. Note how much water has been disturbed when the line is backcast before it's off the water. This frightens fish and spoils good backcasts.

A major reason why fishermen don't catch fish in shallow water—be they bonefish or trout—is an improper line pickup for the backcast. All line should be removed from the surface before you make a backcast. Surface tension grips the fly line. If even a few inches of line is on the water when you make your backcast, it will rip loose and create a noise and disturbance that alerts the fish. *I think this is a primary reason why many dry-fly fishermen don't catch fish—and I know that many bonefish have been lost for the same reason. It's imperative that you lift all your line from the water before making a backcast.* Of course, the lower your rod when you start the backcast, the easier it'll be for you to lift the line free.

A Natural Approach

One of the major reasons why so many fly fishermen fail is that they don't realize the importance of how a fly approaches a fish. A crayfish doesn't attack a smallmouth bass; nor would a minnow pick a fight with an 18-inch brown trout. Yet that's exactly what we do so often when we present a fly to the fish. This applies to all kinds of fishing: trolling, using plugs, spinning, and fly fishing.

Let me cite one example. I fished with an experienced freshwater angler last year at Christmas Island, in the South Pacific. This is perhaps the best place in the world—at least of the places where I've fished—to learn how to successfully catch bonefish. There are days when you'll see well over 1,000 bonefish, usually in singles, doubles, or small schools. Christmas Island also has some of the best wading flats anywhere. When you're wading in such shallow water you're able to closely observe the fish and its reactions.

Inching our way across one of these flats, my friend and I saw three bonefish approaching, swimming very close together. They were going to pass slightly to our right as they headed for a nearby channel. When they were about 35 feet away, my companion made a cast that dropped his fly 4 feet beyond and about 6 feet in front of them. He started to retrieve—when suddenly all three bonefish flushed wildly and tore off into the channel's safety.

What had happened was typical of what I see occurring so many times—yet even after repeated failures, few anglers seem to know what this is. They usually change fly patterns, assuming the fish didn't like their offering. After all, the cast was delivered so quietly that the fish didn't spook. The fly dropped exactly where the fisherman wanted it to. And it's fairly evident that the fish didn't see the angler.

Yet a basic principle of retrieve was violated. That day on the Christmas Island flat, my friend made the same presentation several times—each time frightening the bonefish. He threw only a few feet in front and just past the cruising fish. The retrieve brought the fly toward the fish, but when it got closer, the fish had already moved so far ahead that the fly was actually approaching them from behind. This was, of course, an unnatural way for a prey species to approach a predator, and so the fish instinctively fled.

Here's one of the most important rules concerning retrieving underwater flies: No fly should ever be retrieved so that the predator may think it's being attacked. Predators chase and eat their prey; never in the natural environment does a crab pick a fight with a permit, or a baitfish chase a barracuda. When this happens the reaction of the predator is to back off, or just leave. Predators expect to see their prey (or the fly) act and react in the natural manner of any creature that's in danger.

Whenever we present a fly to a fish, we must retrieve it so that it behaves like all the other prey the fish consumes. More important than the type of fly, the color, its size, or its sink rate is that a fly be retrieved in a natural manner.

Let me give you some more examples. An angler, either wading or in a boat, sees a fish ahead of him. A basic tenet of good presentation is never to throw your line over a fish. So what most fishermen do is place the fly directly ahead of the fish, allowing only the leader to fall to the surface near the fish. Then they retrieve the fly in hopes the fish will strike it. But let's look at this from the fish's viewpoint. It sees the fly swimming toward it; naturally, it expects this fly to try to escape as it gets near and realizes the danger—like all prey does. But instead, this "thing" continues to come straight on, in what the fish has to regard as an attack mode. Of course, the fish bolts.

What should you do in such a situation? Instead of dropping the fly directly in front of the fish, cast so that it falls to the water several feet to one side and a slight distance forward of the fish. Then begin your retrieve. What the fish will see is a creature that appears to be sneaking by off to one side, and it'll bolt forward for the grab.

Let's look at another situation. The angler sees a fish directly in front of him and casts. What happens if the fly lands almost on its nose? The fish sees something directly in front of it, appearing to slowly, or casually, move away. This isn't a natural occurrence, so the fish will often refuse the offering. But when the fly falls to the side, the fish sees what it expects: something trying to sneak by. Impulse will cause the fish to streak forward and hit the fly.

When a fish is lying in a channel or where a tidal current is carrying its food along, it doesn't expect to see shrimp, baitfish, and other creatures swimming upcurrent against the tide. To the fish, this simply doesn't appear normal. Instead, cast so that your fly comes sweeping down to one side of the fish; just before it gets to the fish, the fly should make a U-turn, right in front of the predator. This is what occurs frequently in the current. Shrimp, crabs, and other morsels are drifting with the tide. Then suddenly they see downstream something that might eat them. So they try to go sideways, rather than continuing to drift toward the fish. *A fly that sweeps downcurrent and then turns away directly in front of the fish is the most natural of all retrieves.*

Perhaps where fly fishermen make the most consistently wrong retrieve is with a fish cruising off to their left or right. What generally happens is that the angler drops his fly well ahead of and beyond the swimming fish.

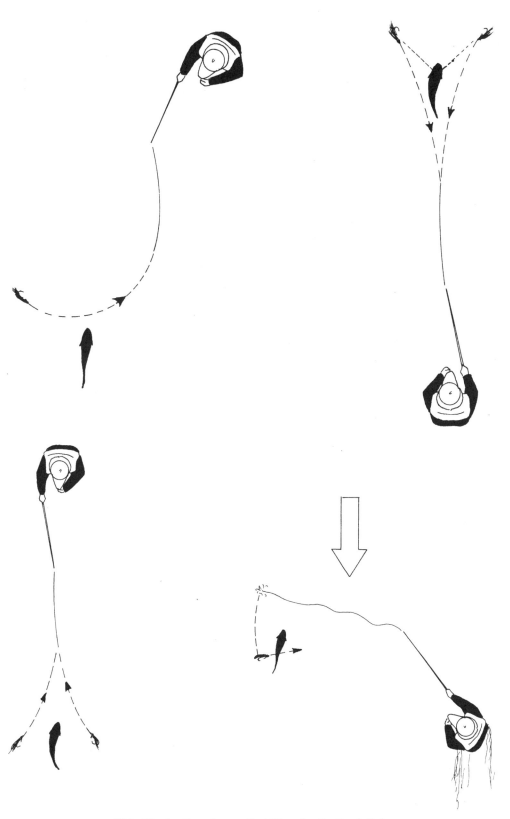

This illustration shows that flies don't attack fish.

He starts his retrieve but while he's bringing the fly back, the fish is swimming forward. Far too often the fish moves far enough ahead so that the fly never passes in front of the fish at all—which would be the perfect retrieve. Instead, the fly approaches the fish from an angle and slightly to the rear. Coupled with spooking bonefish on the cast, I find this the major reason why anglers fail to score. This was the mistake that was constantly being made by my companion at Christmas Island. Each time, his fly approached the bonefish at an angle from the rear.

Here's a final example. A daisy chain is a small group of large tarpon swimming in a tight circle, usually in shallow water. If you use a long leader and a monofilament line, and are an excellent caster, you could cautiously throw the fly into the middle of the circle. But this may spook the fish; it only works with extreme care. A better approach is to throw on the correct side of the circle. If the tarpon are moving clockwise and you're at a 6 o'clock position to them, never throw your fly at 9 o'clock. The fish coming around the circle will see the retrieved fly swimming straight at them—in the attack position. Throw your fly at 2 or 3 o'clock and, as the fish come around the circle, they'll see it swimming away from them. To the tarpon, the fly seems to be attempting to escape.

If you always retrieve your fly so that it appears to be acting like any prey species—trying to elude a predator—your hookup rates will drastically increase.

The End of the Retrieve

You're retrieving the fly when you realize that you'll need to make a longer cast than you have line off the reel. During the retrieve, slip your line hand back close to the reel. Now grip the line immediately off the reel as well as the line you're retrieving. This way, each time you recover line on the retrieve, you'll be pulling the same amount off the reel. This will permit you to make your next cast much longer. Study the photos on page 205 to better understand this.

Here's another important point regarding the end of the retrieve. If you have any amount of on-the-water experience, the following has happened to you, as it did to me for many years: You were fishing a bonefish fly, a streamer, a sculpin, or a similar underwater fly *in the shallows*. As you made your retrieve through a potential hot spot, you either felt or thought that a fish had grabbed the fly. Or perhaps you were fishing in clear, shallow water, and you saw the fish grab your offering.

The instinctive reaction is to immediately set the hook by flipping your rod tip upward to drive the steel home. But too many times when you thought the fish had seized your fly, it actually hadn't. The upward snap that you made to set the hook—which wasn't in the fish's mouth—thus caused the fly to sail upward and out of the water. Since the fish was close to you, if you were to catch it you'd have to present the fly again. At such close quarters in such shallow water fish are very spooky and will flee at the slightest disturbance. *The first cast you make is always the most im-*

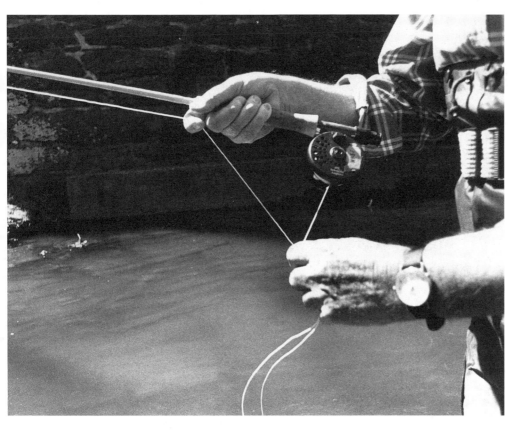

If you make a cast, start a retrieve, and realize you don't have enough line pulled from the reel, you can strip more line off as you retrieve. Grasp both the line you're retrieving and the line coming directly from the reel.

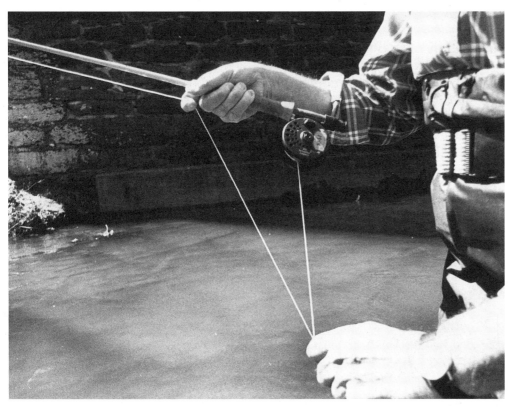

By stripping in line on the retrieve, and at the same time pulling off line from the reel, you can extend the line for a longer cast.

portant—especially in shallow, clear water, where each subsequent cast heightens your chances of alerting or alarming the fish.

By the upward snap of the rod you forced the fly from the water and a second, undesirable cast to be made.

After many such disasters, I've learned a different technique for striking underwater flies. *I might add that this technique applies to just about all types of underwater fishing—except nymph fishing.* It involves manipulating streamers and wet flies to entice fish to strike.

All of us are going to occasionally misjudge when a fish takes a fly and set the hook at unproductive times. But there are ways to set it that won't cause the fly to sail out of the water. In fact, this striking technique will sometimes cause missed fish to actually grab your fly.

There are two methods I recommend for setting the hook on wet and streamer flies: the strip strike and the side strike. Both work, but a special technique is involved with either one. Fortunately, this technique is easy to master once you understand the problems.

Using the strip strike properly you'll almost never break your leader tippet when you drive your hook into a fish. Here's the technique: You're retrieving the fly. You have the line clasped under a finger of your rod hand. Your line hand pulls or moves the line beneath the finger to activate the fly. You think a fish has grabbed your fly. Instead of flipping the rod upward, you leave it just where it was during the retrieve. To set the hook, you release the line from your rod hand, grip it securely with your line hand, and make a short (usually gentle) pull backward. This tightening of the line between you and the fish will set the hook—even in a hard-mouthed tarpon.

When you're using the strip strike, you want to be careful of two things. First and most important is that you don't need much pressure to set the hook in almost any fish; this is especially true with every freshwater species. A gentle set—pulling back no more than 6 inches on the tight line—is all you need. Second, the most panic-stricken moment for the fish is just after the hook is set. The fish will immediately try to escape. This first surge is when it's at full strength, and you must not allow it to jerk your fragile leader tippet. The moment you make your strip strike, then, form an O-ring with the thumb and first two fingers of your line hand; allow the line to flow freely through this O as the fish flees. The O-ring permits you to control the line and slow or stop the fish anytime you desire.

The side strike is just what its name implies: When you think a fish has taken your fly, move your rod gently to the side. There's no need to flip it hard. After all, you're using a lever that's 7 to 9 or more feet long; it will easily set the hook with just gentle pressure. With a side strike, you should also keep the rod *low and parallel* to the water as you move it sideways. And as soon as the hook is driven into the fish, form the same O-ring and follow the procedure described for strip striking.

If you learn to strip or side strike in shallow water when using wet flies and streamers, or any other underwater fly except a nymph, you'll increase your score of hooked and landed fish—in salt or fresh water.

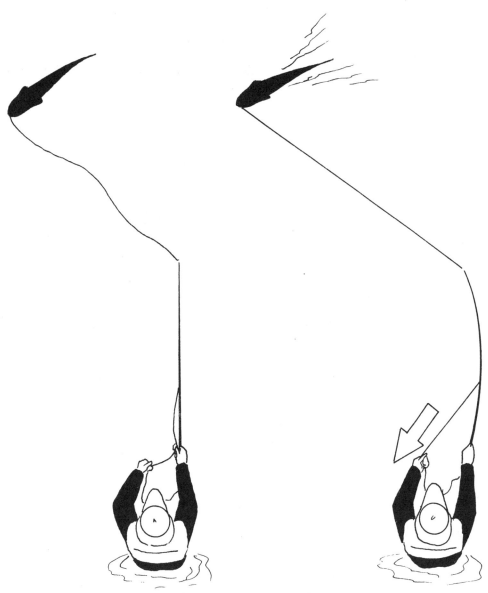

Shallow-water strip strike

A common mistake made by fishermen who seek steelhead and Atlantic salmon with dry flies is to strike improperly. A Bomber or similar surface fly is cast across the water. The current causes the line to drag the fly in a skittering motion that's often attractive to salmon and steelhead. A salmon or steelhead rises to suck in the fly. Notice I said *suck in*. It's important to realize that a salmon or steelhead is not going to bite the fly; it sucks the fly into its mouth. Now consider more fully what's going on during the retrieve. The fly is being pulled across the surface by the tension the current is exerting on the fly line. The fish rises, tries to suck in the fly—and the tension of the line actually moves the fly away from the fish. Then to compound the problem, the fly fisherman sets his hook as the fish takes. Between the line tension and the sweep of the rod, it's easy to see why the fly ends up being pulled out of the fish's mouth. Instead, when the salmon or steelhead takes your fly, you should *drop the rod tip toward the fish* so that slack occurs, permitting the fish to suck in the fly.

The Deep-Water Retrieve

Given their choice, most fly fishermen would likely prefer to fish clear, shallows flats. They can see their quarry here, and often the fly, and—most exciting—watch as the fish strikes. There's no question that all of this is exhilarating. There's the added bonus, too, of seeing all the life on the flats: rays swimming, sea stars, unique vegetation, a fish trying to evade a predator, and much more.

But there's another fly-fishing world that many anglers ignore. This is the world of deep-water fly fishing, both in the salt and in freshwater lakes. Many of the fish you seek in lakes are down deep—more than 15 feet below the surface. Enticing them into taking your offering, and knowing when to strike, require special techniques. The sea is vast, and to the uninitiated so much water can be intimidating. In the shallows you can *see* where to cast and when to set the hook. But in deeper water, unless fish are breaking on bait or right at the surface, it's difficult to know where to cast.

In fresh water it's mainly open lakes that give anglers problems. In the salt, deep-water fishing includes fishing in channels deeper than 10 feet, as well as around wrecks and along coral reefs. Fish holding around bridge pilings well below the surface is another example. Chumming, where the fish may be deep in the chum line and not near the surface, is another deep-water situation. *In a sense deep-water fishing is blind fishing. It means fishing by feel more than anything else. Deep-water fishing requires more concentration than working the flats or shallows with a fly rod.*

But there's another concern. In waters less than 10 feet deep you're usually very much aware when a fish takes your fly. You'll feel a distinct jolt or see visible evidence as to when you should set the hook. In deep water, though, many anglers simply don't know when a fish has taken their fly.

Obviously, if a fish grabs the fly and takes off, there's no doubt. But when you're fishing more than 10 feet deep and a soft take occurs, how do you know? Fortunately, there are some tips that will help you better judge when a fish has taken a fly deep in the water column.

It begins with selecting the proper fly lines. For many years weight-forward sinking fly lines used the same design as every other weight-forward fly line. There was a short level section (usually a foot in length) at the front end, called the tip. Then the line gradually increased in diameter for 6 to 10 feet (called the front taper). Then there was the heavy belly section. The line began reducing in diameter over 7 to 10 feet (the back taper), and finally came the running line, which was a long level line that helped you shoot the head a longer distance.

The problem with this line design was that the heaviest portion sank faster than the rest. *This meant that the tip and front taper were sinking at a slower rate. The leader and fly were attached to this, and so they stayed higher in the water column than the heavier belly section. During the retrieve the fly line, leader, and fly resembled a shallow U, with the belly well below the fly.* When a fish took the fly, the angler wasn't aware of the take until he pulled the sag from the U-shape in the line.

Fortunately, there are now newer lines whose belly and front portions sink at the same rate. The first of these to come out were the Teeny 300 and 400 lines, which feature a thin, level floating line beginning at the rear of the sinking head. Scientific Anglers followed with its Uniform Sink Line. Cortland then introduced a similar line, with a front portion that sinks as fast as the rest. The obvious advantage of this type of line is that all of it remains fairly taut; when a fish takes the fly, you feel it immediately.

If you want to quickly detect a strike, equal in importance to a fly line whose front portion sinks at the same rate is the proper leader. Leaders used on flats are almost always 9 feet or more in length, to prevent the line's impact on the surface from frightening spooky fish. In deep water the problem is reversed. These fish are not nearly so leader-shy, so you don't have to worry about line impact. But a long monofilament leader tends not to sink the way a weighted fly line will. This causes another sag in the line-leader combination and, again, helps mask any strikes by fish.

Leaders for sinking lines should therefore be very short; the fly should sink at almost the level of the line. This way when a fish strikes, it'll be immediately evident. Also, a shorter leader will help you connect faster to the fish, because you won't have to stretch any sag from the monofilament.

Another trick that greatly aids in detecting underwater strikes—even when you're fishing a floating line in 4 or more feet of water—is to end your cast and begin your retrieve by placing the rod tip into the water. Leave it under the water as you retrieve the line. Continue to strip with the tip under water *until you feel wet line crossing your finger.* Then you can raise the rod tip from the water, and the line will remain wet and slick. *Not only is a wet line more comfortable to retrieve, but it also allows your finger to sense strikes much better.*

Another technique that I often use when I'm fishing flies deep in the water column, in both fresh and salt water, is to run a small amount of silicone paste such as line dressing in the groove in my finger that I'm stripping the line across. This permits me to feel the line much better, and detect soft strikes much more easily.

The Crippled Baitfish Retrieve

A neat trick I've been using for years works well in fresh and salt water when the surface is calm. Most of us have watched an injured baitfish struggle on the surface. It rides almost in the surface film, sometimes with a portion of its back protruding above the water. Such commotion on the surface usually draws the immediate attention of any predator in the area.

My trick involves imitating such a crippled baitfish by swimming my fly in the surface film. This only works when the water is calm; the fly will often go unnoticed if the water is rippled or broken. The technique is deadly on trout as well as striped bass and snook. I've never seen anyone else use this retrieve, but I can assure you that under the right conditions it's extremely effective.

You need a special fly, but one that's easy to tie. One of my favorite patterns for this is a Lefty's Deceiver, although many streamer patterns work. *The best streamers are those tied with bucktail—and you do need a liberal amount for the wing on the pattern.* It's important not to place any dressing on the hook shank; tie in a wing, and that's it. A Deceiver will have just the tail and a bountiful collar of bucktail. Now comes the special treatment: Soak the entire fly in dry-fly oil (the same liquid you immerse a dry fly in to make it float). Do not use paste flotant—it doesn't work. It just clumps the material together so that the fly sinks and has little action on the retrieve.

Cast the fly to the target area. Sometimes you'll have to give a little tug on the line to get it to sink. Once it's slightly immersed begin a slow, twitching retrieve to imitate a swimming, crippled baitfish.

There are several advantages to this technique. One is that you can swim this fly in incredibly shallow water, for it rides in or just below the surface film. Retrieve this fly to a cruising redfish, snook, or bass; these and many other predatory fish will rarely fail to take it. Another asset is that the fly comes to the water very softly. The impact is so slight that you can drop the fly very close to a fish without alarming it.

A word of caution: If you use extra-heavy hooks, or dress the hook shank with chenille or similar materials, the fly will not swim in the surface film but sink too deep to be effective. Be sure to use a light hook, and remember that the best material is bucktail. Obviously, this technique doesn't work everywhere. But for many situations, it can be extremely effective— often better than any other retrieve I know.

In this chapter on retrieving the fly I've concerned myself with general observations that cover many areas of fly fishing. In the following chapters I will address specific fishing situations, and I'll either amplify what I've just said or give you new retrieval information.

PART TWO

10

TROUT

More fly fishermen seek trout than any other species. Trout live in a variety of environments: deep cold lakes, fast-running mountain streams, gentle ponds, limestone-fed creeks, and other interesting places. Because of this their food supply varies from locality to locality, and you need different lines, leaders, flies, and techniques to successfully catch them. Fortunately, most of the techniques are easy to master, and what works on one water often does so on many others, too. Learn the basics of trout presentation and you can do pretty well almost anywhere.

The first thing to realize is that *unlike most of the other species fly fishermen seek,* trout are *often regulated by specific food sources in their environment, many of which arrive and disappear on a fairly reliable time schedule.* Northern pike, bass, stripers, bluefish, bonefish, tarpon, and a host of the species we like to catch are opportunistic and eat a great variety of foods. *Trout are not roamers; they usually live in a home pool and are forced to eat what lives with them in that pool.* Most of their food is aquatic insects, usually in the form of nymphs. There may be mayflies, caddis, and stoneflies in their pool. These flies live most of their lives under water then, for a brief moment, rise to the surface and become airborne. They lay their eggs on the water and then die. Each species lives under water in a unique manner, swims to the surface in a very special way, lays its eggs uniquely, and looks different after falling to the surface to die. All of this demands that the trout fisherman know a little about these insects. You don't have to speak Latin or be able to name the genus of every insect—but you should know if it's a caddis, a stonefly, or a mayfly. It's not necessary that you know how to identify a Quill Gordon; if you can identify it as a little gray fly that can be imitated on a size 16 hook, you'll usually get the job done—if your presentation is right.

One of the best collectors of insects in a trout stream is an inexpensive soap dish—cut out the bottom, leaving a ¼-inch ledge around the side. Use hot glue or epoxy to glue the plastic screen to the ledge. To use, open the box, hold it in the stream, get the samples, and close the box.

Realize that no one ever got a heart attack from fighting a trout. It's not the battle that excites most of us who love this kind of fly fishing. It's solving all the problems and finally getting the fish to accept the offering that we love about trout fishing.

Trout are cold-water fish—for good reason. They'll die in the same waters that are comfortable for bass. Understanding how critical water temperature is to trout will help you catch more of them. While trout can live in exceeding chilly water, they do have a temperature range in which they feed more and are most active. The brook trout prefers the coldest waters of all continental U.S. trout—52 to about 56 degrees. Rainbows do well from about 55 to 60 degrees, while brown trout are probably the most active at 60 to 65 degrees. Trout will feed at temperatures below these, but the cooler it gets, the less they feed. They'll also feed more slowly when temperatures rise above the optimum. If the temperature gets too high, they die. Brook trout, for example, cannot survive long if temperatures reach above the mid-70s.

Why is this important to the fly fisherman? During the summer months, especially on small streams, the water temperature will often rise into the dangerous level for trout. Two things occur: The trout stop feeding, and they seek deep holes where the temperature is lower or migrate to spots where underwater springs bring cooler water into the stream.

What this means is that the best time to fish most smaller rivers and streams in midsummer is in the morning, when water temperatures are lower. Sometimes the temperature again drops into a good fishing range in late evening. A wise trout fisherman will carry a thermometer with him. Constantly check the stream's temperature. When it rises a few degrees above what's desirable for the species you seek, realize that you're probably going to do poorly. Then find a tailwater fishery or spring-fed stream that holds a more consistently low temperature.

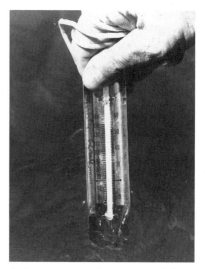

A thermometer is an essential tool for success—especially in trout fishing.

The Leader

In no other area of fly fishing is the leader more critical to success than trout fishing. You can catch bass, snook, and a host of other fish on a dozen different leader designs. For many fresh- and saltwater species, the leader is relatively unimportant as long as it allows you to throw the fly to the fish without alarming it. *But when you're trout fishing, your leader is as important (or more) as your selection of fly, the type of rod and line you use, and the cast you make.*

As I indicated earlier, there are basically two types of leaders. One remains taut most of the time so you can manipulate the fly. *But in much of trout fishing the leader is designed* not *to manipulate the fly, but to allow the fly to drift naturally in the current.* This is an important factor to understand when you're pursuing trout. If the leader pulls on the fly while it drifts, the fly will swim unnaturally, and most of the time trout will ignore it. Instead you need a leader with a special taper. Leaders can be hand-tied, and you should learn how so that you can make or modify your own. *However, some manufacturers today make tapered dry-fly leaders that are really better than you can build yourself.* If you fish where there's a great deal of underwater vegetation, then a commercial knotless, continuously tapered leader may prevent you from picking up this plant life and possibly losing a good fish.

The Dry-Fly Leader

Most trout fishermen want leaders that will cast dry flies properly. Such leaders may be as short as 6 feet, or as long as 18. The most useful are those 7½, 9½, or 12 feet in length. Many commercial leaders don't have a large-enough-diameter butt section *that's also long enough.* Other hand-tied commercial leaders have a butt section made of stiff or hard monofilament. If you review the section "Leaders" in chapter 3, you'll see that I feel a stiff butt on any tapered leader is the wrong concept. When you cast, your fly line unrolls toward the target until it reaches the leader; at this point the better your leader continues to unroll, the better it will deliver the fly. Thus every leader needs flexible weight in its butt section. To properly construct a basic dry-fly leader, I use a butt section that's heavier and longer than has been recommended for years. For anyone who disagrees with this, all I ask is that you read what I'm about to explain and try it. think you'll find that these leaders turn over better and deliver a slack tippet better than any others you've ever used. When I build my own leaders I use limp monofilament, such as DuPont Stren Easy Cast, Berkley XL, o my favorite, Silver Thread. All of these monos are basic spinning lines. My favorite *tippet* material is Scientific Anglers clear mono. It has the prope limpness and high knot strength, and it has worked extremely well for me

I'd like to mention that there's no standard among manufacturers as to how a nylon's diameter relates to its strength. Line of the same pound tes can vary in diameter by several thousands of an inch. For example, I've miked 20-pound test that ranged from .017 to .024 inch. The average diam eter of 20-pound-test monofilament is about .019 inch.

One of the most highly touted formulas for a 9- to 10½-foot dry-fly leade has for decades called for a butt section of .017 inch—approximately 15 to 17-pound test. The butt section is about 10 inches long. In my view thi is entirely too thin, too short, and too lightweight. *Remember, what yo need in the butt section is enough flexible weight to cause the leader t continue to unroll toward the target.*

Here's my suggestion for the best dry-fly-type leader; I'll describe th popular 10½-foot length. If it sounds unusual to you, I suggest you eithe buy or make your own and test it—the results will surprise you. Remem ber, for best results you should construct your leaders with monofilamen that's all the same brand, and high-quality, limp spinning line is a goo choice. *The butt section should be from monofilament approximatel .022 inch in diameter, or about 25-pound test.* **The butt section shoul be about half the length of the entire leader.** Make the butt section fo a 10½-foot dry-fly leader 5 feet long. (For a 12-foot leader, I suggest a 6-foo butt section.) Connect to this butt section 6 inches of 20-pound test (ap proximately .019 inch), then add 6 inches of 15-pound test (approximatel .017 inch). Add 6 more inches of 12-pound test (approximately .014 inch and to it tie another 6 inches of 8-pound test (approximately .009 inch) Connect about 18 inches of 4X, 5X, or 6X tippet (approximately .007 t .005 inch). Remember, if each segment is a few inches off, it won't matter And if you'd like a longer or shorter leader, use these lengths as basi guides and adjust each link accordingly. *Let me emphasize that a continu ously tapered commercial leader will work better than you trying to ti all these strands to the right lengths. I've stopped tying my own, since can use a commercial leader over and over, as I shall explain later.*

The most critical part of a trout leader is its tippet end, where the fly i attached. Remember, you need to cast accurately to where a fish is rising. I the tippet is too long or too thin, the fly will fall back on it; a too-long o too-thin tippet may give you a drag-free drift, but it can't give you accuracy If the tippet is too thick or too short, it will fall straight on the water. Dra will occur, and the trout will usually refuse the fly.

When you're casting where drag may spoil your dry-fly drift, drop the line over a rock to aid in getting a better drift.

Here's the single most important thing to know about using a leader when you're dry-fly fishing for trout: There must be a few gentle waves or curves in the tippet directly in front of the fly. If there are some waves, there will be no drag. But, once the tippet directly in front of the fly is straight, drag is almost sure to occur. Even though you may not see it, the trout will notice that the fly is floating unnaturally and refuse it.

The length of the tippet depends upon several factors: your casting skill, local fishing conditions, the line and rod you're using, the length of your leader, and—most important—the size and air resistance of your fly. A myth that has been floating around for years says that you can divide the size of the hook by 4 to determine which size tippet you need. For example, if you're using a size 12 fly, you'd need a 3X tippet. Nothing could be farther from the truth. Let's take two flies tied on identical size 12 hooks. As an example, we'll use a Catskill-tied Quill Gordon and a Humpy. The Quill Gordon is very sparsely tied and offers virtually no air resistance on the cast. The Humpy is a bulky, heavy fly for its size that offers considerably more resistance on the cast. There's no way that the tippets used for these two flies should be of the same diameter or length, despite their identical hook sizes.

Here's how you determine the right length and size of tippet for your casting skill and fly. Add a length of tippet material to your leader. Attach the fly and make several casts. If the fly falls back on itself in a crumpled mess, the tippet is either too thin or so long that it can't turn the fly over. While you'll get a drag-free drift, your accuracy will suffer. Clip off a section of tippet, reattach the fly, and cast again. If it still falls inaccurately and with many waves, repeat the process. When you get it right, the leader will fall straight toward the target area, creating soft waves a few inches across just in front of the fly. Later, if you switch to a smaller fly, you'll find that this tippet will fall straight because it's too thick or too short for this less air-resistant fly. You'll have to remove the tippet and repeat the process described above until the tippet again falls accurately with soft waves immediately in front of the fly.

Since commercial tapered leaders perform best when they're new, you don't want to destroy the taper. This is what you do when you repeatedly attach new tippets, which use up a portion of the leader with each knot you make. Instead, try this technique, which I've used successfully for years. Almost all continuously tapered leaders of less than 10½ feet have less than 24 inches of tippet. (If the leader is much longer, the tippet may extend to 24 inches, but rarely will it be longer.) Measure back 24 inches from the end of the tippet, cut it off, and discard it. Construct a nonslip loop knot in the end of a tapered leader. Properly constructed, this knot is stronger than the leader you tie it in. Then take a length of tippet material from a spool and build a nonslip loop knot in it. Connect the two loops with a square knot configuration. Now when you have to replace a tippet, all you need do is unloop the current tippet and add a new one with a nonslip loop. With this method, one commercial leader will serve you for many fishing trips. As the knot wears, simply clip if off the tapered section and install another one to get more service from the original tapered leader.

Much has been written about dry-fly leaders, and almost every experienced trout fisherman has strong opinions about which ones are best. The fact is, many leaders can be turned over well *if you can cast well.* The leaders I've suggested work well for both people who aren't good casters and those who are.

But what many fishermen fail to consider about making a delicate presentation to trout, especially with dry flies, is the weight of the fly line. They don't understand why on rough or fast water they can use a short leader, but on very calm water they need a much longer one. Experience has shown them that when casting below a riffle, the agitated water allows them to use leaders as short as 7 feet with dry flies. But when they fish a beaver pond, a limestone stream, or a similar slow-moving, quiet pool, it becomes necessary to switch to a much longer leader. Why is this?

The reason is that it's the impact of the fly line on the surface that frightens the fish—not the dry fly, which usually descends softly. If you fish many waters where there are calm pools, quiet surfaces, or wary fish, you can up your score by switching to lighter lines. I believe that a size 1 or 2 line is impractical. If you want to use one, have at it. But for most delicate dry-fly fishing situations, I feel that a size 3 fly line is the lightest (and the best) tool to use. You can get by with a size 4, but anything heavier, in my opinion, will reduce your chances of success. A size 3 line weighs 120 grains, while a 6-weight line weighs 160 grains. That's considerably more weight, and I believe it can affect your fishing. Some anglers question whether they can adequately cast dry flies with such a small line. Unless there is *excessive* wind blowing (so much that even a 6-weight line might give you trouble), you will be able to cast well with a 3-weight. Consider what a dry fly weighs and you'll realize that a 160-grain line can easily deliver your offering. *Incidentally, I've helped many novice dry-fly fishermen score better by selecting a line 1 size lighter than what their rod calls for.* This lighter line won't generate the same amount of force or speed as a perfectly matched one—hence you get a gentler presentation.

Fishing for Trout with Nymphs

Most of the time trout feed below the surface. While they eat minnows and larger creatures when they can, trout subsist largely on nymphs. Therefore, learning to fish nymphs properly will let you catch fish throughout the season (because you won't need to wait until a hatch occurs), and catch lots more fish than someone who casts only dry flies.

Two important factors should be immediately recognized when you begin nymph fishing. It is vital to have polarized glasses. These glare-reducing glasses allow you to better watch your leader or indicator during the drift. In many situations you'll be able to locate a fish and observe it while your nymph approaches; by measuring the fish's responses, you'll know when to set the hook. You must also recognize that you don't want to make your backcast the same way you would when fishing dry flies. Refer to the section "Casting Sinking Lines, Heavy Flies, and Weighted Leaders" in chapter 8; if you follow these instructions, you'll have fewer problems. While these two factors may not seem important, they form a foundation for good nymph fishing.

Basic Nymph Leaders

Nymph leaders can be as short as 2 or 3 feet and as long as 25 (for fishing *Chironomid* imitations in deep lakes). But in most nymph fishing you'll be working waters from 18 inches to no more than 5 feet deep—with an average depth of 2 to 4 feet. Leaders for nymphs should generally be much shorter than those for dry flies. One major reason is that you're often casting weighted nymphs, heavy Woolly Buggers, and the like. Also your leader may have attached to it an indicator, one or more nymphs, and split shot. The mission of a nymph leader is twofold: It must turn over well on the cast, and it must carry all of these attached items. *Once in the water, the tippet must be flexible enough to allow the nymph or nymphs to drift drag-free.* A factor often ignored by dry-fly fishermen is drag. It's just as critical a part of presentation when you're nymphing—maybe more so. Trout feed briefly on the surface, but most of their feeding occurs under water. *This makes them acutely aware of a presented fly that drags unnaturally. That's why the end of your nymph leader should be flexible enough to allow free drifting.*

If I had to use one leader for all my nymph fishing in flowing water, it would be as follows—and it's simple to make: I use about 4 feet of 20-pound test (approximately .022 inch) and about 2 feet of 12-pound test (approximately .015 inch). Since trout are not especially leader-shy, I then use a 1½- to 3-foot tippet of 6-pound test (about .005 inch). *This tippet length depends on water depth. It should be shorter in shallow water, longer in deeper streams.*

This leader allows me to turn over weighted nymphs, even with attached indicators and split shot. It works well in most river- and stream-fishing situations. On small streams I may shorten all the parts of the leader proportionally. On lakes, I use a much longer leader, as long as 12 to 14 feet—but I use the same proportions. If I fish on very clear, calm waters, where the fish are especially wary, I use a different leader for nymphs. I make the butt section from about 6 feet of 20-pound test, add about 4 feet of 12-pound and about 2 feet of 6-pound, then use a tippet of 1½ to 2 feet of 5X, or about 4-pound test. When I need a slow-sinking line, I use a clear line, such as the Scientific Anglers stillwater line. I've suggested this nymph leader system to help you realize that good nymph leaders must be relatively short, fairly heavy in diameter through much of their length (to carry the load required), yet have a supple, thin tippet at the fish's end.

There are a number of methods for fishing nymphs. They've been designed to meet different fishing conditions. You may thus need to make slight adjustments in the basic nymph leader; I'll explain these further in a moment.

Indicators

But before I discuss the different nymph-fishing methods, let me tell you about indicators. An indicator tells you when an unseen trout below the surface has accepted your nymph. All trout hold in the current and open their mouths to take in the nymphs that drift downstream to them. They can quickly detect the difference between a real insect and your imitation. Here's what happens when a trout takes your nymph: It allows your fly to enter its mouth for a very brief time. You must set the hook during this

A sure sign that a trout has taken your drifting nymph is when you can see the white of the inside of the trout's mouth—then it's time to strike!

time, before the fish expels it. It takes years of fishing experience to know the exact moment when you should set a hook. Fortunately, if you understand indicators, you can quickly learn when to set the hook.

Indicators are actually little bobbers. They're miniature versions of the bobbers used by catfish and panfish anglers. They have to be small so you can cast them with a fly rod, and so they won't splash hard enough on the surface to alert the trout. Yet they must also be visible to you. In some cases they act like a bobber, supporting a weighted fly or leader. You can see that you'll need different indicators for different fishing situations.

Many types of indicators exist, but a few words of caution might help you make your selection. It has been my experience, especially in the air-clear waters of New Zealand (as well as other clear waters where trout are pursued frequently), that brightly colored indicators and larger bobber-type indicators of plastic, balsa, or cork will cause refusals. In such situations the best indicator is often a dry fly, just buoyant enough to float the nymph correctly. A good rule is to use the most subtle indicator you can— the one with the softest impact on the water. *However, when you're using heavily weighted nymphs, what's most important is that the indicator be able to support the nymph—or it'll be drowned.* Indicators that can be adjusted along the leader's length are more useful than those permanently attached. There will be times when you need to move the indicator up or down the line to cause your nymph to drift at the right depth. When using yarn of any type (generally my favorite indicator), use a slip knot; this is

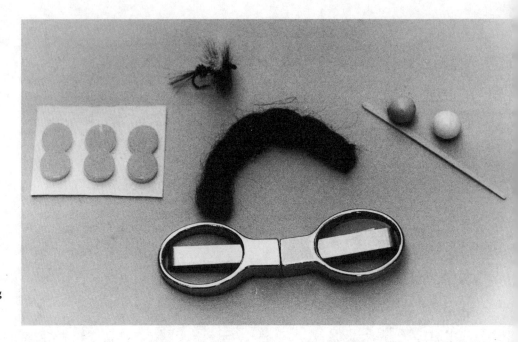

Indicators used when nymph fishing. Top: dry fly. Center, left to right: buoyant plastic tabs, buoyant yarn, and small floating balls (with a toothpick to hold the ball in place on the leader).

quick and easy to tie, but can be opened to let you adjust the yarn on the leader. Another factor to consider when selecting indicators is color. Most commercial indicators are offered in several colors. You'll discover that under different fishing conditions, some colors will show much better than others. While you may not think it, black is often a super color. *What I recommend is that you attach two pieces of yarn, one black and another of a bright, contrasting color, even white. Such a combination of colors seems to show up well under almost all light conditions.*

Indicators serve another purpose: They let you drift your fly where you want it to go. By studying the currents and then casting your indicator to a point where it will drift your fly right where you want it, you can more effectively present the fly to the trout. This is an important point many fly fishermen don't recognize. So indicators have three functions: They allow the fly to be drifted naturally, they help you see the strike, and they permit you to drift the fly where you want.

When you fish an indicator, don't try to fish your fly—*instead fish the indicator.* Throughout the drift concentrate—and I mean *concentrate*—on the indicator. Remember, too, that the water on the bottom of the stream is flowing more slowly than that at the surface. The bottom offers resistance as water flows over it, slowing the current. Either cast so that your fly lands slightly downstream of the bobber—which can then catch up—or add split shot to counter the indicator's upward pull on the fly. You want the indicator to drift a little slower than the surface current. An easy way to check this is to watch any foam near the indicator (which will be drifting at the same speed as the surface). If the indicator and foam are traveling at the same rate, then your indicator is moving too fast for the nymph below, which is in a slower current. Add either a little more split shot or weight to the tippet, or mend the indicator upstream.

In most nymphing situations I like to attach the indicator about one and a half times farther up my leader than the water is deep. Since a stream bottom is not perfectly level, an indicator at this position will keep the fly somewhere near the bottom, which is what you want. *When I fish turbulent waters, I'll often put two or three bright indicators along my leader; I prefer yarn for this. When one of them is hidden by the roughened surface, I can still see the other.* When you're fishing in lakes, where you may use a leader of 20 to 25 feet, set the indicator at the depth at which you want your fly to suspend. In this case the fly is used as both bobber and indicator.

Beneath the indicator is a fly, and often a weight. The weight needs to be adjustable to suit different current flows and fishing conditions. Many times a slight change in the amount of weight can mean the difference between getting a drag-free drift and swimming the nymph at the current's height in the water column. One of the first things to do if you know trout are seeing your nymph and ignoring it is adjust your weight.

Three basic types of weight are used on nymph leaders. The most common is split shot. A split shot is nothing more than a lead ball with a slot in the middle. The leader is slipped into the slot, and the ball squeezed shut to grip the tippet. Many times attaching the split shot just above a leader knot will help it to stay where you want it. Split shot vary in size from those so tiny they're nearly impossible to see to others a little larger than a BB. Most fishermen buy a small container that carries a variety of sizes so they can select what they need.

Another favorite weight for nymph leaders is twist-on lead. This is a lead strip resembling a narrow ribbon. Select a short length and twist it on the

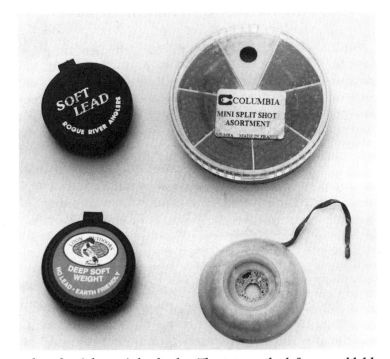

Several examples of weight to sink a leader. The two on the left are moldable putty; on the upper right is split shot. The lower right is flat lead.

---

leader. If you need more weight, simply add some more. Twist-on allows you to easily add or remove weight.

Another very adjustable weight is lead putty, a moldable putty that contains either lead or—better—heavier tungsten dust. To use, pinch off a hunk and mold it around your leader tippet at the desired place. It's easy to remove or add a little of this material to the leader.

Popular Methods of Fishing Nymphs

THE UPSTREAM DEAD-DRIFT METHOD

This is perhaps the most popular method of fishing nymphs. The nymph is cast upstream, or upstream and across. This method works best in water that's less than 3 feet deep; this is close-quarters combat. You rarely fish more than 25 feet away. Streams that flow from slow to moderately fast are best, although once you master this technique you can do well in faster water, too. Normally, you don't fish blind: You either see the fish you want to catch or drift your fly over the water where you feel a trout may be holding. It's target fishing. This is perhaps the best technique to use on small brooks and streams.

I prefer to fish with a small amount of weight built into my nymph—enough to let me make the cast and allow my fly to sink to the desired depth. If the current is a little too fast or too deep, I'll add a small amount of split shot or twist-on lead. Try not to cast your fly line over the fish, and, if possible, position yourself off slightly to one side of it, so neither line nor leader falls over the fish when you cast. The general-purpose nymph leader works fine for this fishing. On smaller streams I use a leader of no more than 7 feet, but on moderate to larger streams I like a 9- to 10-footer. I prefer a rod of 8½ to 9 feet, since I can use this longer length to maneuver my fly. The tuck cast is invaluable for this fishing: It allows the nymph to fall downstream from the leader and sink quickly. Since you're close to the trout, you need to get your fly down to them fast. As soon as your fly sinks to the desired depth, raise your rod as the line drifts back downstream to control any slack. Intently watch the indicator or the end of your line. If it pauses at all, set the hook. When you're using this dead-drift technique you may stand in one position and make a dozen or more fan casts so that your drifting nymph covers every possible pocket of water that might hold a fish. Using a reach cast can often help you get a drag-free drift.

THE HIGH-STICK METHOD

This method is deadly in faster water such as riffles or just below them. Many people refer to it as pocket-water nymphing, because you're fishing at very close range in rough, tumbling water. This water will hold many trout—and often big ones. The currents that swirl around rocks create whirlpools that briefly catch nymphs and other underwater creatures, 'orming a trap where the trout can easily feed. The trick is to get your nymph quickly through the swift, turbulent water and allow it to swirl down there drag-free. Rarely will you cast more than 12 or 15 feet. Your leaders should range from 7 to 9 feet in length, and *you try to keep most of the fly line out of the water.* Generally, several split shot are attached to make the nymph dive quickly. Because you're using the leader and a little line, long rods are best; I favor a 9-footer. Hold the rod aloft (hence the term *high-sticking*) with the leader dangling into the water. *Since usually only the leader is on the water,* you must intently concentrate on it, noting even the slightest pause or twitch. This is one type of nymph fishing in which you don't need an indicator. Because the nymph may swiftly pass by the trout, or the fish may not see it, make repeated casts to the same spot, each time moving the cast a little to either side. The technique is simple; the problem is learning to recognize when a trout has accepted your nymph.

You may think that fishing within a feet few of a trout will cause it to refuse your nymph. But the water is turbulent here, so if you move slowly and carefully, you can take fish consistently with the high-stick method.

THE WEIGHTED-NYMPH METHOD

It was on a stream in New Zealand years ago that I learned it's sometimes inadvisable to place weight on a leader. New Zealand, Argentina, and Chile have the clearest streams I've ever fished. Some of these waters are so clear they appear to have no water in them. When you fish a long, quiet, deep pool of such water, the fish have lots of time and opportunity to detect anything unnatural—such as your drifting nymph imitation.

You have several problems to solve when you find wary trout in quiet, deep pools of exceptional clarity. First, a heavy fly line falling to this water is like a stone thrown at a glass window. A light line without split shot or heavy indicators is called for. Bright indicators also are noticed, so subtle ones are best—my favorite for this is yarn or a dry fly. You need a long leader. I favor one from 12 to 14 feet in length, and this is one time when a very light tippet is advisable. Use the lightest tippet you feel comfortable with; the best results are obtained with numbers 5X to 7X. Nymphs that feature natural, flexible movement will do better for you, with their more lifelike appearance.

But here's the most important point: I don't use shot on my leader. And here's why: When fishing out of Dick Fraser's Cedar Lodge on the South Island of New Zealand, I cast an unweighted Gold-Ribbed Hare's Ear with a split shot a foot above the fly onto two successive pools. In each pool I could clearly see a big trout throughout my nymph's drift. As the split shot and fly approached, the trout simply moved to one side. After the rig had passed, it returned to its holding spot. So I rested each pool for half an hour and then tried the same fish, but using a nymph tied with built-in weight. Both fish slowly moved to the fly and inhaled it. Subsequent tests have convinced me that given ultraclear conditions and smart trout, dangling split shot served as a warning to the fish. Since that time I've used weighted nymphs without split shot in such conditions—and my score has upped considerably.

I use three different amounts of weight in my nymphs. On the ones that are very heavily weighted I tie off the head with black thread. Medium weighted nymphs I finish with a dark brown head. Lightly weighted nymphs get a tan head. *This way I can look in my fly box and know instantly which fly to select.* While I believe that unweighted flies, with split shot on the leader at least a foot away, act livelier in the water, there are times when you'll need a weighted nymph.

THE HINGED-LEADER METHOD

This nymph-fishing method works best where the bottom is level and the water averages the same depth; from 2 to 4 feet deep is perfect. The method is especially effective when the fish are spooky and you need to make a careful drift. It requires a very different type of leader: Start with a 3-foot butt section of 20-pound test (approximately .018 inch); add about 2 feet of 12-pound-test (about .014-inch) monofilament. Then determine the depth of water you'll be fishing, and add about that amount of 5X to 7X tippet.

Attach an indicator where the tippet joins the 12-pound section. Usually, you'll be fishing slick water, so a subtle indicator is called for. My two favorites are a buoyant dry fly and yarn. I favor using two colors of yarn at the same time; one of them is bound to contrast with the surface and be easier to see.

While you can blind-fish with this method, I prefer, when possible, to locate the fish before casting. Throw the nymph well upstream from the fish. The heavier portion of the leader will float on the surface, while the 5X to 7X tippet hangs vertically down in the water. If the leader won't float well, try greasing it with some line dressing. In effect the heavy portion of the leader is like a long bobber. I like to dress all of the leader except the tippet with a paste fly flotant. With this method, by adjusting your casts, you can cover every inch of the water.

THE FRANK SAWYER METHOD

Frank Sawyer, the originator of the Pheasant Tail Nymph, was a legendary angler. He developed a nymphing method on the chalk streams of England that is deadly, but does require seeing the fish and accurate casting.

You should use a light fly line (my favorite is a 3-weight) and a long leader—about 10½ to 13 feet. The water should be calm and clear enough that you can watch the fly during the drift. I prefer to use a weighted nymph, but some anglers use a nymph and a split shot. I find my accuracy suffers when I attach a split shot in addition to the nymph.

Locate a fish; it's especially helpful to find one that's obviously feeding ("on the fin," the English call it). Make your cast far enough upstream that he fly will drift down to the trout at its height in the water column. If your fly is slightly above the trout, you'll often get a take. However, trout apparently don't see nymphs drifting well below them. The keys to this technique are to get the fly to drift at the same level in the water as the trout—and to be aware when the fish takes.

Whenever you're nymph fishing and can see the trout, wait until your fly is near the fish, then strike if the fish moves up or sideways. One of the best hints is seeing the white inside the fish's mouth—a sure sign that it has opened its mouth to grab your fly.

THE LEISENRING LIFT METHOD

A method that's somewhat similar to the Frank Sawyer yet distinctly different is the Leisenring lift. The first difference is the position you fish from. With the Sawyer method you generally fish from slightly downstream of the trout. *Using the Leisenring lift technique, you should be slightly upstream.* You must also be able to clearly see the fish during your presentation. The method works best where the waters move slowly enough that you can see the trout well. You don't want an extra-long leader; you need to monitor your fly during its drift. Make your cast upstream of the trout and drop your rod tip low to the water. Follow the leader and line as they move downstream. Try to allow the fly to drift drag-free toward the trout. When the fly is close to the fish stop the rod's motion; the current, pushing on the leader and fly, will cause the nymph to start rising. This nicely imitates a nymph ascending from the bottom to the surface. Ideally, the upward swing of the nymph will have it rising just in front of the fish. If you time this swing perfectly, few trout can resist a nymph that literally heads for its mouth.

The Sawyer and Leisenring lift methods are just as effective when you're fishing soft-hackle or wet flies. Because caddis use an air bubble to blast them to the surface when they leave the bottom to become winged flies, the Leisenring method is especially deadly during a caddis hatch.

Tips for Fishing Nymphs

1. Know what kinds of nymphs are in the water you're fishing. Examining rocks and debris on the bottom will tell you.
2. Knowing where a trout is can mean a higher success rate. To do this you need to be able to see the fish.
3. Wear good polarized glasses. Frequently tilting your head one way or the other will eliminate even more glare from the surface.
4. A hat with a dark underbrim will allow you to see better. Be sure the hat doesn't contrast your surroundings (wearing a bright yellow hat on a green, wooded stream will tip off the trout).
5. Learn to *look at the bottom* and not at the surface. It's a trick many anglers never learn.

When you're on larger waters, it greatly helps to have someone at a higher elevation point out to you where the fish are. Here the Argentinean guide directs the angler.

6. Watch for "moving windows," which will allow you to see better. A moving window is a flat, calm, small portion of the surface that drifts with the current. In broken water, locate a moving window and let your eyes rove with it. The calm flat, surface, even in riffles, will let you see fish you otherwise couldn't.

7. Have a buddy locator. Position a companion in an elevated place where he can direct your casts to the fish.

8. Be aware of the sun's angle. You can see so much more if the sun is slightly behind and to one side of you. Also, peer into the water where dark trees or a stream bank rise up. This eliminates much sky glare.

9. If you have a choice, select a stream bottom against which it's easier to see the trout. For example, light gravel, sand, or a continuous brightly colored bottom are preferable to a weedy or rock rubble bottom.

10. When you're fishing alone and locate a feeding trout, find an object near the fish you can identify before you move to your casting position. This will allow you to more accurately present your fly.

11. When approaching the fish try not to wade too fast. This forces shock waves through the water that will alcrt the fish. *The slower the current is moving, the slower you must wade.*
12. Get into the correct position before casting. Remember, each successive cast reduces your chances.
13. Never cast fly line over a fish and, if possible, never allow your leader to drift over one. Whenever possible get into a position such that you can cast off to one side, preventing the leader from passing over fish.
14. If the trout have been fished over a lot or you're not having much luck, try using smaller nymphs. Often switching from a size 12, 14, or 16 to a size 20, 22, or even 24 will turn the trick on difficult fish.

Recommended Nymphs

There are thousands of nymph patterns. How do you select what you need? Fortunately, you don't need boxfuls. On most streams, sizes 12 through 22 will serve you well. Remember, presentation is what's most important. Getting the nymph down to the level of the trout, allowing it to drift drag-free, and knowing when to set the hook are the keys to nymphing for trout. Next in importance is lifelike action. I favor nymphs that look alive in the water. Exact imitations, often tied with hard, unyielding materials, have been poor producers for me. I'm also convinced that most nymphs should be tied both with and without beadheads. There are times when a beadhead imitation will catch drastically more fish than the same pattern minus that head; often, I think, this is because the beadhead gets the nymph down deeper. Manipulated gently, beadheads will also imitate the action of a lead-head jig, and this sometimes increases your hookups. Regardless, I am sold on beadheads. *If you tie your own, or when you buy them, I urge you to use beadhead nymphs tied on hook shanks slightly longer than normal.* I'm also never without a few nymphs tied with peacock herl.

Here's a list of my favorite nymphs. All have produced well for me in New Zealand, Chile, Europe, the United States, and many other waters:

Gold-Ribbed Hare's Ear
LaFontaine Sparkle Pupa
Prince Nymph
Pheasant Tail
Zug Bug
Whitlock's Squirrel Tail
Muskrat Nymph
Yellow Stone Fly

I carry all these patterns in sizes 10 through 22; I prefer to slightly weight each of them.

Wet-Fly Fishing

Much of what I've said above about fishing nymphs can easily be said of wet flies. Many of the special techniques used for fishing nymphs also apply to wet. However, most people fish wet flies down and across the stream. I have no way to prove this, but I suspect that the first flies fished for trout were wets used in what's generally referred to as the wet-fly drift or swing.

Before I describe their fishing techniques, let me briefly discuss wet flies themselves. There are two basic types: those with a rather stiff wing (the Leadwing Coachman is a good example; it has a herl body and a duck wing), and those we now refer to as soft-hackle flies. These latter flies usually have skimpy bodies and a soft hackle wound at the front that waves and undulates in the water during the drift. If I had to choose between the two, I'd opt for soft-hackle flies, although the older and more conventional wet flies have caught thousands of trout—and will continue to do so. The reasoning is that wet flies and soft-hackle flies represent drowned insects and nymphs emerging to the surface, respectively.

The wet-fly drift or swing is easy to do. A floating line is generally used. Leaders range from 7½ to 10 feet in length. A rod at least 8½ feet is preferable, since you'll often mend the line. Make your cast slightly down and across the stream. The currents will immediately begin pushing on the line, forming a belly. The larger the belly that develops, the faster your wet fly or soft-hackle will speed through the water. To slow down your fly you can mend the line upstream, or lift some of it from the surface during the drift. There's no one best speed for all fishing conditions; you must experiment and determine what's the best speed for the current conditions. The belly actually controls the drift speed of the fly, and it also helps you set the hook. Many anglers add split shot to obtain the proper drift level.

Most wet-fly fishermen use more than one fly, and it's not unusual to have three flies attached. Generally, the heaviest or largest fly is located at the end of the tippet (called the point). The other flies are located a foot or so apart. One advantage of fishing several flies is that it allows you to offer the trout variety in both size and color. *Important—if you tie more than one fly to your leader, be sure that the section you use to tie in the extra fly (or flies) is no longer than the width of a man's hand, once the fly is attached.* If you make it longer, it will frequently tangle during casting. The easiest way to attach extra flies is to join two sections of tippet with either a blood or a surgeon's knot. Trim one end; use the other tag end to attach the fly.

Recommended Wet Flies and Soft-Hackles

Most wet flies are dressed on size 12 through 16 hooks, but occasionally a size 10 or 18 will turn the trick. Here are some favorite wet flies of mine:

Leadwing Coachman
Royal Coachman

March Brown
Alder
Black Gnat

My favorite soft-hackle flies are:

Partridge and Yellow
Partridge and Green
Partridge and Orange

There are three flies that most experienced trout fishermen carry—two of which they often seem ashamed to use, but they are deadly in many areas. The more popular of these "ashamed-to-use" flies is the Glo Bug or Egg Fly. This is a round fly, tied on a very short-shanked hook to resemble a drifting fish egg. It's most commonly tied with gift yarn, but materials that are translucent are often more effective. For example, an Egg Fly tied with Antron will often outfish the same pattern made from yarn. There are also "Egg Balls," which have tiny sticks of Mylar protruding; these certainly work. Some fly fishermen use a Double Egg: two round egg imitations on the same hook shank. Regardless, almost all species of trout and salmon will fall for the Egg Fly.

Another fly many people don't like to admit using, but usually carry, is the San Juan Worm. This is simply a sticklike piece of yarn, usually tied on an English-style bait hook. The fly represents many of the worms that trout feed on and comes in several colors; bright red or orange is the most popular choice. When all else fails, desperate anglers will reach for a San Juan Worm or an Egg Fly.

Three flies that assure trout fishermen a good catch are the Green Weenie (top), the Egg Fly (bottom left), and the San Juan Worm.

While it's not as effective in the rivers of the western United States, another fly you should always carry is the Green Weenie. This is simply an inchworm imitation. In the Mid-Atlantic area in late spring or early summer, millions of these green fluorescent worms lower themselves from branches on silken strands. They fall into streams in uncounted numbers, where trout gorge on them. Perhaps because they're so brightly colored, they imprint strongly on a trout's brain. Whatever the reason, though, you can catch trout from early spring through late fall on this exceptionally effective fly. It's usually tied on a 2X-long, size 10 or 12 hook. There are some variations, but the basic tie involves winding chenille or another body material the length of the shank, then tying off. Like the Egg Fly, it's simple to tie. If you live east of the Mississippi I urge you to carry a few of these for those days when trout refuse your other offerings.

More than any other fish I've taken on a fly, the trout seems to prefer coming up behind a streamer and nipping at its rear. For this reason I often employ a stinger hook in my patterns. Place the hook in the vise and, with 10-pound-test mono, secure at its rear a regular-shanked stinger hook slightly smaller in size. I tie the stinger hook so that it rides up. I've taken many trout because they nipped my fly and the stinger caught them. Study the photo below to see how the stinger hook is positioned.

If trout fishermen were limited to a single underwater fly, almost all experienced anglers would choose the Woolly Bugger. This fly resembles both none and many of the creatures that trout feast upon. The Woolly Bugger is a variation of the Woolly Worm—it is a Woolly Worm with a tail. It's dressed on long-shanked hooks from as small as size 12 up through size 1/0.

It can be fished as quickly as a streamer, dead-drifted, and worked as you would a wet fly or even as a nymph. For me, the best retrieval method for really big trout is the fast strip. I cast the fly above and across from the trout and then bring it back with a series of fast line strips, which make it look like it's trying to flee the trout. I've caught many fish in both fresh and

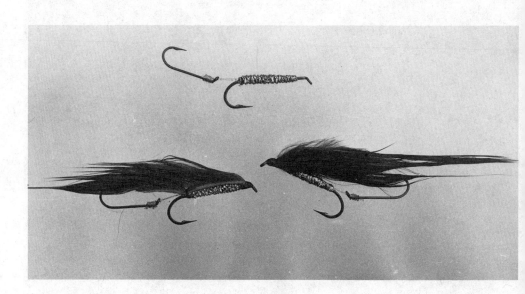

Freshwater trout often nip or strike at the rear of a fly. To catch those "nippers" attach a "stinger" hook, as shown in the rear of the streamer fly here.

When you're using woolhead or deer hair flies, you must often use up fishing time to get the wool or hair wet enough so the fly sinks well. To avoid wasting time, presoak the fly in a Zip-Loc bag before you fish it.

salt water on the Woolly Bugger. In smaller sizes, for example, it's deadly on bonefish. It can be tied in several ways: unweighted, weighted lightly with wire, or weighted with bead-chain or lead eyes. Woolly Buggers are also dressed with beadheads and coneheads of various metals, including very heavy tungsten.

The basic dressing is a marabou tail and a chenille body, over which is spiraled a soft neck hackle. The most popular Woolly Bugger is perhaps the version with an all-black tail and body, plus a grizzly hackle. Not far behind is the all-chartreuse model. However, bodies of tan, brown, and a combination of yellow and black are also favored. Another body material that's becoming very popular is Cactus Chenille. A Woolly Bugger tied with this Mylar chenille is often called a Krystal Bugger. *I am convinced that the most effective Woolly Bugger has a black marabou tail, a fat body of twisted strands of peacock herl, and a grizzly hackle.*

Fishing with Dry Flies

Before I discuss how to fish for trout with dry flies, I urge you to reread "The Dry-Fly Leader" beginning on page 215. My favorite fly line for dry-fly fishing is a weight-forward size 3. If there's considerable wind I'll switch to a weight-forward size 6.

Several trends have emerged in the past few years concerning improving the fly fisherman's score with dry flies. One is that more and more smaller flies are being cast. For years the standard sizes were 12 through

16. Today, few anglers use dry flies of size 12 or larger, except under specific conditions. *More size 16 through 24 flies are now in use, and they do pay off.*

The second dry-fly trend is a shift away from using the conventional-style dry fly—one with the hackle wound on the front in order to support the fly. Observe a mayfly on the water and you'll note that it lies with its belly in contact with the surface. Dry flies constructed so that their bellies lie on the surface draw more strikes from trout than the conventionally tied fly that stands on its tiptoes. If you're working trout that have been fished hard and become wary, I suggest you try using some of the following patterns, all of which sit with the belly of the fly on the surface:

Paradun
Thorax tie
Parachute tie
No-hackle
Haystack tie

Another bonus when you tie these flies is that you don't need grade-A dry-fly necks, which are very expensive.

Finally, for many years we fished mainly overstocked trout—which often took patterns imitating hatchery food pellets better than insect imitations. But that has changed. Much of the change is due to Trout Unlimited and Federation of Fly Fishers, whose memberships have convinced resource managers charged with trout fisheries to allow for natural trout reproduction wherever feasible. This (along with budget cuts for hatcheries) has created a new fishery. Departments of natural resources are finally recognizing that what counts is not how many pounds of fish per acre reproduce, but how much *quality* recreation they can create. Coupled with this is the wise and ever-growing practice of catch-and-release.

All of this means that the fish and the fishing have changed. *We no longer have lots of hatchery fish that don't know the difference between a mayfly and a food pellet. Instead, trout are born in streams and learn from birth to feed on what's naturally available. After being hooked, landed, and released, they become smarter.* Today's trout fishermen have to be better anglers to fool these fish. Thus they use lighter lines, and are more careful with their casts. The use of smaller flies that I noted above is often necessary, too. One good reason for using smaller flies is that they make it a little easier to deceive trout with something that's not a very close imitation.

Consider the flies recommended in books written two decades or longer ago by Bergman, McClane, Leonard, and others. Very few of those patterns are in use today. During the past 20 years vastly new materials have become available and both fly-fishing and fly-tying skills have increased tremendously. This has resulted in far better imitations of the natural insects to use in different situations. Older patterns were often suggestive of an insect;

When you're fishing on flat, calm, clear water, it's imperative to use long leaders and a lighter fly line.

many of the popular modern patterns closely resemble various insects. Even what we used to call "attractor" patterns have changed. Witness the Madame X, Chernobyl Ant, and Turck's Tarantula, which look like nothing I ever saw on a trout stream. Yet these rubber-legged patterns can often fool fish that have refused even the best of imitations.

Not too long ago we could successfully cast almost any small fly when a hatch of midges was on the water. No longer. We now must present much more realistic midge patterns. Emergers are now an important type of pat-

Three flies to carry on days when trout are refusing your offers, or when you can't get a big trout to take your fly, are the Turck's Tarantula (top), the Chernobyl Ant (bottom left), and the Madame X.

tern to carry. You don't need a host of them, but you do need a few, dressed on small hooks. Spinners weren't very effective years ago, but that may have been because most were tied with hackle-tip wings; when wet, these usually disappeared into a thin quill shape. Today, though, we have a number of materials to tie spinners with; they float well, are transparent, and give a good impression of outstretched wings lying on the surface. I consider John Betts to be one of the most innovative fly tiers in the world today. John is hung up on synthetics (thank God). At first I looked askance at some of the stuff he used in his flies, such as Z-Lon. But it makes wonderful wings on mayflies and caddis. His Crinkle Z-Lon is one of my favorite materials for tails, spinner wings, and trailing shucks. I could go on. But if you're a traditionalist who hasn't investigated many of these new materials, you need to.

Having said all this, what I'm about to add may seem like a contradiction. But if I was limited to a single dry fly (and I certainly hope I never am), it would be a Parachute Adams with an upright wing of pearl-colored Krystal Flash. Tied in various sizes and presented well, I believe this fly will catch more trout in more places than any other pattern I've used. Certainly you'll need other patterns from time to time. But don't leave home without this one.

To be able to see a dry fly is a tremendous advantage. This is a major reason why most fly fishermen never cast a dry fly farther than they can see it well. Unseen dry flies often result in missed strikes when the trout takes

Dress your flies well before the season so you don't have to do it on the stream.

your offering. For this reason it's important, whenever possible, to build into your dry flies something that will allow you to see them well. I would also include terrestrials in this statement, since so many terrestrial flies float *in* the surface film and are more difficult to see than dry flies, which float *on* the surface. Many tiers are thus now including wings of bright materials in their dry flies and terrestrials. In some situations, such as fishing a fly where there's glare on the water, *a black wing is better.* Bright-colored paint is used on some terrestrials, such as on the back of a beetle or an ant. A bright fluff of yarn attached to the back of a terrestrial will also let you see it at a long distance. Once, when I was making a film on the Bow River in Alberta, my cameraman wanted me to use a fly bright enough to be seen clearly on film. I tied up some dry flies with fluorescent pink wings that looked like nothing ever seen on the water. Yet when I made good presentations, fish took them readily. Of all the materials I've experimented with, pearl-colored Krystal Flash has best helped me see my dry flies. I got the idea from George Harvey, who some years ago handed me some Trico Spinners whose spent wings were tied from this material. He said I'd be able to see them better than the conventional yarn-winged Tricos. He was right, and the fish seemed to like them as well as any other imitations. The following year I fished the Green River, where the trout were taking small midges. My patterns were so hard to see that I missed many takes. Then I

Some methods of improving the fisherman's sight of the fly on the water (left to right): a Krystal Flash wing, a white calf tail wing, a brightly dyed feather, orange paint, and a bright tuft of yarn.

Small dry flies are hard to see; the smaller they are and the older the angler, the more difficult this becomes. If you tie your own, you can make flies much easier to see by forming the wing from a strand or two of Krystal Flash. This material of twisted Mylar reflects light at all angles.

remembered that I'd tied a few midges whose wings were made from a strand of pearl Krystal Flash. As far as I could cast them, they were still easily visible. Krystal Flash is a strand of spiraled Mylar. *Because of these spirals it didn't matter what angle the fly was floating at—some portion of the twisted Krystal Flash reflected light back to me.* Now I use this trick for many of my smaller patterns. Here's how I use it to tie a parachute fly, for instance: Simply double a strand of Krystal Flash several times. Tie it in as you would any other wing material. Pull it upright, make the post, and let it be. Then finish the fly. When the fly is complete, clip the Krystal Flash strands projecting above the body to the correct height, and you have a fly that almost anyone can see—even at 45 feet or more.

Some General Rules of Dry-Fly Fishing

1. Use the lightest-weight fly line that you can handle well.
2. Straighten all coils from your line and the leader. Never use rubber to straighten a leader—it damages and weakens the monofilament. Draw the leader through a firmly clenched hand to remove coils.
3. Perhaps the most important factor in deceiving trout into taking your dry fly is that most of the time the fly must float drag-free—or naturally with the current. *If you don't have several small waves in the leader directly in front of the fly, you'll almost always get drag.*
4. Never get in the water if you don't have to. Water conducts sound approximately four and a half times faster than air.
5. If you must get in the water, wade as slowly as possible. Any visible waves that radiate more than 12 inches out from your boots mean you're probably wading too fast.
6. Make sure *all* of the fly line has been lifted from the water before you make your backcast. If any line remains on the water, it's being held by surface tension, and ripping it loose with your cast will create a disturbance that alerts trout. *This is a major reason why many people fail to catch trout with dry flies.*
7. When you lift your dry fly from the water, never false-cast over the trout. Two things occur if you do: You flush tiny droplets to the surface that alert a trout, and the fish may see your leader or line.
8. Never get in position to cast until you've determined whether you can make the cast and, if you hook the fish, whether you can land it from that position.
9. Instead of waterproofing your flies with dry-fly oil just before use, try applying it in the off season. This saves time and reduces any chance of leaving an oil residue on the water.
10. Use smaller flies when tempting harder-fished trout.
11. Use lighter leaders when working on very wary fish.
12. The clearer and calmer the water, the thinner or lighter your tippets should be.

The trout fisherman is doing it right here—keeping low so the fish doesn't see him while he casts to it. He also stays out of the water to reduce the chance of the trout hearing him.

13. With exceptionally difficult-to-catch trout, extend the tippet considerably. Often a tippet of a yard or two—or more—will turn the trick. You'll sacrifice accuracy, but you'll be able to get that fish-fooling drift.

14. When you're fishing with very small dry flies or midge pupae, it's advisable to grease the entire leader but only a little of the tippet, to prevent the leader from sinking and drowning your fly. A high-floating, greased leader also experiences less drag.

15. To check if your fly is drifting drag-free, cast it alongside some drifting foam. Fly and foam should have an identical drift—if not, make your tippet longer, or thinner.

16. If you're getting drag after a good cast, your leader tippet is probably too short or thick. Lengthen the tippet, or use a lighter, thinner one.

This angler is wisely staying low and downstream of the dam. Many trout will lie at the breast of a dam when feeding. By dropping his fly line across the rocks on the right side of the stream, he avoids getting line drag during the time his fly floats past the trout.

17. Trout face upcurrent—not upstream. When you approach an eddy, consider where the trout are holding and in what direction they're facing before casting your dry fly.
18. A trailing shuck on a dry fly often produces more strikes.
19. When you're fishing a hopper, don't cast it within inches of the bank—work it at least a foot away, so that fish lying under the bank will better see it. There's enough food in a hopper for a trout to move some distance to take it.
20. Wear clothes that match the background. On eastern wooded streams, olive or dark-colored clothing is advisable. On western rivers, where the banks may be lighter in color, khaki-colored clothing is best.
21. Don't wear bright, flashy tools that can reflect light to the trout.
22. Take your time before casting to rising trout. Unlike saltwater species, trout will usually continue to rise for some time. By carefully

observing a fish, you can determine exactly where it's taking the flies and what kind of flies it's eating—and often you can time its rises, too, so you can drop your fly just as the fish is coming up.

23. On smaller rivers most anglers fish from one bank. Instead, fish from the side that's usually ignored. Often this will produce higher catch rates for you.

24. Always get as close as you can before casting a dry fly. The shorter the distance you cast, the more accurate you can usually be. There's a bonus, too: Having less line on the water will reduce your problems with drag.

25. If you're in doubt as to what patterns are doing well on local streams, ask at a nearby fly shop. Of course, the shop personnel want to sell you flies, but most will sell you only what you need. They want you to come back, so they aren't going to sell you flies that don't produce.

26. Not always, but often, when a trout is taking flies off the surface a bubble will appear after the insect is taken. If after several rises no bubble appears, the fish may be taking nymphs or emergers.

27. When the surface is broken as a fish rises, don't throw at the ring. The trout will be forward of that ring. If you cast at it, your fly will fall downstream of the trout and remain unseen. What many anglers don't realize is how far forward the fish may be. *The depth of the water has much to do with how far ahead you should cast. If the trout rises in less than 2 feet of water, a cast that falls 2 or 3 feet in front of the ring will generally be right. But as the water deepens—depending upon where the trout is holding in the water column—you may need to cast much farther ahead. When in doubt, make it a rule to cast a little farther ahead than you think.*

28. When trout take your dry fly in slow-moving water, they tend to suck it in slowly, so you should delay your strike. But when a fish takes your dry fly in fast water it must get up there, grab the fly, and dive below before being swept away in the current. For this reason you should make it a general rule to strike slowly in slow water and faster in fast water. *However, if you're working over trout that have been fished hard and caught frequently, the rule is to strike as fast as you can. You'll miss some fish, but these pressured trout have learned to quickly eject an artificial dry fly.*

29. It's difficult to see trout when you look toward the sun. To better locate trout (or any fish), then, keep the sun over your shoulder, or look at water that's against a high bank or trees. These darkened areas will let you see through the water better.

30. Water flowing through a pool does not all flow at the same speed; there will be narrow channels of faster-flowing currents. These are what I call food highways. Insects drifting downstream are concentrated into these channels. It pays to start by fishing these swifter flows with dry flies, wets, nymphs, and streamers. To

identify these narrow, fast flows, look for thin lines of *flowing* foam. They'll clearly indicate where you should be offering your flies.

31. Most commercial leaders are good for basic dry-fly work. However, when you're fishing extra-small flies such as midges, it's often advisable to add extra tippet to ensure a good, drag-free drift.

32. Whenever possible, approach a trout stream from the sunny side— you can see the fish better, and they're less likely to see you.

The current doesn't flow at the same rate all through a pool; instead, there are narrow currents that travel much faster. These are what the author calls food highways—they transport most of the insects that come downstream. To recognize and fish these look for flowing, thin lines of foam.

An entire book could be written about how to catch trout on dry flies (indeed, several have been). What I propose to do here is boil down to the essentials: what you need to make a good presentation with a dry fly, followed by a hookup.

Successfully catching trout on dry flies requires the abilities to read the water, locate the fish, determine the correct leader-fly combination, and make an accurate cast that produces a drag-free drift. Sounds difficult as hell, and sometimes it is. Fortunately, most of the time all of the above can be accomplished with a little effort. First, realize that trout don't speak Latin and they don't have a computer for a brain. They have three basic needs: They want something to eat, somewhere to rest, and a safe haven from predators. If you use these three precepts to evaluate your dry-fly fishing—or any fishing, anywhere—you'll be on a straighter road to success.

Certainly, the more you know about entomology as it relates to fish foods and their habits, the better you can determine what a trout is currently eating. This will help you solve the perennial question of what flies you should use and how you should fish them. However, there are other indicators that will give you a good idea as well.

I can't emphasize enough how important presentation is. An experienced trout fisherman using the "wrong" fly pattern will probably catch more fish than one correctly matching the hatch. *Presentation, above all else, is vital to success! The single most important factor is that a dry fly should almost always float without drag. Since most trout feed in a small area, they know intimately the effects that current has on any drifting natural insect. A fish may not know all the currents in the pool, but it does know exactly the currents in the small area in which it feeds. Therefore, it's extremely important that any dry fly you offer a trout float as would a natural. More than anything else, this means that just in front of the floating dry fly there must be slack in the form of waves in the tippet. I try to get into my tippet undulating waves at least 3 or 4 inches across. So long as there's some slack immediately in the front of the dry fly, no drag will occur. This is the most important thing to know and master if you want to become a successful dry-fly angler. It can be accomplished by using the correct leader tippet, as I discussed earlier (see "The Dry-Fly Leader" beginning on page 215). You can also use a number of different casts (see chapter 8) to get that vital slack in the tippet.*

There are two types of insects you'll need to imitate: mayflies and caddisflies. While stoneflies are important in some areas and prevalent in others, most of the time you'll be imitating mayflies or caddis. As I mentioned earlier, many of the old standby patterns of years past are not as effective as these developed in the past decade. Flies whose bellies rest on the surface are usually more successful that those sitting on their hackle tips. Fly patterns that more closely imitate the body shape and wing of the natural will generally outfish older styles that were more suggestive. This is particularly true when fishing midges. Years ago any small fly would be accepted by trout. But fish are warier nowadays, and midge patterns that more closely imitate the tiny flies on the surface will do better. For example, some of the most successful hatching-midge patterns today have a noticeable wing case and a trailing shuck—something unthinkable not too long ago.

Some flies are called attractor patterns. For years, two of the most popular around the world have been the Royal Wulff and the Humpy. But experienced anglers are beginning to believe these were and are so effective because they imitate well a number of different species.

Dry flies with extended bodies are usually much more effective. John Betts was a pioneer in introducing many of the synthetics now used in various fly patterns. He was chastised for it at the time, but many synthetics are now recognized as superior to older and more natural materials. Insects that fail to get out of their husks represent to trout an easier prey than a fly that can lift off the surface and flee quickly. Because trout will often key on these bugs that are dragging their husks along, trying to free themselves, the trailing-shuck fly was developed. The early trailing-shucks consisted of materials tied at the rear of the hook and clipped off at the proper length. *Now it's recognized that, instead of clipping the material into a fat edge, you should twist the material and then tie both ends into the fly. This forms a shuck much like a closed horseshoe, which better imitates the natural shuck than a clipped square would.* This is only one indication of how we need to better imitate insects to fool these wiser trout. Older stonefly imitations worked, but they're no longer as effective; the new stimulator patterns represent a much better imitation.

A few attractor flies do work, especially when there's no hatch occurring. Several of these are tied with rubber legs and would have been scorned years ago by serious dry-fly fishermen. No more. They've saved the day for me and many others when no hatch is on. They're great to search the water with—they'll often show me a fish that won't hit, but that I can catch in another way. Occasionally, when trout are keying on a specific hatch, they'll ignore all your offerings (this often happens when midges are prevalent). Toss a much larger Madame X, Chernobyl Ant, or Turck's Tarantula among the tiny insects and frequently a fish will take it in preference to the actual living midges. Such patterns produce strikes from larger trout, too.

There are a few dry-fly patterns that I consider essential. They should be tied in sizes 12 through 22, *with most of them in sizes 16 or smaller.* If I had to fish with one dry fly the rest of my life it would be the Parachute Adams, and as I explained before, I'd tie the wing with pearl-colored Krystal Flash. In the proper size this fly can represent a host of mayflies that are dark in color. If lighter mayflies are on the water, such as sulfurs, I'd use a Parachute Light Cahill, again with a pearl Krystal Flash wing. I'd have two caddis patterns. To imitate caddis down to a size 16 or 18, I'd choose the Elk Hair Caddis. Still, there are a lot of microcaddis around, and the Elk Hair doesn't imitate these tiny insects the way I like. For caddis imitations smaller than 16, one made with a slender dubbed body, a hackle spiraled over the dubbing over the length of the body, and a wing of polypropylene is my choice. I think it's necessary to carry caddis imitations in several shades, from cream to light tan and dark gray.

Many streamborn trout can be better fooled by a fly whose body sits flush on the water, as I mentioned earlier. One of the best patterns for such fishing is the thorax fly. This is an excellent choice on calm water, where trout get a good view of every fly they may take.

The Griffith's Gnat is one of the older fly patterns I would never be without. It's as easy to tie as almost any dry-fly pattern. It imitates a host of smaller insects—even mayflies and caddisflies. It can also be tied as a cluster midge (essentially a Griffith's Gnat with a CDC wing). It can be fished floating nicely on the surface—or, if the hackle is clipped from the entire bottom of the fly, it does well as an emerger.

Wherever I've found trout, I've found ants, which trout seem to enjoy eating. A number of different materials are used to tie ant imitations. My favorite as a dry fly is the Deer Hair Ant popularized by one of the finest trout fishermen I ever met, George Harvey. When this fly falls to the water, there's a definite *plop* that seems to draw trout; they can recognize when a heavy ant falls to the surface. I prefer to tie a bright chartreuse feather on the top of the ant, since I have trouble seeing it in dim light. I also use dubbed fur ants in very small sizes—16 to 22. There are times when a tiny 20 or 22 fur ant will outfish anything on the water. (And incidentally, don't fail to carry a few cinnamon and black-colored sinking ants, too.)

The hopper is another fly I enjoy using. When a strong wind is blowing across some of the western rivers, the air is filled with hoppers, which then have the unlucky fate of being dropped on the water. One hopper represents a lot of protein to a trout, so an imitation will often pull a bigger trout from the depths that would ignore other dry-fly offerings. I once lay on the bottom of a stream and had someone toss live grasshoppers onto the surface. Every hopper that came by had its legs protruding through the water. For this reason I now use only hopper patterns that have legs. Yes, I've caught many trout on patterns without legs—but I have a greater measure of confidence when I fish hoppers with legs.

Also important is how you present a hopper. Fly fishermen often fish hoppers on streams that have grassy, undercut banks—but too many times they fish the hoppers tight against the banks. This can be a mistake. First, trout will move some distance to get a hopper. If a trout is lying back under the protective bank and you cast a fly tight against the bank, it may drift by unseen. Let me give you an example: If you stand at the front of an open garage and an airplane passes overhead, you can look up and see it. But step back into the garage and it's no longer visible. It's the same with a trout well back under the bank. Therefore, I suggest fishing your hoppers at least a foot away.

Where the water is rough and your dry flies might be drowned, I recommend using two patterns that have produced well for years: the Royal Wulff and the Humpy. Both of these flies stay on top even in very rough water. While they're attractor patterns, they belong in every trout fisherman's box of dry flies.

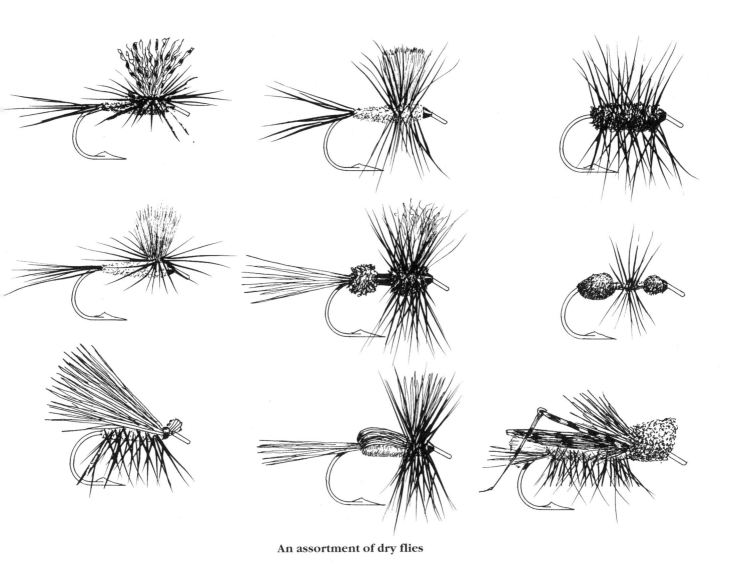

An assortment of dry flies

In a number of situations a two-fly presentation will outfish a single one. There are a number of reasons for this. By offering two sizes or patterns, you can vary your immediate selection. Also, when you combine a large dry with a much smaller one, the larger fly often acts as an attractor and brings a fish up. The trout sees the larger fly, but more often takes the smaller one.

The most effective two-fly combination for me has been a dry fly combined with a nymph or emerger. I also use this combination in summer and fall when trout are taking hoppers. They'll often approach a hopper and turn off. Try attaching an ant or beetle imitation 6 inches from the hopper. It may surprise you how effective this can be. *However, two nymphs, two dry flies, or any combination of two flies can cause trout to strike.*

When trout are very hard fished in extra-clear waters your line should be lighter, your leaders lengthened, and smaller flies selected. Concentrate on getting a good drag-free drift and cast the fly well above the fish.

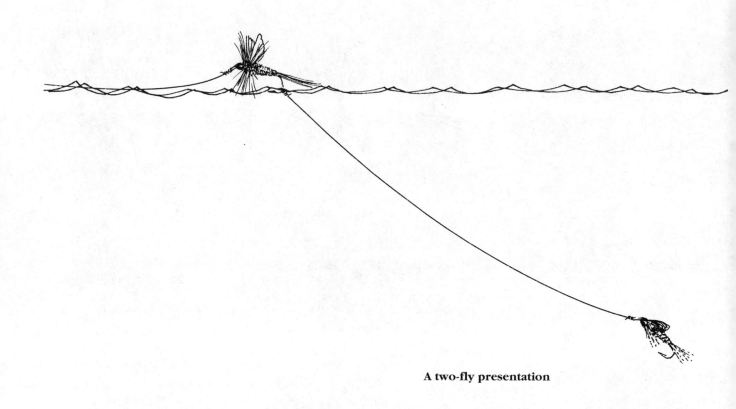

A two-fly presentation

Another common mistake is fishing mainly the center of a stream. On larger rivers much of the trout feeding occurs either close to the banks or in the shallows. That's why I like to carry a small pair of field glasses. By staying well back from the bank and closely examining every inch of the water, I can locate many trout that don't normally get cast to. In particular, remember to fish the banks. Banks hold cover, shadowed areas, and usually a reduced current flow; much of the food in a stream is swept against them, too. There are more terrestrials close to shore than will ever be out in the middle of a pool. It makes sense to fish these areas as hard as or more intensely than the center of a pool.

The best trout-fishing lodge I ever spent time in is Cedar Lodge on the South Island of New Zealand. Dick Fraser is the owner and a superb fly-fishing guide. Many of the fish here are truly smart, and they all live in very clear water. Dick taught me something years ago about presenting a fly to a fish feeding close to the bank, whether it's a dry fly or an underwater type. "Never cast the fly between the bank and the fish," he cautioned. Ever since I have carefully observed his advice. Drift your fly on the outside of the fish.

I was able to fish for trout a few years back at Herb Wellington's place near Ennis, Montana, on what I believe to be the finest dry-fly stream in the United States. Herb allows only a few people a year to fish his water, and the fish are of awesome size and incredibly wary. They feed almost exclusively on small flies—a size 16 would be large here. I was fortunate enough to fish with one of my good friends, Nick Lyons. Nick tells everybody how poorly he fishes, which is a damned lie: Nick's a great trout fisherman. Nick and Herb introduced me to the use of Power Gum.

They explained that we needed to use fine leaders—usually a 7X or 8X—and very small hooks. What this meant was that we were going to have to hook these hefty trout on very small flies (that gripped very little meat) and fragile leaders; then somehow hope to land them. "You need to install a short length of Power Gum in your leader," both of them told me.

Power Gum is a material that I believe originated in Germany—but don't take that to the bank. It looks like conventional nylon monofilament, but the similarities end there. Power Gum stretches like a rubber band. You can take a 6-inch length of .026-inch-diameter Power Gum and stretch it to about 10½ inches before it will break. This is nearly twice its total length!

What's the value of this? Anytime you're hooked to a fish with a very small fly or an especially fragile leader tippet, then Power Gum can serve a useful purpose. It forms a shock absorber that doesn't prevent tippets from breaking or hooks from pulling free, but certainly helps you prevent these problems from occurring. There are several diameters of Power Gum that I'm familiar with: .012 inch, .026 inch, and .040 inch. I find the .012 to be very thin—too thin for my use. The .026 (I'd guess that it's about 15-pound test) is ideal to insert in the butt section of a trout leader. And if you're going to use Power Gum in bass and saltwater leaders, the .040 (about 22-pound test) is recommended. The drawing below shows you how Herb and Nick told me to rig my leader with Power Gum.

Power Gum is also sold under the name Shock Gum. Both Power Gum and Shock Gum come on conventional leader spools and are inexpensive; they can be bought in some fly shops. Also available from some fly shops is a product manufactured by Phil Camera called Bunjeebutt: It's a neat length of Power Gum with conventional leader material smoothly attached to each end. This makes it easy to tie the Power Gum into the butt

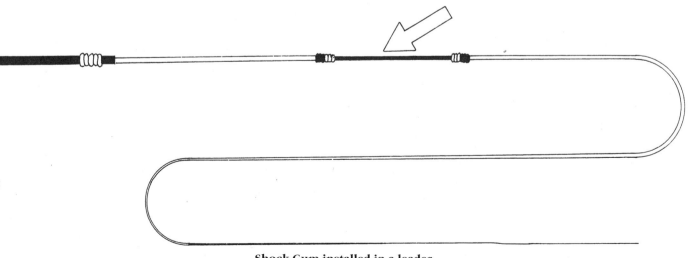

Shock Gum installed in a leader

of your leader. Simply clip the butt section in two and use a standard blood knot to attach both ends of the Bunjeebutt, the same way you would to add any regular leader material.

While Power Gum is often used in trout fishing, it can serve well in other areas of fly fishing, too. *For example, if you're trying to capture a world record in saltwater fly fishing on a light tippet, Power Gum could make a substantial difference in whether you land a fish or not. It's also useful for Atlantic salmon—a species famous for its lightning runs and high-jumping antics. In fact, anytime you use small hooks or light tippets to battle very active fish, Power Gum can offer you a measure of security.*

If you're night fishing for brown trout, it's critical that you be able to fish where the trout are. George Harvey didn't waste time fishing empty pools. Instead, he located his fish just before he cast to them. Here's how he did it—and the technique can immeasurably improve your success catching brown trout at night: As he prowled the banks of a stream at night, George carried with him a five-cell flashlight. He moved its beam quickly back and forth over the bottom. Once he had spotted a brown trout, he quickly

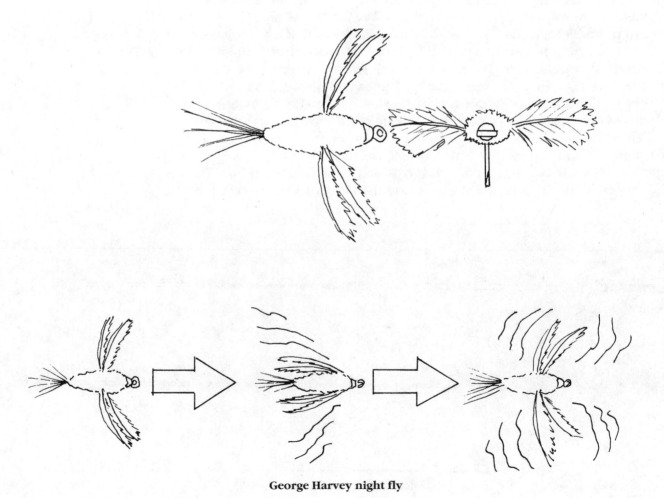

George Harvey night fly

urned the light off the fish. After a full two minutes, he'd make another quick search with the light to see if the trout was still there. He found that f the light didn't remain on the fish, it almost always stayed where he'd seen it.

George then moved upstream a short distance and got into the water, if necessary. Using a floating line with a relatively short leader (long leaders can too easily tangle), he'd cast a special fly he tied—it was torpedo shaped with protruding wings—across and upstream from where the fish was lying. He'd let the fly sink then, using a hand-over-hand or slow, short retrieve, move it toward the trout in a pulsating manner. Study the drawing on page 250; the wings of this fly act like oars when retrieved, sending out vibrations. That's it. It took George years to develop his method. It is simple, but it's oh, so effective!

Many trout fishermen know that wintertime can produce some fine atches. If you can stand the cold, you'll get some great action. Trout feed throughout winter, and though some anglers aren't aware of it, many hatches occur. *Almost all the insects that emerge are either black or very dark in color.* Midges hatch throughout winter. In many watersheds a little black stonefly will emerge when air temperatures reach the 50-degree range for several days. Anglers often refer to these winter hatchers as snow flies since they fill the air despite the blanket of snow covering

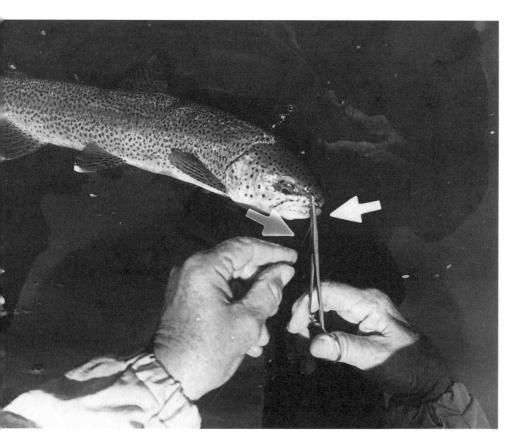

To quickly release a trout, slide one hand down the leader to within an inch or two of the trout, then grasp the hook by the bend with a hemostat or needlenose pliers and turn the hook so the point is toward the water. The trout will quickly fall free.

everything. Blue-winged olives seem to tolerate cold weather very well. Almost all these flies are small; a size 16 would be a big one. But nymph and dry-fly fishing can be fun and effective in the height of winter. Most of your nymphs should be small.

This is the time of year to dress warm and use neoprene waders. Keeping your fingers warm is the biggest problem. For a long time I used wool gloves with the fingertips removed. My hands stayed fairly warm, but my fingers felt like they were frozen. I've tried other materials, but none works so well for me as wool; even when wet it seems to keep me warm. However, I now modify my gloves in a way that allows me to keep my fingers warm on all but the coldest days. I buy a pair of heavy all-wool gloves—usually gray in color. I sew a buttonhole stitch on the inside of the first fingertip on each glove. I sew another buttonhole stitch on the inside of each thumb. Then, with a razor blade, I carefully slit the glove inside the buttonhole stitch. The slit is long enough for my fingertip or thumb to barely push through the buttonhole. When I'm fishing I can slide the end of my first finger and thumb through the slits, allowing me to control the cast and to retrieve. When I'm not fishing I simply slide my fingers back inside the glove. This keeps all of my hands and fingers warm, except the tiny bit exposed through the buttonhole.

If you enjoy fishing tailwaters during winter, you can also enjoy great nymph fishing. While hatches of dry flies emerge at different times, nymphs are here all the time and furnish the bulk of trout's winter diet. My favorite nymph size is 16. If there's some vegetation, such as in many spring creeks, you'll generally need only two flies. The aquatic vegetation holds many shrimp and cress bugs, so a good size 16 cress bug and shrimp

The author modifies a wool glove to keep fingers as warm as possible. See the text for instructions on how to make this excellent winter fishing glove.

Tailwaters and limestone streams furnish good fishing all through the year. Here an angler is fly fishing the Letort Spring Run in Carlisle, Pennsylvania.

patterns are all you need. *Since the air temperature is often well below freezing, it's best not to false-cast; instead, roll-cast to the fish. This keeps your fly under water almost all the time. Roll-casting also prevents ice from forming on the guides or fly, and allows for a very soft presentation.* Many times you'll see a trout nudge its head into the underwater weeds, shake its body vigorously, and then drop downstream. What it's doing is dislodging shrimp and sow bugs. As the insects free-drift in the current, the trout can feast on them. Watch for this and, when the trout drops back after wrestling the weeds, roll-cast a cress bug or nymph imitation a few feet in front of it. You're almost surely going to get a hookup.

11

OTHER
FRESHWATER SPECIES

Bass

More has been written about fly fishing for trout in the United States, but the most sought-after species here—by all anglers—are the large- and small-mouth bass. One or both of these species live in every state in the country and have been caught by fly fishermen for years. It was James A. Henshall who in 1881 wrote, that "Pound for pound, it is the strongest fish that swims." Of course, Henshall never caught a lot of saltwater species (or carp), so he can be excused for his statement. Nevertheless, I confess that my favorite of all the freshwater species I've boated around the world is the small-mouth bass. Perhaps it's because I grew up fishing for them. A smallmouth was the first fish I caught on a fly rod, and I simply love to fish for them.

Bass exist in lakes, rivers, and small streams, as well as Texas watering tanks, farm ponds—virtually anywhere there's clean, fresh water. Large-mouth bass can also tolerate the brackish waters of tidal creeks.

Both species of bass are structure oriented. Largemouths will use vege-tation, old boat docks, stumps, and many man-made structures as ambush spots. In lakes, rocks and aquatic vegetation are the keys to catching small-mouths, although they'll use the same structure as the largemouth. In rivers, rocks are the most popular smallmouth hideout areas, but logs and drowned timber are often good locations to seek these great fish as well.

Smallmouths prefer cooler waters than largemouths, which is a major reason why you don't find them in the shallow lakes or rivers of the Deep South. They do exist in the large impoundments here, though, mainly be-cause the water is cooler in summer. Water temperature is critical to suc-cessful bass fly fishing. I don't subscribe to the idea that bass (or any other

The author's favorite fly-rod target—smallmouth bass. It brings a smile to his face each time he catches one.

fish) are more comfortable at certain temperatures. Yes, I use the word *comfortable* to describe them at times, but this is a figure of speech; please don't take me literally. *Humans have a particular body temperature, and our bodies try to maintain it at all times.* Thus, in a cold room our bodies will strive to keep us at a warmer temperature; the reverse is true when the air surrounding us is very hot. That's why we sweat; so the evaporation will cool us. *All fish, however, take on the temperature of the water that they swim in. Unless it's near freezing or very hot, fish are not uncomfortable, because they're not attempting to maintain a specific body temperature.*

Largemouth bass exist everywhere in the tidal basin in Washington, D.C. It's a great place to fish for them.

But water temperature does have an effect on how bass feed. At optimum temperatures the metabolism of a bass (or any other fish) operates at its fastest, and thus requires the most food. This means that at optimum temperatures, bass will feed more often, giving fly fishermen improved opportunities to catch them. If the temperature falls below or rises above the optimum range, the bass's metabolism slows down and requires less food, so our chances of catching them decrease. Biologists have determined the temperatures at which both species feed the most. Smallmouth bass are most active in temperatures from about 67 to 71

Largemouths prefer lots of warm water filled with vegetation—such as here in the Everglades.

degrees. Interestingly, bass smaller than 12 inches seem to stop feeding when temperatures fall to 50 degrees. Yet from about 40 to 80 degrees, smallmouths can be caught on flies—although the action slows as temperatures fall into the lower range or rise near the upper levels. Largemouth bass feed best in water from about 65 to 78 degrees. They're much more tolerant of higher temperatures and, while they can be caught frequently in waters reaching even the mid-80s, larger bass seem to slow their feeding once water temperatures get into the low 80s. The exception to this is in the Deep South. Here largemouths have over the eons developed resistance to higher temperatures. I've caught some big bass when water temperatures were in the high 80s.

A major reason why smallmouths and largemouths in lakes will hold in 12 to 20 feet of water during the summer months is that the water is much cooler there than at the surface. Here's another example of how water temperature can increase your catch rate. If you're fishing in midsummer when the water temperature is well above the optimum range, and you know where an underwater spring is located, you're in luck. Water exits springs at about 50 degrees, so the fish in the cooler water affected by the upwelling spring *will have higher metabolic rates* and thus be more likely to strike your flies. Conversely, in colder weather you might want to fish the same spring, because the water there may be *warmer* than what surrounds it. In spring when lakes are starting to warm, look for shallow coves with dark bottoms to fish. A darker bottom will collect more heat from the sun and often have a water 5 to 10 degrees warmer than will a nearby lake with a light-colored bottom.

There are two other differences between smallmouths and largemouths. Smallmouths are almost always found near a bottom that's rocky, sandy, or gravelly. While largemouths can also be found near such bottoms, they more often frequent muddy or silty areas. The other difference is that smallmouths prefer clearer waters than largemouths.

Tackle for Bass

Because largemouth flies are usually a little larger, more air resistant, and often heavier, slightly larger rods and lines are needed than for smallmouth flies. I lean toward an 8-weight as a light rod for bigmouth bass; a 9-weight is ideal. I really don't think you ever need a 10-weight for largemouths. For smallmouths, in most fishing situations an 8-weight rod is ideal. If you want to go a little lighter, try a 7-weight, but there will be times when you might want the 8. Many years ago it was said that a slow-action rod was best for bass fishing of any kind. That was never true. The modern medium-fast rods are packed with power and will deliver the best results. I'm often asked which rod to buy. My answer is that any rod you spend $200 or more for today will probably cast better than the person who buys it. There are few really bad rods on the market, although the high-end models from top companies will slightly outperform rods that cost much less.

As for lines, you really need several, depending upon where you fish. In some situations the correct line selection will much improve your presentation and catch rate. If limited to a single line, I'd select a weight-forward floater. There are a variety of weight-forward tapers. If you're a good caster—you can easily throw 70 feet of line—select one of the longer-taper weight-forward lines. This will allow longer casts and more delicate presentations. If you have problems casting more than 50 feet, I suggest one of two lines. First is one I developed for anglers who aren't good casters but want to obtain more distance: the Teeny Pro Series Line designed by Lefty Kreh. It has a very short front taper, a shorter-than-normal belly, and a shorter-than-normal back taper. More important, the first 30 feet of this line weighs 1½ line sizes more than the rod it is designed for. For example, if you're using a rod matched to an 8-weight line, the first 30 feet of this special Teeny Pro line weighs what a 9½ line would weigh. What this line permits you to do is retrieve back to the rear taper, make a pickup, and—with a single backcast (because the rod loads so much better with the heavier line)—come forward and shoot the line back to the target.

False-casting is neither desired nor needed with this line. My second suggestion would be any of the popular bug or bass taper lines. These lines have shorter-than-normal bellies, so you can retrieve closer and still make good casts.

Another line you may want to consider is the Sink Tip or Wet Tip (the same lines, just different names). The first 5 to 10 feet of such lines sinks. The rate of sink can vary, depending on the line you select: A sink rate I line sinks the slowest, and a V descends the fastest. Usually a III or IV sinking-tip is best; the heavier sink rate V tip is often difficult to cast. One problem with sinking-tips is that the remainder of the fly line floats. During a retrieve, then, every strip of the line tends to loft the sinking portion and the fly. The obvious advantage of a sinking-tip line, however, is that because most of the line floats, it's easier to lift it from the water for a backcast. Sinking-tips perform best when you're fishing water less than 6 feet deep. They also have a special place in fly fishing for bass. If you're using an underwater fly where the surface is covered with lily pads or other aquatic weeds with small openings, the sinking-tip is ideal. A full-sinking line fished across such an opening wants to tangle in the weeds on the backcast. A floating line never gets the fly properly down into the opening. But cast a sinking-tip into the opening, let it sink your fly, and then retrieve to the opening's near edge. When you're ready to make a backcast, the floating portion of your line will help you lift the sinking-tip from the opening without tangling in the vegetation.

Another line that every bass fisherman should carry is one that sinks slowly throughout its length. Many writers recommend an intermediate line, which sinks rather slowly. I like the slightly faster sink rate of a II (a Scientific Anglers Wet Cel II, or one of several clear monofilament lines). These lines sink a little deeper and permit the fly to get down better. *The advantage of using any sinking line—or at least one in which a long portion of the front end sinks—is that your fly and line will travel at the same depth during your retrieve.* A floating line or sinking-tip tends to loft a sinking fly upward during the retrieve.

A line especially effective for bass where water depths exceed 6 feet is the Teeny 300. This is matched perfectly with a 8- or 9-weight rod. The first 27 feet of this line sinks very rapidly; the rest is a thin floater. It's a modern shooting head. In calmer water this line will permit you to fish weighted flies, such as Clouser Minnows or weighted Woolly Buggers, down to about 12 or 14 feet.

A line that has special applications is the shooting taper, or shooting head (as it's generally called). This is usually a 30-foot length of fly line (it can be floating, slow sinking, fast sinking, or lead core) attached to a thinner shooting line. The shooting line can be monofilament or a commercial shooting line, which is usually a II or III level floating fly line. Shooting heads allow you to make much longer casts than you could with conventional fly lines. They're especially helpful in large, open, and/or deep bodies of water. Good examples are Lake Erie and similar waters, which hold so many good smallmouths. Because you can make longer casts with these heads, you can get down deeper and retrieve over a longer distance. This allows you to search more water—sometimes essential to getting hookups in large open water.

Modern Largemouth Bass Flies

Most fly rodders are still using underwater largemouth patterns that were developed as much as five decades ago; these are often bucktail or feather-wing streamers. Such older flies will still catch some fish—but modern fly-tying materials and designs have been developed that are much more effective.

The standard popping bug for largemouths has been a cork- or balsa-bodied bug with a bulky tail made from feathers; between tail and body are dense hackles surrounding the hook shank. Usually several strands of soft rubber dangle to represent legs. Such bugs are wind resistant and hard to cast. The soft, undulating tail feathers frequently wrap around the hook in flight, thus destroying your presentation. Even when such a bug gets to the water, its many hackles cause it to sit high on the water—which can sometimes cause a missed strike. And the cupped face on most models makes it difficult to lift the bug from the water without making a loud *whoosh* that frequently frightens any bass in the neighborhood.

My own experience and that of many others has shown that bigger bass (both large- and smallmouths) want what I call groceries—not samples. It's true that elephants will eat peanuts, but that doesn't mean they can make a living on them. To stay big and healthy they need and want large portions. So it is with bass.

If you're seeking smallmouth bass of at least 3 pounds or largemouths topping 4, a switch to larger flies will almost certainly aid in your search. And when you do switch to larger flies, you may be amazed to learn that small bass will also attack them. It's true that you'll get fewer strikes from smaller fish, but many of these little characters will persist in hitting the fly. What's pleasing is the number of bigger fish you'll begin to catch. Trophy largemouth bass do prefer slightly larger patterns than smallmouths. When I say that flies in the 4- to 6-inch range are often better for taking larger bass, some anglers are skeptical. But consider the conventional spinning fishing lure for bass—a 5-inch Rapala, or a plastic worm of up to 9 inches! So a 6-inch fly isn't too large.

Let me tell you about some modern patterns that have been water-tested on big largemouths and work well. For surface work, I suggest two flies. One is the Dahlberg Diver—but not the little models 2 or 2½ inches long. As I said earlier, big fish want big foods. The Dahlberg Diver I recommend is dressed on a 2/0 hook and has a trimmed deer hair head at least 1 inch wide! It should also have a weed guard, since it's frequently fished in dense aquatic vegetation.

The second surface fly is the Marabou Gerbubble Bug. The Gerbubble Bug has been around for more than 50 years; it was developed on the

Chesapeake Bay by angler Tom Loving. The conventional pattern features saddle or neck hackles extending out around the sides and back. Make a slot in one side of the balsa wood body. Strip all the hackle from one side of a feather, then glue the bare part of the feather stem into the slot. Repeat on the other side and on the back. This forms scores of thin legs sticking out all around the bug's body, except the face. For decades it has been a good fly.

But Norm Bartlett, a creative Maryland fly fisherman, recently developed a vastly improved Gerbubble Bug. He substitutes marabou for the conventional feather. Stripping the marabou from one side of the stem, he wets the remainder of the hackle and glues the marabou stem into the slots made along the sides and back. When complete, the rear and both sides of the Gerbubble Bug have a marabou skirt radiating outward (see the photo below). What this fly does in the water is fantastic.

Largemouths, *particularly where there's no current,* such as in ponds and lakes, often hold underneath a popping bug and watch it. That's why there are flexible rubber bands on many largemouth bugs—but these stop moving after the retrieve is finished. Not so with the Marabou Gerbubble Bug. Activate this one and long after you stop moving the bug, the mini currents you created during the retrieve will continue to undulate its supple marabou plumes. Even a bug sitting motionless on the surface will, with the slightest wave action, move its marabou plumes as if treading water. On stillwater this bug outfishes every other largemouth bug I've tried.

Much largemouth bass fishing, especially in the South, is done in waters that have a profusion of vegetation. It goes without saying that you should

On the left is a conventional Gerbubble Bug; on the right a Marabou Gerbubble Bug. You can visualize how much more action is possible from the right-hand version.

carry some bugs equipped with weed guards for such work. But standard popping bugs have a wide face; when fished in thick lily pads, bonnets, or the like, this face frequently tangles in the grass and weeds. For these situations, there's a bug that's much sleeker (so it's easier to cast) that does a great job of threading through vegetation with rarely a hangup: the pencil popper. It doesn't make a lot of noise—just enough to draw the attention of the bass. A simple 30-pound-test monofilament stub works well as a weed guard. Punch a hole in the belly of the bug with a large needle. Touch a little Krazy Glue to the stub and force it into the hole. Deposit a small glob of Krazy Glue where the stub exits the bug body to ensure it stays in position.

Texas largemouth fishermen years ago took a saltwater pattern and began to fish it for largemouths in tanks, ponds, lakes, and rivers. Word spread, and now fishermen seeking big largemouths around the country are using this fly, with happy results. The fly is the Lefty's Deceiver. While a number of color combinations are effective, a version that's mostly black has become the choice in waters a bit murky or cloudy. I also like to add to each side a natural grizzly saddle feather and some purple and black Flashabou or Krystal Flash; this plus a beard of red Flashabou seems to draw more strikes (see the photo on page 266). The pattern is usually tied on a size 1 or 1/0 hook, and is 4 to 6 inches long. A weed guard is almost always tied in, although in open-water situations none is required.

The Clouser Minnow was developed to catch smallmouths but is also a deadly largemouth pattern. My favorite version is one with an underwing of white bucktail, followed by a liberal mix of gold Flashabou and pearl Krystal Flash, and topped with chartreuse bucktail.

Another favorite of mine for both big smallmouths and largemouths is the Half & Half, a pattern that combines the attributes two popular flies. It's a long fly, so it looks like a big meal to a bass. Yet it's light and easy to cast, and has terrific action. The Half & Half combines the Lefty's Deceiver and the Clouser Deep Minnow. At the rear of the hook you tie in a wing as if you were starting a Lefty's Deceiver. Carry the thread forward and secure a pair of metal or lead eyes on the fly, just as you would on a Clouser Minnow. Tie a full forward wing of bucktail or a substitute (Super Hair, Ultra Hair, or the like) on top behind the lead eyes. Add a good bit of sparkle by including some Flashabou or Krystal Flash; I like to mix a little of each.

This fly sinks well because of its metallic eyes; obviously, the heavier the eyes, the faster it'll dive. The feather wing positioned at the tail gives you a longer pattern with a soft wing that swims well on the retrieve. The Clouser-type wing at the front creates the appearance of bulk; to a bass, this looks like a real treat. It's easy to tie, even to 5 or 6 inches.

Another fly that I find deadly for fishing around structure—including fly-snagging drowned timber, aquatic vegetation, boat docks, and drowned stump fields—is the Bend-Back. This ancient pattern was developed in the late 1800s for fishing bass in dense lily pads. With modern refinements I rate this as the single best fly to fish in spots where almost all other flies—

even those with weed guards—will snag frequently. If you fish it slowly, teasing it along, the Bend-Back can be crawled over and among almost all fish-holding structure. You can throw it up on the bank, even into overhanging trees; if gently retrieved it will almost always work itself through the branches and drop to the water.

The fly is easy to tie. Generally a long-shanked hook is best, although many people tie the Bend-Back on a standard-length hook. *Longer-shanked hooks will impale the fish better on the strike than regular length.* Of the several factors that make this fly effective, first in importance is the long-shanked hooks; I prefer one 3X long. To create a Bend-Back, grip the bare hook about ¼ inch behind the hook eye with a pair of pliers and bend it in the opposite direction of the hook point. Apply pressure with the pliers, and as soon as you feel the metal bend—*stop!* If you bend the hook too much it'll dangle below the wing on the completed fly. Fish seem less inclined to strike such a fly, and the excess bend can also mean missed hookups on the strike. *Some time ago I stopped placing any body material on the hook shank.* The fly is easier to cast and fishes better. Body material tied on the shank also tends to wear badly if drawn across a rough-textured bottom. The wing is tied on the unbent portion of the shank. **One of the most important factors in a well-designed Bend-Back is that on the retrieve, the wing hides the body. For best results this wing should be made from buoyant materials. This helps the fly ride with its hook up.** If you want the fly to sink faster, make a number of wraps of lead wire on the bare hook shank as close as possible to the bend. I suggest securing the wraps with thread, then giving them a thin coating of epoxy as a protective shield.

To fish a Bend-Back, simply cast it into the target area and begin your retrieve. If you're fishing in cover that might snag the fly, so long as your retrieve is slow and gentle the hook point (riding up and hidden within the wing area) will rarely snag, and the fly will crawl over the obstacles. A favorite trick of mine with the Bend-Back is to toss it into a tree or bush that hangs over the water of a good-looking bass hideout. Slowly tease the fly out of the tree. Amazingly, it will slither through the branches, almost never entangling. Something that appears to be crawling through the branches then suddenly plopping into the water is hard for a bass to resist. You can also throw a Bend-Back up on a shoreline and crawl it slowly back into the water—sometimes a deadly presentation.

Another very old fly—it was used by bass fishermen in the last century—is the Red & White Hackle Fly. **This is one of the best patterns for both large and smallmouth bass that I've fished in the more than 50 years I've been chasing them.** I never make a trip without some of these in my box. Oddly enough, I've tried many other color combinations, but none is nearly as effective as red and white (some other combos do work in salt water, though). Some years ago it was renamed the Sea Ducer, but many of us still think of it as the Hackle Fly.

It's very simple to tie—even a novice fly tier can make this one. You need only two colors of feathers, a hook, and some thread. To prevent the tail feathers from fouling, I build a small bump with thread at the rear of the straight portion of the hook shank. Tie at least six or eight white saddle hackles directly in front of the thread bump. Add to each side 8 to 12 strands of gold, copper, or pearl Flashabou (or a combination of them). Tie in a red hackle and palmer it closely together on the shank. Sometimes a white feather is then wound in front of the first red palmered hackle, followed by enough red hackle to densely fill all of the hook shank. Lately I've simply filled the entire hook shank with palmered wound red hackle. That's it!

The hook size I use depends upon the size of the bass I'm seeking. If I'm after big ones, I tie the fly on a size 1 or 1/0. For smaller fish I use a size 2. Never use a hook smaller than this. *I tie this in lengths from 3 inches to as much as 8 inches—depending, again, on the size of the fish I hope to catch.* To make the fly longer, use 3X-long hooks. While the fly is generally tied without weight, it can also be fished deeper in the water column. *Lead eyes seem to affect the action of the pattern poorly. If you want to fish the fly deeper, try wrapping lead fuse wire along the hook shank prior to palmering the red hackle.*

Why is this fly so good and when and where should you use it? Because it has nothing but a wing and hackle wound along the shank, the Red & White casts effortlessly. The near weightless tail and hackles wound along the shank allow this fly, when you stop retrieving, to sit at virtually the same level in the water column; it sinks only very slowly. *You can therefore fish this fly about as slowly as any underwater fly. And you can fish it in very shallow water, something impossible with many other patterns.* Many times I've located a fish in calm, shallow water. Realizing that a conventional fly plopping down on the surface would frighten the bass, I switched to a Red & White Hackle Fly, which descends to the water like a thistle seed in flight. I urge you to tie some of these. Remember, too, what I said earlier about red and white in a fly—most of the rear of the fly should be white, with only a short section of red at the front.

The final trophy largemouth pattern I recommend is the Dave's Hare Jig, a fly that's easy to tie and, while a bit tough to cast, deadly on largemouths. Almost every experienced bass fisherman in the country will tell you that the plastic worm is either the best or the near best lure for tempting largemouth bass into striking. Dave Whitlock developed the Hare Jig as a fly fisherman's answer to the plastic worm.

It's usually tied with a weed guard—but in open water that's not necessary. One of the keys to fishing the fly is to fish it slowly, whether you're retrieving it through the water column or crawling it over structure or the bottom. Secure a pair of relatively heavy lead eyes at the front. For a fairly fast-sinking fly I recommend 1/24-ounce (7/32-inch-diameter) eyes. Install the weed guard material if you need it. Then select a 7-inch strip of rabbit fur that's approximately 3/16 inch wide. Tie the fur strip at the rear of the hook shank so that about 4 inches of it extends beyond the fly's rear. Now wrap the rest of the fur strip forward, securing it at the hook eye, and cut off any strip not used. That's it!

A good assortment of largemouth bass flies. Top row, left to right: Dahlberg Diver, pencil popper, and Marabou Gerbubble Bug. Second row, left to right: a Red & White Hackle Fly and a black Lefty's Deceiver. Third row, left to right: Half & Half and Clouser Minnow. Bottom row, left to right: Bend-Back and Dave's Hare Jig.

If you've been longing to catch a really trophy largemouth bass and haven't had any success, I urge you to try the patterns listed here. Almost all of these flies can be purchased from many fly shops around the country. They represent the modern trend in trophy-bass flies.

Largemouth Fly Retrieves

The Dahlberg Diver, Lefty's Deceiver, and other bass flies can be fished in special ways.

DAHLBERG DIVER

You can fish the versatile Dahlberg Diver as a popping bug or a wobbling underwater streamer fly. If you make short, quick strips with your fly line, pausing between each, the bug will pop and gurgle like any popping bug. But if you make a series of long pulls, keeping the line taut with no pauses in your retrieve, the Dahlberg Diver is dragged beneath the surface. As you continue to retrieve the fly line, the Diver will swim like an underwater fly with an undulating motion. When the retrieve stops, the bug floats to the surface. This gives you the option of fishing only on the surface, fishing continuously below the surface, or combining the two retrieves. To make a Dahlberg Diver more efficient grease its tapered head with a paste fly flotant before your first cast. Otherwise the deer hair head eventually absorbs water and restricts the pattern's action.

POPPING BUGS

A retrieve not generally known to bass bug fishermen is similar to the Dahlberg Diver retrieve. If you use a *sinking* fly line and a *leader at least 10 feet long,* with a *popping bug* made of any floating material—balsa, cork, or closed-cell foam—you can get a fantastic retrieve that will often produce well, especially in deep, clear water. Make a long cast and give the line a considerable time to sink. The descending line will pull the popping bug slowly down. When the line is deep in the water column, begin a retrieve. The line, well below the popper, will pull the bug much deeper. Now stop your retrieve; the buoyant popping bug will begin to rise almost vertically toward the surface, if the leader is long enough. Whenever you want begin your retrieve again, and the sinking line will cause the popper to dive again. By alternately stopping and retrieving, you can cause a buoyant popping bug to swim under water with an up-and-down motion. This technique is especially effective in clear-water lakes.

LEFTY'S DECEIVER

This is a very versatile fly. Although I originally designed it for saltwater fishing, it's equally effective in fresh water. Although it's relatively large, in the air it's sleek and offers little resistance, making casting easier. In the water it takes on a baitfish shape. Because the wing is attached at the rear and the collar flows well back along the wing, the Deceiver rarely fouls in flight. It can be tied as short as a few inches or as long as 7 to 9 inches. It can be cast across a current and, with an occasional manipulation of the fly line, will produce a darting motion that bass find exciting. Most of the time the Deceiver is fished as you would any streamer fly: Cast it into a likely pocket. Holding your rod low and pointed at the target area, make short or long strips with your fly line. This causes the fly to dart about as an escaping minnow might when pursued by a bass. In dingy or dark waters, the all-black Lefty's Deceiver is one of the most effective of all underwater bass flies.

Once an angler learns to tie a Lefty's Deceiver he usually ties it the same way each time, and with the same amount of materials. However, the Deceiver can be tied in various ways, so you don't need to limit yourself. First, most tiers are aware that color combinations can be changed. But other variations are possible: If you want a Deceiver to fish near the surface, add several extra hackles to the tail and *use a lot of deer hair to make the collar.* This will cause the Deceiver to float much higher in the water column. If you're imitating thin baitfish, use only two or three saddle hackles in the tail and very little bucktail in the collar. Conversely, if you want a fly that presents a large profile so that it "pushes" water (enabling fish to find it) and sinks well, you can make a Deceiver do this. Add extra hackles to the tail, wrap the shank with lead fuse wire, and then build a heavy collar of bucktail. Some people call this Deceiver the Grocery Fly. These examples should demonstrate that the Deceiver is a very versatile fly that can be used effectively in many fishing situations—so long as you modify how you tie it.

Modern Flies for Bigger Smallmouth Bass

For many years smallmouth fishermen have used basically the same old fly patterns. Popping bugs have generally been constructed with a number of feathers extending from the rear and a lot of hackle wound between the hook bend and the rear of the body. Such bugs popped poorly, were hard to hook fish with, and lifted badly from the surface. New bugs have replaced these—and they cast easier and are more efficient. Old underwater flies were streamers that rarely reached 3 inches in length. Even today, some people who write about smallmouths recommend small flies. Certainly, these small flies will catch smallmouths—just not many of the larger ones. Bigger fish want bigger flies. While large fish will occasionally take a small offering, that's the exception rather than the rule. Anyone experienced at catching brown trout knows that big browns eat other trout and are rarely found sipping dry flies, unless there's an intensive hatch. Big browns are caught mostly at night with larger flies. I'm not necessarily recommending you fish for smallmouths at night (not a bad idea, however). My point is that if you've fished for bigger brown trout, you know they want larger food sources. So it is with smallmouths.

But what is a "bigger" fly? For smallmouth bass I suggest streamers at least 3 to 4 inches long. (For largemouths, add another inch or two.) A very few patterns are exceptions to this rule. For example, if the body of a fly is unusually fat (representing a lot of food sources), its length can be reduced a little. The Clouser Crayfish—which I consider the best of all imitations of this very important food, especially for bass—may measure only 2 inches long, yet it's often taken by larger bass of both species. Still, I think your chances of interesting the real trophy bass will improve if you use the same pattern in sizes a bit larger.

Let me describe some effective modern flies. Each of the patterns below will catch either smallmouth or largemouth bass; some are much more effective on smallmouths than largemouths. Beginning at the surface and working down, here are the six top flies I recommend if you're after larger smallmouths:

LEFTY'S BUG

I hate to seem immodest, but this bug—which I spent many years designing—is one of the best for both species of bass. It's become very well known; it's sometimes called the Potomac Bug. Good popping bugs should have several important characteristics.

1. They should appeal to the fish—that's the most important attribute.
2. They should be easy to cast. If you can't get the bug to the bass, you have a problem.
3. Their tails shouldn't tangle under the hook in flight.
4. They should pop easily and every time.
5. They should lift from the water easily.

The Lefty's Bug has all these attributes. Look at how it's designed. A long-shanked hook is used—one that extends well behind the body. As the bug sits on the water the hook is well below the surface and so is the first point of contact when a fish strikes. The cork body is glued on so that the very base of the bug's face is flush with the hook eye. Positioning the hook eye higher up in the face tends to drown a bug on the pickup and backcast. The tail is usually of squirrel tail. This hair clings together in flight, reducing air resistance, and flares out on contact with the water. *Important factors when you tie this bug are to make sure that the tail is short, and to wind thread only from the rear of the hook body to the end of the straight portion of the hook shank. This keeps the tail in the correct position so it* never *fouls on the cast.*

RED & WHITE HACKLE FLY

This is one of the oldest bass flies—it was popular with fly fishermen in the 1880s. The difference between what was used for decades and what we now use is size! Formerly, a Red & White Hackle Fly was only about 2⅓ to 3 inches in length. Now experience has taught us to tie this fly at least 4 to 5 inches long—and it can be as long as 7 inches. (Think about it: A Rapala double-jointed plug is nearly this size and takes bass.) The addition of 8 to 12 strands of gold, silver, or copper Flashabou on each side is helpful in drawing strikes. This fly fishes very shallow. If you want to fish it in weed-filled areas, add a monofilament or wire weed guard. For occasions when you want to fish deeper in the water column, add lead wire to the shank.

CLOUSER DEEP MINNOW

This fly, often called the Clouser Minnow or just the Clouser, has helped revolutionize smallmouth bass fishing—and it's deadly on largemouths, too. Tie lead or metal eyes on top of the hook. Then remove the fly from the vise, turn it over, and replace it in the vise. Tie on the wing. With the lead or metal eyes on the bottom, the fly swims with its hook point up. This allows you to fish right on the bottom with little fear of snagging. The Clouser can be tied in whatever length you desire, and in many colors. It's often tied to imitate a baitfish or small fish. A version with an olive top-wing, a thin black center wing, and an underwing of white is called the Baby Bass—it represents a small bass. Another great version has a white bottom and gray top. This is a fine imitation of a minnow. The Clouser Deep Minnow is one fly you should not be without; I consider it the most effective streamer fly pattern developed in the past 30 years. With this fly, in fact, I've taken 84 different salt- and freshwater species around the world in the past three years.

Bob Clouser, who invented the Clouser Minnow. You'd think he doesn't like to catch bass; look at the grin.

CLOUSER CRAYFISH

This is another smallmouth fly you need! Many scientific surveys of smallmouths' food preferences list the crayfish as the most important. The best way to fish it in rivers is simply to throw it across and slightly down-current and *let it drift freely.* Sometimes a sinking-tip or even a slow-sinking line is best to get the pattern deeper. In lakes I use a sinking line; I throw the fly out, permit it to sink, and then slowly retrieve it close to the bottom. For this reason it's advisable to use a weed guard on the fly.

This fly is a little difficult for a novice to tie. It can be purchased in many fly shops, however—and you can also buy directly from the man who developed it. He also sells instructions for tying it. Call or write: 101 Ulrich Street, Middletown, PA 17057, (717) 944–6541. I suggest buying a number of his Clouser Minnow variations right from Bob Clouser, and keeping them as samples you can tie from.

CACTUS MINNOW

This easy-to-tie fly can be used on smallmouths ranging from 6 inches to 6 pounds. I coined the name Cactus Minnow for it many years ago; it has been called by many other names since then, including the Cactus Bugger. Regardless of the name, though, this is a great smallmouth fly. In larger sizes it's also effective on largemouths, pike, and striped bass. It can be retrieved almost at a dead drift in current, or it can be fast-stripped to imitate an escaping minnow.

Aside from the hook you need only three materials, and with a little practice you can tie the fly in less than three minutes. Use either a long-shanked or a regular-shanked hook. Secure a set of lead or metallic eyes to the shank as you would to begin a Clouser Minnow. At the rear of the hook tie in a 1½- to 3-inch tail of light-colored chartreuse marabou. Secure some Cactus Chenille (also known by many other names, including Estaz chenille) and wind it forward and back until you've built a body of the diameter you want. That's it. The best color combination by far in my experience is a yellow-chartreuse tail with a shank of darker chartreuse. Two other combinations are also very effective; I think smallmouths take these flies for crayfish. The first uses a marabou tail of light tan and a Cactus Chenille body of root beer color. The second has a white marabou tail, half the hook shank of pearl Cactus Chenille, and, at the front of the hook shank, a hank of bright red Cactus Chenille. This fly doesn't look like much, but on some days it's the hottest pattern I cast.

WOOLLY BUGGER

Many smallmouth bass fishermen wouldn't be without the Woolly Bugger. It can be fished very slowly, stripped rapidly, or—if there's a good current—dead-drifted. It can be dressed on a bare hook shank, or you can add

A good selection of smallmouth flies. Top row: Lefty's Bug. Second row, left to right: Woolly Bugger, Cactus Minnow, and Red & White Hackle Fly. Third row, left to right: Baby Bass Clouser and Clouser Crayfish. Bottom row, left to right: Clouser Minnow and Half & Half.

lead eyes to give it a dipping motion during the retrieve. When I want it to go deep, I prefer wrapping lead wire along the hook shank.

Basic Rules of Bass Fishing

There are some fundamental rules of fly fishing for bass. Both small-mouths and largemouths are structure oriented. If there's one place you're likely to find smallmouth bass throughout their range it's where there are rocks. Fish an area of a lake or flowing water that's virtually without rocks and you may have lean times seeking smallmouths. They hold near sunken wood, too. Largemouths prefer to hide in aquatic weeds, or near stumps; they're often found around drowned timber. In a lake they'll be found around boat docks and holding on points, as well as drop-offs from shallow to deep water.

FISHING BASS IN LAKES

Lakes are not a static environment, though they may seem so to a novice. There are many changes occurring. Lake waters become dirty from muddy rivers that flow into them. The water can lose much of its oxygen in places in summer, and algae can build. Weeds furnish a natural cover that comes and goes with the seasons. While some lakes have a uniform bottom devoid of cover or undulations, most lakes have drop-offs, points of land projecting into the water, and other features. To be a successful lake bass fisherman, it pays to know something about all of the

Streams, and especially lakes, that experience a large dropdown exposing the bottom should always be photographed. The photos will help you locate fish-holding structure. Just be sure to include in the photo some sort of shoreline as a reference point.

above. Here are some tips that may help you locate and catch large and smallmouth bass in lakes.

1. Very Clear Water

    Clear monofilament sinking lines and lighter tippets will catch you more fish in water that's extra clear. Longer casts are required—the farther you can stay away from the bass, the better. When water temperature is near 60 degrees and the lake is very clear, the best time to fish is when light levels are low. This could be on cloudy days, when it's raining, or at dawn and dusk. Gurgling surface poppers slowly across the shallow flats on warm summer nights can be very effective.

    In lakes where the water is exceptionally clear, your flies should be subdued, with little flash and lots of action on a slow retrieve. Excellent imitations of baitfish and crayfish will give you an edge. Remember, the crayfish is almost always the prime food of a lake bass, whether smallmouth or largemouth.

    Many clear lakes have areas that aren't so clear. Carp will root in some places; other factors can also cause the water to get slightly dirty or tinted. Try fishing these areas. If a clear lake has a lot of vegetation, the feeding bass are usually more easily deceived when you fish for them in the grass.

2. Dirty Water

    Odd as it may sound, when lakes are discolored from high rains or other elements, there will often be some places that are much clearer. For example, coves that didn't receive much of the dirty water may be much clearer. Clear water may also be found where streams enter the lake, or where there are upwelling springs.

    You'll need special flies to fish dirty water, and you can expect a lower success rate. Flies that have bulky bodies and large heads will create small vibrations as they're retrieved, allowing the bass to better locate your offering. Some fly fishermen are big on rattlers, but I've never found them to be effective. A wobbling bass plug with rattlers is certain deadly. The Rat-L-Trap, I'm told, is the best selling of all casting plugs around the world. Such plugs wobble on the retrieve, and this back-and-forth motion allows their rattlers to make a lot of noise. When you retrieve a fly, it travels pretty much straight ahead, creating little noise. On several occasions I've fished in salt and fresh water with a friend who used rattlers in his flies, while I didn't. I never felt that one fly outfished another. However, in dirty water—especially if it's shallow—a slow-worked popping bug will often cull you fish when nothing else seems successful.

3. Clear Lakes with No Visible Cover

    A depth finder is an extremely useful tool to a fly fisherman working lakes. Try locating grass beds (if there are any), along with any structure in the lake that lies less than 12 feet deep. If no cover can be found, the bass will be difficult to catch. I recommend a shooting head, which lets you cast longer distances and search more water with each cast. Also, fish when it's raining or very overcast—or at night, when the fish will be roaming and more likely to find your flies.

4. Lakes with Lots of Cover

These can be difficult, since the bass can be almost anywhere in the lake. This is the time to cast and move, cast and move. Don't stay in any one place for long unless you're getting strikes. The bass will generally be scattered, because food should be abundant throughout the lake. Look for openings in the vegetation and then use a sinking-tip line technique (see chapter 8).

5. Bright Sunny Days

Bass shun bright light, so the key is to fish shady areas. Try around or under boat docks, on the shady side of a shoreline, or around any structure (boulders, weed beds, and so on). You may have to locate spots where the bottom drops from 5 to 8 feet, and descend into deeper water. Fish the side of the lake where the drop-off will be shaded.

6. On Windy Days

This may sound foolish, but if it's possible you should fish the shoreline onto which the wind is piling. Don't fish the lee side, which is the natural tendency. This is especially true in summer, when water is warmer and doesn't hold as much oxygen. The churned water will be much more highly oxygenated. On cooler days in spring and fall you can seek calm coves and lee shores, however, since the colder water will hold oxygen and bass will be comfortable there.

7. Fish the Points

Fish underwater land points that slowly move away from shore into deeper water. Be sure to fish on top of an underwater shelf, as well as on both sides. Underwater projections of land are favorite hangouts of lake bass.

8. Weed Beds

Fish weed beds whenever they're present. These are one of the best places for bass to hide and ambush their prey. On sunny days fish the shady side. Try to fish as close to the weeds as possible. When you can, it's best to fish along the edge of the weeds, rather than casting into the weeds and bringing your fly directly away from them. An important point to remember is that in fall, when the weeds start turning brown, they're no longer giving off oxygen; they're using it to decay. *Bass will leave aquatic weed beds as soon as they start turning brown.*

9. Approach

A lake is a quiet body of water. Too often fishermen roar into a quiet cove, throwing bow waves that wash up on shore. Instead, use an electric motor, which will allow you to get into position and within casting range of potential hot spots as quietly as you can.

10. Fish Logs

Many lakes contain logs, with one end stuck in the bottom and the other end tilted up or close to the surface. Most anglers tend to cast at right angles to the log—which means they're usually fishing only the log's upper end. But the bass holding near the log will almost always be under it and fairly deep. Thus you should position your boat so that you can make a cast (a sinking line is almost always best for such work) where your fly will descend laterally along the log. On the retrieve bring your fly back along the length of the log, instead of passing at right angles to its top.

11. Fish Boat Docks

On some lakes the most prevalent cover will be boat docks and anchored boats. It pays to fish these docks. If you're using a floating line, try using the skip cast (see chapter 8), which enables you to get the fly well back under the dock where the best fish will be hiding. A low side curve cast (also described in chapter 8) will also allow you to place your fly back in that area. Early in the morning and late in the evening, when everything is so quiet, a deer hair popping bug with a weed guard is ideal for fishing boat docks. It's much better than a harder-bodied (cork, balsa, or plastic) popper. Get in position and throw your deer hair popper up onto the dock. *A hard-bodied popper would make too much noise, but a deer hair popper drops silently onto the decking. And because you have a weed guard on the deer hair bug, you can tease it off the dock and drop it gently to the water. This can be extremely effective on an early-summer morning.*

12. Spawning Temperatures

Since lakes are almost always clear in spring, having a knowledge of the spawning habits of bass can be helpful. *I don't believe you should be catching bass off spawning beds. And if you do, return them to the bed area quickly.* But if you're aware of the temperatures and times at which bass spawn, you can catch some great fish in spring as they move to spawning areas, or leave it when they've finished. Temperature, more than anything else, controls when bass spawn, so it's helpful to know the spawning temperatures of bass. The range is not large. Smallmouth bass spawn a little earlier than largemouths. The smallmouths spawn when the water temperature ranges from 55 to 70 degrees; largemouths spawn from 64 to 75 degrees. *Remember, not all bass spawn at the same time.* Bass start moving into spawning areas 6 to 8 degrees before actual spawning occurs. And new fish continue to move in throughout the spawning temperature range.

13. Distance Casting

While little has been written about distance casting when fishing for bass, it's important. There are few chances to sight-fish for bass. You can cast around visible cover but only rarely will you actually see the bass you're seeking, unless it's in the shallows of a clear lake. What this means is that much large- and smallmouth fishing consists of searching the water with your fly. The longer you can cast, the longer your retrieve will be and the more water you can probe. If you enjoy bass fishing, I urge you to practice until you can make long, effortless casts. It will produce more fish for you.

Making long casts, as Ed Jaworowski is doing on the Potomac River, allows him to search more water with his fly.

FISHING FARM PONDS FOR LARGEMOUTH BASS

Look at lists of state-record fish—the largest caught—and you'll find that an amazing number have been taken from local farm ponds. Of the 10 biggest largemouth bass caught each year in many states, there's a good chance that at least half of them, and maybe more, were from farm ponds. This is especially true in the Midwest and Northeast. Best of all, there's no need to make a distant journey to fish these ponds, because there are hundreds of them in most states. In Maryland, where I live, some counties have more than 100.

The best and most productive ponds for bass fishing usually fit several criteria. One is that they're fairly clear. Ponds that remain constantly muddy are generally poor producers. *Another criterion is size: Most ponds of less than ¼ acre will produce bluegills but few bass.* Ponds surrounded by green pastures almost always fish better than those with mud banks where cattle can walk, roiling the waters. Because these bass are aggressive, ponds can be "fished out" of them. Farm pond owners, if they want to continue to have good fishing, should insist that most bass be returned after being caught.

Something else occurs with some ponds. Now and then a pond gives up good fish for a number of years, and fishermen work its waters frequently. Then, because of the pressure, fewer bigger fish are caught, and anglers begin to believe the pond is fished out. What has really occurred, of course, is that the pond has been overfished—but a few bass remain. Anglers stop fishing because their success rate is so low. But the few bass, no longer pursued by anglers, grow fat and big. Then one day someone throws a bait, lure, or fly into the pond and hooks a real trophy. This happens more often than you might think.

Another reason ponds produce large crappies, bluegills, and bass is that so many contain a wonderful food supply. The bass grow fat on the abundant small bluegills, which in most areas produce two or three spawns, or more, each season. Larger bluegills and crappies also feed on their young—as well as small bass. The tiny food also needed by young crappies, bass, and bluegills is plentiful in most ponds—they're great fish factories. In fact, it's generally recognized that farmers will have a better pond if they allow anglers to catch and *remove* many of the bluegills, which reproduce so effectively that they can create a problem of overpopulation. This results in thousands of small bluegills that will never reach appreciable size, simply because too many are eating the available food.

Many ponds are also underfished, because anglers don't know they're there. They may be well off the road and hidden from view. Local or federal topographical maps can lead you to many ponds that the general fishing public has no knowledge of. Some pond owners also restrict the numbers of fishermen—which means that bass get a chance to grow larger. Cultivating a friendship with such farmers can mean you have virtually your own private fishing water. All of this adds up to a great fishery close to many anglers.

There are a few tricks to fishing farm ponds. I learned one of the best lessons about catching bass back in the 1950s when I read a pamphlet produced by the U.S. Department of Agriculture. The pamphlet explained how you could use certain chemicals to poison and rid your pond of an overpopulation of bluegills. It said,

> The bass move in to feed along the shorelines mainly during the early and late hours of the day. From midmorning until mid-afternoon the bass generally retreat to the greater depths of the pond. The bluegills move along the shoreline about the time the bass are departing for deeper water and leave as the bass return to the shallows. Therefore, you should spread your chemicals in the water near the shoreline about midmorning on windy days. The wind helps to disperse the poison. The bluegills will then move into the treated area and be killed. If prescribed amounts are placed in the water on windy days, the chemicals will be dispersed by wave action before the bass return late in the afternoon.

This was a textbook from a scientist—but it told me how to fish for bass in ponds. Now I knew where the bass and the bluegills would be at different times of the day. Following the pamphlet's suggestions, I found that

If you backcast over land, you'll probably snag your line in trees and other obstructions—such as the tree behind this angler.

On farm ponds casting over the water reduces your chance of snagging the backcast.

fishing early and late in the day along the shorelines indeed helped me make better catches of larger bass. And of course fishing the shallows during the middle portion of the day helped me score better on bluegills.

Bass also seek cover. In many ponds the only real refuge is deeper water. If a standpipe controls the level in the pond, it's usually located in one of the deepest parts of the pond. This greater depth is desirable to bass, and the pipe also furnishes shade and a place to ambush whatever unsuspecting food swims by. Trees that overhang a pond can also be a hot spot. The shade is certainly an attractor, and insects fall off the trees—another food supply. If there are rocks along the shoreline, these are always good spots to investigate with your fly.

Good lures for farm pond bass are simple. Fly rodders can use poppers during the warmer months and when the fish are near the edges. For much of the year, and when fishing deeper water, long streamers do very well; carry some that are slightly weighted and that have undulating feathers in darker colors. My all-time favorite choice for ponds is the Red & White Hackle Fly. And when I'm seeking bigger bass, I tie this fly at least 5 to 7 inches long. Lefty's Deceivers are great, especially when you want to work along the shallow banks of a pond. In deeper water Clouser Minnows and Half & Half patterns are deadly; the most effective color combination in these is a white underwing with a topping of chartreuse. Use plenty of flash in the flies, too. It pays to dress some of your farm pond flies with a weed guard, since vegetation is common. During the heat of summer in warmer climates, the best time to hook a truly big largemouth bass is at night. Pond waters reach high temperatures during the day and the bass seem reluctant to move much, since their metabolisms have slowed. But at night the water cools, and they become more active. A slow-moving popping bug is the best, but I've done well with Red & White Hackle Flies, too.

If you haven't tried your local farm ponds, you may be missing some of the best bass fishing in your area.

Fishing Rivers for Bass

We are blessed in this country with many great river systems that hold bass. The slow-moving rivers of the Deep South hold largemouths; they're too warm for smallmouths. But farther north and to the west are great smallmouth rivers. For far too long many departments of natural resources in the more northerly states were vitally concerned with their cold-water (trout) fisheries but ignored their bass rivers. Fortunately, this is changing. For nearly 20 years I worked as an outdoor writer for the *Baltimore Sun-papers,* one of the biggest newspapers in the country. In the mid-1980s, I wrote several editorials arguing for a catch-and-return section on the Potomac River. It was scoffed at by most state officials. But about 10 years later, under pressure from many bass fishermen, Maryland's Department of Natural Resources has now indeed established a catch-and-return section of good length on the Potomac River. Pennsylvania angler Bob Clouser has led the fight to establish slot limits on bass in the wide Susquehanna River, one of the finest smallmouth rivers in the world. The stretch of river that Bob and his companions worked so hard on is now producing better catches than anywhere else on the Susquehanna. In fact this stretch is doing so well that much of the rest of the river is now being considered for more stringent regulations regarding keeping bass. The John Day River in the West is another of the finest smallmouth rivers in this country. But it's being overfished, and we will soon see the demise of many of its larger bass—so abundant here for decades. Unless we move to put regulations on this fine river, and others, we'll lose some of our best smallmouth fishing.

I've been writing columns for various newspapers since 1951. Couple that with my travels (I think I travel about as much as any fisherman I know) and I've learned a few things. One thing I'm sure of is that for generations fisheries biologists have been taught to manage fisheries so that a certain number of fish can be harvested, yet enough be left for recreation. What we desperately need is a change in that basic philosophy. *It's time for biologists and state officials to recognize that of primary importance is the recreational value of bass (and other) fisheries. Of lesser importance is how much can be harvested. We should no longer think of our fisheries as "grocery shelves." But until this philosophy changes, I see bass fishing declining.*

Here are some tips on how to locate and fish for both species of bass in rivers:

1. In northern rivers you can catch bass on spinning and plug tackle when water temperatures are as low as 38 degrees. But fly fishing really doesn't become effective until the temperature rises to at least 55 degrees, and it improves with every degree above that. Ideal temperatures when you're fly fishing rivers for both species are about 62 to 82 degrees. When temperatures are below or above that, fly fishing generally slows. Of course, in the Deep South these temperature ranges don't apply.

2. The best time to fish in rivers in the *Deep South* is usually from December through March. This is, again, mainly because of water temperature. While southern bass often feed in water as warm as 90 degrees, such temperatures do slow them down. From sometime in December until late March, waters are cooler and contain more oxygen. This increases the largemouth's metabolism, which means that bass will be feeding more actively.

3. In the spring of the year on northern rivers, when water temperatures are in the high 50s, a unique opportunity occurs. Along many of these rivers, grass beds grow from late spring through summer. Where they die back, they leave only thick stubble. This stubble along the shoreline resembles a harvested wheat field. In spring the rivers usually run a little above their summer levels, covering these stubble patches. At this time minnows have few places to hide—there are no aquatic weed beds or lush shoreline weeds. But the stubble offers them some protection.

I have thus had some great fly fishing in the spring of the year by drifting on a river that's a foot or so above normal and casting to the drowned stubble of the weed beds.

4. Cypress and other trees standing in the water furnish some of the best cover for bass in southern rivers. Learn to throw a curve cast (see chapter 8) and you'll be able to fish around all sides of these trees. By using Bend-Back flies you can throw way back into areas that may hold some fine bass.

5. Southern rivers are often discolored from tannic acid and plants. Use flies with more than the normal amount of flash in them.

6. A good rule to remember is that when you're using streamer flies for bass, it's important to match the material the flies are made from *to the water's clarity.* I favor bucktail for most streamers; it has lifelike action, and all fish seem to approve of flies tied with it. The exception is when I'm fishing very clear water. *When waters are exceptionally clear, I switch from using bucktail for streamer wings to the more translucent synthetic materials, such as Super Hair. This applies to flies for other fresh- and saltwater species as well. Time and again I've had slow fishing in clear water, but when I changed to more translucent flies my ratio of strikes increased.*

7. Bass in rivers, especially smallmouths, will be found near current-breaking structure. This can be broken-down dam rubble, single boulders, rock ledges, sunken logs, and similar underwater structure. *If there's one good rule for smallmouths it's that you should fish where there are rocks, ledges, and boulders. However, the shape of the rock has a lot to do with where the fish will be holding. More about this later (see page 285).*

8. During warmer weather many insects hatch on rivers. This is especially true on limestone-type rivers, such as exist in the Mid-Atlantic region. Often only bass of 4 to 10 inches will feed on these emerging insects—but not always. Again, more about this later (see page 287).

9. During the heat of summer bass fishing is often best early and late in the day. Early morning is usually better than dusk, since water temperatures cool during the night.

10. When water temperatures rise in summer, and a river has a shoreline with high banks or tall trees, it's often best to fish early in the day on the western bank, or the bank that's shaded. Bass seem to feed better when there's no bright sunlight. Remember, bass don't have eyelids to protect them from the sun's glare.

11. In a river locate carp rooting in the bottom. These spots can furnish some great trophy-bass fishing. I'll explain more later (see page 287).

12. Just as in deep-water fishing, in rivers it's often important to adjust the swimming depth of your fly. At times bass will be feeding close to the bottom; at others they may prefer the middepths or just below the surface. When you're not getting the strikes you think you should, experiment with weighted flies and lines with different sink rates.

13. Locate seams of water—spots where two currents collide or where the river rushes past a location with calmer water adjacent to the current. The bass will be holding just inside the quiet water waiting for food to sweep by.

14. Popping bugs should be retrieved almost continuously when you're fishing a river with a current. Poppers allowed to float dead, without much motion, often pass right over fish—which aren't aware that a bug floated by.

15. A drag chain is often a good idea when you're drifting a smallmouth river. It can regulate your drift speed as well as preventing your boat from spinning in the current. A drag chain can also be used in a lake. While it doesn't touch the bottom, its resistance in the water tends to keep the boat floating in the direction of the drift and not turning or spinning.

16. When a river is slightly roiled or dirty from recent rains, seek out spots where clearer streams enter it. Fish this clearer section along the river's shoreline.

17. During the colder months in northern climates, you can often enjoy great bass fishing by working the warmer waters emitted from local power plants.

If it's possible, I recommend that you always carry two fly rods armed with different lines and fly patterns. Unless a bass river is very deep—and most of them aren't—I suggest carrying a weight-forward floating line, which is the one you'll probably use the most. It's ideal for working popping bugs, for flies close to the shoreline, and in water depths not exceeding 5 feet. Incidentally, if you're fishing sinking flies on a floating line and you need to get a little deeper, you usually have to do two things. One, you need to change to a fly with a bit more weight. Two, you need to increase the length of your leader. A conventional leader will be buoyed by the floating fly line; with a longer one you'll give the fly a better chance to swim deeper in the water column.

I favor a brightly colored floating line for bass fishing. Much bass fishing is done in the early morning and late evening, when light is low and things become difficult to see. Brightly colored (especially fluorescent) lines permit you to better monitor both your cast and your retrieve. Also, remember that floating lines fish better if they're clean and float high on the surface. If the front end sinks, it's a good idea to clean the line. Commercial vinyl cleaners are sometimes used to clean fly lines. But most are water soluble and, while they will clean your line, the slickness soon washes away. I suggest using one of the fly-line manufacturers' line cleaners. These products were developed for this special purpose and will not only clean your line but also allow it to shoot through the guides better.

The other fly line I recommend for river fishing is not an intermediate (with an approximate sink rate of 1 inch per second) but a line that sinks slightly faster. Use a Scientific Anglers Wet Cel II, which sinks about twice as fast; even better, I think, is to cast one of the new all-monofilament lines designed for cold-water fishing (lines designed for tropical fishing in cooler waters will tend to coil and make casting difficult). These lines cast superbly and will permit you to retrieve your fly several feet deeper than an intermediate line—often a decided advantage.

While I'm discussing lines for river fishing, I'd like to make another point. Unless you're casting to specific targets *and you're a good caster who's trying to cover a lot of water,* I suggest not using a bass bug taper or conventional weight-forward taper. Instead, get one of the lines that has a longer belly and front and back taper. Such lines as the Scientific Anglers Steelhead Taper or Cortland Rocket Taper allow you to make longer casts than you normally could with a conventional weight-forward. If you cast well and haven't tried these lines in situations when you need to make frequent long casts, you may be pleasantly surprised.

When it comes to popping bugs, I long ago decided that the color of any bug that's moved fairly quickly on the retrieve is unimportant. Eyes are put on poppers for anglers, not fish; they're almost always located on top of the bug above the water, and go unseen by bass. However, I find that it's to my advantage to color the front or face of my popping bugs with bright yellow paint. This is the portion of the bug that faces me during the retrieve. I feel it's important always to know the location of my bug, and a bright yellow face helps me see it better.

Many trout fishermen are aware that if you grease almost all of your leader with fly flotant (the exception is the tippet, when you're fishing midges), the leader floats or at least stays near the surface. This trick works well with popping bugs, too. This can be helpful in slick water, but where it really shines is when you're working vegetation, and especially in swift water. *A greased leader stays on or near the top and allows the bug to be worked better. In swifter water, an ungreased leader often sinks. This tends to drown your popping bug, and it ruins your presentation.*

When retrieving any underwater fly or popping bug, one basic mistake that even experienced fly fishermen make is to use the tip of the rod to manipulate the fly or bug. By flipping the tip upward, the fly or bug is swept forward. The rod tip is then lowered so another flip can be made. The problem with this is that as the rod is dropped, slack develops in the line between the fly or bug and the tip. Should the fish take the offering at this moment, the accumulated slack often leads to a missed strike. Another common mistake is to work an underwater fly or popping bug with the rod tip held several feet above the surface. The problem is especially apparent with a popping bug, which you can see throughout your retrieve. What occurs is this: You manipulate the fly or bug by either stripping in line or flipping the rod tip. As you pause in your retrieve, the line immediately outside the rod tip sags downward. So instead of the fly or bug stopping, the sagging line continues to pull it forward. If you're aiming for a stop-and-go retrieve you'll thus never get it by holding the rod tip high. *Instead point the rod tip at the fly or bug and hold it no more than a few inches above the surface. This way during any pause in the retrieve, the line is always taut and ready for a good strike. Also, the bug or fly will stop when you stop moving the line.* **This applies not just to bass fish-**

ng but also to retrieving under water in almost all fresh- and salt-water situations.

Fishing seams of water is important. A river rarely flows at the same speed throughout its width. Underwater obstructions slow the current or create eddies, big or small. Where the slower-moving water meets the faster-flowing current is what's called a seam; it's clearly visible to anyone looking for it. Bass will hold just within the quiet water, waiting for any food being swept downstream on the current. Seams can occur in the middle of a river or close to shore. They're an important structure that you should constantly be looking for.

I mentioned earlier how important rocks are in bass fishing. But it's the shape of the rock that determines where bass may be holding. If a rock slants downstream, current rushes up on the slant and then swirls around the rock's downstream end. Bass will almost never hold in front of such a rock—they'd have to fight the current. Instead, they'll lie in the water behind the rock. If the rock is very wide, they'll usually be in the quiet water out near one of the seams formed by the meeting of the calmer water with the current. The best way to approach such a fish with your fly isn't from downstream, or by casting into the quiet water and working the fly out into the current. These would be unnatural approaches. Instead toss your fly upstream from the rock and retrieve it down past the rock, the way nature would carry any creature with the current.

One of the most effective places in a river to fish bass is any barrier—look for a ledge, a small dam, or the head of a riffle that has a rock barrier with water flowing over. Such barriers form a dead flow of water immediately in front of them. They can be only a foot or two high, so long as the water slows as it approaches one and then flows over it. Bass can lie at rest in this dead water and watch for incoming food. I try to anchor upstream and at an angle from the barrier. Then I make a cast several feet above the barrier and retrieve my fly across the current so that it swims immediately above the barrier. This is an exceptionally good way to take nice bass.

One of the finest of all rock structures that hold bass is a ledge slanting upstream, with a recess on its upstream side. A bass can lie in the dead water of the recess with the overhanging stone roof making it feel secure. It doesn't need to work in the current—it just watches the food approach. Cast upstream from the ledge and bring your fly back just the way Mother Nature would deliver prey to the bass.

Bob Clouser gave me a great tip for catching larger river bass. Bob guides daily in summer on the Susquehanna River. Here carp root in the bottom to get their food. As each tears at the bottom, it leaves a plume of downstream mud that's easily seen. Bob noticed that he frequently saw big bass swimming right beside the carp as they rooted. He began looking for rooting carp and any nearby bass. Incidentally, when bass are following rooting carp they turn almost black and very visible; many fish change color like this just before they attack their prey. Anyway, when Bob located a bass following a carp, he dropped a fly just in front of the bass and was

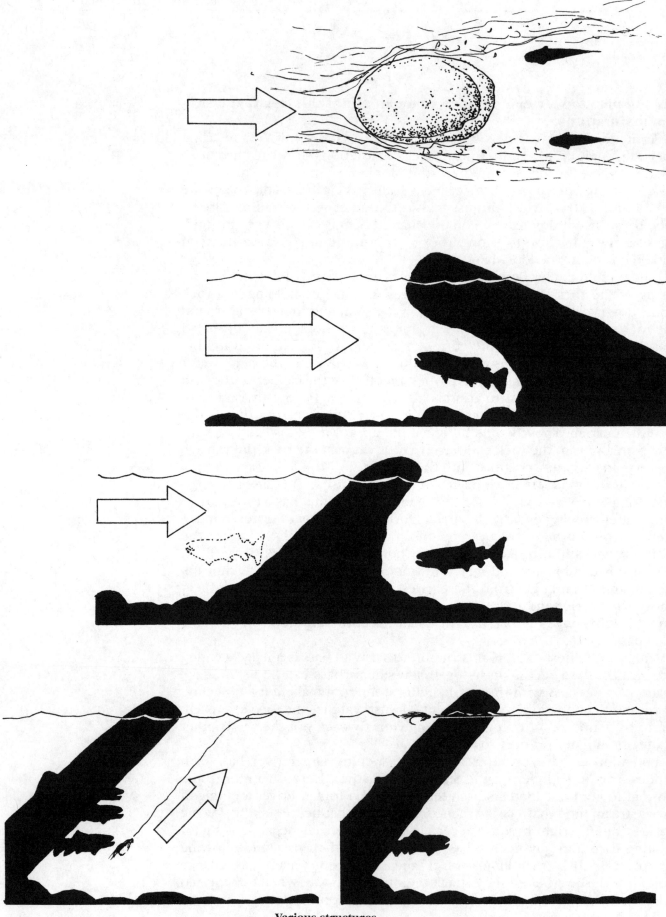

Various structures

ewarded with an instant strike. Apparently the rooting carp dislodge or frighten crayfish, which flee. The bass know this and follow the carp. Oddly enough, the carp don't have to be rooting; if an individual carp is swimming among other carp that are rooting, bass will frequently follow this individual. Perhaps the bass feel this loner will soon start to root and furnish a meal.

Casting to bass cruising near rooting carp is very effective; in summer a good river bass caught with this technique will weigh 3 pounds. I recall taking my son and grandson on the Susquehanna River one August day. Using this method we managed to catch five bass of more than 3 pounds, two of them exceeding 4 pounds. We caught them in less than 3 feet of water—a very difficult accomplishment in the heat of a midsummer day.

During the summer months (usually July and August) there occurs in many northeastern U.S. bass rivers an insect hatch that no avid fly rodder should miss. Similar hatches also occur on many rivers throughout the United States, harboring both bass and trout. This is the white miller hatch (genus *Ephoron*); on many rivers these mayflies emerge in near blizzard numbers. The height of the hatch looks like a snowstorm, so many large white flies are in the air. Usually the hatch begins on the lower portion of a river and, over a two-week period, progresses upriver. White millers begin coming off at about dusk. They're unusual mayflies so far as mating is concerned: The male nymphs shed their skins within minutes of emerging, and sometimes can be seen with a portion of this skin trailing along behind them in flight. The females don't molt at all. These *Ephoron* emerge from the water ready to mate.

The first two indications that this hatch is about to occur are tiny rings appearing on the surface where fish are quietly sipping on emerging nymphs, and a few white mayflies fluttering in the air. The total hatch time is short—from about sundown to no more than an hour after dark. Of all the bass-triggering insect hatches I've fished, the white miller is the most phenomenal. It's usually so intense that it causes large bass (some better than 4 pounds) to feed avidly. *This is one of the rare times when you have a good chance of catching a very large bass on a dry fly.*

To catch bass during a white miller hatch is easy once you know where the bugs are emerging, which is usually over a gravel bar. Use a floating line; a 7- or 8-weight rod is ideal, but you'll be casting less than 30 feet, so an even lighter rod is okay if you choose. Your fly choice isn't critical, but it should float. Many people tie large, buoyant white or Royal Wulff–type flies on size 8 or 10 dry-fly hooks. Even small popping bugs will work. My favorite fly is one that's durable, quick to tie, and floats well. I've successfully used this pattern during white miller hatches since the early 1950s. If you can spin deer hair on a hook, you can make this one: Attach a sparse, short tail of white deer hair to the shank of a size 6 or 8 standard dry-fly hook. *Then spin white deer hair onto the hook shank, being sure to pack it firmly.* Trim the body to a rodlike shape approximately ¼ to ⅜ inch in diameter. *To make the fly float better, I grease it well with fly flotant.* Locate a fish taking either nymphs or adult millers on the surface. Immediately cast a few inches above it. *Bass will*

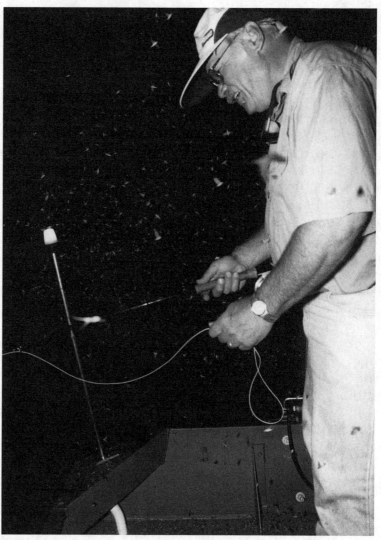

Bob Clouser with a swarm of white millers around him during a July hatch on the Susquehanna River.

cruise, so your cast should be directed to the target area as soon as possible. That's it. Take a light with you, because the fish will feed for at least a half hour after dark.

Fishing Streams

The same techniques that work on rivers also work on small streams. There are a few differences, however. First let me say that some of the most enjoyable days I've ever spent fly fishing have been on small meadow streams. Such streams run warm in summer, so they support few or no trout. What they do hold are scrappy sunfish, rock bass, and smallmouths.

Some of the most enjoyable fly fishing the author does is on small meadow streams like this one.

A big bass on most of these streams would weigh 2 pounds; a true trophy, close to 3 pounds. I wet-wade these streams and, on a warm summer day, there's nothing finer for me than to be alone with a light fly rod, sneaking up on these fish.

Tackle has to be scaled down. Panfish-sized popping bugs dressed on a size 6 or 8 hook are the ticket. Streamers and nymphs dressed on size 6 or smaller hooks are recommended. Use a size 4, 5, or 6 weight-forward line. (Basically, this is your trout tackle.)

The most important difference between fishing a small stream and a bigger river is your approach. Because you'll be wading in rather thin, quiet water, your approach must be much more silent and careful. Most important, you should wade upstream. In a narrow, small stream, the wading fisherman flushes silt and mud downstream before him, which apparently alerts the fish. Make it a point to wade upstream.

In pools bass will almost always be holding in one of three places. If there's a large rock in the pool, that will be the prime location to find bass. If there's no rock, the best spots are usually at the head of the pool, just below the riffle, or at the pool's tail.

One other factor needs to be considered. On small streams all flies should be worked gently, including popping bugs. These fish are not huge and they aren't sure whether a fly will hurt them or they can hurt it. So gently working the bug or fly brings better results.

Peacock Bass

The peacock bass is becoming a prized quarry for fly rodders. Peacocks have existed in the canals of southern Florida for many years, because the state stocks them. In the beginning they planted a subspecies that didn't grow very large—but this has been corrected. There are enough of them in these canals now for full-time guides to take you after them.

But the best peacock bass fishing occurs in Central and South America. I've fished for them in a number of places, and I've found that the best trophy-peacock fishing is in the upper Amazon basin of Brazil. Many of the waterways and rivers of this region have been lightly fished—or haven't been fished. On my last trip here we caught several bass that we weighed at just under 20 pounds. Now, if a lot of 20-pound peacock bass were put on a scale, they'd weigh 12 pounds or less. Ours were tested on a scale. Colombia has some fantastic peacock opportunities, if that country ever becomes safe to travel in. Venezuela also has some great fishing. However, a fly rodder won't do as well on this country's lakes with drowned timber; it's difficult to fish a fly among standing dead trees.

If you fish for peacocks in their home range, Central and South America, here are some tips that I've found helpful. First, a peacock has a huge mouth in relation to its size. But you don't need large hooks for this fish. *My biggest hook is a size 2/0, with which I've taken many peacocks heavier than 12 pounds.* Large hooks are more difficult to cast and to set properly on the strike. Best of all, you simply don't need them. However, larger streamer flies will catch bigger fish. My favorite large peacock pattern is a modified Deceiver (I call it a Magnum Deceiver, and an example is shown on page 91) at least 9 inches long. But because it's tied on a 3X-long 2/0 hook, it can easily be cast with a 9-weight rod.

Popping bugs will catch peacock bass, but I urge you to use them only as a last resort. The favorite lure of spin and plug casters who seek monster peacock bass is the Wood Chopper or a similar plug. These are huge wooden lures, as thick as a broom handle, with one or two propellers on them. They're thrown out and retrieved to create as much disturbance as possible. Some huge peacocks have been caught on these monster plugs. *But every time I've been at a camp with fishermen who used plugs, jigs, spinner-baits, or spoons, I've found that fly fishermen outfished them. The anglers always caught bigger and more peacocks—providing they used large flies.*

Why? Much peacock fishing is done either in rivers, along banks, around fallen trees, in deep holes, or in lagoons (small lakes off to the side of a river). Visualize one or two anglers going into a quiet lagoon and making 30 or 40 casts with those noisy lures. Any wise peacock will be alerted that something very abnormal is going on.

A nice peacock bass taken on a fly rod by the author in the north-central Amazon basin of Brazil.

But if two fly fishermen using streamers move quietly into a lagoon, they can cast for an hour or more and cause little disturbance. Because of their silence, they'll catch more and bigger peacocks. I've seen this occur time after time.

What tackle should you use for peacocks? A good 9-weight is enough, even for a 20-pounder, if you have any fish-fighting ability. If you're in doubt bring along a 10-weight, but know that it'll get tiresome to cast. You should have two lines. A weight-forward floater is ideal for fishing a popping bug, or when fish are in shallow water. There are times when peacock bass will either be spawning, or in 1 to 3 feet of water and cruising like bonefish. At such times a long cast with a 10-foot or longer leader and a fly that drops quietly to the surface is ideal. Most of the time, a floater and a Teeny 300 fast-sinking line are the ticket. You'll probably use the

Teeny 300 more than the floater. Peacock don't have big teeth, so a shock leader of 20-pound test at the tippet is all that's needed.

Fortunately, fly patterns are simple. Several Lefty's Deceivers in red, yellow-and-red, black-and-yellow, and—best of all—chartreuse-and-white will all produce well. Put plenty of Flashabou or Krystal Flash in the wings. Large Clouser Minnows dressed in chartreuse-and-white, yellow-and-black or white with a touch of red at the front are excellent. Add to these some Magnum Deceivers and you have all the fly patterns you'll need for peacock bass. However, native peacock waters also contain all sorts of toothy fish—payara, (which have two huge teeth protruding through their skulls), piranha, morocoto, jacunda, and many other species. For these take along some smaller versions of the above, along with braided 30-pound-test wire.

Northern Pike

I caught my first northern pike on a fly rod in 1947. It was such fun that I can still vividly remember it. For many years the northern was shunned by fly fishermen, but fortunately, we've recently discovered what a wonderful fly-rod fish this is. Last year my friend Bill Anderson and I fished at Lake Maria (pronounced "Ma-RYE-ah") in the North Seal River Preserve of Manitoba. In six days of fishing we caught more 50 northerns of 12 pounds and up—all on fly rods. Some were quite a bit bigger. It would be hard to match such fly-fishing fun.

Four patterns have worked for the author for decades wherever he fished for northern pike. Top: Rabbit Leech; middle: Clouser Minnow; bottom: Lefty's Deceiver and Bend-Back.

There are many features about fishing for northern pike in the far north of Canada of interest to any fly rodder. First, long casts are often unnecessary; many northern pike can be caught with a cast of less than 25 feet. Also, much of this is sight-fishing. This is especially true in spring, when pike move into the shallows. And northerns are not selective when it comes to flies. Every fly rodder I know has several favorite patterns. Truth is, these fish, when in the mood—which is most of the time—will eat anything you put in front of them. For some years outdoor writers insisted that you needed huge flies to encourage larger pike to hit. But I've found that a fly of 5 inches will draw as many strikes as a 9-inch fly—and the 5-incher is so much easier to cast. I believe that four flies is all you need. Lefty's Deceivers in red-and-white, chartreuse-and-white, and olive-and-red are excellent. Also try orange-and-black and yellow-and-red. The same colors of Clouser Minnow do well; when pike are in deeper water, add lead eyes.

Most northern pike lakes hold leeches. Pike must feast on these leeches, because the best fly on many occasions is so shabby looking you wouldn't use it unless someone suggested it. Place a 2/0 hook in your tying vise. Cut a black rabbit fur strip 3 inches long and ¼ inch wide. Attach it at the front of the hook and finish the fly. Add a light coat of epoxy to the thread—and that's it. Looks like the devil, but tease it in front of a pike and you'll almost always get a strike. If the pike are lying in shallow bays, drop the fly a few

Many fish, such as this pike, are found in weeds. One of the best flies for this is the Bend-Back—a few are shown.

feet beyond one and retrieve it slowly up to the fish. If it shows interest but doesn't strike, let the fly go to the bottom, then slowly drag it through the silt. Few pike will resist this. If the fish are in deeper water, I add a pair of ¼-ounce lead eyes and fish this deep and slow.

The final fly that you should always carry is a Bend-Back. I use a size 2/0 long-shanked hook and tie only a wing on the fly—with a lot of flash. Don't bother with any body material on the shank. This fly can be fished among sunken weed beds, lily pads, and drowned logs or rocks without fear of snagging. In fact it's one of the most important flies you should carry for northern pike above all others. The best colors are, again, the same mentioned for the Deceiver.

Tackle requirements are simple. An 8- or 9-weight rod is ample—there's no need for anything larger. Pike rarely make long runs, so a good freshwater bass reel is okay. What you do need is the right leader. Most of the time I use a straight piece of 15- or 20-pound-test monofilament for the butt section. Leaders with many knots tend to tangle in the weeds so often found where there are northern pike. For a floating line I use a leader of about 7 or 8 feet. For a sinking line, such as the Teeny 300, a leader 3 to 4 feet long is ample. What is important is the bite tippet. It should be 30-pound-test braided wire (solid wire kinks too quickly). Any pike has a big mouth, and a 15-pounder has a huge one. They frequently strike from the rear of the fly. Surging forward, they suck it in or deeply inhale it. Because they have sharp teeth—which also cover the roofs of their mouths—you need a long wire leader. I suggest starting with a 14-inch bite leader. As flies get destroyed, you'll have to retie a number of times, which means shortening the wire. When it reaches 10 inches or less, I replace it with another 14-inch length. Attaching the leader is simple: Clinch-knot the smallest barrel swivel you can find to the end of your monofilament leader. Then tie the braided wire to the other end of the swivel with a figure-8 knot (see chapter 5). Then attach the fly with another figure-8 knot.

Just after ice-out in northern Canada (usually in late May), northern pike move into the shallows. They gather outside 2- to 5-feet deep coves and small bays when the water temperature rises above 55 degrees. As soon as it hits 60 degrees they move into the bays, where they'll remain until the water reaches about 70 degrees. This is some of the most exciting fly rodding you'll ever do. It's like fishing for freshwater barracudas. Your boat quietly moves into a bay and you search for the pike, which are usually lying motionless. Once you've located one, place your cast so the fly is about 5 feet past and 2 or 3 feet in front of the fish. Begin a slow retrieve. That's it!

As soon as water temperatures hit 70 degrees most fish move out of the bays. At these times—and also when the bays are colder, in the high-50-degree range—pike can be found just outside the mouths of the bays and coves in deeper water of 6 to 12 feet. This is where the Teeny 300 line and a weighted Clouser are ideal. Since these lakes are so clear, much of the time you can still sight-fish. Pike can also be found where there is a profusion of lily pads.

Heavy rods are not necessary for big pike. The author landed this 16-pounder on an 8-weight and a Teeny 300 line.

During much of July and August the fish will gravitate to underwater weed beds, rocky shorelines, or spots where streams enter the lake. You can still sight-fish, but usually you'll be blind-casting. If you haven't tried fly rodding for northern pike, you've missed one of the most interesting aspects of our sport.

12

FISHING INSHORE AND BACKCOUNTRY WATERS

It has been written that in the United States, about 80 percent of the population lives within a four-hour drive of salt water. When you consider that many freshwater fishing areas are either crowded or overfished, you can understand why fly fishermen are gravitating to the coast. There are other reasons, too. In salt water there are almost no stocked fish. Fish in the sea live only if they can escape their predators. The way most species do this is being able to swim faster than whatever's chasing it. Thus almost everything in the sea is a faster and more powerful swimmer than freshwater species. Another reason fishermen are heading to the salt is that it offers more open water, space, and opportunities to fish without crowds. I could go on, but already you can see why so many fly fishermen are now fishing in the sea, especially inshore waters. I define inshore, by the way, as roughly those waters within a few miles of a coast and averaging in depth from 1 foot to no more than 40.

Perhaps the four most popular inshore species sought by fly fishermen are striped bass, bonefish, redfish, and tarpon. I might also include the permit in this category, since it's rapidly becoming the most prized of all tropical flats species.

In the following pages I'll discuss some presentation problems—and solutions—in fishing for most inshore species.

A quick way to straighten coils from a fly line is to make a large loop, place your foot in it as shown, and pull firmly on the two ends.

Understanding the Tides

There are a number of differences between fresh- and saltwater fishing. One of the greatest is the way tides can determine saltwater fishing success. If you want to be proficient in the salt, you'll need at least a basic understanding of the tide and what it does.

The tide is the rising and falling of water. It has two major effects: It changes the height of the water in any location it affects, and it creates a current flow. Both of these factors are very important to fish and fishermen.

There are three major reasons why the tide affects fishermen:

1. It floods areas that fish normally can't get to. For example, on a low tide shallow flats either are dry or have so little water that fish can't get up onto them.
2. It transports the prey species that fish feed on.
3. Tidal current often concentrates the food sources. The ability to recognize where these concentrations occur can make a big difference in how well fishermen fare.

Of all the factors that cause tide to affect fishing success, the most important for fishermen to realize is that much of the food that saltwater species prey upon doesn't live in specific locations. Let me explain what I mean. In a freshwater stream crayfish, sculpins, minnows, and other prey species live in a particular pool. When rains swell the stream, these creatures seek shelter so that they can stay in their home pool. *Most will live and die in the same pool.* In salt water, the very opposite is true. *Most creatures that are a food source for the predators fishermen seek are nomads.* Shrimp may be transported by the tide several miles in a given day. Mullets, menhaden, alewives, bay anchovies, and dozens of other saltwater baitfish are constantly changing their location. Crabs are being forever swept along with the current.

Perhaps the most important reason you should understand the tide is to realize that much of the food of predatory fish is being carried by it. Once you understand this, you can look at the tides in a different light. You can begin to understand, for example, that if the tide is flowing over a coral flat, oyster bar, or reef, there's likely a vertical eddy on its downtide side. The water on the downcurrent side swirls somewhat like a moving waterwheel. Baitfish are momentarily trapped here. This in turn will lure gamefish. Here's another example of how understanding tidal function can mean more hookups. If the banks of a creek or river are flooded at high tide, baitfish will seek shelter and food among the drowned trees. But eventually, when the tide begins to fall, the baitfish will have to return to the river. They sense that predators will be lurking close, waiting to eat them, so they'll wait until the last possible moment before coming back to the river. The last water pouring off these drowned flats will run out through depressions, small creeks, and ditches. The baitfish will stay until they must finally swim down the ditch into the river. Thus it's a good idea to fish on a falling tide at the mouth of any creek or drainage ditch.

While there are more than 30 factors that influence the rise and fall of tide, the main one is the gravitational pull of the moon and sun on the earth—and its waters. Another factor—less important but still worth considering, particularly where the water is shallow—is wind. I'll discuss the effects of wind on the tide a little later.

During each 28-day period, most locations see four major tides cycles. For one seven-day period there will be little rise and fall in the water. This

The tide radically affects saltwater fishing. Here's a tidal flat at high tide. Compare this to the same flat at low tide.

This is the same flat at low tide—very much different.

is followed by a seven-day period when the tide will rise much higher and fall much lower. Then there is another seven-day period when waters rise and fall only a little. This is followed by a seven-day period when waters again rise and fall markedly. Each of these cycles is approximately seven days in length. *The period when the tide only rises and falls a little is called the* **neap** *tide phase (always pronounced "nip" tide). The seven days when the tide rises much higher and falls much lower are called* **spring** *tide. Some people remember this by saying the tides "spring up and down."* There are a few places that see only one low and high tide a day. And in rare places there's no real tide at all—such as in Fiji. *But most saltwater fishermen can figure that wherever they fish, there will be four tides during a 24-hour period—two highs and two lows.*

How do you know whether a neap or spring tide is occurring? Most newspapers give a daily listing of the local tidal rise and fall. Many fishing publications do the same, and local fly shops can inform you. But there's a simpler way of knowing which tidal phase is occurring: Just look at the moon. If there's a full moon or no moon, then the maximum gravitational pull is being placed on the earth and there will be spring tides, which rise and fall considerably. In the quarter-moon phase, gravitational pull is diminished—and neap tides occur.

How does all of this help you as a fisherman? **First, understand that tides repeat themselves every two weeks!** Let's assume that you were at Lucky Ledge Light on the Sunday the 10th of the month, and fishing was terrific. You realized that the best fishing came at noon. If you returned the following Sunday at noon and tried fishing here, you'd find the tidal phase to be almost exactly the opposite, and you'd probably have little success. But come back 14 days—two Sundays—later, and unless there's been a major weather change, tidal conditions will be almost identical. *It's important to realize that generally, the tidal phase is repeated every two weeks.*

In most places there are four high and low tides in a 24-hour period. Approximately every six hours you'll see a change from the prevailing tide. For example, the tide will fall for about six hours; then it'll rise for about six hours; and then the cycle is repeated. *It's important to remember that tides are about one hour later each day.* Thus, if a high tide occurred at 10 o'clock today, tomorrow that high tide will be at 11 o'clock, unless there's a major weather change (winds, for example, can hasten or delay the rise in the water). But if weather and conditions stay approximately the same, each succeeding day the tides will occur about one hour later.

In summary, here are some of the important points to remember about the tide:

1. Tides that rise and fall very little and last for seven days are called neap tides. The seven days following a neap tide period the water will rise much higher and fall much lower; these are called spring tides. Then the cycle repeats itself.

2. The moon will tell you whether neap or spring tides are occurring. During quarter-moon phases neap tides occur. During the dark of the moon, or a full moon, spring tides occur.
3. Tides are roughly one hour later each day—so plan your fishing accordingly.
4. The tidal conditions will usually repeat themselves every two weeks.

As I've mentioned, the wind can be a major factor affecting the flow and the height of water in an area. Regardless of whether the tide is in the neap or spring phase, wind can sometimes have a major impact on the water. In areas with a lot of shallow water, especially large basins (Currituck Sound in North Carolina is a good example), wind blowing strongly from one direction can actually push or shove a lot of the water in a downwind direction. For example, if a stiff wind blows for a day or two from the west, the water on the eastern side of a shallow bay may rise several feet higher than it would with no wind. And the western side may have little or no water. While wind is usually not a major factor in tidal rise and fall, it happens often enough that you should be aware of it.

Many people think that the incoming tide is always the best for fishing. Of course, that's not true. Writers have often said that the incoming tide is best when bonefishing. While this is certainly true in many situations, the reverse can also be true. For example, imagine a flat that rises from deep water to a ridge; beyond the ridge is a large bay. Bonefish will often feed up on this flat as the tide rises. After the water rises above the ridge the bonefish may well cross over the ridge and follow their prey, *feeding all during the falling tide as it recedes into the bay beyond.*

In a large basin or bay with a narrow neck that connects it to the main body of water, the fishing may be excellent on both the incoming (rising) tide and again as the tide falls. On the incoming tide the baitfish and creatures that gamefish prey upon will be swept with the tidal current into the opening of the bay. The best feeding situation for predator species will be on the *inside* of the mouth of the opening. Think of the inside of this mouth as the opening of a funnel as the bait is carried from the larger body of water into the bay or basin. The fish will take up a feeding position as water is brought into the bay. But when the tide falls the reverse is true— the fish will move to the outside of the bay and await the prey species being swept out of the bay at the "funnel mouth."

There are also many situations in which a slack tide (no current or rise and fall is occurring) can produce the best fishing. This is particularly true if you seek fish that prefer to hang around buoys, markers, and other such structures. When the tide is racing past such formations certain fish, such as snook, tripletails, cobia, jewfish, and others that live near these structures, will simply hug the bottom and not fight the current. *But when the tide goes slack these species often rise and hold near the markers and buoys. This is the time to fish them.*

The tide can have a major impact upon the water temperature in an area, too. Let me cite two examples of how tide and temperature can affect your fishing success. During the warmer months the sun will beat down on water in a shallow bay. If the bay's bottom is covered by dark turtle grass or black sand, this water will heat up rapidly. The increased temperature may cause fish normally here to leave the area. A falling tide will drain this extra-warm water from the bay. A rising tide will flood cooler water into the area, and the fish will often return to feed. One of the best places to fish for stripers in early spring when they arrive along the New England coast is in dark-bottomed bays. The water temperature rise in these bays attracts both baitfish and stripers. During the winter months in the Caribbean a cold front will often cool the water on flats, causing permit and bonefish to flee to deep water. *For a fishing vacation in the winter months, you may want to consider areas that are adjacent to deep water.* Suppose you're booked into a lodge well away from deep water in an area where there are large, shallow flats that bonefish feed on. A cold front arrives as you get to the lodge. The water temperature drops and remains low for several days. You'll see few fish. But if you choose a lodge whose fishing flats are close to deep water, you needn't worry about water temperature. Cold fronts will have no effect on the deeper water. Each incoming tide will bring a flood of warm water onto the flats, which can maintain an acceptable temperature for bonefish and other species. Flats located well away from deep water, on the other hand, may be devoid of fish. During the hottest days of summer, flats adjacent to deeper water will also deliver cooler water to the flats—the reverse of winter conditions.

Tidal flow can have a major effect upon water quality, too. Wind or other factors may so dirty the water that fishing is impossible. During neap tidal phases you often won't see this water change much. But during a spring tide, so much water is sucked out of the area to be replaced by clear water that fishing can again be great.

Tides can also affect fishing in another way. Along many shorelines and around mangroves and other trees lining the banks, all sorts of grass and floating debris will collect on a high tide. This is left stranded on the banks. When another spring tide occurs that rises high enough to refloat the grass and debris, fishing can get complicated. So much debris is floating on and in the water that it can spoil your retrieves. Knowing that this can happen will alert you to avoid areas where these conditions exist, or to be armed with weedless fly patterns.

Knowing when tidal currents flow rapidly, such as through inlets and around projecting points of land, can help your fishing. Inlets and projecting points of land create eddies in the water, much as does a rock sitting in a river's flow. Predatory fish will lie either in the eddy or along the edge of the quiet current, waiting for any prey species to be swept past them. This is why a rock jetty usually holds fish. Not only is there fish-holding cover among the rocks, but the jetty also creates an eddy on the downcurrent side that helps trap baitfish.

The author with a nice bonefish caught on a Bahama flat near deep water. The fish was caught during a cold spell, but the nearby deep water kept the temperature warm enough for bonefish.

Many people chum for a host of species in salt water. The tidal phase can have a major effect on chumming success. Unless you're chumming fish up from considerable depths, a slack tide will usually produce poorly. Any chum placed overboard on a slack tide will fall almost vertically to the bottom—attracting few fish. If the tide runs very slowly, your chum line won't reach out as far as you want, and so the number of fish alerted to your chum is also reduced. If the tide runs too fast, though, you need to use more chum to keep the chum slick from being dissipated. (For more information about chumming, see page 311.)

To be a successful fisherman in salt water you must understand that the tide will affect your fishing. The better you understand this, the better you can plan and cope.

Being Ready

Perhaps the outstanding difference between fly fishing in fresh and salt waters is that the angler working the salt has to be ready to react faster and, often, more accurately. Being ready is the hallmark of an experienced saltwater fly fisherman; the angler unaware of this vital requirement will see far too many missed opportunities.

Being ready starts before you leave the house, motel, or camp. Saltwater fly fishing demands sharper hooks. Freshwater fish have relatively soft inner mouths, while many saltwater species have mouths that seem tougher than a bank vault door. Instead of sharpening your hooks just before you cast the fly, you should presharpen them at home. At times you'll hook a fish but see the point dulled or the fly badly mangled during the fight. You land the fish but there are others nearby, hungry and eager to strike. Take the time to check the point. Barbed flies can also be damaged when you try to remove them from fish. I've been using barbless hooks since 1956 and I don't believe I've lost fish because of this. However, it sure allows me to release fish easier.

Make up spare leaders beforehand so that they're quickly available should the one you're fishing with break. A heavy shock or bite leader attached in front of the fly must swim straight if the fly is to travel correctly on the retrieve. Most experienced tarpon fishermen know that quickly getting the coils out of 80- to 120-pound monofilament bite leaders is nearly impossible. For this reason they prepare their leaders ahead of time, straightening the heavy monofilament and attaching the tippet and fly. The completed and ready-to-use leaders and flies are then stored in various types of containers so that the stiff monofilament remains straight. When you need one, just lift it from its storage compartment and attach it to the butt section.

Pliers should always be available instantly—and on your hip. You need them to tighten knots, cut wire or heavy monofilament, remove hooks from fish, and many other chores. *If you have them stashed away, it may take you too long to get them.*

Especially in the Tropics, rain can descend on you in a hurry. It boggles my mind to see people go on any *kind of fly-fishing trip without carrying rain gear.* If there's one thing every angler should have in addition to his tackle, it's good rain gear. I prefer the type with separate jacket and pants. You can slip on the jacket as a windbreaker when you need one; also, a two-piece suit usually gives you more freedom of movement. When

you buy rain gear, make sure you can put the rain pants on without removing your shoes. Some rain pants have legs so tight you have to sit down,
take off your shoes, put on the pants, and then the shoes—a good opportunity to get wet. Keep rain gear where you can grab it quickly. I've seen
people store it in the bottom of their carrying bag—where it's difficult to
get to.

A hat with a brim allows you to see fish so much better. Every flats fisherman has had the experience of speeding along in a boat and seeing the
breeze tear his cap off. You *know* it's going to happen, so be ready—have a
dry spare. Many people use a lanyard to clip the hat to their jacket or the
collar of their shirt—not a bad idea. And remember never to nod your
head up and down while wearing a hat and cruising at high speed. I try to
keep my head tilted forward so that the wind keeps my hat pushed tightly
onto my head.

Polarized glasses are an essential piece of your fishing tackle. If you have
only one pair—especially if you're on a distant trip—and you break or lose
it, your fishing is going to be tougher. Carry a spare pair. If you wear prescription glasses and can't afford a second pair, at least carry a pair of clip-
ons for your regular glasses. Clip-ons come in several tints. For most fishing
situations a pair of glasses or clip-ons that're brownish tan in color seems to
be best. But offshore many of us prefer the darker blue-gray tint. This same
darker coloring is also generally better for fishing brightly lit, white-
bottomed flats. *Christmas Island is a good example—the flats are so
white they appear to be covered with snow. I find that long hours of
searching for fish on such bright flats creates painful eyestrain with any
polarized glasses except those tinted blue-gray.* On dark or overcast days, I
find that a pair of yellow polarized glasses is a decided asset in seeing fish.

Take an emergency rod repair kit with you to any fishing camp. Include
in it a few rod guides and tiptops, along with a fly-tying bobbin, a spool of
thread, and some melt-type glue. Make sure that the tiptops are slightly
larger than those on your rod tip—this way, if your tip breaks off, the over-
sized tips will still fit. Should the tip guide be too large you can wrap
thread firmly around the rod tip to fill the space, and then add your melt
glue to secure it firmly.

I always carry a large Zip-Loc bag with a number of similar small bags inside. I use these for all sorts of things. They're perfect for carrying spare
napkins that can be kept dry to wipe your glasses. Your wallet and paper
money will be kept dry inside one of these bags. In the large Zip-Loc bag I
also carry an assortment of rubber bands—something you'll always find
uses for.

In my pocketbook are always two or three Band-Aids. They're handy for
stopping a bleeding small cut, and every fly caster has at some time or
other had his line cut a groove into his stripping finger. Without a Band-Aid
the fishing is going to get miserable. I've used the tape on Band-Aids for
other purposes, too. For example, a friend had a fly rod whose ferrules
wouldn't stay together. So we pushed them as tightly as we could, then I
wound a Band-Aid around the joint. It worked for the rest of the day until
we could get home and have the rod repaired.

Flats boats are designed for fly fishing. They have no line-tangling devices, and John Zajano and his Bahamian guide are able to work in water only inches deep.

Masking tape is something else you should carry if you fish from boats. I'm convinced that there are some third world countries where it's against the law for a boatbuilder to drive his nails all the way into the boat. Cleats, ropes, boat pole holders, and many other things in a boat will also grab your fly line—especially during a critical cast. With a roll of 2-inch masking tape, though, you can virtually eliminate these problems. Even the guy who owns a fancy yacht won't object to you placing a little masking tape over an annoying cleat.

When I'm fishing from a small boat that has many line-tangling devices I eliminate the problem by throwing a small mesh net over the trouble spots. A common minnow seine, available in many tackle shops, or a 7-foot square of ¼- or ⅜-inch-mesh commercial fish netting is ideal. Place a small sinker on each corner and another between each corner along the netting edge. Toss it over the obstructions and you can cast almost trouble-free.

When you're sight-fishing the flats for fish such as bonefish, tarpon, or permit, keep checking the line that lies on the deck. This should be a constant chore. I can't tell you how line manages to creep underfoot. Even when I could swear I haven't moved my feet, somehow the line is under one, making a cast impossible. You'll especially encounter trouble if there's a breeze. The wind constantly shifts loose line around. It tangles on itself, around cleats, around gear in the boat, and even with your shoestrings. To avoid much of this trouble, first of all don't strip any more line off than you need to cast with. Additional line only means more chances for tangles. Then plan in advance where you'll drop all loose line. I clear the area where the line will reside. I also try not to drop line on the same deck I'm standing on. I prefer to stand on what's called the casting deck (I like to think of it as the "observation" deck). Then I can make a cast and strip the line back so that all the loose line falls on the lower deck *behind* the casting deck. This lessens my chances of standing on the line. An added advantage of depositing the line on the lower deck is that when the wind is blowing hard, the line tends to remain where you put it: The lower deck is in a lee because of the higher boat sides. Other anglers opt for a stripping basket to store the line.

When standing in the bow of a flats boat, hold some of your line ready for a cast. The line that drops from the reel often will tangle with the line held in your hand—especially if a breeze develops. To eliminate this tangle, loop the line under your belt or in your pants, as shown here.

The wind is blowing from the left of the angler. When flats fishing, always lay your line downwind so you don't stand on it with your feet and spoil your cast.

Mike Murphy was able to cast to some breaking fish because he had previously stored his fly line in the bucket on the deck.

Finding the Fish

Birds

Birds are essential to locating inshore fish. Most anglers know that gulls and terns can lead them to fish. But the actions of the birds can also tell you whether you're going to see fish. If the birds are diving quickly to the water, then predatory fish are pushing bait to the surface; you'll score if you get there quickly. Birds that are slowly circling an area may indicate fish deep below, or they may be searching, just like you. If a considerable number of birds are sitting on the water, chances are they know bait lies below; they're waiting around for bigger fish to find it.

Here's another tip about birds. Areas that flood during a rising tide generally drain during a falling tide. The last bits of water often run out through ditches, gullies, or indentations in the bottom. Baitfish know that predators await them as they travel these lanes—so if you see wading birds congregating around such structure, you can be sure that baitfish are using it to get back to deeper water. And if predator birds are there, predator fish will probably be there, too.

Feeding Fish

If the water is slightly rough from wave action and you spot a smoother slick on it, fish are probably feeding below on oily bait. The residue oil from the chopped-up baitfish rises to the surface and calms the water. Try fishing a deep-sinking line and weighted fly under the slick.

When you arrive at a scene full of birds and breaking fish, don't make the mistake of getting too close to the fish. Often your boat will cause the fish to dive deep—too deep for you to reach them. Instead, try to anticipate the direction the school is moving as they tear into bait on the surface. Approach the school from an upwind position, which will help you make a better cast. Cut the engine and allow the fish to come to you. If the fish are moving too fast for this, try to stay on the outer edge of the school and on the upwind side. If you're moving up on breaking fish that are obviously small, try using a sinking line and fly. After you cast, allow the fly to sink deep beneath the small fish. *Many times (especially with stripers and bluefish) there will be much larger fish below the smaller ones on top.* When you're casting to breaking fish and aren't getting the strikes you feel you should, check what size bait the predators are feeding on. *It may seem foolish, but in the presence of a huge number of a baitfish of a specific size, predator fish will frequently key on that size and refuse any flies that are smaller or larger.* Often it's not exact imitation that's important—simple size or length is the ticket. If there's a slight chop on the water, you can often see breaking fish better from an upwind position. Wind causes the waves to break off and form white water; from the downwind ide, this can make breaking fish tough to see. Never hesitate to use field glasses inshore. You can see breaking fish, locate a cobia near a marker, examine weed lines, and much more. These glasses are an essential tool of the inshore angler.

Chumming

Earlier I discussed chumming a little. There are a number of ways you can use chum to lure fish to your boat. For example, there are two techniques for using ground chum. First, inedible parts of fish can be ground into small particles and then frozen. Later, you place the frozen block in a mesh bag and hang it overboard, where it will slowly melt—forming a chum line. The second method of using ground chum is much more effective: Grind up fresh-caught fish on board and deliver them overboard with a large spoon to form a chum slick. Fresh chum will outperform frozen chum.

The fishing technique you should use depends on whether you're using frozen or fresh-ground chum. When tiny pieces of ground chum are melting off a frozen block, they attract small baitfish. Of course, large fish are there to feed on both chum and baitfish. One of the best fly patterns to use in this situation is thus a small baitfish fly. You can recover your fly by stripping it through the melted chum bits. But when fresh-ground, bloody chum is being thrown in the water, flies that resemble this bloody meat will outperform baitfish patterns. Here's how to tie them: Use a size 1/0 or 2/0 hook. Tie some flies with several wraps of lead wire; others should be more heavily weighted, and some left unweighted. Surround the hook with plumes of bloodred marabou about 2 inches long. You can also use rabbit fur, dyed to the color of the freshly ground chum. That's it. The tricks are to drop this chum fly where the actual bloody fish parts are being tossed onto the water, and to *let the fly drift at the same speed as the natural chum.* It's much like nymph fishing for trout: Watch your line and if you see any indication that a fish has taken, set the hook. Sharp hooks are a must for this kind of fishing.

When you're fly fishing in a chum line you need to use some sort of sinking fly line; a floating line is usually not ideal. A sinking-tip works well when the tide is running rather slowly, but you'll need to change to a faster-sinking line as the current speed increases. *The trick to successful chumming is to keep your fly drifting at the same depth and speed as the chum you've placed overboard. This means constantly being aware of what the tidal current is doing.*

If you locate fish on a depth finder that are more than 20 feet down, you can sometimes lure them close to the surface if you have a downrigger unit and a block of frozen chum. Attach a mesh bag filled with the ground chum to the depth finder ball. Always tie it with cord; never wire the bag to the ball. Otherwise, if a shark decides to take the chum bag, you may also lose your downrigger weight. Lower the ball and chum bag to the bottom. Allow them to remain there for a few minutes. Then gradually lift the ball and bag for a few feet, and stop. Repeat this procedure a number of times. You can often lure bottom-hugging fish to the surface as they follow the ball and bag.

Another excellent way to chum is to obtain a large number of silvery baitfish. The species will vary from sea to sea, but the liveliest local baitfish will do. Usually you get them with a cast net, then store them aboard in a good live well or large, well-aerated garbage can. Anchor over a good wreck or other structure (sometimes you can drift in deeper water) and begin throwing the baitfish overboard one at a time. Keep the baitfish coming in a steady flow. Soon the predators will show. They could be barracudas, mackerel, striped bass, a host of species. So long as you keep a steady flow of the tiny baitfish falling into the water, the predators will stay, and more will come. Then toss a fly such as a Lefty's Deceiver into the same area you're throwing the baitfish. Most of the time, allowing the fly to dead-drift with the tide is fine, although sometimes a retrieve improves your score.

If you chum for bonefish on a flat, shrimp can be expensive. You can effectively chum with fewer shrimp, however, if you use a 12-inch length of PVC plastic pipe. Cement a cap on one end. Drill a number of holes into the sides of the pipe. Attach a length of stout cord to the cap for the other end, fill the pipe with cut-up shrimp, and secure the cap. Attach a stout

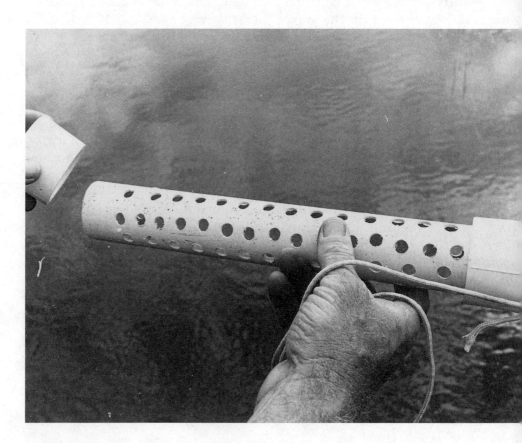

Stuff this pipe with cut chunks of shrimp and throw it into a light sand hole to chum fish to your boat.

ine to the pipe and throw it into the water where you want to attract
bonefish. A good place to put the pipe is over a white sand bottom, where
you can better see bonefish approaching. The bonefish will smell the
shrimp and approach the pipe, but they can't get to the bait. After you've
fished through an area slip the pipe, still loaded with shrimp, into a bucket
and transport it to the next chumming spot.

Structure

Buoys, channel markers, and other structures standing in deeper water
are favorite hangouts for many species of fish. When the tide is running
fast, these fish will lie near the bottom, out of the swift current. But when
the tide goes slack, they'll often rise and rest within inches of the surface.
Species that are very likely to be found around markers when the tide is
slack include cobia, tripletails, jewfish, snook, jacks, and snappers. It's important to approach the marker quietly; best is to drift down on it and
make your cast. If you don't see any fish, a popping bug will often lure
them to the top. Once you hook a big fish, start the motor and try to keep
your boat between you and the hooked fish. If possible, herd the fish away
from the downtide side of the marker—it can smell the marker from
downcurrent and swim back to it to break you off. Never pass up markers
on slack tides; they can offer some real thrills.

Special Flies

A basic tool of the inshore fisherman is the hookless chugger—a casting
plug with a scooped face. You want to tease a fish with this lure, not catch
it. Remove all hooks. It often improves the action of the lure if you attach
a ⅛-ounce sinker at its rear end. Have a companion use a spinning or
plug rod to cast the hookless chugger out, then bring it back with sweeps
of the rod. This results in loud *whoosh* sounds as the plug traps water in
its scooped face. The noise attracts many species of fish from around markers, in channels, over rock piles, around coral heads—it can even bring
them up from deep water. This trick has been used for years in tropical
waters, but is also extremely effective in luring larger stripers to the surface. Once the fish are attracted to the noisy chugger, throw a popping bug
or a streamer fly as close to it as possible. Even if a fish has grabbed the
hookless lure without holding on, it will frequently take the fly or popping
bug. This is one of those tools every inshore fly fisherman should avail
himself of.

Along the same lines, here's a trick you can use on species such as sea
trout, striped bass, mackerel, ladyfish, and many others: a popping bug
with a streamer fly as a trailer. Attach a short length of 15-pound monofilament to the rear of the popping bug hook. I prefer to make a nail knot
on the hook shank, but you can also tie the mono to the bend of the hook.

At top left is a chugger-type plug whose noise will bring fish to the surface. A popping bug (top right) is then thrown in. On the bottom is a popping bug combined with a Clouser Minnow—very effective.

Attach a streamer fly to the other end of the mono. The best fly I've found for this is a Clouser Minnow, simply because it has good action and is weighted. If you're after sea trout use a bright fluorescent-colored streamer, such as a chartreuse-and-yellow; for other species a good baitfish imitation seems to be best. The fly-streamer combination is cast out and retrieved. The popping bug makes noise, and often fish will strike it. More often, however, a fish will approach the nervous bug, then see the dangling streamer fly and accept that. This is a deadly way to take sea trout, but works on many other fresh- and saltwater species.

In many inshore waters the bottom is rather muddy or silty. These same areas may be affected by higher-than-normal tides; the excessive amounts of water rushing across such a bottom cause the water to be roiled or cloudy. Wind can do the same thing, as can waves washing onto a shore. Some jungle rivers never clear; seeking tarpon in the rivers of the northeastern coast of Costa Rica means fishing in waters that are always muddy to some degree. Swift-flowing tides can roil water. Some inshore waters are also stained from plant life and existing vegetation. In all of these situations, light-colored flies are usually not the best producers. This is the time to use very dark flies—either dark brown, purple, or black. Sleek patterns such as the Clouser Minnow are not as effective as those that make noise and have a wide profile. One of the best flies for dirty-water conditions is the Whistler. A black Lefty's Deceiver with some gold Flashabou is also deadly, especially if the head of the fly has been coated in epoxy—which helps it create more sound waves as it travels through the water.

Night Fishing

Fishing lighted structures at night can produce some exciting fly fishing. Manufacturing plants that are located on the water often have many lights shining on the surface. Boat docks frequently have lights installed either on the end or along the sides. Bridges, of course, are often lighted, and if there's a channel or boat passage under a bridge it'll have lights, too. Wherever light is cast onto the water there is potential for some good fly fishing. Of course, the reason for this is that the lights attract baitfish, which in turn lure fly rod targets.

There are a few tips that will make night fishing around lights more productive. You should match the size of your fly to the size of prevalent baitfish. Often the bait will be tiny. If the fish are feeding on 2-inch bait and you're throwing a 6-inch fly, you're probably not going to do well. You also need to consider whether the fish are right on top or down a few feet. It pays to carry both a fly rod rigged with a floating line and one with a slow-sinking or Wet Tip line. Attach a lightly weighted fly to the sinking line. Also important is that night fishing frequently involves casting around boat docks, piers, markers, and other structures that can snag your fly. *I prefer to fish Bend-Back flies most at night.* If you need to get down, try tying a Bend-Back-style Clouser Minnow. If you throw the fly upcurrent and retrieve it with the flow, you'll almost always catch more fish. This is another example of the old rule that you should bring the fly to the fish the same way Mother Nature would. I fish flies that resemble minnows when working under lights, and I believe some extra flash (Flashabou or Krystal Flash) produces more strikes. Finally, if the bridge lights are on, remember that there will be a shadow line where the bridge blocks them. Predator fish will be lying just inside the outer edge of the shadow and on the uptide side. For example, if the tide is flowing from north to south, the fish will be holding just inside the shadow line on the northern side. If you can examine such an area from an elevated position, look carefully and you should be able to barely see the fish holding there.

GPS

Scientists keep producing more tools for fishermen. The array of electronics available to fly fishermen today is almost overwhelming. If you fish inshore or in any large, open body of fresh water, GPS is a tool that will certainly increase your fly-fishing fun—and your catches. *GPS* stands for "Global Positioning System." It was primarily developed for scientific and military use, but it has become an essential tool of fishermen everywhere.

This instrument is now available to fishermen for less than $200. Of course, more sophisticated models will cost more, but a $200 unit will do for most anglers.

It works this way: Say you run across a difficult-to-find wreck, drop-off reef, or other underwater structure that holds fish. Using a simple procedure you can then enter the location into your GPS and give it a name. Later just punch in the name and the GPS will lead you directly to the spot. It's also a valuable safety tool: If fog slinks in and you're not sure how to find the boat landing again, you can easily get there even in total darkness if you punched in the ramp location beforehand. If you're an inshore fisherman not inclined toward electronics, I believe a few minutes with a friend who understands GPS will make you competent enough to use it. You'll never regret it.

Tips for Inshore Fly Fishing

Here are some suggestions for improving the quality of your inshore fishing:

1. If you fish an area regularly, keep a logbook recording the time of day, type of tide, weather conditions, gear used, and so on, for every trip there. All experienced guides do this.
2. Be aware of the tidal phase. Remember, in most places a seven-day period of extra-high and extra-low tides is followed by seven days with a lesser rise and fall of water. Also, tides usually repeat themselves every two weeks, and in most places the tide comes about one hour later each day.
3. Tide carries bait—this is the main reason it's important. Learn where tide concentrates bait and you'll improve your fishing.
4. Tide can clear muddy water, cool it down, or warm it up. All are sometimes important factors.
5. Fishing around channel markers and buoys is usually best on a slack tide.
6. Use the lowest spring tides, when bottom structure is exposed, to study the areas you fish. Use your GPS to mark these fish-holding locations.
7. When you're seeking bottom-feeding species, it's best to start with a fly that closely matches the color of the bottom.
8. When you're fly fishing from a boat that has line-tangling devices, carry a mesh net or roll of masking tape to cover these problems.
9. Be ready. Saltwater fly fishing offers opportunities that must be capitalized on immediately.
10. Try not to run into a school of breaking fish. Always approach a school of breaking fish from its upwind side to make casting easier. If possible, get ahead of the fish, kill your engine, and wait for them.

11. When gamefish are breaking, it's often important to match the size of the baitfish they're preying on.
12. Many times when small fish are breaking on the surface, much larger ones will be lying deeper, so allow your sinking line and fly to bomb below.
13. Birds are one of your most important allies in inshore fly fishing. They signal breaking fish, or at least indications of fish.
14. Carry a good pair of field glasses to help you locate birds and/or fish.
15. When you're using fresh-ground, bloody chum, it's often best to use a fly pattern that imitates the bloody chum. If you're using ground and frozen fish, the small, melting particles attract many smaller baitfish; often a streamer fly that imitates this bait is best.
16. When you're fishing dirty water, flies with head profiles large enough to produce underwater vibrations, and flies in darker colors, will help fish find your offering.
17. A hookless chugger worked noisily on the surface can often draw fish from the depths. Present a fly near the chugger to catch them.
18. In very clear water, streamers whose wings are constructed of translucent, synthetic materials are often better producers than those with bucktail wings.

Backcountry Fishing

Some of the most interesting saltwater fly fishing is in the backcountry—the boundary between open saltwater bays and seas and the mainland. This habitat is generally bordered by mangroves, and the water can be salty, brackish, or even fresh. The backcountry in Florida is usually considered that area from about Naples to the southern end of the Ten Thousand Islands. This is a world that few fly fishermen have explored. The water isn't always clear; it's frequently stained a tea color. Snook, redfish, and tarpon are the main targets, but a number of other species inhabit this area too, including jewfish, snappers, ladyfish, and black drum. All of these fish will take flies.

But backcountry exists in many other parts of the Tropics, too. One of my favorite backcountry fly-fishing areas is at Bathhurst Island in northeastern Australia. There are also some great backcountry waters in Central America and the lower Yucatán coast; Ascención Bay is typical backcountry. Suffice to say that there are many backcountry fishing waters scattered in Tropics all over the globe.

Fortunately, your fly selection for these areas is simple—just five flies are really all you need. This is not to say that you can't use other patterns—you can. But if you carry the five flies I recommend here, in various sizes and color combinations, you'll be able to fly fish effectively anywhere in the backcountry. Check with almost any experienced backcountry fly fish-

Redfish are one of the most popular of backcountry fish.

erman and you'll find these five patterns in his box: a popping bug, Bend-Back, Lefty's Deceiver, Sea Ducer, and Clouser Minnow. For most backcountry work, flies seem most effective if they're about 3 inches in length—give or take ½ inch. The color combinations that seem to produce the best are olive, light tan, red-and-white, red-and-yellow, and chartreuse-and-white; add a little flash material to each. The Lefty's Deceiver has also been developed into a special backcountry fly with the addition of a single wire weed guard. The fly is 3 inches long and known as the Glades Deceiver.

Let's examine each fly, along with how, when, and where it's used.

POPPING BUG

This fly is best used on snook and small tarpon. The redfish has an inferior mouth—one located low on the face so it can grab things off the bottom. While redfish will certainly hit a popper, they're often unable to grab it—despite their desire to.

Poppers have several advantages. An important facet is that when worked on the surface, they make enough noise to fish that might not have noticed a silent, swimming streamer fly. Another great asset is that a popping bug, when worked rather continuously, puts up enough surface disturbance that fish will often think it's a larger food source than it is. Thus big fish that ignore a streamer will take a popper. Another advantage is that you can work a popping bug slowly, allow it to sit in one spot to tease a fish, or move it along quickly to resemble a crippled bait.

After more than 50 years of using popping bugs, I believe that color has almost nothing to do with whether a fish will hit one or not. I favor bright colors, simply because I can see them. Since most popping bug eyes are on the top of the bug, fish never see them—I believe they're of no use to the angler. The best bugs seem to be made from cork or balsa, although Live Body and other tough closed-cell-type foams (such as beach sandal soles) are used. Still, nothing beats cork or balsa wood for a lively popper body. Because balsa and cork bugs are so light, they're also easier to cast than some of the heavier closed-cell foam bugs.

BEND-BACK

This ancient pattern was first used in the Mid-South for bass fishing in heavily weeded waters, where other flies would foul on the vegetation. A Bend-Back is any pattern tied with the hook reversed. Properly constructed, the wing hides or encloses the hook. Some tiers bend the hook too much, and it dangles below the fly—often causing refusals from sharp-eyed fish. *Several years ago I stopped tying any material on the hook shank.* If you're working over gravel or oyster bars, sharp shells will often shred the body material from the hook shank. By not having material on the shank, the fly is basically all wing—which makes the hook ride up much better. It also gives the fly a softer impact on the water.

Where and how would you use a Bend-Back? *First, larger tarpon have a very tough upper mouth, so I rarely use a Bend-Back for tarpon of more than 60 pounds; I have problems sticking the hook.* But a Bend-Back is superior to all other flies if you're throwing into "dangerous territory"—such as mangrove roots, which will snag your fly if its point even touches bark. With a Bend-Back you can throw into the roots of a mangrove, across a weed-strewn white hole in the flats, or over a bottom so shallow that regular fly patterns would snag. Weed guards are okay, but Bend-Backs are better tools for really snaggy situations.

LEFTY'S DECEIVER

This fly has been used for years in the backcountry. Flip Pallot and that great fly tier Steve Bailey codeveloped a variation that's perfect for the backcountry: a small Lefty's Deceiver with a calf tail wing and a single wire weed guard. It's a killer on redfish, snook, smaller tarpon, or any other species that will eat baitfish in the backcountry. It almost never fouls on the cast, and it can be thrown effortlessly. They call it the Glades Deceiver.

SEA DUCER

This is another ancient fly pattern first developed for bass fishing that also meets the special conditions of the backcountry. Because of the many hackles radiating from its hook shank, and its long, undulating tail, this fly comes to the water as softly as any pattern I know in salt water. And the hackles and tail act like miniature outriggers, letting you suspend the fly in the water. This allows you to fish in virtually no water and at a really slow speed. Many times this fly's soft presentation and ability to be held almost stationary in front of a fish can make it irresistible to a redfish, snook, or tarpon.

CLOUSER MINNOW

No fly has had such an impact on saltwater fishing in the past three decades as the Clouser Minnow—often called just the Clouser. This pattern is a method of tying, not a specific recipe; it features metallic eyes located on the bottom (the hook rides up or reversed) and a wing constructed to hide the hook point. This fly sinks quickly—the sink rate is determined by the weight of the attached metallic eyes. In the backcountry many people attach a weed guard of some type.

If I had to choose just two flies for the backcountry, I suspect I'd go for a Glades Deceiver and a Clouser. If I had to further specify color combinations for the Clouser, my first choice would be a fly with a white underwing, a chartreuse upper wing—and a bit of pearl or bright flash material between the two colors. A second Clouser would feature a tan underwing, topped by copper or gold flash, and an upper wing of darker brown.

But you needn't limit your own flies. Use all five of these flies in various color combinations and sizes. You'll have all the flies you'll ever need to fish the backcountry.

13

SOME SALTWATER SPECIES AND A WORD ON CONSERVATION

Striped Bass

While some of us have been fly fishing for stripers for decades, no species has brought more people to saltwater fly fishing in the United States in the last 10 years than the striped bass. Management restrictions placed on the species have allowed it to come back from near extinction. Today, especially on the East Coast, the striped bass has to be the single most popular target of fly rodders.

Much of what I've said about inshore fishing applies to the striped bass. Still, there are some special considerations concerning this grand fish.

On the East Coast stripers mainly overwinter in the Chesapeake Bay, with smaller populations in the Hudson River and off North Carolina. In early spring, after spawning, they leave their wintering grounds and migrate along the coast. Stripers are definitely an inshore fish; they're rarely found far from the coast. Knowing the migration patterns in your area is important. An important point is that there would be no striper migration if the baitfish they feed on didn't also migrate. The wise angler will notice when bait begins moving into the shallows of his fishing area. Within a week or so the stripers will follow. As in other inshore fisheries, shallow bays that have a darker bottom will see temperatures rise much faster than deeper or light-colored bays. Look for such places for early-season fishing. *Popping bugs are usually poor producers for striped bass until water*

John Zajano battles a fish caught in the surf at Hatteras, North Carolina. Fly casters working the surf here can experience some of the greatest beach fly fishing in the United States. *Photo credit: Dave Zajano.*

temperatures get into the 70s. Early-spring fishing is usually done with streamer flies, and often with a slow- or fast-sinking line.

I can't think of another inshore fish in the United States that can be fished for in so many different ways. You can catch stripers by standing on the beach, wading shallow bays or flats, standing on a jetty being pounded by turbulent waves, and from big and little boats. You can chum them, you can cast to breaking fish, you can fish white water (perhaps my favorite method), or you can simply blind-fish in deep or shallow water. If all that isn't enough, during summer northeastern striped bass fishing is probably most productive at night. This is a fish for everyone!

In most striper situations a 9- or 10-weight rod is best, although there are times when trout-sized rods will take smaller stripers. You can also use a weight-forward floating line, a full-sinking line, or a shooting head—each offers special advantages. If I had to choose only two lines for all my striper fishing, though, I'd opt for a special shooting head (which I'll explain in a moment) and one of the Teeny sinking heads—the Teeny 300 is the most popular for an 8- to 10-weight rod. My personal favorite fly line when stripers are within a few feet of the surface is a floating shooting head. If you can't easily cast 60 feet, I suggest you buy a commercial floating shooting head that's *2 sizes larger* than your rod calls for. For example, if you use a 9-weight rod, buy an 11-weight floating shooting head (which is about 30 feet long). Attach one of the shooting lines by Scientific Anglers or Cortland, which are made especially to be used with shooting heads. *Be sure to get one that has a diameter of at least .035 inch.* A shooting line with a smaller diameter than this may have a breaking strength of less than your leader.

If you can easily cast 60 feet or more, however, I suggest you make your own shooting head. Buy a double-taper 1 size larger than your rod calls for. Measure from the front end back 34 feet and cut off the line. Attach this to the special shooting line with 50-pound Cortland Braided Mono Running Line (see chapter 5). With either a commercial head 2 sizes up or a homemade line, you'll be able to cast much farther than you could with a conventional weight-forward line. The 34-foot head is my favorite for distance casting when stripers are near the surface.

If you must fish deep, then I recommend either a Teeny-type sinking head or a lead-core shooting head. *If you make your own lead-core heads, my experience indicates that the Cortland LC-13 lead-core trolling wire is best.* It weighs 13 grains per foot; the plastic coating on this line eliminates almost all tangles. I'm a great proponent of lead-core heads for deeper fishing. See chapter 8, "Casting," for information on how to cast weighted lines and flies. *Once mastered, the lead-core or Teeny-type lines are the easiest of all fly lines to cast.*

Unlike many other forms of inshore fishing, I believe that when you're seeking striped bass, the use of a stripping basket (also called a shooting basket) will enable you to perform better. Wading baskets are a must for wading and beach fly fishermen. They keep the line from tangling and help you produce trouble-free casts. Even in a boat a stripping basket is an aid, since it allows you to move around freely. This is especially helpful when you're trying to get to breaking fish. I've never had satisfactory results from wading baskets that fold up or have a mesh container. I'm sure some good ones will be developed, but at this writing I've only been disappointed. The most popular is the plastic dishpan type supported by a belt. This basket is usually positioned directly in front of the angler. The cast is made, the rod is tucked under the arm, and the line retrieved hand-over-hand. Some of the finest striper fishermen I know prefer this method. Personally, I think a basket supported low on the hip is best most of the time. With this I can make either hand-over-hand or a conventional stripping motion, if I choose. Still, this is a personal choice; you should try both types of baskets and then make your decision. A side basket does need to have many holes in it so that any water that gets into the base drains immediately. When fishing in deeper water some anglers also modify the dishpan

The Boga Grip is a fine tool for holding fish prior to release. Here Dan Marini grips a striped bass before release.

stripping basket by placing a closed-cell foam support under each side. This way the basket rides on the surface when you encounter deep water. Regardless what type of stripping basket you use, it should have some device in its base to prevent the line from tangling when it's dropped there. This can be stiff monofilament stubs, plastic cones, artificial turf, or loops of monofilament.

Striped bass can be caught around power plants throughout winter. Such plants exist from the Carolinas to New England; warm water at their outflows attracts baitfish and then stripers. A great winter striper fishery exists on the Outer Banks of North Carolina. I've enjoyed some fantastic

A shooting basket (sometimes called a stripping basket) eliminates many of the problems associated with casting.

December and January fishing here, on stripers averaging 15 to 20 pounds—often larger. The only problem is weather. If you live close by you can take advantage of the opportunity, but so often you travel here only to find that weather has ruined your trip. Streamers are usually best during the very cold months. But the real fly-rod action starts in spring, when the fish begin migrating. One of the most unique of the migrating striped bass fisheries in the United States is in North Carolina's Roanoke River. The fish move up the river and begin spawning in early to mid-May; they'll hold here for several weeks. This is one of those places where even a 14-foot jon boat is big enough to allow you to fish for stripers.

Captain Brian Horsley holds a striper that was caught in mid-December at Nags Head, North Carolina, on the Outer Banks. Striped bass fishing in the cooler months can be superb here.

Watch for the clam worm hatch that usually occurs near the full moon at the end of May or the first week of June; it's most intense in the shallow bays of New England. The hatch begins just at dusk and continues into the night. Billions of these small worms come to the surface and mate. Stripers go wild when this happens. It can be some of the most frantic action of the entire striper season. It can also be frustrating, since you're throwing your imitation in among so many of the real thing. But if you get lucky you'll catch stripers as fast as you can hook and release them.

A floating fly line is necessary. It's possible to catch stripers with a sinking line, but a floating line lets the fly ride high, and allows you to quickly backcast and throw in another direction. A 9- to 10-foot leader is ideal. While many anglers tie a single fly on the tippet, you can improve your chances if you add a dropper fly. Make the dropper length no more than 8 inches, or you'll get frequent tangles. There are many clam worm imitations available in local New England fly shops. I favor those that are a bit translucent, such as the one Kenny Abrames features in his terrific book, *Striper Moon.* Cast where you see stripers feeding avidly, and make fast, 6-inch-long strips on the line.

Perhaps the finest all-season striped bass fishery along the East Coast is the Bay Bridge-Tunnel at the mouth of the Chesapeake Bay. In spring, stripers migrate out of the Chesapeake Bay to move up the Atlantic coast.

They can be caught in good numbers and sizes beginning sometime in March. Once the major schools of larger stripers (called rockfish by Maryland, Virginia, and North Carolina fishermen) have left the Chesapeake, fish of up to 15 pounds will hang around the rock piles and bridge abutments, remaining through spring, summer, and fall. Late fall witnesses the big fish returning to the bay; these can be caught (weather permitting) all winter.

During summer one of the most interesting ways to catch stripers is to fish the flats, just like you would for bonefish. In a number of areas in New England (and a few in the Chesapeake Bay) stripers roam across light-colored sand flats in 3 to 5 feet of water seeking bait. Pole or drift your boat across these flats and, when you see fish, cast to them just as you would to tarpon or bonefish in Florida. The best fly line for this is a clear monofilament, which several manufacturers produce. *When you're fishing stripers in shallow, ultraclear water, I believe that these clear monofilament lines produce more strikes.* Many times the fish are in schools; if you cast to a lead striper and other fish encounter the more visible rear of the line, they'll flare away. A clear mono line should thus be in every striped bass fly fisherman's arsenal. One problem with these lines is that it can be difficult to determine where you can easily pick up the slow sinking line to make your backcast. *Place a nail knot on the line at the point where you can most easily lift it to make an easy backcast.*

I was introduced to white-water fishing for stripers by Captain Greg Weatherby, who runs the Saltwater Edge fly shop in Newport, Rhode Island. Greg has a boat with a pulpit at its bow. The fly rodder stands in the pulpit, ready to cast as the boat approaches a shoreline where waves crash against the rocks. Such fishing demands great skill of both the angler and the boatman. Experts, like Greg, can maneuver the boat on the rising and falling swells as the shoreline nears. When the boat is on a wave crest close to the target area, the captain has the angler cast into the melee of white water and crashing waves. Baitfish are swept into this white water trapped there until they can escape; striped bass know this, and they work these waters like a cafeteria line. As soon as the cast is made the boatman begins to move the boat backward, away from what could be disaster. But the fly fisherman soon learns that just throwing the fly into the white water is not the best technique. Instead, you need to study the rock formations as you approach the white water. Wherever the rocks taper into a V with the narrow end of the V at the surface is a great spot. And a large boulder lying a few yards offshore from a rocky wall is another searching spot, for a swirling eddy often occurs behind the rock. What you look for is how the water *drains* away from the rocky shoreline. Anywhere that ebbing water is concentrated (such as in the V or behind a boulder), more bait will be momentarily trapped and this draws in stripers.

Many flies are productive for such fishing. Three of my favorites are the Clouser Minnow, the Lefty's Deceiver, and a crab pattern. I fish all of these in varying weights. Sometimes an unweighted or very lightly weighted fly turns the trick, especially if the boat can be held close to the white for an extended period. And while few anglers use it, the Del Brown's Crab Fly

When fishing crashing waves or white water, a pulpit such as this is used to steady the fly fisherman. It also permits him to get close and make accurate casts.

pattern is very effective in white water: Baitfish trapped in white water can get out of there pretty quickly, but a crab will be trapped in the turbulent water much longer. Also, stripers love crabs.

The striped bass, as much as any species I have caught in salt water, is selective as to what size of fly it will strike. There are many times when changing from a 4-inch to a 3-inch fly, for example, will produce many more strikes. This is especially true when you're fishing Lefty's Deceivers. *I suggest carrying the same fly pattern in a number of different sizes— and also weights.* I've also noticed that stripers seem to be more adversely affected by bright sunlight than other fish. The brighter the day, most of the time, the poorer the fishing. This is especially true in extra-clear waters. During warmer months stripers seem to prefer feeding at night. This is not to say they don't feed during the day—they do, of course. But overcast days, early in the morning, or late in the evening, when the light level is low, is definitely the better time to fish for stripers.

A good striped bass fly assortment. Top row, left to right: popping bugs, Crab, Glass Minnow. Second row, left to right: Spread Fleye, Sand Eel, Surf Candy. Third row: two colors of Lefty's Deceivers. Fourth row, left to right: Bend-Back and Whistler. Bottom row, left to right: Sar-Mul-Mac and Half & Half.

If you fish striped bass in many places, even in freshwater lakes, I believe that some of the following flies will work for you. Here's my list of suggested striper patterns:

Popping bug
Clouser Minnow
Lefty's Deceiver (also include a black one)
Sand eel imitation
Del Brown's Crab Fly
Whistler
Surf Candy
Sar-Mul-Mac
Bend-Back
Glass minnow imitation
Spread Fleye

The Spread Fleye was conceived of by Bob Popovics and nicely imitates baitfish whose bodies are wide from top to bottom, such as alewives.

There's one extra fly I'd suggest if you're interested in catching larger stripers. To interest these fish you often need to present a much larger-than-normal fly pattern. The problem is that such flies are usually too wind resistant and bulky. You'll find a huge number of flies by different names that are simply variations of the Lefty's Deceiver. Most of these bigger flies are horrible to cast; in fact, a size 12 rod and line is frequently recommended—which is simply too heavy for many fly fishermen. Still, if you can get a big fly to the fish, you have a chance of getting a hookup. So I've developed a fly that has helped me catch some very large stripers and yet is easy to cast on a 9-weight fly rod. The fly is not only effective on stripers but also deadly for northern pike, cobia, and many offshore species—any predator fish that are looking for bigger imitations of baitfish. I call it the Magnum Deceiver. It's sold by Umpqua Feather Merchants through many fly shops, but it's easy to tie.

False Albacore

A fish often found with the striper is the false albacore, which can be found from southern Maine all the way down the East Coast. Autumn—when albacore mass to gorge on the migrating bait—provides the best fishing. Albacore have small mouths and the generally feed on baitfish of 4 inches or less. The best flies for them are thus sleek Surf Candies, Clouser Minnows, or Lefty Deceivers—and *sleek* is the important word. The hottest fishing begins in New England sometime in September. The fish are easy

Young Taylor "Nick" King successfully battles an albacore at Cape Lookout, North Carolina.

o locate: You'll see them skyrocketing a foot or two above the water as they push bait to the surface. Rush the boat so you can get ahead of the school. Stop and then throw to them as they sweep by. This is an exciting fish; a 12-pounder can peel off 150 yards of line very quickly. While most people use a floating line (which does allow you to make a quick correction cast), the wise angler also has aboard a fast-sinker. Sometimes a line like a Teeny 300 will be more effective, getting down into schools that aren't showing. Albacore have such sharp eyes that a leader bigger than 12-pound-test will get a lot of refusals.

The greatest of this albacore fishing occurs at Cape Lookout on the southern coast of North Carolina. Beginning sometime in late October, the albacore show up in incredible numbers. If weather stays warm they'll remain into December. This can be some of the most exciting East Coast fly rodding north of Florida.

Use your knowledge of spring tides—when the water rises higher and falls lower—to your advantage in albacore fishing. During the lowest stage

Jessica Van Rens readies an albacore for release that she caught with Captain Sam Sellars at Cape Lookout, North Carolina.

of an extra-low tide, go to the areas you fish. More of the bottom will be exposed, and you'll be able to see where underwater channels drain flats, and where to find many structures hidden during higher tidal phases. If you beach-fish you'll see where the sandbars (hidden at higher tide) form a depression on the shoreline side, where bait can hold when waves are crashing. Using the lowest tides to locate good fishing areas like this is important. And here's where GPS (Global Positioning System) can really come into play: Mark good fishing locations so you can return to them during higher tides.

Permit

The permit is regarded as the most difficult of the tropical flats species to catch on a fly rod. (Of course, a mutton snapper offers a greater challenge, but then so few are encountered on the flats.) For years we thought permit simply couldn't be caught regularly, but the last decade has seen a technique perfected that will allow you to catch permit with some confidence. Several factors account for this. First, a fly has finally been developed that appeals to this wary fish. Second, we've also perfected a technique that works—about one-third to one-half of the time. Know from the beginning that you'll scare a lot of permit, and still get a lot of refusals, with your offerings.

The important fly is a crab pattern. The best crab flies, in my opinion, are those with a soft base. Any crabs whose base is coated with epoxy or a similarly hard material will make a loud splash that spooks many permit. A crab pattern made from acrylic yarn, wool, or similar soft materials alights much more quietly and, I believe, enhances your chances of drawing a strike. The Del Brown's Crab Fly (often called a Merkin) has probably produced more permit than any other.

When you make a crab pattern there are three factors that I feel are important. I believe that the crab should be weighted on one end: This way it enters the water, tilts to the side, and dives for the bottom at an angle, just as a swimming crab would. You should also have crabs in at least two or three colors. On light-colored flats there are ghost crabs, which are a creamy white color. On other flats the crabs are very dark; you'll also find many crabs of an olive color. I feel it's important to carry crabs that are unweighted, lightly weighted, and heavily weighted—in the same sizes and colors. I prefer lead eyes in the following weights: $\frac{1}{50}$, $\frac{1}{36}$, and $\frac{1}{24}$ ounce. There are times when crabs will be swimming near the surface; it's not just permit but also all sorts of fish that will take them. When fishing in very skinny water, you need a lightly weighted fly. Of course, in water more than 2 feet deep, a more heavily weighted crab fly will often produce more strikes. While many people throw huge crab patterns to permit, I've found that you don't need one larger than a quarter in size. Just be sure you use a hook with large enough gap that when a permit grabs it, there's ample space for a hookup.

What's the retrieve technique for permit? You'll need a rod that throws at least a size 9 line—and many experts prefer a 10. The reason is that many fish are cast to at short distances and to get a weighted crab fly into action quickly, you need a line heavy enough for the purpose. Many people use an intermediate line; others prefer a floater. The advantage of a floating line is you can more quickly recast to a permit, if needed. Still, both lines work. Del Brown has caught more than 350 permit on a fly—more than any other angler. I've fished with Del several times and his technique is simple: When he sees a permit, he casts as close in front of it as he can. He scares the hell out of more than half of them, and they flee. The crab fly is allowed to drop to the bottom. **Del believes that if you begin to strip-retrieve the fly you'll frighten the permit and rarely get a strike.** Once the fly reaches the bottom, the permit will often circle it to see what's there. *Del keeps the line taut. If the permit ignores the fly it may require a* very gentle move-*ment of the fly with your stripping hand. Don't make any sudden strips; give just enough life to the fly to get the fish believing that here is a live crab.* Permit can pick up a fly and blow it out of their mouths quickly, so you have to be ready. If the fish takes the fly, Del simply strip-strikes by pulling back on the line in his hand. If the fish moves away and Del is certain that it's leaving, he picks up and cast again in front of the fish. This retrieve method is repeated as often as possible and has allowed Del to become the king of permit-hunting fly fishermen.

Here are some more tips for catching them. Permit action seems best when water temperatures are between 72 and 75 degrees. Permit can tolerate water temperatures a little lower and higher than bonefish. Small permit can often be found in a foot of water, but larger permit require a flat to be at least 2 feet deep. Of course, spring tides are better then neap tides for them, too. Many anglers fish the flats directly against the keys. But some of the best permit fishing is well away from shore, as much as a mile or more. Such distant flats may be dry on spring low tides, but carry several feet of water during high spring tides. Because they're less frequently fished, the permit on these flats are often more easily approached. Permit frequently follow low underwater ridges that can corral or trap bait. Look for a flat that's dry on a low tide, but well watered on a high one. If there's a shelf that drains the falling water into the depths, permit will prowl the deeper side of the shelf grabbing any foods that wash over. Many times a permit will swim with the same wobbling back-and-forth motion of a shark. Don't be fooled by this—as I have several times.

Because of their silvery sides, permit are often difficult to see. What's often most visible is the black line on the top of the body, or the edges of the tail. On a flat most permit will travel in the same direction during each tidal phase. If you see one or two swimming northward, chances are all the others will be doing the same thing. You can often locate permit in the shallows from a distance by watching low-flying birds, such as pelicans and cormorants. If these pass immediately over a permit, it will spook and show itself. Yet this is a natural occurrence, and the permit will soon settle down so you can approach it. There are a number of locations where you can reliably catch small permit. But if you're seeking a trophy permit on the flats then undoubtedly Key West, Florida, offers you the best chance.

Bonefish and Redfish

The techniques for fishing for redfish (commonly called reds) and bonefish are much the same. These species are generally sought in depths of less than 4 feet. Most of the time you don't cast to a fish until you see it. You can wade or fish from a boat. Wading offers the advantage of a more silent approach; you can also get closer. Fishing from a boat, on the other hand, allows you to cover more water, see farther (because of your height above the water), and move faster when pursuing a fish. If you wade, try to do so as slowly as you can. Remember, water transmits sound about four and a half times faster than the air. A shooting basket will help you hold your line. If you don't have such a basket, use a floating line. An intermediate or other sinking line tends to descend and foul on the bottom. When I'm wading, I'll often keep about 15 feet of line, plus the leader, outside my tiptop. Instead of holding this line, I simply make frequent roll casts in

A tailing bonefish—one of the most exciting sights in fly fishing.

front of me. This way the line is ready for an instant cast. Carry spare leader material, clippers, and extra flies, as well as a pair of pliers. To hold all this I prefer a fly-fishing vest designed for hot-weather use, which is made mostly from a mesh material. These vests are cool, and carry the tools you need. I believe you should purchase one that also lets you store a rain jacket in the back. Unless you've been exposed to tropical flats rains already, you've no idea how cold they can be. When wading, I also carry in my pants pocket an Umpqua Feather Merchants ceramic sharpening stone. This little 2-inch by ½-inch stone isn't affected by saltwater exposure, and can touch up a dull hook.

Most fishermen seek bonefish from a boat. One of the advantages of fishing from a boat is that you usually have a guide who knows where the fish should be and can help you see them. Another factor is that you can take with you all sorts of extra tackle, gear, food, and so on.

Let me give you some tips that will help when you're fishing from a boat. First, if you want your guide to like you, don't wear black-soled shoes into the boat. These leave marks that are very difficult to remove; the boat owner will hate them and you. Be sure to clean your shoe soles off before entering a boat, too. Sand and grit deposited on the floor can ruin your fly line and will certainly reduce your casting efficiency. Many fly fishermen strip 60 or 70 feet of line off the reel when flats fishing. Then a fish is hooked, it takes off, the excess line on the deck tangles—and the game is over. Instead, make a 6- to 10-inch mark with a permanent pen on your line at whatever length you feel appropriate—for most anglers I suggest between 35 and 40 feet. Pull off line until you encounter the mark. Let's assume that you made the mark at 35 feet. If you're using a 10-foot leader, you now have a total of 45 feet of line available for a cast. For most bonefishermen that's enough. *What's especially important is that every time you step to the bow of the boat and strip off line, be sure to make a cast and retrieve the line. If you don't, the line you last removed from your reel will lie on top of the heap. If you make a cast, there's a chance that the forward end of your fly line—on the bottom of the pile—will tangle.*

If you're fishing with a companion, whoever isn't currently fishing should monitor the line lying on the deck. If one constant partner checks it to make sure it doesn't get underfoot or tangled in something in the boat, the angling partner will be better able to make a tangle-free cast when he sights a fish.

If you don't have a guide, avoid poling toward a white cloud. The cloud's reflection on the surface will make it nearly impossible for you to see fish. The best direction to pole, when possible, is so that the sun is either behind the caster or behind and to his side. This really improves visibility. Most of the time polarized glasses tinted yellow-brown will allow you to see better. But on overcast days I prefer a pair of bright yellow polarized glasses. At this writing the only company I know selling such glasses is Hobie.

A number of indicators will tell you if bonefish are around. One is muddy water. In many areas, especially off the Bahamas and Belize, bonefish gather in basins or open bodies of water and root in the bottom for food. During the process they create great patches of milky or roiled water that somewhat resemble 2 percent milk. These are referred to as muds. While many fly fishermen don't enjoy fishing in muds (they consider it like shooting fish in a barrel—and I agree), it's certainly productive. Locate a mudding area, and then find its brightest or freshest mud. Cast into this brighter mud, allow your fly to get to the bottom, and retrieve it in slow strips. *Another mud that can often produce bonefish, even under poor visibility, is a single mud made by a bonefish blasting food out of the bottom.* If a shrimp, crab, or other creature sees a cruising bonefish, it'll bury itself in the bottom to hide. The bonefish locates the hiding place and, with a hydraulic blast of water from its mouth, dislodges the creature. This creates a small "puff" of mud that's easily seen by knowing fly fishermen. The bonefish moves on, and the process may be repeated several times. The earliest mud puffs will begin to slowly dissipate. After the bonefish has created several such puffs of mud the oldest ones will be barely visible, and each successive puff a little more distinct. By following the mud puffs you can track the bonefish down and get a presentation.

As time passes the mud puffs disappear—but they leave behind what I call blowholes, which are another bonefish giveaway. The photo below shows a fresh one. If you look carefully you'll soon be able to distinguish fresh from older blowholes. Obviously, if there are lots of fresh ones, bonefish have been using this flat frequently.

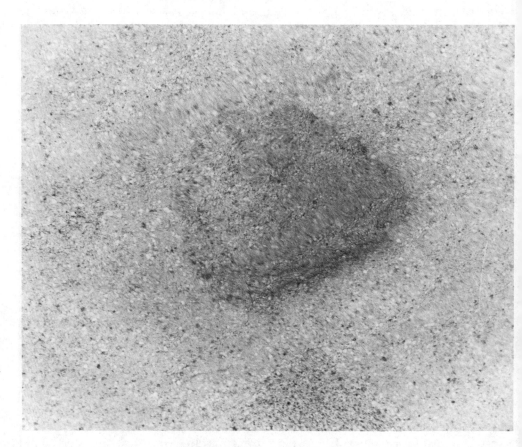

The circular hole in the sand is a tip-off that bonefish have been feeding recently. The hole is caused by a bonefish squirting a blast of water to flush out food.

Mike Wolverton points his rod at the place where the guide says there's a fish. Pointing the rod like this is the fastest way to locate a difficult-to-see fish on the flats.

Anytime you see a wave moving in the opposite direction of other waves, it could be swimming fish. Nervous water is another indicator. A shimmering of the surface tells the experienced angler that bonefish are probably cruising. A tail tipping up a or a spray of small minnows often indicates a bonefish. Redfish will often chase shrimp in shallow water, causing them to go airborne in an escape attempt. Drop a fly in front of a redfish that's frightening shrimp like this and you can be assured of a strike.

Keep boat noise to an absolute minimum. A boat acts like a drum and resonates any sound over a long distance. Quickly stepping down from the front of the boat, or noisily moving a tackle box, can spook any fish for quite a ways.

A guide will often describe the boat in terms of a clock face to explain to you where to find a fish he's sighted. Think of the bow as noon and the stern as 6 o'clock. If your guide sees a fish cruising at about 10 o'clock he'll tell you to look in that direction. You'll find the fish faster if you point your rod in the general direction that the guide indicated. Then he can tell you if you need to move right, left, or whatever. By doing this you'll be looking down your rod almost like a rifleman looking down the barrel of a gun; you'll see the fish much more easily.

On calm days use a cast other than one directly overhead. Such casts allow the fly to fall many feet to the surface, and sometimes fish will see the unrolling line. Instead try a curve cast, which will get you many more fish when you're very close to the quarry. The curve cast allows you to present your fly so that it swims not back toward the boat, but at a right angle to the fish, for quite a long time. This prevents the fish from getting close enough to see you. If a fish that's following the fly does get too close to the boat, kneel down to lower your profile. Also, when you find redfish or bonefish that are especially wary, cast your fly 30 or more feet ahead of the direction the fish is swimming. This will prevent the fly's impact from frightening the fish. But here's the key to this technique: *Note where your fly falls. It may be near a mangrove shoot, a conch shell, or a dark spot on the bottom. Remember the spot. When the fish approaches the fly, make two quick strips and then a series of short ones. I've often been able to take bones and reds this way that seemed uncatchable with normal presentations.*

Another tip has helped me almost double my score on bonefish. Many times as you're making a series of strips on the fly line during a retrieve, you'll feel a fish pecking at the fly. What's really happening is this: When you dropped the line to pick it up for another strip, the fish had your fly. The peck you felt was the fish dropping it. So try this trick, which has really helped me. A fish very close to your fly will often tilt downward; at this point begin a slow and constant retrieve. I start with my stripping hand well out in front of me, and then begin a long, slow, continuous pulling on the line. *What I want to do is keep the fly barely moving—ever-so-slowly on the bottom. The slight disturbance made as my fly drags on the bottom often triggers a strike. And because I've kept the line taut, I can feel every such pickup by bonefish. All I need to do is make a gentle strip strike to hook the fish.*

I prefer bright-colored fly lines for bonefish and redfish, unless these fish have been worked over hard by others. In this case a clear monofilament line will produce more strikes from especially wary fish.

Tarpon

The techniques for fishing tarpon are much like those for bonefish and redfish. However, there are also a number of special tricks that will help you get more hookups. Almost all tarpon fishing is done from boats. The fish can be found in water depths of 2 to 15 feet. They roll on the surface to breathe; this allows you to locate them and also tells you what direction they're moving. If you see a tarpon roll, but it disappears once it drops below the surface, cast well in front of the fish with a sinking line and allow the line to descend before beginning a strip. I prefer to use clear monofilament lines for tarpon; they're far less likely to cause fish to flare away. If tarpon are daisy chaining (several fish circling near the surface) it's best to throw your fly in front of an oncoming tarpon, which will think the fly is escaping. If you throw the fly so that circling tarpon see it coming at them, they'll often flush away. If you use a clear monofilament line and are careful with your casts, then casting into the center of a daisy chain and bringing the fly back will often produce more strikes.

The best sight-fishing for giant tarpon occurs on the flats of the Florida Keys. Nowhere else can you find such large numbers of tarpon on such a reliable basis. But these fish are frequently offered many flies each day. I've stopped using conventional tarpon flies for these fish; I've gotten so many refusals that I think the tarpon have come to recognize the same old style of flies. Instead, I've been using flies that look more like baitfish, and having much greater success. Good imitations of baitfish in lengths from 2½ to as much as 4½ inches have been producing well. In very clear water I prefer to build the flies from Kinky Fibre or Super Hair, a synthetic fly-tying hair that's translucent and really imitates baitfish. Try this and I think your strike ratio will improve, too.

It's important to use the correct leaders for permit, bonefish, redfish, and tarpon. When I'm seeking the first three species on days when wind ruffles the water I prefer approximately a 10-foot leader—nothing shorter. When tarpon are especially spooky, or are cruising over white sand, a 16-foot leader is often necessary. On very calm days under a bright sun, I find that bones and reds can be highly spooky. I then use a 14- to 18-foot leader. If you use the formula shown in chapter 5 (a heavy leader butt that's half the length of the leader), you'll have no difficulty turning over your fly. The longer that leader under difficult conditions, the more likely you are to catch fish.

One of the most common mistakes made by anglers fishing for tarpon, redfish, bonefish, or permit is looking at the fish while making the cast. Experts teach shotgunning by having a student look intently at the target, bring the gun to his shoulder, and—while still looking at the target—pull the trigger. Instinctively, all of us tend to hit what we're looking at. If you cast while looking at a fish cruising across a flat, chances are you're going to hit too close to the fish. *Instead, look at your target, and you'll be able to see the fish in your side vision. If you do this, your casts will become much more accurate.* (See the illustration on page 190.)

Sharks

Almost every tropical flat holds sharks. They can be very small or huge. I've seen hammerheads in 4 feet of water that were longer than the boat I was in. Naturally, I didn't cast to them—but sharks do make great fly-rod targets. First, let me warn you that you should never pick up a shark by the tail. Sharks have no bones; if you grasp one by the tail, it can curl around and bite you. I've seen this happen twice in my fishing career. In fact unless you have a competent guide who'll handle the fish for you, don't angle for sharks at all.

Fortunately, the technique for catching sharks is pretty simple. Popping bugs aren't your best fly choice. They certainly attract the fish—but because a shark's mouth is located well back under its head, a shark attacking a popper often pushes it away. I've seen sharks attempt several times to grab a popping bug, finally leaving in frustration. Sharks also have poor eyesight, so offering them flies they can see makes sense. I have two favorite patterns. Both are easy to tie, but must be tied right. For sharks from 3 to 5 feet long I use a size 3/0 hook; for larger sharks, a 4/0 or 5/0. Make sure the hook is well sharpened. For the first fly, place the hook in the vise and tie in a liberal amount of bright yellow bucktail (the longest you can find) along the bottom and sides of the shank. Turn the hook over and add 15 or 20 strands of gold or copper (or a combination of the two) Flashabou on top of the yellow bucktail. Be sure to allow some of the flash to extend an inch behind the bucktail wing. Then add a liberal amount of bright red bucktail on top of that, so that you've constructed a fly that resembles a dense hula skirt. Tie the second pattern the same way, but using white bucktail on the bottom, and a dense top of chartreuse bucktail.

When you're casting to a shark try to get in front of the fish, and make the cast so that you can retrieve the fly alongside the eye. Try to keep the fly close enough to the eye that the shark can see it well. The head will sweep sideways to engulf the fly. Naturally, you need to have a wire trace in front of the fly. Braided wire doesn't work well for larger sharks. The fish's teeth will sever one strand during the battle, then another, and another, until finally the braided wire leader will part under stress. The wire leader should be at least 10 inches long. When the shark takes your fly, try to see on which side of the mouth the fly is impaled. If you can keep to this side during the battle, you have a better chance of landing the fish. Remember, too, that a shark's skin is like rough sandpaper; if your leader or fly line rubs across the head of the shark, it will probably fray through.

Incidentally, there's a way to lure sharks to the boat so that they're in a mood to take your flies—but I don't approve of it and would like to see the practice discontinued. It involves catching and killing a barracuda and hanging it overboard. If you've never been near a 'cuda, you don't know how strong the odor from one is. Apparently, sharks can smell this from a long distance, and be easily lured to boatside. However, I just don't think we should kill a barracuda in order to catch a shark.

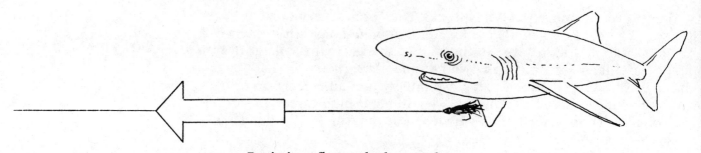

Retrieving a fly to a shark correctly

Barracudas

The barracuda used to be scorned, but it's now recognized as a first-class flats species for fly rodders. I once wrote an article about catching 'cudas on a fly. I wrote that I had seen a 'cuda before and after it struck, but never while it was striking. It's true. These fish are so fast that even if you're looking right at one, it can hit your fly without your ever seeing it move.

For barracudas I use the same two flies I mentioned for sharks, plus one other—a popping bug. *I don't recommend using the various long, skinny flies that imitate needlefish. These present little profile, tangle like hell during the cast, and are not nearly as effective as the shank flies and popping bug—which never tangle in flight and are easy for you and the 'cuda to see.*

There's no way you can retrieve fast enough for 'cudas. I've tried all methods—hand-over-hand, sweeping the rod, and so on. It can't be done. Once you realize this, you modify your retrieve. *The method I'm going to describe will work on about 40 percent of all the 'cudas you'll cast to.*

Once you locate a barracuda, get close enough so that you can make a cast and easily pick up all the line you've thrown for a backcast. It's important that you be able to do this. Throw the fly about 4 feet in front of the 'cuda and slightly past it. *As soon as the fly hits the water, lower the rod tip almost to the water and make a long drawing of your rod so that the fly rips across the surface and comes out of the water for the backcast. Repeat this.* One of two things will happen. The 'cuda may streak away—which happens more often than not. Those 'cudas that don't escape are apparently ready to strike. Make a third cast to the same spot. Immediately begin an erratic retrieve,

Three 'cuda flies. Top: popping bug. Bottom: white, chartreuse, and orange flies. The bottom two are also the author's favorite shark flies.

never allowing the fly to remain still. It doesn't have to be retrieved at a high speed—simply kept moving. On the flats this method works better than any other I've tried, especially with either of the shark flies I mentioned earlier. If the 'cudas you try don't hit one of these two, switch to a popping bug. The key here is to throw the bug at least 10 feet in front of the 'cuda—any closer will alarm it. Begin a nonstop retrieve. The bug doesn't have to move far on each strip—but it has to be kept in constant motion.

If you can locate an underwater wreck, the most successful method of catching 'cudas on a fly is yours. You must first obtain several good-sized baitfish—at least 8 or 10 inches long is best. The best of all baits is the blue runner, which is so tough that it can live for a long time. Small jacks will work, too, and I've used snappers and groupers. You're going to tease the 'cudas to your boat. Use a stout stick; a gaff handle works fine. Tie onto its handle about 3 feet of heavy monofilament, and to this attach a hook. Impale a blue runner with the hook just under its dorsal fin, and in about the top middle of its back. Lower the baitfish so that it just contacts the surface and allow it to swim. Blue runners will swim vigorously and create a disturbance on the surface, which is what you need.

Be alert—for soon you'll see a number of 'cudas arrive from the wreck below to catch the struggling bait. *You must not allow a 'cuda to grab the bait. Each time one surges, lift the bait from the water. This really turns on the 'cudas.*

The fly rodder is standing by with his outfit, including a fairly large white fly such as a big Lefty's Deceiver attached to at least 5 inches of wire. When it's obvious that the 'cudas are in a greatly excited state, allow one to catch the bait. The 'cuda will chop off part of the body. *Here's the key to success: The angler must immediately throw the large fly beside the remaining piece of baitfish.* The 'cuda will come back and take it—but only if it's first had a taste of the baitfish. Of all the methods I've tried for 'cudas, this one is the most reliable. And it's very exciting!

Flats Tips

When you're fishing from a flats boat, there are a number of procedures that can make your day more productive. But if you ignore them, it can result in a spoiled cast or a lost fish. Here's a checklist of what you should do when you step into the boat:

1. Lines should be cleaned before you enter the boat. Dirty lines will often drastically reduce casting distance and can mean lost opportunities. Many newer fly lines have a thin outer coating that won't take the abuse older lines could; we used to scrub our lines with Bon Ami or other abrasive soaps. *Modern fly lines can be cleaned by washing in warm water and a gentle liquid soap.* Just make sure you rinse them well enough to rid them of all soap.

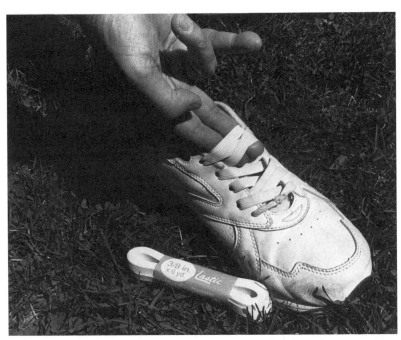

Remove your shoestrings and replace them with ⅜-inch elastic. Start at the top of the shoe, lace to the front, and tie off securely. You'll never again catch a fly line on a shoestring—or ever have to tie this shoe again.

2. Your footwear shouldn't have long shoestrings. Moccasins are the worst line grabbers of all. I can't tell you how many times I have seen a cast fouled in midflight because the shooting line tangled in a shoestring. Instead, use ⅜-inch elastic. Begin at the top of your shoe, and lace the elastic toward the front. Tie off and you'll never tangle another cast in your shoelaces.
3. Always wear a hat with a dark underbrim. Many fly fishermen stand on the bow of a flats boat wearing no hat—but the glare from the sun will reduce how well they can see. Any hat will be an aid. Still, if it has a light underbrim, sunlight will bounce off the water, up and under the brim, and then into your eyes; this will also impede you from seeing well. A cap with a dark underbrim is a real asset.
4. Before entering a boat, clean your shoe soles. This will not only endear you to your guide but also keep the deck clean. Any dirt carried onboard tends to stick to a fly line, reducing casting distance and also wearing your rod guide and fly line. You want the deck to be super clean at all times.
5. On tropical flats mosquitoes, and particularly some biting flies, can make life hell. You can never seem to kill them—especially those biting flies. I now carry a fly swatter. People laugh when they see me get into a boat with one. But it sure helps my concentration and presentations.

It may seem foolish, but you'll make better presentations if you carry a fly swatter aboard to kill insects that may spoil your cast.

6. Pull off only the line you'll need to cast to a fish. Too many anglers step up on the casting platform and strip off 70 to 80 feet of fly line. Never pull off more line than you'll need for your next cast. Any extra line lying on the deck is a potential trouble source. Del Brown, master permit fisherman, has a great idea. He figures that 50 feet of line, and a 10-foot leader, is all he'll need for most situations. He makes a foot-long mark at 50 feet on his fly line. When he steps up to the casting platform, he simply strips off line until he reaches that mark.

7. Stretch all the coils from the line before making your first cast. Fly lines stored on the reel will usually come off in tight coils and can cause tangles on the cast. One of the quickest ways to get rid of coils is to hold about 8 feet of the line in your hands so that it hangs down to the deck. Place your foot on the bottom of the loop and give a firm upward pull with both hands. This will remove all coils.

8. Make a cast with all the line you have stripped from the reel and then retrieve it. When you first strip line from the reel the forward end of the line is on the bottom of the pile, and as you continue to drop line from the reel, it ends up on the top. If you made a cast, the forward line on the bottom would likely tangle. By making a long cast and then retrieving line, the rear of your fly line ends up on the bottom.

9. Never drop retrieved line on the deck where you're standing if you can help it. Any flats fisherman can tell you about scores of times he's made a cast, only to see it ruined because the line was

underfoot. The perfect casting platform (in my opinion) is one that's relatively small: a 2- or 3-inch elevated platform for you to stand on. Behind this should be a lower platform where you can place your line. When you're on the average flats-type boat I recommend that you stand a little back from the bow and drop the shooting line into the well or onto the main deck below the casting platform.

10. Clear the area of the deck where you'll drop fly line. Protruding fly-rod handles, spinning-reel handles, and other items in the boat should always be placed so that line won't grab them on the shoot.

11. On windy days use a stripping basket. It's unfortunate that only in the Northeast do fishermen regularly use stripping baskets in boats. I favor a hip-mounted basket for flats fishing. This is a basket or plastic container held on the hip and suspended on a shoulder strap, permitting you better control for retrieving and striking. Anyone who's ever fished a tropical flat on a windy day knows how much the wind can blow the shooting line around, ruining the cast. Try a shooting basket; you may be pleased.

12. When you're on the flats, you're sight-fishing, and most of the time you must make your cast soon after you locate a fish. Flats fishing demands a speedy cast that's also accurate. The time to practice this type of casting is when you're at home—even on a lawn. Far too many northern fly fishermen don't practice, and so they fail when the opportunities arise.

13. Don't stare at one spot when you're searching the shallows for fish. Constantly shift your eyes. By staring at one place you'll likely fail to see tiny wakes, moving fish, minnows skipping, muds, tailing fish, and much more.

14. A great tip-off to the presence of fish is low-flying birds. Gulls, cormorants, and other birds see fish chasing bait and go there. On some flats where there are lots of shrimp, you'll see gulls inches above the surface. These gulls are grabbing shrimp that have been pushed up by redfish, snook, and other species. When birds fly low over the shallows, they often spook fish—but usually such a spooked fish will only swim a short distance and settle down.

15. Constantly check the line around your feet for tangles. No matter how carefully you placed the line in the beginning, it somehow moves around. Keep checking to make sure it's not underfoot or trapped on something in the boat.

16. Use your rod to locate a fish the guide is trying to show you. When the guide says the fish is at 10 o'clock, point the rod in that direction. The guide can then tell you to move left or right. This is the fastest way I know of for locating a fish that your guide has spotted.

17. Unless your guide insists, don't cast until you see the fish. Never throw your fly where you *think* the fish is. This almost always results in a bad cast.

18. If a fish is directly ahead of the boat (at the 12 o'clock position) don't cast until your guide has had time to move the rear of the

boat to one side. If you cast straight ahead, you'll almost always hook your guide—not a good idea! Give him a chance to move the boat off to the side before you cast.

19. Don't cast too soon or wait too long. Making a cast too soon means you'll probably have to frantically retrieve line and recast. If you wait too long, the fish has frequently come close enough to see the boat. If you see the fish, cast when the guide tells you.

20. If you cast to a fish that obviously doesn't see the fly, cast again. Most of the fish we seek on flats with a fly are sight feeders. If you make a cast behind a fish too far to one side—or if for any reason the fish is not likely to see your offering—don't continue to retrieve. Instead, quietly pick up and cast again.

21. If on a cast your fly hits the boat pole, motor, or any other hard object, check the fly. Make sure that the point hasn't been dulled. It's also a vital rule that if you strike two fish without a hookup, you should check your hook point.

22. Never make a backcast if there's any line on the water. Surface tension grips your fly line. If even a foot of line is on the water when you make the backcast, the sound of that line ripping loose from the surface tension will frighten many fish. *This is one of the major reasons why many people fail to catch fish in the shallows.*

23. When you're false casting, never let the fly hit the surface. This happens most often with redfish and bonefish flies—their lead or bead-chain eyes make them a little difficult to cast. The disturbance of the fly striking the water between you and the fish ruins many opportunities.

24. Retrieve your fly with your rod pointed at the fish. Don't hold the rod tip well above the water—the subsequent sag in the line will create too much slack for an effective strike, and can also spoil your retrieve. Never use the rod tip to manipulate the fly, either—this also increases the chances of having too much slack when the fish strikes. Keep the rod pointed at the fish and manipulate the fly by stripping in line.

25. Never strike upward with your rod on a fish in shallow water. If a fish grabs your fly here, the tendency is to flip upward with your rod tip. If the fish then misses the fly, you've missed the strike—but you've also removed the fly from the water. If the fish is close by, another cast may spook it. To properly strike, move your rod sideways or use a strip strike: Simply grasp the line during the retrieve and pull back a few inches to set the hook. If you miss a fish on a side or strip strike, your fly will remain in the water near the fish.

Being aware of all these things will increase your chances for success on the flats.

To close this book, I would like to add a brief conservation message. We must take better care of our natural resources. For far too long sport fishermen have been overruled in state legislatures by commercial fishermen,

Mike O'Brien releases a smallmouth bass as Bob Clouser looks on. Putting our catches back helps ensure good future fishing.

who cite the economic importance of continuing to harvest fish from the sea. The truth, of course, is that in most areas of the United States much more money is spent by recreational fishermen than the total earned by commercial fishermen. But the commercial fishermen's toll on the resource is appalling. Only where sport fishermen have stepped in are fish stocks showing any kind of recovery.

I have been an outdoor writer since 1951 and it's been my observation that not all, but most commercial fishermen are like buffalo hunters. They will take the last fish from the sea then go get another job. *The* only way *we can ensure that we'll have fish to fish for in the future is if we have paid lobbyists in our state legislatures.* Commercial fishermen already have paid lobbyists, who make "friends" with those who make the laws. When a piece of legislature then comes up that might adversely affect commercial fishing, the politicians say to themselves, "Am I going to vote against my friends or 'rich sportsmen'?"

What we need is our own paid lobbyists who also become lawmakers' friends so that we can get a fair hearing and just laws. Until we do this, it's my belief that it will be extremely difficult to get the kind of laws governing our fisheries resources that we need.

Finally, we long ago stopped fishing as a way to get food. Most people today regard our fisheries as recreational resources. For this reason, we need to put back most of the fish that we catch. Someone once asked me why I put my fish back. I answered, "You don't burn your golf balls at the end of the day, do you?"

I hope that this book helps you master presentation, the key to almost all fishing. And that our fisheries become even healthier in the future.

INDEX

for gills, 72
on Lefty's Deceiver, 92–93
for night fishing, 315
on wings, 89, *238*

ladyfish, 313, 317
LaFontaine Sparkle Pupa, 229
lakes, 15, 195, 213, *273,* 273–76, 294
Laptew, Mike, 71, 72
largemouth bass, 22, 58, 81, 195
 environment of, 51, 57
 in farm ponds, 277–78, *279,* 280
 flies for, 261–66, *262, 266*
 fly retrieves, 266–68
 mouths of, 67, 196
leaders, 44–45
 color of, 45
 length of, 50, *197,* 197–98, 209, 251
 level, 50–52
 materials, 45–46
 for nymphs, 219–20
 tapered leaders, 46–50
 for trout fishing, 215–19, *217*
lead eyes, 68, 75, 196, 197, 233
lead weights, *223,* 223–24
Leadwing Coachman, 230
leeches, 101
Lefty's Bug, 269, *272*
Lefty's Deceiver, 89, 90–92, *91,* 210, *292*
 for backcountry fishing, 317–18, 320
 black, 71, 263, *266*
 for dirty water, 315
 for largemouth bass, 267–68
 for northern pike, 293
 for peacock bass, 292
 for pond fishing, 280
 for striped bass, 327, *329,* 330
 tying method, 92–93
Leisenring lift method, 227
level leaders, 50–52
Lewis, Bob, 17
logs, 16, 275–76
long-line pickup cast, 175–76
loop, casting and, 139–41, *141,* 185–86
Loving, Tom, 262
low tide, *300*
lubrication, 27, 33
Lyons, Nick, 249

mackerel, 37, 312
Madame X, 235, *236,* 245
Magnum Deceiver, 290, 292, 330
maintenance
 of backing, 38
 of reels, 33
Marabou Gerbubble Bug, 81, 195, 261–62, *262, 266*
March Brown, 231
Marinaro, Vince, 16
masking tape, 307, 316
mayflies, 66, 213, 244, 246
meadow streams, 16
Merkin, 332
metallic eyes, 75
Micron line, 35, 36
midges, 243, 244–45, 251
midsection (leader), 44, *44*
monofilament
 knots and, 103, 105, 106, 111
 leaders, 216
 lines, 35, 37, 45, 47, 60
 weed guards, 97, 99
moon, tides and, 299, 301, 302
morocoto, 292
mosquitoes, 343
motion, approaching fish and, 125, *126–30,* 129
mousetrap exercise, casting and, *19,* 189
"moving windows," 228

muskies, 44
Muskrat Nymph, 229
Mustad hooks, 85
mutton snappers, 332
Mylar, 71, 72, 233, 239

nail knot, 55, 63, 104, *104*
neap tide, 301–2
New Zealand, 221, 225, 229, 248
Nicholson Smooth files, 41
night fishing, 315
noise, 11, 133
nonslip loop knot, 111, 113–14, *113–14,* 218
northern pike, 22, 67, 292–95, *293, 295*
 casting to, 154
 environment of, 51
 food of, 213
 mouths of, 196
 popping bugs and, 76
 retrieve speed and, 199
 sharp teeth of, 44
nymphs, 155, 242
 downstream retrieving and, 199
 sink rate and, 196, 197, 198
 trout fishing with, 219–29, *221, 222*
 weighted, 68, 70, 75

obstructions, 154
Ocean Hair, 74
Offshore Popper, 82
overhand knot, 104
overhead casting, 63

Pacific salmon, 57
Pallot, Flip, 320
panfish, 78
Parachute Adams, 236
Parachute Light Cahill, 245
Partridge soft-hackle flies, 231
payara, 292
peacock bass, 290–92, *291*
Pencil Popper, 81, *266*
permit, 52, 75, 154, 303, 332–34
piers, 15
pike. *See* northern pike
pile cast, 170
piranha, 292
pliers, 305
plug casting, 33, 155
pocket-water nymphing, 224–25
points, 275
polar bear hair, 74
polarized sunglasses, 119–22, *120–22,* 219, 227, 306, 335
Popovics, Bob, 329
popping bugs, 76–77, *83*
 backcountry fishing with, 318, 319
 for barracudas, 341, *341, 342*
 boat-dock fishing with, 276
 combined with Clouser Minnow, 313–14, *314*
 fly lines for, 51
 for largemouth bass, 267
 materials for, 77–79
 for peacock bass, 290
 quick-change heads for, 83–87, *84*
 retrieving with, 193, 195, 199
 river fishing with, 283, 284
 rods for, 22
 shape and design of, 79–83, *80*
 for sharks, 340, *341*
 with sinking-tip lines, 57–58, *58*
 stream fishing with, 289–90
 for striped bass, 39, 321–22, *329*
 used around structures, 313
Potomac Bug, 269
Power Gum, 45, 249–50
power plants, fishing around, 324
"power stroke," 143, 162

predator-prey behavior, 200–2, *203,* 204, 209
presentation
 best times to fish, 9–12
 color of fly line and, 63
 fly-rod handles and, 24, 26–27, *27*
 guidelines, 5–7
 reel seats and, 23
 rods and, 22
 with sinking-tip lines, 56
 tapered line and, 55
 two-fly, 247, *248*
Prince Nymph, 229
puddle cast, 170
pulpits, *328*

quick-change popper heads, 83–87, *84*
Quill Gordon, 218

rabbit fur flies, 99–101
Rabbit Leech, *292*
rain, 11, 119, 120, 121, 305
rainbow runners, 95
rainbow trout, 11
rain gear, 305–6
rattler flies, 73, 76
reach cast, 224
redfish, 70, 297, 334
 in backcountry waters, 317, *318,* 320
 casting to, 154, 193
 flash and, 72
 flies for, 96
 mouths of, 67, 196
 shrimp and, 337, 345
 tackle for, 36
 time of day for fishing, 11
Red & White Hackle Fly, 264–65, *266,* 269, *272,* 280
reefs, 316
reels, 27–34
reel seats, 23
retrieving, 51
 accuracy, 189–90, *190*
 color of flies and, 70
 crippled baitfish retrieve, 209–10
 debris and, 303
 deep-water, 208–9
 downstream "retrieve," 199
 end of the retrieve, 204, *205,* 206–8, *207*
 line manipulation, 190, *191,* 192–93, *194,* 195
 natural approach to, 201–2, *203,* 204
 for permit, 333
 rod position in, 284–85, 346
 sink rate, 196–99, *197*
 speed of, 56, 99, 199–201, *200*
 for trout, 232
right-angled cast, 173, *174*
riverbanks, 16, 242
rivers, bass fishing in, 280–85, *286,* 287–88, *288*
rockfish, 327
rods, 21–27, *24–27*
 for bass fishing, 259
 direction of during retrieve, 193, 195
 pointing to locate fish, 337, *337,* 345
 repair kits for, 306
 for striped bass, 322
 weight of, 59
roll cast, 22, 59, 135, 142–49, *144–47,* 253, 334
Royal Coachman, 230
Royal Wulff, 245, 246, 287
running drag, 30

sailfish, 22, 85
salmon, 22, 27
saltwater fly fishing, 132, 184, 298
 hooks for, 42
 popping bugs and, 81